Regional Cohesion and Competition in the Age of Globalization

Regional Cohesion and Competition in the Age of Globalization

Edited by

Hirotada Kohno

Professor Emeritus, Institute of Socio-Economic Planning, University of Tsukuba, Japan

Peter Nijkamp

Professor of Regional, Urban and Environmental Economics, Free University, Amsterdam, The Netherlands

Jacques Poot

Professor, School of Economics and Finance, Victoria University of Wellington, New Zealand

Edward Elgar
Cheltenham, UK • Northampton, MA, USA

Published by
Edward Elgar Publishing Limited
Glensanda House
Montpellier Parade
Cheltenham
Glos GL50 1UA
UK

Edward Elgar Publishing, Inc.
136 West Street
Suite 202
Northampton
Massachusetts 01060
USA

A catalogue record for this book
is available from the British Library

Library of Congress Cataloguing in Publication Data

Regional cohesion and competition in the age of globalization / edited
    by Hirotada Kohno, Peter Nijkamp, Jacques Poot.
        1. Competition, International. 2. International economic
    integration. 3. Regionalism. 4. International trade. I. Kohno,
    Hirotada, 1932–   . II. Nijkamp, Peter. III. Poot, Jacques.
    HF1414.R44 1999
    337.1—dc21   99–33955
                                                            CIP

ISBN 1 85898 918 3

Printed and bound in Great Britain by Bookcraft (Bath) Ltd.

Contents

Figures

Tables

Contributors

Jim Bumgardner, Regional Economic Models Inc., USA

Kenneth Button, Institute of Public Policy, George Mason University, USA

Li-Lu Chen, College of Commerce, Feng Chia University, Taiwan

Hsianghoo S. Ching, Department of Public Finance, Feng Chia University, Taiwan

Fabienne Corvers, MERIT, University of Limburg, The Netherlands

Mustafa Dinc, Institute of Public Policy, George Mason University, USA

Eduardo Haddad, Regional Economics Applications Laboratory, University of Illinois, USA

Kingsley E. Haynes, Institute of Public Policy, George Mason University, USA

Geoffrey J.D. Hewings, Regional Economics Applications Laboratory, University of Illinois, USA

Yoshiro Higano, Institute of Agricultural and Forestry Engineering, University of Tsukuba, Japan

Dapeng Hu, Zell/Lurie Real Estate Center, The Wharton School, USA

Ryoichi Ishii, Regional and Urban Planning Department, Nomura Research Institute, Japan

Masamichi Kawano, Department of Economics, Kwansei Gakuin University, Japan

Hirotada Kohno, College of Applied International Studies, Tokiwa University, Japan

Tesshu Koshiba, Department of Economics, Tohoku Gakuin University, Japan

Yoshinobu Kumata, Department of Social Science and Engineering, Tokyo Institute of Technology, Japan

Jisheng Liu, Institute for Systems Science, Soka University, Japan

Takafumi Matsuba, Faculty of Economics, Nagoya City University, Japan

Guoping Mao, Asahi University, Japan

Ronald W. McQuaid, Department of Economics, Napier University, United Kingdom

John M. Munro, Department of Economics, Simon Fraser University, Canada

Birgit Nahrstedt, Department of Economics, Odense University, Denmark

Peter Nijkamp, Department of Regional Economics, Free University, The Netherlands

Paul Parker, Department of Geography, University of Waterloo, Canada

Jessie P.H. Poon, Department of Geography, State University of New York at Buffalo, USA

Jacques Poot, School of Economics and Finance, Victoria University of Wellington, New Zealand

Piet Rietveld, Department of Regional Economics, Free University, Amsterdam, The Netherlands

Tatsuro Sakano, Department of Social Science and Engineering, Tokyo Institute of Technology, Japan

Gustav Schachter, Center for European Economic Studies, Northeastern University, USA

Michael Sonis, Department of Geography, Bar-Ilan University, Israel

Makoto Tawada, School of Economics, Nagoya University, Japan

Suminori Tokunaga, Department of Economics, Nagoya City University, Japan

Frederick Treyz, Regional Economic Models Inc., USA

Jie Zhang, Research Center of Bornholm, Denmark

Preface

Modern economic development is positioned at the interface of strengthening global forces and a stronger orientation towards regional competitiveness. Against this background, we are now witnessing an increasing interest among scholars and policy makers in the indigenous regional potential, which is required to survive in this new economic force field.

The description and analysis of the restructuring phenomenon in the new global and regional economic order is still in its infancy. There is a variety of challenging research questions. For example, what is the nature of the underlying spatial competitive mechanism? How can regions attain the critical mass to become powerful players in the new spatial configuration? The nature of support systems and institutional backing must also be re-evaluated. Other important questions concern the convergence or divergence among regions and the consequences of industrial hollowization in major parts of the developed world.

Against this background, this book aims to shed light on these and other issues of regional competition and cohesion in the age of globalization. The authors of the chapters of this book presented their first drafts under the theme of 'Regional science in the process of borderless globalization of the world economy – preparing for the 21st century' at the Fifth World Congress of the Regional Science Association International, held in Tokyo in May 1996. At the conference, an abundance of topics was addressed that are at the heart of this theme, such as the rapid economic changes in the Asia-Pacific region, the widening of Europe and perspectives from developing economies. A selection, review and revision process of papers took place following the conference. This resulted in the nineteen contributions which make up the menu of this volume. The book aims to provide a balance of descriptive overviews, pertinent theoretical modelling and empirical research regarding specific relevant issues.

On behalf of all the contributors, we would like to thank the Japan Section of the Regional Science Association International for their professional organization of the World Congress and their warm hospitality at Rissho University in Tokyo.

Many people would need to be thanked for their help during the preparation of this volume, too many to be mentioned here. However, we should mention explicitly the authors for their efforts to meet deadlines in preparing the final versions of their papers.

Finally, the camera-ready material was expertly prepared out of the usual confusing variety of word-processing formats by Dianne Biederberg of Contact Europe.

Hirotada Kohno, Peter Nijkamp and Jacques Poot
Editors

PART ONE

Introduction

1. Globalization and Spatial Diversity: an Overview

Hirotada Kohno, Peter Nijkamp and Jacques Poot

1. INTRODUCTION

It has almost become a cliché to refer to the growing integration of the world economy as globalization. For globalization is not a new phenomenon. Trade with faraway places is as old as written history and the transborder mobility of labour and capital dates back to the age of exploration and the establishment of colonial powers. Economic activity at a truly global scale had emerged already as the fruit of the nineteenth century innovations of the steamship, transcontinental railroads and the telegraph.

Yet the rapid changes in the nature and patterns of international economic activity which have taken place in recent years warrant a pronouncing of the end of the twentieth century as the age of globalization. The global changes are driven by the pervasive influence of new information technologies such as the microchip, parallel processors, the Internet, fax machines, cellular phones and electronic money. These technologies have not only led to a vast array of new final and intermediate goods and services, but they have also profoundly affected the spatial dimension of economic activity. While claims of a 'death of distance' (Cairncross 1997) are exaggerated, since the costs of transportation and storage of resources, goods and people have by no means been reduced to zero, the invisible transaction costs of economic activity such as coordination and communication have fallen sharply indeed.

Commentators with an optimistic perspective on globalization (usually economists) have pointed to several other positive features, in addition to an avalanche of product and process innovations plus the lower costs of communication and transportation. One of the most important is that the growth in international trade does not only lead to an enhanced economic welfare from countries being able to exploit comparative advantage, but the efficiency gains from economic integration may also fuel technological progress and scale economies which in certain circumstances may lead to permanently higher global growth rates (Rivera-Batiz and Romer 1991; Rivera-Batiz and Xie 1993).

Another advantage is that the increasing fluidity of innovation diffusion and absorption contributes to the convergence of living standards between regions or countries which share common technologies and this convergence is reinforced through trade and factor mobility. Convergence is in the standard neoclassical growth models due to diminishing returns to capital accumulation but evidence is now emerging that trade can also contribute to the catching up of the lagging regions and countries (Slaughter 1997).

Furthermore, an increased openness forces governments to carry out prudent fiscal and monetary policies and, for example, to maintain low rates of inflation. That the discipline of the international marketplace reduces the degrees of freedom in economic policy is clear, for example, from the political difficulties that surrounded the introduction of the European Monetary Union (EMU). Finally, rather than being a threat, rising incomes in huge emerging economies such as China and India open up vast export opportunities for the developed world.

Yet there is also an emerging school of thought which emphasizes the costs of globalization. Its proponents are found primarily among protectionists, politicians and adversely affected sectors. One of the most often quoted problems is globalization-induced structural change. Globalization may have accelerated the sectoral structural change in of the economy in a way which has led to large adjustment costs both for capital and labour. In the developed economies these have often taken the form of a decline in manufacturing. This process is commonly referred to as deindustrialization or hollowization. Not only are resources withdrawn from declining industries but they are increasingly taken abroad to reap higher rates of return to capital. The effects of globalization on the service sectors are not unambiguously positive either, as for example the Internet may substitute for local intermediaries such as real estate agents or travel agents.

Moreover, the speed of change is faster than ever before which has led, due to limited substitution elasticities between different types of occupations and the time-intensive processes of upskilling and retraining, to growing unemployment. Restructuring has led to growing wage premiums for highly skilled internationally mobile people in professional and managerial occupations, while it has marginalized blue collar employment in traditional industries. There is therefore little dispute that globalization has led to growing income inequality, despite the national welfare gains (for example, Burtless 1995).

Moreover, Rodrik (1997) points out that to address inequities with tax-funded redistribution policies increases the share of government transfer payments in the overall income allocation which, in turn, may lead to distortions (inefficiencies) in resource allocation.

Another strand of literature warns that increasing returns in information-related industries may lead to a monopolization of large enterprises in certain areas (for example, Microsoft in the software industry) or the widespread adoption of suboptimal technologies due to network externalities (Arthur 1996). An opposite force is the re-emergence of the small firm as falling communication costs permit specialization, niche marketing and outsourcing (Brynjolfsson et al. 1994). The global trend in the growth of small firms encourages competitiveness and innovation. The two forces of market concentration and dispersion operate at the same time and lead to a growing complexity and diversity of global market structures.

Finally, globalization has also contributed to the growing severity of global environmental problems as the increasing global output, trade, mobility and real incomes have led to unsustainable exploitation of natural resources such as tropical forests, the accelerated emission of greenhouse gases and the irreversible damage to the ecosystem.

How are the regions of the world faring under these far-reaching global changes? It is hard to find regional islands of stability amidst the global turbulence. Some regions (for example, California, Ile-de-France, Bavaria, Randstad Holland) have become 'world regions' with a far-reaching impact on the world economy as a whole. Others have become important specialized areas providing services or manufacturing to a significant part of our world (for example, Third Italy, the Greater London area, Silicon Valley, Tokyo Metropolitan area). And yet others have become the losers in the new competitive world economy (for example, regions in Central and Eastern Europe, Greece, parts of Latin America). And finally, there are also peripheral regions which, due to historical or ecological advantages, are booming as a result of global tourism flows (for example, the Greek islands and the Turkish coast, the Caribbean, northern Queensland). Virtually all regions in the world seem to be in a state of transition as a result of global forces (economic, geopolitical, cultural, demographic).

Although the exact nature of this global change cannot as yet be easily and precisely mapped out, there is no doubt that development prospects, uncertainties and interdependencies of regions are key features. Research into the major issues, challenges and problems of the regions has only recently commenced. The regional configuration in the age of globalization appears to turn into a multipolar spatial system, in a partly fragmented way (following the end of the cold war) and in a partly uniform way (following the diminishing of North–South conflict). The global picture of the regions is rather heterogeneous (see also European Commission 1997).

Thus, the core theme of this book is that the consequences of globalization, both positive and negative, are spatially differentiated. At the national level, the winners appear to be emerging manufacturing nations, newly industrializing economies (NIEs) and developed countries which specialize in transshipment, distribution and producer services (such as the Netherlands), while the losers are countries strongly affected by deindustrialization (such as Japan, Germany, France).

Yet, we have already given several examples above about the different impacts of globalization on the different regions within or between nation states. In particular, regions with a traditional export base of manufactured goods may now witness an outflow of labour and capital. Venables (1995) shows that economic integration may theoretically trigger agglomeration either within industries or in an economy-wide form. In the latter case, a growing regional inequality is likely. This theme is taken up in Part Two of this book.

The appropriate response to the globalization-induced regional diversity is not straightforward. The nature and target of the subsidy, if any, to less advanced regions, may influence whether the subsidy leads to welfare gains and higher growth overall. Theories of endogenous growth suggest that a trade off may exist between equity and the average growth rate in an open system (Walz 1996). Growing economic integration may lead in some cases, such as in the European Union (EU), to a higher average growth rate but also to growing regional disparities which are at present not yet adequately addressed (Taylor 1996).

Given the context described above, it was felt appropriate that the theme for the 5th World Congress of the Regional Science Association in Tokyo in May 1996 would be 'Regional Science in the Process of Borderless Globalization of the World Economy – Preparing for the 21st Century'. Regional science provides a multidisciplinary problem-focused approach to spatial issues. Its strength lies in the synergies which can be reaped from combining the insights of core disciplines such as economics, geography, engineering and managerial sciences into a framework for the study of spatiotemporal phenomena.

This point is reinforced by Haynes and Dinc in the next chapter. Haynes and Dinc note that much intellectual progress has been made at the interface of disciplines with other fields of knowledge and that regional science can similarly provide a better understanding of phenomena such as globalization.

The abstraction of nations as 'one point economies' is becoming an increasingly untenable assumption in the age of globalization. While national borders still matter for trade or migration, even in common market areas (McCallum 1995; Poot 1995), industrial or high-tech clusters may transcend borders and the intranational spatial inequality may be greater than international inequality.

Modern regional science research builds on three principles. The first is that space is a non-reducable characteristic of economic activity. Consequently, the region is the core paradigm of a regional science approach to globalization, as will be elaborated by Haynes and Dinc in Chapter 2. In addition, regional science adopts a predominantly dynamic perspective. This is not simply a matter of attaching a time subscript to variables in economic systems, but regional science is instead primarily concerned with the causes and nature of processes of change. Finally, regional science has adopted a problem-solving approach in which it attempts to identify concrete solutions to specific economic problems.

Thus, regional science has been in the present context of globalization concerned with, for example, decisions on company location – the location of head offices and the 'slicing' of enterprise activity by outsourcing and the shift of manufacturing to locations abroad. Secondly, regional science has studied transportation infrastructures such as international networks of high speed trains, the deregulation of the airline industry and the emergence of hub-spoke routing.

The development of mega cities and the hierachy of cities under centripetal forces of agglomeration and centrifugal forces of congestion and pollution are also popular themes. The location of major administrative centres such as the proposed move of the Central Government of Japan away from Tokyo is a specific example in this context. In addition, much research has been devoted to the impact of new information and communication technologies. Finally, regional scientists have studied the continual shaking up of the international trading patterns by the changing spatial allocation of productive resources and the generation and diffusion of new technologies.

The present volume contains a selection of congress papers which specifically aimed to shed light on such key theoretical and empirical aspects of the spatial consequences of globalization. The papers were revised in the light of comments made by discussants in the conference sessions and by a subsequent anonymous refereeing process.

The papers have been grouped into four parts. Part One, Introduction, is concerned with the main issues with respect to the regional impact of globalization and the contribution which regional science can make to studying these issues. Following this overview already given above, we will proceed in this chapter with summarizing the main points of the remainder of the book. Chapter 2 explains why the age of globalization offers extensive opportunities for new advances in regional science.

Part Two of the book consists of five chapters concerned with theoretical models of the relationship between trade, welfare and economic growth. Some empirical evidence for the role of agglomeration effects in this context is also provided. Part Three is concerned with international and interregional patterns of trade. Finally, Part Four focuses on the implications of globalization for regional policy.

Haynes and Dinc describe in Chapter 2 of Part One briefly some of the key features of the globalization phenomena which we are witnessing at present. They also reinforce and expand the comments already made regarding the opportunities for regional science to provide better insights into this multifaceted process. Regions will matter more than nations in the twenty-first century, yet the functional region will be polycentric and possibly have a 'flattened' regional periphery.

Like many other commentators, Haynes and Dinc stress the importance of human capital investment as a driving force of economic growth but they also note that a better understanding of the process of development requires an appreciation of the influence of culture. In this respect, there is a scope for contributions from, for example, sociology and anthropology – disciplines which have traditionally had little contact with regional science.

Finally, the dynamic orientation of regional science is aided by the new mathematical theories of, for example, self-organizing behaviour and complexity. However, a development of managerial and operational decision-making support tools for regional policy makers is still badly needed.

2. TRADE, WELFARE AND GROWTH

Despite trade liberalization having taken place only gradually after an era of staunt protectionism earlier this century, growing regional economic integration and the freeing up of global international trade have been two of the major achievements of the late twentieth century. The authors in this part of the book focus on short-run and long-run welfare implications of economic integration and growing trade.

The standard case for free trade is that in competitive markets any form of trade barrier will lead to welfare losses. The gains from liberalized trade in the short-run are, however, small compared with the potential gains which can result from a positive impact of trade liberalization on the long-run rate of growth. Part Two of the book focusses primarily on theoretical explanations for various phenomena associated with global trade, development and restructuring. The method of analysis is that of the new international trade theory (see for example, Krugman 1988), which has in common with the new theories of economic growth an emphasis on product differentiation, innovation and imperfect competition (see also Nijkamp and Poot 1998). In the current context, however, the trade theories are extended to search particularly for trade and factor mobility-related causes of spatial agglomeration and uneven development.

In the presence of countries imposing external tariffs, the creation of a free trade area (FTA) among some of them, may generate welfare benefits for some participants in the FTA agreement, particularly for those countries which benefit from the resulting trade diversion from low-cost to high-cost suppliers, but the overall welfare gain will depend on a range of factors. These include the demand and supply elasticities, the tariff rate imposed on countries excluded from the FTA, and on the difference between the world price under free trade and the equilibrium price within the FTA. In Chapter 3, Koshiba studies these familiair situations, and more complex ones, by means of a simple graphical exposition of the welfare effects, following the tradition established by Viner (1950).

Koshiba discusses a variety of regional economic integration arrangements (REIAs), including free trade areas (FTAs), custom unions (CUs), preferential trading arrangements (PTAs) and unilateral trade liberalization (UTL). However, much of his analysis refers to the North-American Free Trade Agreement (NAFTA), which is of particular interest due to being a FTA which involves both developed (Canada and the USA) and a developing economy (Mexico).

In general, there will be winners and losers after the introduction of an FTA, despite the aggregate welfare gains. However, the compensation issues are complex and the welfare effects depend also, for example, on whether trade and migration between members are substitutes or complements when labour migration is permitted (see, for example, Nana and Poot 1996).

Koshiba also notes that PTAs can theoretically lead to a greater welfare enhancement than FTAs, but because of the high related transaction costs, the discriminatory elements of such a policy and its potential for trade diversion, PTAs are not a practical solution. This issue is similar to that of the impracticality of implementing optimal Ramsey taxes (Ramsey 1927; see also, for example, Evans et al. 1996, p. 1868).

Instead, Koshiba notes that the best policy aims for an advantage-developing FTA in which innovation, product differentiation and human capital accumulation lead to higher growth in the FTA which spills over to non-member countries. One means of spillover is foreign direct investment (FDI), such as was the case with an inflow of foreign capital at the introduction of NAFTA. By the gradual expansion of FTAs, these arrangements can become a stepping stone towards freeer global trade, although Poon provides evidence in Chapter 8 of the current realignment of trading nations into five world trade regions.

The dynamic benefits of economic integration may have their root in scale effects in production or in positive externalities such as technological spillovers. Both sources of increasing returns generate imperfect competition. Consequently, many of the new trade models are concerned with cases of imperfect competition and scale effects (for example, Grossman and Helpman 1991). However, a seminal contribution with respect to scale effects is Krugman (1981) and with respect to imperfect competition Markusen (1981). Extensions to both these contributions can be found in this volume, namely in Chapter 5 by Kawano and in Chapter 4 by Matsuba and Tawada respectively.

Markusen studied a two-country two-good general equilibrium model in which the market for one of the two goods is a Cournot duopoly. He found that a smaller country would export the good sold in the imperfectly competitive market, while the larger country would export the good sold under perfect competition. In Chapter 4, Matsuba and Tawada return to this situation, but assume instead that the duopoly is of a Stackelberg leader–follower nature. This is a more realistic situation, particularly when the firms which act as leaders in the market are also in the larger country.

Matsuba and Tawada find that the results are then generally quite different from those of the Markusen model. A smaller country would only export the good sold under imperfect competition if it had a very strong leadership in the market. It is more likely that the larger country exports the good sold under imperfect competition, particularly when it is also the Stackelberg leader. In this case, the larger country will also reap the gains from trade.

This type of analysis suggests that economic integration, particularly among regions or countries which have a leadership role in some imperfectly competitive market, can generate strong welfare gains for the integrating economies by reaping scale benefits. However, there is still much scope for further theoretical work with these types of general equilibrium models, particularly when differences in factor endowments are considered explicitly and when the impact of the *ex ante* pricing behaviour of the imperfectly competitive firm on other prices in the economy is taken into account. Work in this direction has already been undertaken by Kemp and Okawa (1995).

A key issue is whether the globalization process is leading to convergence or divergence among regional economies. Neoclassical growth models with a stable steady-state growth path suggest that such convergence is inevitable among closed economies, whether productivity growth is exogenous or not, as long as economies share the same initial technologies. In practice, estimates of convergence suggest that this process is very slow. One reason is that human capital growth may contribute to diminishing returns to capital setting in very slowly, but there may also be other causes (for example, Barro and Sala-i-Martin 1995; Quah 1996).

However, diffusion of innovations, factor mobility and trade can all be shown to speed up convergence. The globalization process, which mobilizes inputs and outputs on a global scale, is therefore expected to be the main driving force for a catching up of the developing economies. Yet the empirical evidence on convergence is still far from conclusive. Convergence appears to be present most clearly among economies which are not only highly integrated, but also have similar cultural, legal and political traits. Among more heterogenous economies, the dispersion of living standards does not appear to be diminishing and there are as many economies 'falling back' as there are 'catching up'.

Consequently, there remains much interest in explanations of uneven development due to spatial differences in productivity, which are reinforced by scale and agglomeration effects and other sources of cumulative causation. These have a long tradition in the literature on regional economies (for example, Myrdal 1957; Kaldor 1970), but they have also theoretical support in the new trade theories. Krugman (1981) describes a very simple two-sector (manufacturing and agriculture) 'North–South' model in which there is only a saddle point equilibrium of equal development, and the more likely theoretical outcome is a complete specialization which is fully determined by the initial conditions.

As complete specialization is not a theoretically attractive outcome, several extensions have been suggested in the literature to describe mechanisms which would generate more plausible equilibria. One such extension is given in Chapter 5. In this chapter, Kawano introduces two manufacturing sectors and an agricultural sector which has exogenous productivity growth. Moreover, the two manufactured goods have different income elasticities of demand. The agricultural productivity growth increases the real wage and this leads to a change in the demand for the two manufactured goods, which may enable the South to obtain a comparative advantage in the production of one of the two. The Kawano model can generate a rich diversity in development patterns and, for example, the South overtaking the North is one of the possibilities.

Hu describes in Chapter 6 a general equilibrium model of the trade and capital mobility between two economies of which one is relatively well endowed with capital and professional workers (for example, a developed economy) and the other economy is relatively well endowed with unskilled workers (for example, a developing economy). There are two production sectors. The first is a manufacturing sector which uses capital, unskilled labour and producer services. An increase in the variety of producer services generates a spillover benefit for manufacturing. Producer services use only professional labour as input. Labour is assumed immobile, but capital and manufactured goods are perfectly mobile. However, the key feature of Hu's model is that the trade in producer services is subject to transaction costs.

It is clear that under these assumptions the developed economy will export producer services and import manufactured goods. Hu then studies the effect of a decline in transaction costs. In his model this will lead to an increase in the exports of producer services to the developing economy as well as a capital flow in the form of foreign direct investment (FDI) to that economy. In this way, Hu can explain that in practice FDI and trade in producer services are complements rather than substitutes. Any agglomeration then results from pronounced spatial variations in transaction costs. These spatial variations are due to regional differences in communication and information infrastructures, and the availability of professional labour. Moreover, spatial economic diversity is also due to cultural factors when institutional and business practices are very different between trading nations or regions.

Hu's theoretical conclusions are partially confirmed by empirical research reported in Chapter 7. In that chapter, Tokunaga and Ishii study the locational choices of Japanese multinational firms in the electronics industry. They used two approaches to study the decisions which led Japanese firms to FDI in East Asia. Firstly, Tokunaga and Ishii reported the results of several surveys of motives for locational choice regarding FDI (some of the surveys also included also the USA as a potential destination). Secondly, the authors of this chapter estimated a conditional logit model of locational choice using the observed spatial distribution of 74 new plants in East Asia. These choices are explained by several country-specific characteristics.

As the new trade models – such as the one formulated by Hu in Chapter 6 – would predict, the Japanese firms indeed located where they would obtain a competitive advantage in terms of low wage costs. Moreover, the importance of scale economies was revealed by the positive effect of market size (measured – on the grounds of an income effect – by real GDP per capita). Openness of an economy in terms of the export to GDP ratio also attracted FDI. Furthermore, the importance of agglomeration advantages was confirmed by the significance of intraindustry trade with other Japanese firms at the foreign location. This appears to encourage FDI, presumably through lowering transaction costs. Finally, the availability of public infrastructure also plays an important role.

However, it is somewhat surprising that the conditional logit model did not confirm that the average level of education of the local labour force and economic/political stability are FDI attraction factors, although these factors did score relatively highly in surveys of managers of multinational electronics firms.

3. SPATIAL INTERACTION AND COMPETITION

Part Three of this book focusses on the opportunities and threats for regional economies due to the growing international economic integration. Functional regions are of course not necessarily confined to subnational entities. Globalization is leading to a clustering of nations into what Poon in Chapter 8 calls 'World Trade Regions'. Thus, globalization is not just a matter of the removal of trade barriers and a more geographically dispersed distribution of the exports of nations. Instead, large world trade regions of fairly contiguous nations emerge. These 'natural' regions (Krugman 1993a) are not just the result of the active pursuit of regional free trade areas such as NAFTA or EU. They are also a consequence of technological change and the changing ways in which firms operate.

Poon studies the changing global trading patterns by means of the intramax method and the computation of trade intensity indices. She finds that these patterns can be well understood by the neoclassical paradigm of comparative advantage, provided comparative advantage is seen in the dynamic framework of the new theories of trade and endogenous growth (for example, Grossman and Helpman 1991). Thus, there is no need to replace the meta paradigm here by that of the 'competitive advantage' of nations, as introduced by Porter (1990), which is – by having its roots in the theory of the firm – more suited to empirical micro level analysis than the macro level study of globalization. In addition, Porter's focus on product differentiation may in fact lead to the wrong policy recommendations for countries or regions at an immature level of development (Warr 1994).

Poon finds that the emergence of five global trading regions by 1990 (with hubs in Japan, Germany, the UK, the former USSR countries and the US), compared with eight in 1965, is not thwarting a trend of extra-regionalization, although the latter trend was downward in the 1980s. Thus cosmopolitanization and the emergence of world trade regions are not incompatible forces and have led to the popularity of 'open regionalism' as a new basis for trade policy (for example, Garnaut 1996).

A popular model in regional science to study any type of spatial flows (migration, shopping trips, trade, and so on) is the gravity model. Linneman (1966) provides an early contribution to use the gravity model to explain gross international trade flows and a recent application is Sanso et al. (1993). Some behavioural microeconomic foundations for this macro level descriptive model are provided by Bergstrand (1985). Nahrstedt and Zhang use the gravity model in Chapter 9 to analyse the bilateral total trade flows between the individual member countries of the EU and ten East Asian (EA) countries (Japan, China, Hong Kong, Singapore, South Korea, Taiwan, Indonesia, Malaysia, Philippines and Thailand) over a period of 20 years (1971 to 1990).

Equations were also estimated separately for food products and for manufactured goods.

Nahrstedt and Zhang find partial support for the gravity property of trade flows: the volume of trade is positively correlated with the scale of the trading economies (as measured by GDP) and with the per capita income levels. Moreover, trade is negatively correlated with the difference in per capita income between two trading countries, which is referred to in the literature as the Linder effect (see Linder 1961).

Linder suggested that a similarity in preferences and demand structures would lead to greater trade. This may in fact be one reason to explain why economic convergence, aided by trade, appears to have been greater among sub-national regions (with similar incomes and demand structures) rather than among countries.

Nahrstedt and Zhang consider a range of gravity model specifications. Those which take into account a stochastic influence of location-specific factors and/or time (referred to as one and two factor random effects models respectively) tended to perform better than Ordinary Least Squares (OLS) models. One, at first sight rather curious, result in the context of gravity models is that distance appeared to have no significant influence on the trade flows. However, as Nahrstedt and Zhang's gravity model was only estimated for bilateral trade flows between EU and EA countries rather than also among these groups of countries, the coefficient of variation of the distance variable would have been much less than in most gravity model applications.

Another application of the gravity model can be found in Chapter 10. Ching and Chen study in this chapter the effects of Taiwanese immigration in Canada on the bilateral Taiwan–Canada trade flows, following a similar study to link bilateral trade to US immigration by Gould (1994).

In recent years there has been much research on the various impacts of immigration on host economies (see for example, Poot et al. 1988; Borjas 1994; Gorter et al. 1998). One of the key issues is the question whether immigration does not simply generate economic activity on a larger scale in a constant returns to scale economy, but if it instead may contribute to a higher long-run growth rate. This could be the case, for example, when there are positive feedback effects from immigration to investment and technological change. Another mechanism may be export-led growth: if immigrants can contribute to greater exports due to their informational advantages and linkages with the home country, the resulting export-led growth may generate an external benefit to immigration. Alternatively, immigration may lead to more imports from the home country due to taste effects and the lowering of barriers to trade by the emergence of importing agencies run by immigrants.

Ching and Chen test these effects by means of a time-series regression model based on the gravity equation and estimated with quarterly data from

1980 to 1995. They find that a 10 percent increase in the stock of Taiwanese immigrants in Canada increases Taiwan's exports to Canada by 3 percent. However, no significant effect could be detected of Taiwanese immigrants on Canadian exports to Taiwan. They also find that the import effect is stronger for Taiwanese immigrants in the 'self-employed' and 'entrepreneurial' classes than in the 'investor' class of immigrants admitted only on grounds of passive financial investment in Canadian assets. This suggests that relative prices and taste effects are not the sole reasons for the growing imports from Taiwan: Taiwanese business people would have a competitive advantage in the establishment of firms importing Taiwanese goods.

The fourth chapter in this part of the book shifts the attention from the estimation of international merchandise trade flows to interregional flows of trade in services. Treyz and Bumgardner derive in Chapter 11 a model for the estimation of the 1992 trade in services between the 83 counties of the state of Michigan in the US.

Survey data on trade in services are often unavailable, particularly at this spatial level, and the method developed by Treyz and Bumgardner provides therefore a means to fill this data gap. The theoretical foundation for their empirical work is the monopolistic competition model for the spatial allocation of economic activity developed by Paul Krugman (for example, Krugman 1993b).

As noted earlier in this introductory chapter, the monopolistic competition model has become a popular tool for formulating trade and growth models in which there are increasing returns at the level of the firm. Increasing returns necessitates a departure from the assumption of perfect competition. In monopolistic competition models, equilibria can still be computed under zero pure profit assumptions. Firms are assumed to produce different varieties and there are well-defined substitution possibilities between varieties both in terms of preferences for final demand and in terms of intermediate inputs in production. In a spatial context, such models generate both agglomerative/centripetal forces (local scale effects on production costs and the range of varieties available) and dispersive/centrifugal forces (land scarcity and transportation costs). The equilibrium spatial allocation of economic activity is the result of the balance of these forces.

The data requirements for the Treyz and Bumgardner procedure are modest: county level expenditure, output and employment data, inter-county distances, unit transportation costs and an estimate of the substitution elasticity. They find that the effect of distance on services transportation costs is rather large (11 percent for every mile of distance travelled). Given the decline of the role of transportation costs due to new communication and information technologies, the model may be capturing consumer services better than producer services. Consequently, Treyz and Bumgardner find that inter-county trade in services is low for highly urbanized counties in which a large variety of services is supplied locally, but also in remote counties where the transportation cost deters inter-county trade. The authors suggest several possible extensions of this type of analysis and a comparison with survey data, where available, would of course be essential to test the predictive ability of their model.

The relative demand for locally provided versus imported services is an issue which also returns in the next chapter. Sonis, Hewings and Haddad describe in this chapter a method for measurement of the extent of linkages between sectors and regions in a multiregional input–output (IO) system through a partitioning of the IO matrices into intra-regional and external flows. The method is applied to 1975 and 1985 multi-country input–output tables for eight EU countries (Belgium, Denmark, France, Germany, Ireland, Italy, The Netherlands and the United Kingdom).

While the extent of local versus external supplies in sectors and regions can be informally gauged from, for example, average direct IO coefficients, the advantage of the IO multiplier methods is that it derives such measures of openess based on the new equilibrium which can be computed with the Leontief inverse. Sonis et al. find that the large countries are, as expected, relatively more self-reliant and self-absorbing of internally generated economic shocks, with the exception of Denmark. The standard deviation of the distribution of this relative self-reliance across sectors is also smaller in the large EU countries (again with the exception of Denmark). Yet intra-country dependence is greater for the non-manufacturing sectors such as services, construction, commerce and restaurants and food production rather than for manufactured goods.

Variations in relative self-sufficiency tend to be greater across sectors than across countries. Finally, the growth in the trade in services, economic restructuring and actual and anticipated futher enlargement of the EU (by Greece in 1981 and Spain and Portugal in 1986) would have contributed to the growing inter-EU interdepencies in the multi-country IO analysis.

European structural change is also the focus of Chapter 13 written by Munro and Schachter. These authors study the variation in unemployment rates across 55 regions in 7 EU countries (Belgium, The Netherlands, France, Germany, Italy, Spain and the United Kingdom) in 1986 and 1993.

Munro and Schachter revisit one of the prominent issues in the early development of the field of regional economics, namely the relationship between unemployment and sectoral composition. They test the hypothesis that the unemployment rate will be higher in regions which are more specialized.

The analogy with portfolio analysis is obvious. If employment varies over the business cycle in each sector by a random variable with mean one, and these random variables are not perfectly correlated across sectors, the variance in aggregate employment (and therefore unemployment) will be less in more diverse economies. Due to hysteresis effects, the more specialized regions may then suffer from higher natural rates of unemployment after times of economic restructuring (for example, Cross 1988).

Munro and Schachter test the specialization effect empirically in two ways. First they identify those regions with persistently high unemployment in 1993. These regions are indeed primarily among those with a relatively high degree of industrial specialization, as measured by the Gini index, although there are some notable exceptions (such as the North of The Netherlands).

Further confirmation of the detrimental effect of regional specialization on the regional unemployment rate was found by regression analysis. This also revealed an industrial base (or perhaps a non-agricultural base) effect: the larger the share of industrial employment in total employment, the lower the unemployment rate.

Munro and Schachter suggest several policy options for reducing regional unemployment. These are primarily concerned with supply side solutions such as increased labour market flexibility, retraining programmes, the improvement of regional infrastructure (see also Chapter 6 of this book) and the adoption of new technologies.

4.   GLOBALIZATION AND REGIONAL POLICY

Following a brief excursion into regional policy by Munro and Schachter in Chapter 13, Part Four of the book is wholly devoted to new roles for regional policy in the age of globalization.

Corvers and Nijkamp consider in Chapter 14 the effects of globalization on regional inequality in Europe and suggest that, without new policies, greater economic integration may increase regional dispersion. This point is reinforced by McQuaid in Chapter 15, who argues that in particular the gap (in terms of economic indicators) between existing core and peripheral regions may grow after enlargement of the EU. The European situation is a particularly good case study because of the socioeconomic and cultural diversity within the economically integrated area and the presence of several cross-border agglomerations. The key criteria for succesful new policies are accessibility (determined by infrastructure and networks) and receptivity (a function of institutional and technological parameters).

Corvers and Nijkamp develop, on the basis of eight observable phenomena (so-called 'force-fields'), four scenarios for Europe in the twenty-first century (that is, Mobile Europe, Techno-Europe, Homebound Europe and Eco-Europe). Whichever of these scenarios eventuates, there is no doubt that the institutional set up for policymaking is likely to change from a rigid top-down one to a flexible bottom-up one, in which public–private policy networks will play a major role. Given that the breaking down of existing traditional and hierarchical policy systems may be difficult, the emergence of a radically different decentralized policy framework may take considerable time.

In the meantime, the enlargement of the EU to include Central and Eastern European Countries (CEECs) is expected to have detrimental effects on existing peripheries even though overall welfare will be increasing. However, McQuaid notes that there is more than one possible interpretation of peripherality. Physical distance from core areas is still one way to define peripherality, but as declining transportation costs (for example due to deregulation) and new information technologies lower the impact of distance, there remains the problem of low population densities in remote areas. Remoteness may lower the local growth rate through the detrimental impact of low local demand on agglomeration potential (see also Ciccone and Hall 1996).

McQuaid notes that the expansion of the EU to include CEECs will shift the economic centre of gravity in Europe eastwards. The economic gains will disproportionately accrue to Germany and least to southern and western peripheral regions. However, as policies directed to address these imbalances may be targeted at core urban areas, intraregional disparities may also widen.

Both McQuaid in Chapter 15 and Corvers and Nijkamp in Chapter 14 make the point that infrastructure is a necessary but not sufficient instrument to equip firms in regions to compete in global markets. How important is infrastructure? Button and Rietveld assess in Chapter 16 the impact of infrastructural policies on regional development by means of meta analysis.

Major infrastructural investments in recent decades, either by governments or in private–public partnerships, have contributed to a lower real cost of the long distance transportation of raw materials, goods, people, money and information. This has provided a major impetus to growing world trade. Conversely, the benefits of further economic integration may be diminished if adequate infrastructure in ports, airports, roads and telecommunications is not put in place – particularly with respect to linkages between emerging economies and the high income countries.

There is little doubt that infrastructure is welfare enhancing, although the social costs are likely to be underestimated (see for example, Morrison and Schwartz 1996). The estimated rates of return are often high and it may also be expected that infrastructure can increase the long-run real rate of growth of the economy through, for example, its impact on technological developments (see for example, Aschauer 1989).

However, the spatial impact of infrastructural investments is by no means yet fully understood. On the one hand, the increasing accessibility of lagging regions may offer an increased potential for external trade and factor mobility. Subsidized infrastructural investment is often a major instrument of regional development policy. Yet, the reduced spatial friction in the economic system may favour on the other hand existing core regions through scale and agglomeration effects and a cumulative causation process of regional divergence may emerge. Most studies of the impact of infrastructure take a partial equilibrium approach and spatiotemporal general equilibrium studies are still rather rare.

Button and Rietveld review in Chapter 16 empirical studies of the impact of infrastructural investments on total factor productivity. Rather than simply describing similarities and differences between 28 comparable studies verbally, they adopt a meta analysis approach in which the elasticity of interest is 'explained' by means of a regression model in which the explanatory variables represent certain features of the various research projects. Meta analysis is not without problems, but it is nonetheless probably more informative than a literure review on its own. Button and Rietveld find an average elasticity of 0.343 for the effect of infrastructual investments on productivity growth, which is similar to the finding of other surveys.

However, this type of analysis has not as yet shed any light on the causation in this relationship. Given the public nature of much infrastructural investment is it very well possible that such investment primarily takes place in times of high economic growth when (unexpected) taxation revenues relax government budgetary constraints Consequently there may well be empirically a causal relationship from economic growth to investment in infrastructures.

An issue not unrelated to the role of infrastructure is the impact of the stock, generation and distribution of information in the economy. As globalization is providing an extra stimulus for the evolution of the information-oriented society, the role of information in economic development warrants special attention. Following early work by Machlup (1962) and Porat (1977), Higano and Mao in Chapter 17 construct measures of the information intensity of the economy and then test the effect of information development on economic development by means of a production function approach. Higano and Mao apply this methodology to a recently rapidly developing urban economy (Shanghai) and a highly developed country (Japan) over the period 1952–1991.

Higano and Mao construct five measures of information development (capabilities, education, information industries, information in society and information in daily life) on the basis of a principal components analysis of a range of statistical indicators for each of the five areas. The five information measures are subsequently combined into one synthetic indicator of information intensity, again by means of principal components analysis.

The same technique is also used to compute an economic development index which takes into account the growth in Gross National Product (GNP), per capita national income, technical progress (the trend of total factor productivity growth in a Cobb-Douglas production function) and life expectancy.

Higano and Mao show subsequently that their economic development index can be explained by the capital–labour ratio and the information intensity index. The elasticities of about 0.4 and 0.3 respectively are remarkably similar for the two economies (Shanghai and Japan). However, the contribution of the growth in the capital–labour ratio to development has been much greater in Shanghai than in Japan. This demonstrates that a growing information intensity of the economy is a sign of maturity of economic development.

Consequently, creation of the right environment for growth in information development to may be a necessary condition for market-led growth to take off in lagging regions of developed economies. Due to the positive externalities associated with the information development, there will remain important roles for national and local governments to foster research and development (R&D), transportation and telecommunication infrastructure, education and training for 'high-tech' and other sunrise industries.

What policy measures can be taken to promote such 'high-tech'-led growth? Parker describes in Chapter 18 two policy models (top-down and bottom-up) and then proceeds to outline and compare a case-study of each of these two models. The two cases considered by Parker are the Australian Multi Function Polis (MFP) on the outskirts of Adelaide and Canada's Technology Triangle (CTT) (formed by Cambridge, Guelph, Kitchener and Waterloo in south-west Ontario) respectively.

Both initiatives started in 1987 and Parker notes that MFP (the top-down approach) was generally considered a failure by the mid 1990s while CTT was considered a success. However, the MFP concept does have certain appealing features such as the international networking and the emphasis on making a high environmental quality part of the innovative milieux. Thus, despite, for example, the withdrawal of federal funding from MFP, the project may not yet be lost – provided a stronger link is established with local research park inititatives, local universities and businesses.

Despite its overall success, the CTT project also has its weaknesses. Its business networking is still strongly within the southern Ontario industrial belt, which makes CTT sensitive to regional business downturns. Given the relative strengths and weaknesses of both the top-down and bottom-up models as identified by the MFP and CTT case studies, Parker suggests an alternative 'global–local partnership' model which combines the best of the two approaches into a superior model for high-tech development.

The last chapter of this book reinforces Parker's call for devolved regional initiatives, yet within a network of global–local partnerships. Kumata, Sakano and Liu provide in Chapter 19 a case study of the changes in the regional planning process in Japan during the second half of the twentieth century. The planning process has been a product of its time and Kumata et al. provide an overview of interesting paradigm shifts during the last half century, which are not dissimilar to those observed in many other developed economies.

Comprehensive planning at the level of municipal governments was introduced in Japan in 1969, but – given a tradition of top-down government – it took some 20 years for the three tiers of the plans (from broad goals in the first stage to action plans in the third stage) to be realized. The authors suggest that globalization now warrants the commencement of a fourth stage of planning in which an effective new vision for the region is formulated.

Vision formulation requires interactive consultation with all stakeholders: officials, community leaders and local residents. Consequently, barriers in the dissemination of the vision statement and the plan may reduce the effectiveness of the consultative process. To test this empirically, Kumata et al. report the results of a survey of 47 prefectural and nearly 700 municipal governments in Japan. The visions formulated by the planning departments of the local governments were generally not well understood by the local residents, but the diffusion of the vision to community leaders was also low. One problem is that the opportunities for citizen participation decline beyond the early stage of plan formulation, yet the closing of the window of consultation is rational from the planner's perspective. Kumata et al. use the metaphor of language to pinpoint the communication problems in the formulation of regional plans. A redesigned legal and institutional framework and the use of new communication technologies may facilitate the use of a 'common language' by all interested parties.

5. FINAL COMMENTS

The world seems to evolve into a new spatial economic configuration, although it is as yet unclear whether this can be regarded as a 'new world order'. It seems also plausible that, with the disappearance of major ideological conflicts in our world, regional conflicts and tensions are gaining importance. In any case, the global economy is to a large extent characterized by interdependent small open economies. This interdependence is not only of an economic nature (trade, transport), but also of an environmental nature (cross-border pollution, global environmental change), of a strategic and political nature (regional strategic realignments) and of a cultural nature (for example, tourism, entertainment, sport). As a consequence, there is a major problem of sustainable development in the new world configuration, with tensions on resource availability, food supply, environmental quality and socioeconomic welfare. Multilateral agreements may be necessary to safeguard sustainable and stable development of all regions.

There are still many uncertainties in the emerging new spatial configuration of the global system of regions. It seems highly unlikely that reliable blueprints for the future regional system can be created at present. From a policy perspective, it can be argued that at best some meaningful strategies can be advocated. These might ensure a sound and stable spatial evolution. They may include: regional self-reliance policies (exploring indigenous and human resources), market-oriented policies (stimulating efficient economic organization of both business and the public sector), infrastructure policies (shaping the necessary conditions for reaping competitive advantage), and overall-balanced macroeconomic policies (favouring a stable socioeconomic development, non-bureaucratic institutional support systems and a satisfactory social security system).

All in all, the future space economy seems to evolve towards a broad spectrum of possibilities with respect to socioeconomic, cultural and political outcomes. Tendencies towards co-movement and convergence with respect to some socioeconomic phenomena are likely to coexist with tendencies towards divergence and complexity in others.

The trend towards an interconnected global network – linked by means of multilayer networks – will probably provoke the emergence of niche markets with open access to the rest of the world. In this way, regions may become islands of new opportunities in a spatially connected global network configuration.

REFERENCES

Arthur, B. (1996), 'Increasing returns and the two worlds of business', *Harvard Business Review*, July, pp. 412–16.
Aschauer, D.A. (1989), 'Is public expenditure productive?', *Journal of Monetary Economics* **23**, pp. 177–200.
Barro, R.J. and X. Sala-i-Martin (1995), *Economic Growth*, New York: McGraw Hill.
Bergstrand, J.H. (1985), 'The gravity equation in international trade: some microeconomic foundations and empirical evidence', *The Review of Economics and Statistics* **67**, pp. 474–81.

Borjas, G. (1994), 'The economics of immigration', *Journal of Economic Literature* **32**, pp. 1667–717.

Brynjolfsson, E., Malone, T., Gurbaxani, V. and A. Kambil (1994), 'Does information technology lead to smaller firms?', *Management Science* **40** (2), pp. 163–74.

Burtless, G. (1995), 'International trade and the rise in earnings inequality', *Journal of Economic Literature* **33** (2), pp. 800–816.

Cairncross, F. (1997), *The Death of Distance*, Boston Mass.: Harvard Business School Press.

Ciccone, A. and R.E. Hall (1996), 'Productivity and the density of economic activity', *American Economic Review* **86** (1), pp. 54–70.

Cross, R. (1988), *Unemployment, Hysteresis and the Natural Rate Hypothesis*, Oxford: Blackwell.

European Commission (1997), *The Future of North-South Relations*, Brussels: Archives of the Forward Studies Unit, no. 1, European Commission.

Evans, L., Grimes, A. and Wilkinson, B. with D. Teece (1996), 'Economic reform in New Zealand 1984–95: The pursuit of efficiency', *Journal of Economic Literature* **34** (4), pp. 1856–902.

Garnaut, R. (1996), *Open Regionalism and Trade Liberalization: An Asia-Pacific Contribution to the World Trade System*, Sydney: Allen and Unwin.

Gorter, C., Nijkamp, P. and J. Poot (1998), *Crossing Borders: Regional and Urban Perspectives on International Migration*, Aldershot: Ashgate.

Gould, D.M. (1994), 'Immigration links to the home country: empirical implications for U.S. bilateral trade flows', *The Review of Economics and Statistics* **6** (2), pp. 302–16.

Grossman, G. and E. Helpman (1991), *Innovation and Growth in the Global Economy*, Cambridge, Mass.: MIT Press.

Kaldor, N. (1970), 'The case for regional policies', *Scottish Journal of Political Economy* **17** (3), pp. 337–48.

Kemp, M.C. and M. Okawa (1995), 'The gains from free trade under imperfect competition', in Chang, W. and S. Katayama (eds), *Imperfect Competition in International Trade*, Dordrecht: Kluwer, pp. 73–91.

Krugman, P. (1981), 'Trade, accumulation and uneven development', *Journal of Development Economics* **8** (2), pp. 149–61.

Krugman, P. (1988), *Strategic Trade Policy and the New International Economics*, Cambridge Mass.: MIT Press.

Krugman, P. (1993a), 'Regionalism versus multilateralism: analytical notes', in De Melo, J. and A. Panagariya (eds), *New Dimensions in Regional Integration*, New York: Cambridge University Press, pp. 121–38.

Krugman, P. (1993b), 'First nature, second nature, and metropolitian location', *Journal of Regional Science* **33** (1), pp. 129–44.

Linder, S.B. (1961), *An Essay on Trade and Transformation*, Uppsala: Almqvist and Wiksells.

Linneman, H. (1966), *An Econometric Study of International Trade Flows*, Amsterdam: North-Holland.

2

Machlup, F. (1962), *The Production and Distribution of Knowledge in the United States,* Princeton: Princeton University Press.

Markusen J.R. (1981), 'Trade and the gains from trade with imperfect competition', *Journal of International Economics* **11** (4), pp. 531–51.

McCallum, J. (1995), 'National borders matter: Canada–U.S. regional trade patterns', *American Economic Review* **85** (3), pp. 615–23.

Morrison, C.J. and A.E. Schwartz (1996), 'State infrastructure and productive performance', *American Economic Review* **86** (5), pp. 1095–111.

Myrdal, G. (1957), *Economic Theory and Underdeveloped Regions,* London: Duckworth.

Nana, G. and J. Poot (1996), 'Trans-Tasman Migration and Closer Economic Relations', in Lloyd, P.J. and P.S. Williams (eds), *International Trade and Migration in the APEC Region,* Oxford: Oxford University Press.

Nijkamp, P. and J. Poot (1998), 'Spatial perspectives on new theories of economic growth', *Annals of Regional Science* **32** (1), pp. 7–37.

Poot, J., Nana, G. and B. Philpott (1988), *International Migration and the New Zealand Economy: a Long-Run Perspective,* Wellington: Institute of Policy Studies.

Poot, J. (1995) 'Do borders matter? A model of interregional migration in Australasia', *Australasian Journal of Regional Studies* **1** (2), pp. 159–82.

Porat, M.U. (1977), *Information Economy,* Washington: Report to the US Department of Commerce.

Porter, M.E. (1990), *The Competitive Advantage of Nations,* New York: Free Press.

Quah, D.T. (1996), 'Empirics for economic growth and convergence', *European Economic Review* **40** (8), pp. 1353–75.

Ramsey, F. (1927), 'A contribution to the theory of taxation', *Economic Journal* **37**: pp. 4–61.

Rivera-Batiz, L.A. and P.M. Romer (1991), 'Economic integration and endogenous growth', *Quarterly Journal of Economics* **106** (2), pp. 531–56.

Rivera-Batiz, L.A. and D. Xie (1993), 'Integration among unequals', *Regional Science and Urban Economics* **23** (3), pp. 337–54.

Rodrick, D. (1997), *Has Globalization Gone Too Far?* Washington DC: Institute for International Economics.

Sanso, M., Cuairen, R. and F. Sanz (1993), 'Bilateral trade flows, the gravity equation, and functional form', *The Review of Economics and Statistics* **75** (3), pp. 266–75.

Slaughter, M.J. (1997), 'Per capita income convergence and the role of international trade', *American Economic Review* **87** (2), pp. 194–9.

Taylor, J. (1996), 'Regional problems and policies: a European perspective', *The Australasian Journal of Regional Studies* **2** (2), pp. 103–31.

Venables, A. (1995), 'Economic integration and the location of firms', *American Economic Review* **85** (2), pp. 296–300.

Viner J. (1950), *The Customs Union Issue,* New York: Carnegie Endowment for International Peace.

Walz, U. (1996), 'Long-run effects of regional policy in an economic union', *The Annals of Regional Science* **30** (2), pp. 165–83.

Warr, P. (1994), 'Comparative and competitive advantage', *Asia-Pacific Economic Literature* **8** (1), pp. 1–14.

2. Globalization and the Borderless Economy: Perspectives for a Twenty-first Century Regional Science

Kingsley E. Haynes and Mustafa Dinc

1. INTRODUCTION

Recent literature in regional science has focused on its evolution and its future in a twenty-first century globalized and borderless economy. This literature has been laudatory about the past, critical about the present and pessimistic about the future. Following the lead of past Regional Science Association Presidents (Jensen 1991; Isserman 1993; Plane 1994; Ledent 1995), the recent volumes of the *Papers in Regional Science* (1994) and the *International Regional Science Review* (1995) have also discussed the past, present and future of regional science. From the present height of regional science success and before and after its fortieth birthday, there has been a number of thoughtful voices celebrating the past but criticizing the present with some intensity. To some extent, they have asked where do we go from here and where can we do better. This has set off an international self-critical debate within the field (for example, Bailley and Coffey 1994; Isserman 1995; Bailley et al. 1996). These voices have recommended a paradigmatic shift but with many voices suggesting many different directions.

Although diverse, the views have been defensive and often appropriately sceptical about the transition into the next century. What is needed is an appreciation of where regional science has been and a road map of where it might go. Central to this map is an exploration of how the disciplinary, academic and intellectual landscape is changing and some specification of an alternative future. Within that context of alternative futures different regional science paradigms become possible. Therefore, this chapter attempts to provide a map of the regional science landscape and its routes to the twenty-first century.

The next section of the chapter briefly discusses the evaluation of regional science in the context of a changing world economy. This section also underlines the increasing importance of globalization, of regional economies and hence of regional science. In the third section, the potential for regional science to aid the understanding of the regional impact of globalization is explored. The fourth section advocates a future role for regional science in a global economy. The final section provides some concluding remarks.

2. GLOBALIZATION AND REGIONAL ECONOMIES

The world economy has been going through unprecedented changes in terms of its organization, composition, integration and interdependency. In the last couple of decades, expansion of market boundaries and reduction or elimination of trade barriers have brought new opportunities to regional industries while simultaneously exposing them to increased competition from both domestic and foreign producers. Within the context of an increasingly integrated world economy, regional economies have become more and more crucial for national economies and in some cases dominate the national economy from a leading technology or entrepreneurial perspective. The Third Italy (Italy), West Jutland (Denmark), Bangalore (India), Silicon Valley and Route 128 (US) are among some examples of such regions.

This trend is increasingly recognized as the spatially decentralized but economically functional technological region. The rise of regional economies as the building blocks for international competitiveness has been widely recognized by scholars across the world, even outside of regional science (for example, Ohmae 1993; Sabel 1989; Porter 1990 and Krugman 1991a, 1995). Further, some of these scholars have suggested that competition and cooperation among these dynamic technology regions will dictate the future more than nation states themselves. Such a perspective is driven by the recognition that nation states through bilateral, multilateral and international agreements such as the Economic Union (EU), North American Free Trade Agreement (NAFTA), Asia Pacific Economic Cooperation Council (APEC) and the General Agreement on Tariffs and Trade (GATT) are increasingly constrained by what they can do to adjust national, let alone regional, competitive advantage.

Manufacturing continues to decentralize as high access value added information functions compete for nodally advantageous locations. The composition of intra and interregional economic systems continues to show strong specialization but significant and continued interdependency. New manufacturing methods, including flexible manufacturing, just-in-time production, short and niche-specific production runs and closer customer-focused production increase sensitivity to markets in most sectors while information technology makes response to that sensitivity increasingly global. In order to take advantage of these new production technologies effectively, rapid response is required in the value added production chain, all the way from suppliers to customers. This means that hard infrastructure becomes a central foundation to production support. Telecommunications and information infrastructure becomes increasingly central to the support of efficient high-end services. The result is that the interdependency across regions in terms of interregional trade increases the interdependency of regions on each other's basic infrastructure support. Congestion in Bombay means a delay in production in Tokyo which, in turn, means that the access to a new market in the Netherlands may be lost to a competitor. Hence, there is an increased interdependency with respect to the quality and effectiveness of infrastructure across trading regions as just-in-time delivery of inputs gives away to just-in-time production. Such manufacturing globalization is the latest outcome of the globalization of financial markets that respond quickly and relatively efficiently to small differentials in short-run returns to internationalized capital, often in spite of central bank interventions.

Such regions are increasingly polycentric rather than monocentric and, in spite of the best efforts of planners and urban policy makers, they continue to expand and decentralize toward lower residential and even lower employment densities. In support of such regions, communication and transportation technologies continue to enable lateral growth across the flattened regional periphery rather than in the traditional hierarchical monocentric radial fashion of the past.

Terms such as globalization, re-engineering, restructuring, decentralization, organizational flattening, corporate downsizing, the end of traditional jobs, consumer focus, flexible manufacturing, the agile organization, networked production, the virtual corporation and the information economy are all not only indicators of this new pattern but also a part of our daily lives. It is a pattern that challenges, fractures and flattens large organizations – be they public or private entities – but where communication, cooperation, learning and skill sharing are central to social and technologically led research, development and innovation. In such a world there continues to be a need for some kind of organizational activity framework greater than the individual but less burdensome, gargantuan and centralized than national governments or vertically integrated, centrally controlled mass production systems.

3. REGIONAL SCIENCE

Within such a globalizing and increasingly borderless economic environment, an evaluation of regional science is timely and appropriate for two reasons. First, the increasing importance of regions and regional economies creates new opportunities for both regions and regional science to explore. Second, these opportunities suggest increased responsibilities for regional science and regional scientists to provide guidance for these new forms of regional developments.

Isserman (1995) provided a comprehensive analysis of 'the roots and dreams' of early regional science and an assessment of its present standing, though some argue that his analysis is a little too pessimistic (Richardson 1995; Yezer 1995). Since the first Regional Science Association meeting in Detroit in 1954, regional science has expanded slowly but with great academic and intellectual fervour. The time since then proved that regional science has, in fact, been remarkably productive and influential (Yezer 1995). One important reason for its success and influence is that from the beginning regional science has been open and hospitable to diverse disciplines and methodologies and to scholars from the physical as well as the social sciences. It has employed empirical as well as theoretical approaches and paid close attention to policy and analysis (Bolton and Jensen 1995). This gave regional science openness and transferability to other disciplines and provided both a theoretical and methodological door through which other disciplines could contribute to regional science thinking. Its abstract, theoretical and methodological rigour made transferability across nations possible.

Consequently, regional science has grown in terms of scholarship and prestige. Regional science journals and journal articles related to regional science have been growing. Today there are about 17 regional science journals and 12 of them have regional science in their title (Isserman 1995). Several well-known publishers publish regional science book series (for example, North-Holland, Springer Verlag, Sage and Kluwer). Its membership at the level of individuals grew substantially and parallelled the growth in the number of national Regional Science Associations. Today 75 national associations are clustered into three megaregional blocks in North America, Europe and the Pacific and into three multinational linguistic associations. The North American and European meetings of Regional Science Association International occur annually, while the Pacific meetings occur every other year. A world congress is held every four years. In addition, countless localized–regional science meetings take place each year around the world.

In such a healthy and active intellectual environment, it is worth examining the above mentioned self-evaluation and criticisms because they could provide further insights for the future orientation of regional science. Three themes of concern emerged through the many articles and statements. These three related areas of concern are:

- regional science has failed to become a discipline as its originators had promised;

- regional science has not become institutionalized as a set of departments or colleges in most universities;
- regional science has been accused of being too theoretical, abstract and divorced from the reality of application.

Let us look at each of these statements from an alternative perspective.

3.1 Disciplinization

The desire by many regional science scholars, including some of the founders of regional science, is that it should become a discipline. A discipline is a body of knowledge recognized as a fundamental area of intellectual inquiry with specific and relatively narrow tenets and with a well-ordered leadership hierarchy and a vast array of acolytes we refer to as followers, believers or disciples. On the contrary, regional science has been a voluntary association of scholars and practitioners with an equal interest in a specific topic, each bringing different insights and analytic and theoretical perspectives to the same topic.

The disciplinary approach fits the undergraduate, lecture oriented, top-down hierarchical framework from the late eighteenth until the mid twentieth centuries. The latter associative approach, represents the future dynamics of the information economy where the exchange of new ideas, not positions, dictates the outcome and where contributions are assessed, not in terms of who said it but in terms of what is said. In that sense, perhaps Longman's Dictionary of Geography defines regional science more accurately. 'Regional science is an interdisciplinary field of study within the social sciences, linking economics, geography and planning, concerned with economic and social phenomena in a regional setting, making use especially of mathematical models in the forming of theories.'

Instead of being a discipline, it is the focus on interdisciplinary linkages and problem-oriented experience and dual identities of regional scientists with their teaching contributions in areas of societal interest which provides several advantages in today's economy. Recently, a number of mainstream economists have been publishing books and articles in economics journals that have traditionally been in the domain of regional science. The implication of this trend is that regional analysis and regional science is a 'hot' field because disciplinary groups are now working in the area. The business scholar Porter (1990), for example, has emphasized the importance of regional concentrations of innovative economic activity. Similarly, Krugman (1991a, 1995), a mainstream economist, has rediscovered the fact that transportation costs, localization economies and agglomeration economies are more regional issues than national (Isserman 1996; Martin and

Sunley 1996). These are good indicators of influencing disciplinary thinking through interdisciplinary leadership. As in all other fields of science, new perspectives and fresh ideas are needed to progress. Some of the questions we ask of a new idea are: Is it new? Is it relevant? Does it provide new insight? Will it work? How do we test it? What are the implications if it is extended? What happens if the assumptions are changed? This is an exchange of ideas and approaches among equal searchers rather than the structured dusty pedagogy of the past and it is this approach of associative learning that plays a central role in the new information economy.

3.2 Institutionalization

Regional scientists have criticized themselves and even each other for not institutionalizing this study area and not making it a fundamental department in universities and focusing it as a degree granting programme. It is true that regional science has not become a department in most universities and the closing of an existing department in the University of Pennsylvania in 1994 contributed to these pessimistic views. However, an alternative view is that departmentalization is against the very interdisciplinary nature of regional science. We can, however, convincingly argue that regional science has been institutionalized – not as a discipline or department – but as an interdisciplinary association of regional analysts. Further, if we return to our theme of borderless globalization and its attendant characteristics – flexibility, responsiveness, niche production – why should regional science become embedded in slow-changing, disconnected institutions such as universities? Given that the danger of becoming increasingly defensive and irrelevant by an institutionalized and disciplinary straight jacket, is it not better to be non-institutionalized? Is institutionalization not just another word for the intellectual equivalent of tariffs and trade barriers?

Therefore, regional science is better off living with turbulence and change, which create both dangers and opportunities for regional science and regional analysts. If it can utilize these opportunities and survive, regional science will be more flexible and responsive and it will keep regional scientists relevant. On the other hand, if it cannot succeed then at least we will not have added more bones to the intellectual graveyard of disciplinary irrelevance. It should be remembered that in the past few decades intellectual progress has been made not so much in the core of disciplines but at their interfaces with other fields of knowledge, for example, genetic engineering, biophysics, geographic information systems and self organizing behaviour in complexity theory. Hence, anything that limits regional science's ability to interact with its disciplinary neighbours, such as institutionalization and disciplinization, should be avoided. Perhaps the creators of research centres in biochemistry and molecular biology could give advice to regional scientists on how they have faced the handicaps created by institutions and disciplines in their attempts a few decades ago to create these centres. We should not have to learn these lessons twice.

3.3 Application

The charge that regional science has been too theoretical, abstract and divorced from the reality of application is somewhat problematic because it depends on who is criticizing. Since most of the interdisciplinary interactions occur among regional science, geography, economics and urban planning then for economists regional science is too application oriented, but for geographers and planners it is often too theoretical. The theory and abstracting from reality in order to generalize are very important, but without application theory would not be able to go forward. Theory and application are two sides of the same coin; they can be examined separately, but they cannot be separated. Much of this criticism has been misdirected and is a response to the disciplinary boundaries many regional scientists have in their fields of primary affiliation.

However, this is an issue of some sensitivity and it is intensely felt in those areas where regional differentials are particularly acute and where the public sector plays an important levelling role. In that context it is a fair criticism and requires our attention. Such a criticism is appropriate given our dominant simplistic paradigm of short run economic efficiency in the face of stubborn regional inequities. The interplay between culture and regional economic development is under-appreciated in our regional science models, although recently there are some signs of growing concern.

Historically, we have focused on lagging regions in relatively well developed and highly integrated economies where cultural differences are minimal and within this context our pronouncements have been narrowly economic. The political, social or cultural transformations that often accompany attempts to remove regional economic differences have had almost no role in our models. This is very troubling because as we have seen in Eastern Europe, in the former Soviet Union, in the Balkans and potentially in China, there are deep cultural cleavages that make regional economic transformations very difficult. Even within highly integrated and economically advanced economies – US, Canada, Italy and Spain to name a few – there are regions resistant to economic transformation. Here local culture and political leadership does not appear to have the economic strategy or the political will to implement a successful regional development process that will close the gap between the lagging region and the nation. Further, it seems clear that the pattern of massive transfers from central governments to these peripheral regions has not been a successful strategy socially, politically or economically. Hence, regional science and regional scientists need to pay close attention to these issues and to include them in their models.

4. THE FUTURE ROLE OF REGIONAL SCIENCE IN A GLOBAL ECONOMY

We all now know that regional science is not in a state of crisis; on the contrary, it is safe and sound (Yezer 1995 and Richardson 1995). However, this does not necessarily mean it will be keeping its present status. In this changing and globalizing economic environment, if regional science cannot develop and adopt new ways to deal with problems, it will not be able to keep pace with this fast changing world. In this section, we discuss some of the important areas where regional science needs to pay closer attention to other fields.

4.1 Joining Together with Other Social Sciences

Regional science should enrich its interdisciplinary structure by strengthening the bridge between other relevant disciplines and fields of sciences. It should reach out to scholars in the 'softer' social sciences like anthropology, sociology, political science and cultural and historical geography. In particular the role of institutions needs to be assessed directly. By joining together with other social science and professional analysts it will be possible to produce more realistic and useful models. Hence it could be possible to handle more complicated and richer quantitative models of places capturing the cultural and social diversity among regions (Bolton and Jensen 1995).

For example, in recent years political scientists have produced a spate of books and articles on regionalism in national politics and national identities. An important conclusion is that there is a close relationship between forms of government and political culture (Higgins and Savoie 1995). The character of political institutions develops in such a way as to coincide with the cultural characteristics of the local population. This has led, for example, to the recognition that all federal systems develop a flexible non-legalistic arrangement labelled cooperative federalism within which interactions between the core state and the region takes place. Further, in spite of designs to the contrary, these federal systems are modified over time to fit the regional cultures they link together. For example, the original Canadian constitution (the British North American Act) designed a centralized federal system but because of culture cleavages and a highly dispersed regional system, one of the most decentralized federations in the world has evolved. In contrast, next door in the US an intentionally highly decentralized federal system was designed but evolved into a much more centralized system. This is only to say that culture matters and is reflected in the political and economic base of regionalism.

Sociologists examining regional leadership, on the other hand, have noticed a relationship between a region's economic base and successful strategies of inclusion and building bases for managing economic change (Hamm 1985). They suggest that effective leadership is a dynamic process driven by an interactive local elite. However, if the regional leadership is dominated by a single individual, corporation, or even a single economic sector, such dominance will lead to defensive strategies of consolidation, growth through risk spreading and market force insulation. Sociologists hypothesize that such dominance leads to increased regional vulnerability and decreased responsiveness to new trends and changing global economic dynamics (Friedrichs 1986, 1987). The opposite would be, therefore, that diversity, range and variety of regional economic leadership drawn from a wide economic base would produce strategic flexibility and more rapid response to global trends and challenges. These are clear indicators that joining together regional science and other fields of social sciences could provide better answers to regional questions.

4.2 Regional Efficiency and Competitiveness

With different economic endowments, regions, in a competitive environment, have taken an increasingly active role in economic development policy via local, state or province governments. For example, since the Great Depression, the states in the US have developed or adapted several different policies to restructure and improve their economies. Many of these policies involved some kind of low interest loans, tax breaks, industrial recruiting, assistance in labour force training, hard and soft infrastructure or combination of other traditional economic development tools, such as the Appalachian Regional Development Commission (Isserman 1994). European nations have similar patterns (Haynes et al. 1994). As discussed earlier most of the government aided regional development programs have failed or have not provided expected outcomes.

In that sense, to develop and support sound development policies it is necessary to understand the region's economic, cultural and social structure. First, policy makers need to understand the industrial structure of their region, that is, which sectors are the leading sectors in terms of volume of activity, value added or share of labour demand, and which ones are growing or declining sectors regionally and nationally. Second, they should know whether or not the social and cultural structures of the region complement and support such programmes. More importantly, they also need to appreciate how industrial sectors of the region are performing relative to other regions in terms of efficiency and productivity because productivity growth is one of the most important sources of competitiveness in an interactive economy. Productivity is the source of the rise in output and income per person employed. It is argued that if regional productivity grows at just 1.5 percent per year, which is modest growth, output doubles every 47 years with factor inputs held constant. Regional development policies would have difficulty generating such a powerful effect on economic growth (Gerking 1994).

Further, policy makers also need to understand how much a given industry, firm, regional economy or the nation can increase its output without absorbing additional resources, thereby improving its competitive status. In that sense, efficiency becomes an important control parameter for assessing the utilization level of inputs in the production process. Just as the viability of firms in a long-term competitive environment depends heavily on their efficiency, the overall efficiency or productivity of the economy of countries, states, or localities determines the general well-being of their people (Krugman 1991b and Rivlin 1992).

Therefore, understanding, measuring and explaining productivity growth and its impact on a regional economy is very important and should be a main concern of regional policy makers. Any economic development policy, in one way or another, involves allocation and/or reallocation of resources. To develop sound development policies it is necessary (i) to assess a region's (county, state or a greater region) overall economic performance relative to other regions, (ii) to assess which sectors are performing better in the region, and (iii) to assess any given sector's efficiency relative to other sectors' performance in the region (Ali and Lerme 1990). For example, in the short term an industrial sector in a state may be 'leading' in terms of volume of activity, value added or share of labour demand, but if it is not operating efficiently compared to the same sector in other states sooner or later it will become uncompetitive and begin to wither away from external competition. Alternatively a less dominant sector may be a better candidate for growth and development because of its competitive efficiency.

Successful regional evolution is led by a regional experience that develops by increasing efficiencies in reducing the rate of system leakage, that is, reducing allocative, technical and managerial inefficiencies. This is done by effectively capturing proper production technologies, and as they mature, increasingly supplying backward and forward linkages locally (Jacobs 1984). However, those kinds of efficiencies (that is, locally internalizing production externalities) may make the rates of return in new small-scale innovative activities look low unless a long-term perspective is taken. Such a perspective comes from observations of long-term changes and appreciation of waves of regional economic succession.

Another important issue related to efficiency and productivity is regional infrastructure. When designing, locating and building infrastructure, it is essential to be focused on its reproductive capacity (Lambooy 1985). Such reproductive capacity is related to investment not simply in human capital and local R&D but in the capacity to produce or reproduce that capital and expand R&D. This means investment in and maintenance of institutions with these reproductive roles and the utilization of these institutions will generate the capacity to absorb and adapt to change. So it is hypothesized that regional centres with high levels of investment in, or a historically long-term pattern of support for, institutions with this role of generating reproductive capacity will do better than centres that have a thinner veneer of development. This is a reference to institutional infrastructure.

Still another perspective is directly related to factors of production and hence efficiency and productivity. There will be continual realignment with respect to growth within regional systems of complex modern societies responding to underutilization of capital or human resources whether government policies intervene or not. In terms of the former, the scale of access to undervalued resources is important, as is the ability to either transform those resources into factors of production or utilize those resources in substituting for higher cost production factors elsewhere. This relates both to an urban centre's region (that is, its character, resources and factor utilization levels) and its ability to do labour–capital substitution. Government policies can be seen as a complement to these changes easing transformations and maintaining investments for the future.

These are the areas that regional science and scientists should provide guidance to regional policy makers. These are the areas whose success or failure will certainly affect both regions and regional science.

4.3 Human Capital

In such a globalized, interdependent, borderless economy, human capital becomes a central differentiating asset. It is an asset that is mobile, responsive to price differentials in wages and in the short run this demographic reality is only augmentable at the margins. The quality of this human capital is not simply a function of formal education and on the job training – although that is extremely important. The quality of human capital is also related to occupation and work experience in an industrial structure. Further, its capacity for reskilling and acceptance of innovation is centrally important. Human capital quality is also a function of age and gender within a specific cultural context that is often reflected in participation rates but that differs from one region to the next.

The rapid pace of technological development demands an increased input of human capital with more skills, knowledge and related supporting capital investment. The highly competitive international economic environment forces firms to adopt new production techniques and to improve productive efficiencies of their workers.

Human capital can broadly be defined as the accumulation of knowledge and skills and is seen as a major contributor to the well-being and living standards of individuals who possess it. The level of human capital or education determines not only lifelong earnings of individuals but also contributes to the general well being of the society.

In addition to private returns to human capital, there appears to be a considerable amount of social return to human capital, that is, positive externalities such as well-informed and responsible citizens, communication skills, improvement in health and child care, lawful behaviour and lower crime rate (Haveman and Wolfe 1984). Although it is difficult to measure such externalities, it is suggested that the gain to society is substantial and positive (Mincer 1984). Returns to human capital vary geographically depending on the ambient level of human capital and the level of capital investments needed to make maximum use of it.

Isserman (1994 p. 73) reports in his survey of various state economic development programmes in the United States that 'many states have initiated programs to improve education, touting them as part of an economic development strategy'. The main message is that education is necessary for people to have good jobs in an increasingly competitive world economy. According to Isserman (1994) states are placing renewed emphasis on their vocational schools and community colleges, and have been competing to improve their universities as an element of economic development policy. Beyond their traditional teaching roles another function of universities is that their contribution to economic development by providing consulting and leadership training programmes to businesses, operating research parks and assisting in the adaptation of new technology. Silicon Valley and Route 128 are seen as outcomes of Stanford and MIT. In addition, several other regions of the United States, such as San Antonio/Austin in Texas and Raleigh/Durham in North Carolina have explicitly tried to build development centres around their universities (Jaffe 1989). As the then President of Harvard Derek Bok (1990 p. vii) stated 'in the long run, economic vitality of countries, regions and states depends on three important elements: expert knowledge, new discoveries, and highly trained personnel'. Regional science has a crucial role in connecting regional development and human capital requirements in regions.

4.4 Environmental Issues

Environmental regulations and increasing public awareness have two important impacts on regional economies. First, heavy regulations could force firms to relocate into unregulated regions or nations resulting in high unemployment in the regulated region. At the same time, because of the global impacts of the pollution, the problems remain unsolved. Second, sometimes exaggerated environmental problems may prevent useful investments. In such cases, both region and the nation lose.

Many neoclassical economists have sometimes too much confidence in the Coase theorem which states that market forces will internalize the externalities. However, there is no existing theorem that guarantees that even a perfect market will lead to sustainable development and the preservation of life support systems. Regional science and scientists should increase the realism and relevance of their studies by incorporating ecological economic approaches to address growing evidence of the above mentioned problems. In so doing, regional science and scientists could help the region, the nation and the world.

4.5 Modelling and Mathematization in Regional Science

Some have argued that the formal axiomatic and analytic perspective of regional science is what keeps it from absorbing new ideas and perspectives from adjacent, less quantitative social science fields and hence regional science has not been able to fit its findings into particular real world situations. In short, it is argued that this keeps regional science in theory rather than in problem solving. Regional science must not fall prey to the scolasticism of the medieval monks, but it needs to equally avoid today's more common error of solving the wrong problem perfectly due to the lack of direct observation and tacit knowledge. Obviously some of this criticism is correct, but the formal systems of regional science provide us with methodological rigour and allow us to sort the 'chaff from the wheat'. This makes its findings transferable and testable.

It can even be argued, as Krugman (1995) has, that regional science was not advanced enough in formal analytic methods to recognize and incorporate the breakthroughs in nonlinear, multiple equilibrium dynamics that made possible increasing return economics, self-organizing behaviour and the formalization of complexity theory. These breakthroughs made possible the new trade theory and the new economic geography. In spite of Krugman's perspective, regional scientists have already been working in this area but they could not project their findings well enough, partly due to under-utilization of mathematical presentation to make it theirs alone.

However, if one looks at the roots of some of these issues it will be seen that many of these contributions are regional science related.

Therefore, as Jackson (1995) argued, the use of complexity theory should be encouraged in regional science to deal with increasingly complex problems of today and the future. Skipping a mathematical definition and following Rosser (1991), a dynamical system can be described as 'complex' if it is nonlinear and has at least one of the following characteristics: (a) discontinuities in state variables over time, (b) sensitive dependence on initial conditions, (c) aperiodic (erratic) fluctuation patterns. Further and most important, the characteristic must be internal to the dynamical system being specified and not the result of an exogenous impact such as from a series of random shocks as in business cycle models. A short list of the types of complex dynamics with applications in regional science includes catastrophe theory, chaos theory, interacting particle systems, strange attractors, fractal basin boundaries, and evolutionary synergetics.

Catastrophe theory, due primarily to Rene Thom (1972) provides an explanation of discontinuities in structure and dynamic paths. Now often derided after a period of great faddishness, it has been applied, for example, in macroeconomics by Varian (1979) to a model of Kaldor (1940) and by Fischer and Jammernegg (1986). For a full discussion see Rosser (1991).

Chaos theory, drawing on the work of Lorenz (1963) and Li and Yorke (1975) to name but a few, depends on the idea of sensitive dependence on initial conditions (SDIC). A small change in a starting value will make a system behave very differently. This is known as the 'butterfly effect' from Lorenz's idea that a butterfly flapping its wings in China could cause a hurricane in the USA. This SDIC is seen as fundamentally destructive of the possibility of forming rational expectations in a noisy environment (Rosser 1995a, b), especially because chaotic dynamics can arise even in models with rational expectations (Benhabib and Day 1982; Grandmont 1985). They thus can be seen as a source of fundamental uncertainty. Chaotic dynamics also exhibit endogenously generated aperiodicity.

Interacting particle systems models draw on statistical mechanics theory (Kac 1968) in which there are critical thresholds in the interaction of entities which can lead to discontinuous changes in the outcomes of their activities. These models can be used to represent coordination failure in multiple equilibria situations. This idea can be applied to various economic situations (Brock 1993), including economic collapse in transitional economies (Rosser and Rosser 1994; Jin and Haynes 1997).

An attractor is the set toward which a dynamical system asymptotically tends if it is inside the basin boundary of the attractor. An attractor will be strange if it possesses a non-integer dimensionality known as fractal dimensionality (Mandelbrot 1983). It has often been thought that chaotic dynamics and strange attractors coincide, but this is not true in general, although there are many models in which both do occur. Lorenz (1992) has developed a model based on the Kaldor (1940) model with a strange attractor but without chaotic dynamics.

Even though a dynamic system may be non-chaotic and possess non-strange attractors, if it has multiple attractors they may be separated by basin boundaries which themselves possess a fractal dimensionality. Lorenz (1992) has noted that in such cases a trajectory can remain in a saddle zone for a long time appearing to track one basin and then suddenly jump into another basin. Isomaki and Kantola (1995) develop such a model for ecological-economic dynamics and Thompson (1992) provides a more complete discussion of possible dynamics in such systems.

Evolutionary synergetics was developed by Haken (1977) and his associates in Stuttgart (Weidlich and Haag 1983) and is closely related to the Brussels School models (Prigogine and Stengers 1984). These models emphasize out-of-equilibrium phase transitions in nonlinear dynamical systems which can generate systemic evolution in a punctuated form.

The positive nonlinear complementarities involved suggests a comparison with the path dependency models (Arthur 1990), with their multiple equilibria arising from positive feedback. In synergetic models slow variables 'slave' fast variables with critical evolutionary phase transitions arising when fast variables, destabilize to become controlling slow variables – the 'revolt of the slaved variables' (Paelinck and Stough 1996). Long-wave dynamics applications of something similar to this have been articulated by Berry (1991), Goodwin (1986) and Rosser and Rosser (1994). Hence, nonlinear dynamical systems with increasing returns have been tracked by regional scientists for years.

Another major area of application which has a strong theoretical and operational perspective that appears to be missing in regional science is a focus on a Decision Support System in a regional context. Though economic models of regional science provide normative guidance for goal setting, they often do not provide support for the decision making steps needed to reach those goals.

Such a regional decision support strategy goes beyond mathematical programmes associated with multicriteria and multi-objective analysis and focus on the processes of regional decision making in a group setting. It focuses on how to generate and display information to decision makers and how to evaluate good decisions not simply in terms of outcomes but also in terms of processes such as stability, cohesion and inclusion. This is a complex and difficult area but it is particularly important for regional, political and economic processes. It is vital in linking regional theory to regional reality.

Increasing computational power provides regional scientists with new paths in this area to explore and develop improved models. These developments will provide better answers to the complex and nonlinear problems in the twenty-first century.

4.6 Public Sector and Regional Science

One consequence of public sector interventions is that they strengthen urban centres at the location of governmental decision making even if the purpose of intervention is quite the opposite. The quaternary sector cushions local and regional systems from the broad spectrum of changes in the global economy. This generates a basis for continued growth and steady – and sometimes high – returns on service related investments. Under recent circumstances that have encouraged and led the shift to the service and information economy the quaternary sector has supplied strong growth leadership in capital regions.

However, difficulties lie ahead for regional science and scientists in terms of resolving the division of decision making between markets and the public sector. In an economic environment in which centrally planned economies collapse and similarly financial institutions and markets in a liberal system fail, regional science needs to take responsibility. Regional science has enough experience that enables it to contribute methods beyond its primary focus on spatial issues (Harris 1995). With its sound spatial methodology base regional science could provide guidance in such cases where public and private sectors need to act together, that is, in infrastructure, transportation service planning and housing development.

In addition to the above listed issues, there are several areas in which regional science can and should play an important role. One of these is in World Bank projects in Third World Countries. The World Bank, in addition to providing stabilization and structural adjustment loans to developing countries, supports specific development projects such as energy, transportation, education and trade. Regional science and regional scientists in such cases can provide the interdisciplinary insights and experience which are critical for success (Leinbach 1995).

Another issue is that the role of local and regional leadership is becoming more and more important to develop and implement regional economic development programmes. As Stough (1994) suggested, regional science and scientists need to incorporate the leadership – be they individuals, organizations or institutions – variable into their next generation of theories.

Finally, the role of technology and innovation in the regional development process and the fundamental issue of information and telecommunications in terms of their impact on regional processes of spatial organization and patterns of change are vital concerns. These issues are at the core of regional dynamics in the twenty-first century but they require advancement in theory in order to develop problem-solving methodologies. They will require theory and application to go hand in hand. Regional science needs to intensify its involvement in these issues.

5.   CONCLUSION

Regional science is not in state of crisis instead, it is in a position where great opportunities lie ahead of it to explore and benefit. As Knox (1987) pointed out, regional science has a comparative advantage – the ability and interest to work on real world problems and the rigorous and sophisticated methods that can address problems of structural change. This is understandable given the interdisciplinary structure of regional science. Further, strengthening ties with other fields of science will increase these comparative advantages. As long as regional science and regional scientists keep producing high quality, rigorous research and providing solutions to real world problems they will continue flourishing and attracting young scholars into the field.

REFERENCES

Ali, A.I and C.S. Lerme (1990), 'Determination of comparative advantage for the economy of states in the US', The University of Massachusetts, (mimeograph).
Arthur, W.B. (1990), 'Positive feedbacks in the economy', *Scientific American* **262** (2), p. 92.
Bailly, A.S. and W.J. Coffey (1994), 'Regional science in crisis: a plea for a more open and relevant approach', *Papers in Regional Science* **73**, pp. 3–14.
Bailly, A.S., Coffey, W.J. and L.J. Gibson (1996), 'Regional science: back to the future?', *Annals of Regional Science* **30** (2), pp. 153–63.
Benhabib, J. and R.H. Day (1982), 'A characterization of erratic dynamics in the overlapping generations model', *Journal of Economic Dynamics and Control* **4**, pp. 37–55.
Berry, B.J.L. (1991), *Long-Wave Rhythms in Economic Development and Political Behavior*, The John Hopkins Baltimore: University Press.
Bolton, R. and R.C. Jensen (1995), 'Regional science and regional practice', *International Regional Science Review* **18** (2), pp. 133–46.
Bok, D. (1990), 'Foreword', in Hanson, K.H. and J.W. Meyerson (eds), *Higher Education in a Changing Economy*, New York: Macmillan Publishing Company.
Brock, W.A. (1993), 'Pathways to randomness in the economy: emergent nonlinearity and chaos in economics and finance', *Estudios Economicos* **8**, pp. 3–55.

Fischer, E.O. and W. Jammernegg (1986), 'Empirical investigation of a catastrophe theory extension of the Phillips Curve', *Review of Economics and Statistics* **68**, pp. 9–17.

Friedrichs, J. (1986), 'Neue Technologien and Raumentwicklung: Eine Theorie der Sozial-Raumlichen Folgen', *Deutschen Soziologentag* Hamburg (29), pp. 9–21.

Friedrichs, J. (1987), *The Impact of Innovation on Urban Spatial Change*, West Germany: Institute of Sociology, University of Hamburg.

Gerking, S. (1994), 'Measuring productivity growth in U.S. regions: a survey', *International Regional Science Review* **16** (1-2), pp. 155–85.

Goodwin, R.M. (1986), 'The economy as an evolutionary pulsar', *Journal of Economic Behavior and Organization* **7**, pp. 341–9.

Grandmont, J.M. (1985), 'On endogenous competitive business cycles', *Econometrica* **53**, pp. 995–1045.

Haken, H. (1977), *Synergetic Non-equilibrium Phase. Transitions and Social Measurement*, Berlin: Springer-Verlag.

Hamm, B. (1985), 'Nations and cities–societal influences on urban development', in Haynes, K.E., Kuklinski, A. and O. Kultalahti (eds), *Pathologies of Urban Processes*, Finland: Finn Publishers Tampere.

Harris, B. (1995), 'An expanded role for regional science', *International Regional Science Review* **18** (2), pp. 165–70.

Haveman, R.H. and B.L. Wolfe (1984), 'Schooling and economic well-being: the role of nonmarket effects', *The Journal of Human Resources* **XIX** (3), pp. 377–407.

Haynes, K.E., Dignon, T. and L. Qiangsheng (1994), 'Regional development strategies and industrial policy making: a European example', in Cuadrado-Roura, J.R., Nijkamp, P. and P. Salva (eds), *Moving Frontiers: Economic Restructuring, Regional Development and Emerging Networks*, UK: Avebury, Aldershot.

Higgins, B. and D.J. Savoie (1995), *Regional Development Theories and their Application*, Transaction Publishers, New Jersey: New Brunswick.

Isomaki, H. and S.P. Kantola (1995) 'Bifurcation and chaos in an environmental macroeconomic system', mimeo, Helsinki University of Technology and University of Turku.

Isserman, A. (1993), 'Lost in space? On the history, status and future of regional science', *Review of Regional Studies* **23**, pp. 1–50.

Isserman, A.M. (1994), 'State economic development policy and practice in the United States: a survey article', *International Regional Science Review* **16** (1&2), pp. 49–100.

Isserman, A.M. (1995), 'The history, status, and future of regional science: an American perspective', *International Regional Science Review* **17** (3), pp. 249–366.

Isserman, A.M. (1996), '"It's obvious, it's wrong, and anyway they said it years ago?" Paul Krugman on large cities', *International Regional Science Review* **19** (1&2), pp. 37–48.

Jacobs, J. (1984), 'Cities and the wealth of nations', *The Atlantic Monthly* (March).

Jackson, R.W. (1995), 'Directions in regional science', *International Regional Science Review* **18** (2), pp.159–64.

Jaffe. A.B. (1989), 'Real effects of academic research', The *American Economic Review* **79** (5), pp. 957–70.

Jensen, R.C. (1991), 'Quo vadis, regional science?', *Papers in Regional Science* **70**, pp. 97–111.

Jin, D. and K.E. Haynes (1997), 'Economic transition at the edge of order and chaos: China's dualist and leading sectoral approach', *Journal of Economic Issues* **31** (1), pp. 1–23.

Kac, M. (1968), 'Mathematical mechanisms of phase transitions', in Chretien, M., Gross, E. and S. Dreser (eds), *Statistical Physics: Phase Transitions and Superfluidity, Volume 1*, Brandeis University Summer Institute in Theoretical Physics.

Kaldor, N. (1940), 'A model of the trade cycle', *Economic Journal* **50**, pp. 78–92.

Knox, H.W. (1987), 'The nonmetropolitan South in the 1990s: convergence or stagnation?', *Review of Regional Studies* **17** (3), pp.1–4.

Krugman, P. (1991a), *Geography and Trade*, Cambridge: MIT Press.

Krugman, P. (1991b), *The Age of Diminished Expectations*, Cambridge: MIT Press.

Krugman, P. (1995), *Development, Geography and Economic Theory*, Cambridge: MIT Press.

Lambooy, J. (1985), 'Urban theory and urban planning: an institutional approach', in Haynes, K.E., Kuklinski, A. and O. Kultalahti (eds), *Pathologies of Urban Processes*, Finland: Finn Publishers Tampere.

Ledent, J. (1995), 'Regional science futures. Presidential address', Canadian Regional Science Association, Ontario, CA: Brock University, St. Catherines.

Leinbach, T.R. (1995), 'Regional science and the third world: why should we be interested? What should we do?', *International Regional Science Review* **18** (2), pp. 200–210.

Li, T.Y. and J.A. Yorke (1975), 'Period 3 implies chaos', *American Mathematical Monthly* **82**, pp. 985–92.

Lorenz, E.N. (1963), 'Deterministic non-periodic flow', *Journal of Atmospheric Sciences* **20**, pp. 13–41.

Lorenz, H.W. (1992), 'Multiple attractors, complex basin boundaries and transient motion in deterministic economic systems', in Feichtinger, G. (ed.), *Dynamic Economic Models and Optimal Control*, Amsterdam: North-Holland.

Mandelbrot, B.B. (1983), *The Fractal Geometry of Nature Second Edition*, San Francisco: W.H. Freeman.

Martin, R. and P. Sunley (1996), 'Paul Krugman's geographical economics and its implications for regional development theory: a critical assessment', *Economic Geography* **72** (3), pp. 259–92.

Mincer, J. (1984), 'Human capital and economic growth', *Economics of Education Review* **3**, pp. 195–205.

Ohmae, K. (1993), *The Rise of the Region State Foreign Affairs* **72**, pp. 79–85.

Paelinck, J. and R.S. Stough (1996), 'Fast and slow-moving variables as a Lotka-Volterra process', Working Paper Center for Regional Analysis, The Institute of Public Policy, Fairfax, Virginia: George Mason University.

Plane, D.A. (1994), 'On discipline and disciplines in regional science', *Papers in Regional Science* **73**, pp. 19–23.

Porter, M.E. (1990), *The Competitive Advantage of Nations*, New York: The Free Press.

Prigogine, I. and I. Stengers (1984), *Order Out of Chaos*, New York: Bantam.

Richardson, H.W. (1995), 'Not a funeral but a wake: regional science in perspective', *International Regional Science Review* **17** (3), pp. 333–6.

Rivlin, A.M. (1992), *Reviewing the American Dream*, Washington, DC: The Brookings Institution.

Rosser, J.B., Jr. (1991), *From Catastrophe to Chaos: A General Theory of Economic Discontinuities*, Boston: Kluwer.

Rosser, J.B., Jr. (1995a), 'Chaos theory and rationality in economics', in Elliott, E. and J.D. Kiel (eds), *Chaos Theory in the Social Sciences*, Ann Arbor: University of Michigan Press.

Rosser, J.B., Jr. (1995b), 'Chaos theory and post-Walrasian macroeconomics', in Colander, D. (ed.), *Beyond the Microfoundations of Macro: Post-Walrasian Macroeconomics*, Cambridge: Cambridge University Press.

Rosser, J.B., Jr. and M.V. Rosser (1994), 'Long wave chaos and systemic economic transformation', *World Futures* **39**, pp. 197–207.

Sabel, C. (1989), 'Flexible specialization and the reemergence of regional economies', in Hirst, P. and J. Zeitlin (eds), *Reversing Industries Decline*, New York: St. Martin's Press.

Stough, R.R. (1994), 'Comment on: regional science in crisis', *Papers in Regional Science* **73**, pp. 25–8.

Thom, R. (1972), *Stabilite Structurella et Morphogenese*, Reading: Benjamin.

Thompson, J.M.T. (1992), 'Global unpredictability in nonlinear dynamics: capture, dispersal and the indeterminate bifurcation', *Physica D* **58**, pp. 260–72.

Varian H.R. (1979), 'A catastrophe theory and the business cycle', *Economic Inquiry* **17**, pp. 14–28.

Weidlich, W. and G. Haag (1983), *Concepts and Models of a Quantitative Sociology: The Dynamics of Interaction Populations*, Berlin: Springer-Verlag.

Yezer, A. (1995), 'Intellectual space for regional science', *International Regional Science Review* **18** (2), pp. 153–8.

PART TWO

Trade, Welfare and Growth

3. A Welfare Analysis of Regional Economic Integration

Tesshu Koshiba

1. INTRODUCTION

Regional economic integration arrangements (REIAs) are not new to international economics. They have been a continuing part of the IMF-GATT international regime since World War II. However, REIAs have recently attracted growing interest. Three decades ago, under the impetus of REIAs in Europe, countries of the third world launched the first wave of REIAs, customs unions (CUs) and free trade areas (FTAs). Unfortunately, expectations of economic developments through REIAs were not realized, and now virtually almost all REIAs in the third world seem to have failed.[1]

By the early 1980s, multilateral tariff cutting by developed countries and multilateral trade liberalization by developing countries/regions had substantially weakened the incentive to forming REIAs. Paradoxically, however, it is then that a second round of regionalism got under way. This was partly because gains from trade, as the fruits of international economic transactions based on the multilateral trade liberalization under the IMF-GATT system, were smaller and more time-consuming than expected for negotiations among countries. In fact, more REIAs were signed during the 1980s (namely eight) than during the 1960s and still more arrangements (several dozen) are now under consideration, not only by the Western and Eastern European nations, but also by Latin American countries and those participating in NAFTA (the North American Free Trade Agreement). From the viewpoint of the third world, current regionalism differs from the regionalism of the 1960s in two aspects. First, the regionalism of the 1960s was an extension of the import-substitution strategy. The current regionalism is, by contrast, taking place in an environment of outward/inward-oriented strategic policies involving foreign direct investment (FDI). Second, in the 1960s, developing countries pursued REIAs exclusively with other developing countries. Today these countries, especially those in Latin America, have their eyes on integration with large developed countries, particularly the United States. From the viewpoint of industrialized nations, the difficulties in starting the WTO (World Trade Organization) and moving it forward after concluding the Uruguay Round of multinational trade negotiations, have created a concern that the world trade system may gravitate towards a regional trade bloc aligned around the EU, the United States, and Japan (see also Chapter 5).

After a brief review of the welfare economics of a CU in Section 2 of this chapter as one of the most basic and typical forms of an REIA, Sections 3 and 4 will focus on the gains from trade obtained, from a static viewpoint, from welfare improving FTAs with quantitative restrictions and on the welfare benefits earned by the member countries of such welfare improving FTAs with qualitative restrictions as NAFTA, respectively. NAFTA is one of the most comprehensive free trade pacts with the local content requirements, and the first reciprocal trade pact between developed countries and a developing country. It has positive benefits for member countries. However, it has negative and exclusive impacts on non-members. Section 5 will focus on trade and commercial policies of integration such as NAFTA for drawing dynamic and positive impacts from the union, not only on members but also on non-members.

2.   THE WELFARE ANALYSIS OF A CUSTOMS UNION[2]

First, we review the basic Vinerian analysis[3] of a CU with a 3-country (Countries I, II and III) and one-commodity (Commodity X) model under the condition that trade is balanced at the outset among these countries. We assume further that I and II will form an REIA. III represents the outside world. I may import X either from II and from III depending on the import prices.

Figure 3.1 shows general equilibrium conditions for trade among the three. D_I and S_{II} are a general equilibrium import demand line (curve) for I and a general equilibrium export supply line for II, respectively. The horizontal line S_{III} is a general equilibrium import demand line for III. Also, it is III's export supply line at price P_{III}. P_{III} is, then, the price at which I is willing to buy and sell X in the world market with no trade barriers. P_{III} is assumed to be perfectly elastic as shown in Figure 3.1. Under free trade, the total quantity of X which I will import is C_1C_6, of which C_1C_2 will be imported from II and C_2C_6 will be imported from III. I's gains from trade are represented as consumers' surplus by the area under the import demand line and above the world price, that is, $P_aC_6C_1$, and those for II are expressed as producers' surplus by the area above the export supply line and under the world price, that is, $C_1C_2P_c$. Given constant cost and free trade, III neither gains nor loses from trade, because its average cost of production is always equal to its average revenue at any point on S_{III}.

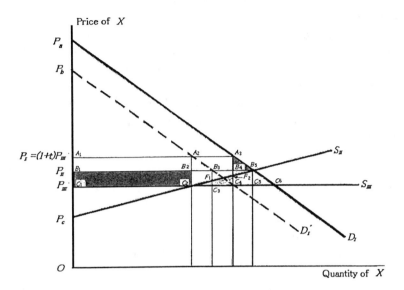

Figure 3.1 The welfare effects of a customs union

Assume now that initially I levies a non-discriminatory tariff at rate t on imports from II and from III. I's import demand line is now D_I' which lies below D_I by the amount of tariff per unit. Now, I's total imports at P_{III} will be C_1C_4, of which C_1C_2 will still be imported from II. Imports from III are C_2C_4 which have decreased by C_4C_6. The domestic price in I is presented by $P_I = (1+t)P_{III}$. The gains from trade for I are now the combination of two areas: $P_aA_3A_1$ (representing I's consumers' surplus) and rectangle $A_1A_3C_4C_1$ which represents I's tariff revenue. No changes occur in the gains from trade both in II and III, respectively.

Now introduce a CU (or an FTA in general) between I and II. Import from II is no longer subject to a tariff. The quantity of I's demand for imports from II is now equal to that of II's export to I at P_{II}. According to Viner's terminology, this has happened from trade diversion which leads to a switching of imports from a low-cost country to a high-cost country. C_2C_4 is I's imports which was switched from III to II after integration. Also, II's exports to I grew by B_4B_5. What does a CU bring to each of the partners? I increased its consumers' surplus by $A_1A_3B_5B_1$, of which $A_1A_3B_4B_1$, however, was I's previous tariff revenue. I's additional gains from trade are expressed in Figure 3.1 as a consumers' surplus of $A_3B_5B_4$. II increases its additional producers' surplus by $B_1B_5C_2C_1$. The area $B_1B_4F_2C_2C_1$ was part of I's previous tariff revenue. Now, the triangle $F_2C_4C_2$, being another part of I's previous tariff revenue, represents II's production cost of X and it is supposed to be distributed among the people who contributed to the production in II. Nothing is imported from III. The triangle $B_4B_5F_2$ is another part of II's additional producers' surplus. Trade diversion from III to II increases II's gains from trade at the cost of I. II's export to I grew by C_2C_5. The CU benefits II both because of the amelioration of its terms of trade and of an export expansion.

The net effect on the union is evaluated graphically by the comparison of two areas: $A_3B_5F_2$ and $F_2C_4C_2$. As seen from Figure 3.1, it is ambiguous to calculate the exact net effect. However, the following three conditions are important to estimate the net effect, other things being unchanged. First, the higher tariff rates I levies the larger consumers' surplus I can enjoy after the introduction of a CU. Second, the lower the prices of X in the world market the larger losses the union suffers from integration. Third, the closer to unity I's price elasticity of demand is, the larger triangle $A_3B_5B_4$ (an additional consumers' surplus in I) becomes. And also the closer II's price elasticity of supply is to unity the larger each of those triangles $B_4B_5F_2$ (II's additional producers' surplus) and $F_2C_4C_2$ (the net dead-weight loss of the union) becomes.

3.   A WELFARE-IMPROVING CU (FTA) WITH QUANTITATIVE RESTRICTIONS

Kemp and Wan (1976) considered a welfare-improving CU (FTA) in the presence of quantitative restrictions. According to them, under the same assumptions as in the previous section of this chapter, I and II can adopt a set of common external tariffs which improve their welfare benefit without hurting the outside world. The gist of their analysis is that a set of common external tariffs may be levied in such a way that the quantity traded with outside non-member countries is unchanged while internal trade is rearranged to maximize the gains from trade.

Suppose first, again in Figure 3.1, that I restricts its total import to A_1A_3 at P_I by a global quota. Let us assume next that quota licenses are auctioned competitively to domestic residents, and that the quantities of A_1A_2 and A_2A_3

will be imported from II and III, respectively. Assume further that the introduction of a CU (FTA) does not alter I's imports from III, namely A_2A_3. If such a CU (FTA) is introduced between I and II such that III is subject to have a quota which restricts III's total exports to I to the initial quantity, that is, A_2A_3, and such that I's imports from II are freed of any restrictions, total imports will expand under the standard assumption of any normal import demand schedule in I (strictly downward-sloping demand curves). Subtracting the same quantity of A_2A_3 horizontally from D_1 on any point at different prices, we now obtain $D_1{}'$ as a demand line facing II and III after integration. As a result, I will import B_1B_3 from II, along with the same quantity as before from III, that is, $B_3B_5 (= A_2A_3)$. The imports from II expand by B_2B_3 $(= B_4B_5)$ due to the reduction of the domestic price in I.

What happens in these countries? There is a positive effect on I, because I can increase its consumers' surplus by $A_1A_3B_5B_1$. However, the rectangles $A_1A_2B_2B_1$ and $A_2A_3B_4B_2$ out of the whole area, were initially parts of I's tariff revenue. The shaded triangle $A_3B_5B_4$ is, then, I's additional benefit. Conversely, there is a negative effect on I. It consists of two parts relating to the loss of the tariff revenue which I used to obtain before the union. One is $A_1A_2C_2C_1$, a small rectangle $A_1A_2B_2B_1$ out of it became I's consumers' surplus. So I's net welfare loss is the shaded rectangle $B_1B_2C_2C_1$. The other relates to $A_2A_3C_4C_2$. Area $A_2A_3B_4B_2$ became I's consumers' surplus, so that $B_2B_4C_4C_2$ is another net welfare loss for I. Thus, the net welfare effect on I is ambiguous. It will be positive or negative whether I's lost initial tariff revenue (the shaded rectangle $B_1B_2C_2C_1$) is larger or less than its additional consumers' surplus (the shaded triangle $A_3B_5B_4$). The net welfare effect on II is clearly positive. Because its producers' surplus grew by trapezoid $B_1B_3F_1C_2C_1$. From the trapezoid, II can receive an additional producers' surplus $(B_2B_3F_1C_2)$ due to the elimination of I's tariffs on imports from II and to the higher price of the good in the union than that in the outside world. II's net welfare effect is the aggregated area of these two. II suffers nothing from attending the union. Nothing is perceived as the net welfare effect on III, keeping still the same quantity of production as before at P_{III}.

Finally, it is interesting to note that I can increase its tariff revenue by $C_2C_3B_3B_2$ if I could divert importing C_2C_3 from II to III. This leads to income transfer and compensation issues. If I could do so, it would yield an additional net welfare benefit expressed by $F_1C_3C_2$ in the sense that the diverting imports from a high-cost country to a low-cost one encourages production in the world market. This is a good example to show that it is efficient for the union to enhance the welfare benefits of the member countries by an open door policy to the rest of the world. This policy often makes cumbersome compensation issues less serious between them.

A union provides a large amount of welfare benefits. But this comes from the union's point of view as a whole. As seen in Figure 3.1, II is the only partner who can gain a large amount of welfare benefits. We implicitly rely in our argument on lump sum redistribution between partners to ensure that neither partner losses. As De Melo et al. (1993) state, in practice, compensation mechanisms are cumbersome and not easy to handle, particularly in developing countries or in such a union in which developed and developing members are involved, because developing member countries in a union often have very diverse levels of per capita income. For example, in NAFTA, the difference between the US per capita income and Mexico's is huge. If integration leads to a migration of industries from the poor to the relatively more advanced economies, compensation is essential. In some cases, special funds are created to help the industrial development of the poorest members (De Melo et al. 1993, p. 165). In fact, the NAFTA countries seem to try to overcome these issues by providing the partners with opportunities to access to the integrated large domestic markets as much and as early as possible. Compensation issues easily emerge due to immigration from Mexico to the United States and Canada and due to a relocation of industries between them. Although the net welfare benefit in I is ambiguous, the net welfare benefit of the union as a whole surely grows by the areas of $B_2B_3F_1C_2$ and $A_3B_5B_4$. Therefore, there are many opportunities for each of the partners to gain from trade and to enjoy a welfare benefit when more countries are introduced into the union.

4. A WELFARE-IMPROVING FTA WITH QUALITATIVE RESTRICTIONS

Now we step forward to build a simple model of a welfare-improving FTA with qualitative restrictions to study, from a static viewpoint, the welfare benefit of REIAs such as NAFTA. NAFTA is one of the most interesting REIAs both with quantitative and qualitative restrictions. The NAFTA members try to lower and finally eliminate tariffs within the territory. At the same time, NAFTA's rules of origin are an effective means of trade barrier, protecting production, employment and income in the union. One of the most strict socioeconomic impacts on non-members is that the NAFTA members impose higher tariffs on imports from outside and even on products manufactured in the territory if those products do not comply with local content requirements. Our interest is to consider whether this type of REIA can be designed as a welfare-improving FTA for each participant.

Here again we assume, as in the previous sections, the same simple three-country settings. Figure 3.2 shows a simple graphic model for such an FTA of this kind.

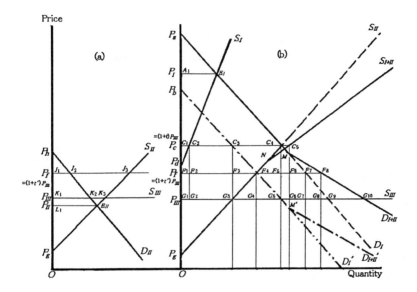

Figure 3.2 The impact of qualitative restrictions

I's supply and demand lines are drawn in Figure 3.2(b) as S_I and D_I, respectively. Economic information shown in Figure 3.2(b) is horizontally connected with that in Figure 3.2(a) in such a way that II's supply and demand lines are transposed from Figures 3.2(a) into 3.2(b) to have union's total supply and demand lines (that is, S_{I+II} and D_{I+II}) for X, by aggregating, horizontally, the quantity of I's supply with that of II's for S_{I+II} and by doing the same for the quantity of demand to have D_{I+II}, respectively, at any price level. Again, horizontal line S_{III} is III's general equilibrium demand and supply schedule (line) for X, which is assumed to be completely elastic at price P_{III}. Total quantity of I's supply is equal to that of its demand at P_I, yielding equilibrium point E_I. So is equilibrium point E_{II} at P_{II} for II's. The union's total supply line kinks at point N, because I's quantity of supply is involved in the union's total supply for any price level higher than P_d. Likewise, union's total demand line kinks at point M, because I's quantity of demand is included in the union's total demand for any price level lower than P_h. The union's kinked broken line D'_{I+II} is drawn as its total demand line imposing tariffs at t.

Under initial autarkic economic circumstances, each of these countries can maximize its welfare benefit at the intersection of its supply and demand lines. Assume, at the outset, that I levies a non-discriminatory tariff at rate t on imports from II and III. I's import demand line, $D_I{'}$, imposed tariff rate t as perceived both by II and by III, is drawn below I's demand line D_I with the same vertical distance from any point on D_I and/or D_{I+II}. The border price facing I is P_{III} and I's total import is G_1G_5. It does not matter to I as to whether to import the quantity either from II or from III. Because in either case I can obtain a tariff revenue shown by $C_1C_4G_5G_1$ ($= C_2C_5G_6G_2$) provided that I does not produce C_1C_2 ($= C_4C_5$) at P_c [$= (1 + t)P_{III}$].

There are two ways in which I can import G_1G_5. One is the importation from both II and III: G_1G_3 from II and G_3G_5 from III. The other is to import the whole quantity exclusively from III. In either case, I can earn tariff revenue $C_1C_4G_5G_1$. In the former case, however, II can gain producers' surplus $G_1G_3P_g$, other things being unchanged. I has another option, namely, it will get producers' surplus $C_1C_2P_d$ by producing $C_1C_2(= C_4C_5)$ at P_c. But this is not lucrative for I, from a static viewpoint. The reason is that I's total benefit expressed by the following three areas: $P_aC_4C_1$ (consumers' surplus), $C_2C_4G_5G_2$ (tariff revenue) and $C_1C_2P_d$ (producers' surplus) is clearly smaller than $P_aC_4G_5G_1$ by the trapezoid $C_2G_2G_1P_d$. The product value expressed by the trapezoid is supposed to be distributed among the production factors contributing to the production in I. In other words, the production has generated a cost of the equivalent value as long as I produces the good. I only gets its producers' surplus in exchange for a higher opportunity cost, meaning a net dead-weight loss.

Now introduce an FTA between I and II in such a way that imports from II are not subject to a tariff and that III is subject to a quota at the initial level of imports (C_3C_4). Assume that the FTA imposes a tariff at rate t'. The prevailing regional price in the union is $P_f = (1 + t')P_{III}$. Total import of the FTA will expand both because of the elimination of tariffs and of the lowering prevailing price in the union. At P_f, the quantity of FTA's total demand is F_1F_8, F_1F_7 out of the demand is derived from I and F_7F_8 comes from II, while the quantity of FTA's total supply is F_1F_4 which is much smaller than its total demand. Therefore, F_4F_8 can be imported from III at P_{III} which is the border price.

I's consumers' surplus grows by $C_1C_4F_7F_1$. Also, I receives tariff revenue $F_4F_7G_7G_4$ which is just the same in size as $F_3F_5G_5G_3$. The net welfare effect on I is ambiguous because, on one hand, I's previous tariff revenue

$(=F_1F_4G_4G_1)$ is eliminated while, on the other, I obtains an additional consumers' surplus $(= C_4F_7F_5)$. If the former is smaller than the latter, I will be better off, and vice versa. II's net welfare consists of the following three parts at P_f. First, its consumers' surplus being MF_8F_7 in Figure 3.2(b) $(=P_hJ_2J_1$ in Figure 3.2(a)), the second is the producers' surplus $F_1F_4P_g$ in Figure 3.2(b) $(= J_1J_3P_g$ in Figure 3.2(a)), and the third is tariff revenue $F_7F_8G_8G_7$. II's producers' surplus grew by $F_1F_4G_3G_1$ in Figure 3.2(b) $(=J_1J_3K_3K_1$ in Figure 3.2(a)). II's net benefit, therefore, increased by $J_2J_3K_3K_2$ in Figure 3.2(a). Integration between I and II increases their welfare benefits as a whole by expanding their imports from III through lowering the prevailing regional price even though the external terms of trade remain the same. The additional welfare benefit of the FTA is reckoned by subtracting areas $F_4G_4G_3$ (an additional dead-weight loss for the production in II) from $C_4MF_8G_8G_5$. Areas $C_4F_7F_5$ and $F_5F_7G_7G_5$ are the consumers' surplus and a tariff revenue for I, respectively.

The welfare benefit of the FTA depends either, first, on its supply and demand schedules, secondly on the level of t´ tariff rates the union imposes, thirdly, on the difference between P_c and P_f, and finally on the price elasticity of supply and demand for member and non-member countries, other things being equal. The closer to unity the price elasticity of supply and demand is for members the larger benefit the union can enjoy, ceteris paribus. The less elastic the price elasticity of supply and demand is for non-members, on the contrary, the larger welfare benefit the union will obtain.

Now, let us compare a welfare-improving FTA with a preferential trade arrangement (PTA). First, suppose further that I imposes a tariff at any lower rate, say at rate t´, on imports from II and at any higher rate, say at rate t, on those from III. Now, in the case of PTA, I will import C_1C_4 from I and II at P_e, receiving tariff revenue $C_1C_4G_5G_1$. Then, I will import F_5F_7 from II at P_f, having tariff revenue $F_5F_7G_7G_5$. A PTA allows I an additional net welfare benefit $F_1F_4G_4G_1$, compared with that in the case of FTA. I is now better off in exchange for a welfare loss for II. This is one of the important points to consider in compensation issues between participating members which enjoy, on one hand, gains from integration and suffer, on the other hand, from it. A PTA can get rid of these cumbersome compensation issues. A PTA makes welfare conditions better for participants than welfare-improving FTAs do. It is shown by de Melo et al. (1993, pp. 71–2) with the help of a three- good model that a PTA can be superior to a FTA. However, there are two important reasons, according to Viner (1950), why PTAs were prohibited by the GATT Article XXIV which permitted both FTAs and CUs, even though PTAs providing partial preferences can yield a better outcome than FTAs which can supply 100 percent preferences among the participants. First, there are likely to be burdens, such as administrative costs for importers and exporters in meeting the customs regulations and costs involved for the governments which levy tariffs in administering the customs machinery. Second, PTAs can be, and usually are, selective and discriminatory. The preferences selected tend to be trade-diverting rather than trade-creating (Viner 1950, pp. 850–51). So, we come back, in a moment, to the main topic of FTAs. We can confirm, under these static settings, that free trade brings the largest gains from trade to all participating countries. Let us suppose now that the members of a welfare- improving FTA eliminate tariff t´ and they will take their trade policies toward UTL (Unilateral Trade Liberalization). This is the case of free trade. Putting it differently, if these countries adopt free trade policies, what happens to them? I's consumers' surplus grows by $F_7G_9G_7$. II's net welfare benefit, on the contrary, decreases by $J_2J_3K_3K_2$. However, both countries can increase their consumers' surplus altogether by $F_8G_{10}G_8$. From this observation, free trade is often called the 'holy grail', meaning the most attractive and efficient welfare-improving trade policy in the short run.

5. DYNAMIC BENEFITS OF AN ADVANTAGE-DEVELOPING FTA WITH QUALITATIVE RESTRICTIONS

It is clear from our review of FTAs with qualitative restrictions that integration of this kind benefits member countries as a whole. Most of the welfare benefits are likely to go, from a static viewpoint, to the member countries that have comparative advantages in production at the expense of the other members having comparative disadvantages in production. Is there any room for the union to develop, from a dynamic viewpoint, welfare benefit for members who have comparative disadvantages?

NAFTA member countries have contracted the elimination of trade and non-trade barriers within the territory and are aiming for an expansion of business activities not only within the union but also with the other non-member countries. However, the members still preserve rights to levy taxes and tariffs on imports from non-members. One of the strongest and the most sensitive rules of NAFTA is the rule of origin which prohibits trade access from outside the union. NAFTA is an FTA not only with quantitative restrictions but also with qualitative restrictions in this sense. Qualitative restrictions are more serious and have more severe impacts on non-members for the expansion of foreign trade and international transactions. In this sense, NAFTA departs from the free trade principles. The negative aspects of such integration like NAFTA lead to retardation of the world economy, unless appropriate trade and commercial policies for economic development can be formulated. What kinds of trade policies can overcome those negative influences?

REIAs may lead not only to one-time increases in income and in gains from trade but also to dynamic gains in terms of growth in trade and FDI. Our interest here is, from this dynamic viewpoint, to design a comparative dynamic scenario for such an advantage-developing FTA with qualitative restrictions in order to overcome the negative impacts which REIAs usually hold particularly both for member countries and non-members with comparative disadvantages.

An advantage-developing FTA with qualitative restrictions is defined as an FTA that can be designed to increase partners' welfare benefits by developing partners' comparative advantages in creating opportunities for new employment, production and investment opportunities. Also, this type of FTA can extend global economic linkages beyond the initially integrated economies. Dynamic impacts on the FTA partners arise not only through various channels such as economies of scale, scope and speed but also through spillover effects like transfers of managerial resources and knowhow, which spur competition including more effective investment climates and accelerated rates of technological developments and so on.[4] These dynamic aspects are greater to the extent that integration goes beyond a one-time increase in gains from trade and production.

An advantage-developing FTA is designed to develop and to enhance a country's advantage, from a dynamic viewpoint, in producing goods and services in such sophisticated and high-tech manufacturing industries and high value-added sectors such as the so-called sunrise industries like computers, automobiles, telecommunications, along with some services characterized by a high elasticity of income, which encompass transport, tourism, sports, banking, insurance, and so on. One of the main characteristics of these industries is that goods and services are fairly differentiated and they are processed by using high-tech production techniques and technologies, advanced managerial skills and knowhow and so on. These differentiated goods and services always need advanced new technologies and sophisticated information, more processed and more specialized managerial-skills-oriented businesses which require more specialized roundabout production processes and techniques in a sequential network of sophisticated production. These sophisticated production patterns and systems are effective only when they are achieved by means of a stream of articulated different production processes. Such effectively arranged articulated production processes with highly specialized techniques require a horizontal and quasi-horizontal division of labour, intra-industry trade (IIT) or an intra-industry international division of labour. These business circumstances naturally enforce the member countries of an FTA to develop more productive and effective managerial resources not only within the territory but also in non-member countries. This leads to more intricated global business networks in the world. Also, advanced production technologies and business systems can often be transferred by multinationals through FDI. Running businesses in these modern industries utilizes economies of scale, scope and speed. There are many opportunities and possibilities for any member country to find, learn and develop any one of those sophisticated techniques or advanced technologies in the framework of a horizontal and quasi-horizontal division of labour. An advantage-developing FTA model helps us to comprehend why countries with different levels of economic development have incentives of participating in a new type of integration such as NAFTA.

Let us consider the dynamic impacts on member countries in NAFTA. Mexico has the opportunities to foster expected sunrise industries by introducing advanced production methods, technologies and business systems of the developed partners. Also, Mexico has more opportunities to create new jobs by encouraging FDI from abroad. These opportunities exist not merely for the developing partner but also for the developed partners. There are more opportunities for the developed member countries by creating new employment opportunities in sophisticated new industries rather than by protective strategies. Basically, NAFTA seems to have strong incentives both for the developed and for the developing partners to form an advantage-developing FTA. In fact, one of the most important objectives declared by NAFTA is to accomplish an advantage-developing and employment-creating FTA by: (1) eliminating barriers to trade in, and facilitating the cross-border movement of, goods and services *between the territories of the partners*; (2) promoting conditions of fair competition *in the free trade area*; (3) increasing substantially invested opportunities *in the territories of the parties*[5]

NAFTA's markets are, however, fairly protected by politico-economic barriers such as the rules of origin. In other words, the more strongly protected the integrated markets of integration are from the outside, the harder it is to break through the barrier. But this means that a closed FTA economy attracts FDI from abroad. In fact, FDI from Asia rushed into the United States just before the integration. The amount of Japan's FDI in the United States was $96.2 billion at the end of 1993. The corresponding amounts for Hong Kong, Korea and Taiwan were $20.2 billion, $8.0 billion and $12.7 billion, respectively. The FDI of these economies in NAFTA surpassed in most cases those of their NAFTA counterparts in these countries.[6]

These dynamic aspects of REIAs are, unfortunately, easy to associate with the so-called 'closed regionalism' and protectionism. One of the main reasons why such closed regionalism has been pursued by countries with inward-looking commercial policies is that they have been looking for better economic performances and higher rates of growth and development. However, it is important for the member countries of REIAs to implement commercial policies for encouraging and fostering strategic business operations and alliances, particularly in sunrise industries, by establishing advanced and intricate business networks and by achieving IIT and horizontal and quasi-horizontal international division of labour. It is clear that all the NAFTA members along with the other non-members, can benefit in a dynamic way from an international division of labour based on an advantage-developing FTA with qualitative restrictions. This is the real meaning of one of NAFTA's main objectives, namely as stated in the agreement, as one of its main objectives: (to) establish a framework for further trilateral, regional and multilateral cooperation to expand and enhance the benefits of the agreement.

ACKNOWLEDGEMENT

The author wishes to thank an anonymous referee and the editors for their helpful comments and suggestions. Of course, the author is responsible for all mistakes contained in this chapter.

REFERENCES

De Melo, D., Panagariya, A. and D. Rodrik (1993), 'The new regionalism: a country perspective', in De Melo, D. and A. Panagariya (eds), *New Dimensions in Regional Integration*, Cambridge/New York: Cambridge UP.
Kemp, M.C. and H.Y. Wan (1976), 'An elementary proposition concerning the formation of customs unions', *Journal of International Economics* **6** (February), pp. 95–8.
OECD (1995), *International Direct Investment Statistics Yearbook*.
Torre, A. and M.R. Kelly (1992), 'Regional trade arrangements', *IMF Occasional Paper 93*, Washington DC: IMF.
U.S.G.P.O. (1993), *The NAFTA*, Volumes I and II.
Viner, J. (1950), *The Customs Union Issue*, New York: Carnegie Endowment for International Peace.

NOTES

1. Torre and Kelly (1992) provide some important information on economic performances of REIAs in both developing and developed countries.

2. To avoid confusion, it is better to define, at the outset, the terms 'free trade
    agreement' (FTA), 'customs union' (CU), 'preferential trading arrangement
    (PTA)', and 'unilateral trade liberalization' (UTL)'. An FTA refers to an
    arrangement under which partner countries impose no tariffs on imports from
    each other but levy positive tariffs on imports from outside non-member
    countries. A CU is an FTA with a common external tariff by partner
    countries. A CU is one of the forms of FTA which is more widely defined on
    integration. A PTA represents an arrangement under which partners impose
    lower tariffs on imports from each other than imports from the outside
    countries. Both a PTA and an FTA allow for different tariffs by partners on
    imports of similar goods from the other world. UTL is a non-discriminatory
    reduction in trade barriers.

3. We will follow Viner's model (1950).

4. There are some non-economic channels such as political leadership and
    national sovereignty. The following discussions will focus on some
    economic channels.

5. Refer to U.S.G.P.O. (1993), Chapter one: Objectives. According to the
    document, other important objectives of NAFTA are to: provide adequate and
    effective protection and enforcement of intellectual property rights in each
    party's territory; create effective procedures for the implementation and
    application of this agreement, for its joint administration and for the
    resolution of disputes; and establish a framework for further trilateral,
    regional and multilateral cooperation to expand and enhance the benefits of
    this agreement.

6. Refer to OECD (1995). According to this, the positions of FDIs in Japan,
    Hong Kong, Korea and Taiwan at the year-end in 1993 were much less than
    those in the United States; $31.4 billion, $10.5 billion, $3.0 billion and
    $31.0 million, respectively.

4. A General Equilibrium Analysis of International Trade with the Stackelberg Duopoly

Takafumi Matsuba and Makoto Tawada

1. INTRODUCTION

The aim of this chapter is to analyse the pattern of trade and the gains from trade in a general equilibrium trade model with the Stackelberg duopoly in an international good market.

Originally, Markusen (1981) applied the Heckscher–Ohlin model to a general equilibrium trade analysis in the case where imperfect competition of Cournot type exists in one international market. Then he showed that a smaller country exports the imperfect competition good while a larger country exports the perfect competition good. Moreover, he proved that the smaller country can enjoy the gains from trade.

In some analyses of oligopolistic competition in game theory, it has been shown that Cournot competition is not necessarily dominant but the Stackelberg duopoly is also possible (see, for example, Albaek 1990; Hamilton and Sketsky 1990). Therefore, it is important to treat the Stackelberg type of imperfect competition in the theory of international trade (see Collie 1994). In our present model which is based on Markusen's model but with the Stackelberg duopoly, we show that the Stackelberg follower country exports the imperfect competition good and can enjoy the gains from trade if two countries are the same in size. So we propose some conditions under which a country exports the imperfect competition good and can gain from trade, when the size is different between countries.

In the next section the model is proposed and the autarkic equilibrium situation is investigated. Then, Sections 3 and 4 are devoted to the analyses of the pattern of trade and of the gains from trade, respectively. Concluding remarks are presented in the last section.

2. THE MODEL AND THE AUTARKIC EQUILIBRIUM

In this section we present the model and explain the autarkic equilibrium.

Suppose an economy with two countries, two goods and two factors. The two factors are labour and capital. And the two countries have the same factor endowment ratio. Thus, these two countries are distinguished by the difference in the absolute amount of factor endowment. The larger (smaller) country is endowed with the larger (smaller) amount of factor endowment. We call the larger (smaller) country country l (f).

Two goods are labelled X and Y. The good X is produced by a monopolist in each country. The good Y is produced under perfect competition in each country. Production technologies are the same between the two countries. Preferences are also identical between the two countries. The production functions of both goods are assumed to be linearly homogeneous as well as strictly quasi-concave with respect to the two factors. The factor endowments in each country are inelastically supplied and supposed to be given. Under these suppositions, we can derive the well-known result that the production possibility frontier in each country is concave-to-origin (see, for example, Quirk and Saposnik 1966). Thus, the production possibility frontier for country i, i = l, f, will be described as

$$Y^i = F^i(X^i),$$
$$(4.1)$$

where x^i and y^i are respectively denoted as the product X and Y in country i, $dF^i(X^i)/dX^i \equiv F^{i'}(X^i) < 0$, and $d^2F^i(X^i)/dX^{i2} \equiv F^{i''}(X^i) < 0$.

The aggregate utility function of country i is $U(D_X^i, D_Y^i)$, where D_X^i and D_Y^i are demands for X and Y in country i, respectively. This utility function is assumed to be homothetic and strictly quasi-concave with respect to D_X^i and D_Y^i. Now consider p as the price of X in terms of Y, that is, $p \equiv p_X/p_Y$ when p_X and p_Y denote the prices of X and Y, respectively. Then the aggregate consumers' behaviour in each country can be described as

$$\underset{D_X^i, D_Y^i}{\text{Max}} \ U(D_X^i, D_Y^i) \qquad \text{s.t.} \ \ I^i = pD_X^i + D_Y^i,$$
$$(4.2)$$

where $I^i \equiv pX^i + Y^i$ and I^i means the level of the national income of country i.

Following this consumers' behaviour, the demand for X is expressed as the function of p and I^i. In particular, the homotheticity of the utility function makes it possible to express the demand function as

$$D_X^i = D_X^i(I^i, p) = I^i g(p),$$

(4.3)

where $g' \equiv dg/dp < 0$. We now introduce the following assumption.

Assumption 1: $g' + pg'' < 0$, where $g'' \equiv d^2g/dp^2$.
By (4.3), the inverse demand function is represented by

$$p = P\left(\frac{D_X^i}{I^i}\right),$$

(4.4)

where $P' \equiv dP/d(D_X^i/I^i) < 0$.

Next, consider the firm's behaviour in industry X in autarky. The behaviour of the monopolist of country i in autarky is

$$\underset{x^i}{\text{Max}} \; P\left(\frac{X^i}{I^i}\right)X^i - C_X^i(X^i), \quad i = l, f,$$

(4.5)

where $C_X^i(X^i)$ is a cost function of good X in country i. We assume that in each country the monopolist does not have a monopsony power in factor markets and considers the level of the national income as given in his profit maximization.

Therefore, the optimal condition of (4.5) is obtained as

$$p(I - \varepsilon(p)) = \frac{dC_X^i(X^i)}{dX^i} \equiv C_X^{i'}(X^i),$$

(4.6)

where $\varepsilon(p) \equiv - [g(p)/p]/[dg(p)/dp]$ which implies the inverse of the price elasticity for demand.

In equation (4.6), $p[1-\varepsilon(p)]$ means the marginal revenue. The marginal revenue must be positive in equilibrium since $C_X^{i'} > 0$. Thus, we assume that $\varepsilon(p)<1$ everywhere. Moreover, under Assumption 1, we can show

Lemma 1

$$\varepsilon'(p) \equiv d\varepsilon(p)/dp < 0.$$

Proof. It is obvious from the fact that

$$\frac{d\varepsilon}{dp} = -\ \frac{p(g')^2 - (g' + (pg''))}{(pg')^2}\ ,$$

and the assumption that $g' + pg'' < 0$. Q.E.D.

Denoting $C^i_Y(Y^i)$ as the cost function of Y in country i, the production equilibrium of industry Y under perfect competition is $1 = C^{i'}_Y(Y^i) \equiv dC^i_Y / dY^i$.

By this equation and equation (4.6), we have

$$-[F^{i'}(X^i) = p[1 - \varepsilon(p)], \tag{4.7}$$

since $-F^i(X^i) = C^{i'}_X / C^{i'}_Y$.

Consequently, for any given p, the supplies of both goods, X^i and Y^i, are determined by (4.1) and (4.7). These X^i and Y^i give the value of I^i as $pX^i + Y^i$. Then the demands for two goods are also determined as

$$D^i_X = I^i g(p) \ .$$

Then, the autarkic equilibrium price p is determined in order to satisfy the market clearing condition $X^i = DX^i_X$. Let the autarkic equilibrium values of p, X^i and Y^i be p^A, X^{iA} and Y^{iA}, respectively. Figure 4.1 shows the relationship between the autarkic equilibrium price P^A and the quantities for X^{iA} and Y^{iA}.

Let us make it clear how to distinguish the autarkic equilibria of countries l and f. By assumption, the difference between countries l and f is in factor endowment. Suppose that the labour and capital endowments of country i, i = l,f are as L^i and K^i, respectively. The assumption that the factor endowment ratio is the same between countries means that $L^l = \alpha F^f$ and $K^l = \alpha K^f$ for some $\alpha \geq 1$. By this assumption and the linear homogeneity of the production functions, the production possibility frontier of country l is obtained by the α-time proportional expansion of that of country f from the origin. This, together with the fact that the indifference curves have the homothetic property, brings forth that the autarkic equilibrium price is the same between countries and that the autarkic equilibrium quantities of the products of country l are α times larger than those of country f.

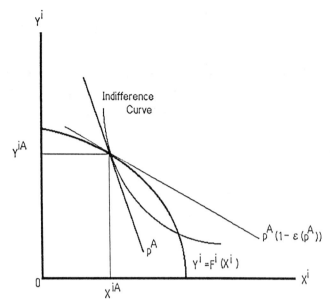

Figure 4.1 Equilibrium in autarky

3. INTERNATIONAL TRADE WITH THE STACKELBERG OLIGOPOLY

Markusen (1981) analysed the case where each country's monopolist chooses the Cournot-type behaviour in the international market. This section will analyse the problem of international trade under the Stackelberg oligopoly. Thus, we suppose that the monopolist in the smaller country behaves as a follower and the monopolist in the larger country behaves as a leader.

Consider the production of good X in the case where international trade becomes possible. We first derive the follower's reaction function. The profit maximization problem of the follower in industry X is formalized as

$$\underset{x^f}{\text{Max}}\; P\left(\frac{X^f + X^l}{I^f + I^l}\right) X^f - C_x^f(X^f),$$

where the world income $I^f + I^l$ and the leader's output X^l are considered to be given for the follower.

Keeping in mind the optimal condition for the profit maximization in industry Y, the production equilibrium condition in country f is obtained as

$$p[1 - \sigma^f \varepsilon(p)] = - F^f(X^f), \qquad (4.8)$$

where $\alpha^f \equiv X^f/(X^f + X^l)$.

The equation (4.8) gives the reaction function of country f to the level of output in country l, which we denote as $X^f = \phi^f(X^l)$. Defining $Q \equiv X^f + X^l$ and $I^w \equiv I^l + I^f$ we calculate $p(1 - \sigma^f \varepsilon(p)$ and obtain

$$[1 - \sigma^f \varepsilon(p)] = P(\frac{Q}{I^w}) + P'(\frac{Q}{I^w})(\frac{Q}{I^w}) \sigma^f.$$

Bearing this in mind, we differentiate (4.8) and obtain

$$\frac{dX^f}{dX^l} \equiv \phi^{f'}(X^l) = - \frac{P' + (X^f P''/I^w)}{P'(X^f P''/I^w) + P' + I^w F^{f''}}, \qquad (4.9)$$

where $P'' \equiv d^2 P/d(Q/I^w)^2$.

The following lemma can be established.

Lemma 2
Under Assumption 1,

$$-1 < \phi^{f'}(X^l) < 0.$$

Proof. Notice that $P'' < 0$ and $F^{f''} < 0$. Then equation (4.9) furnishes Lemma 2 straightforwardly, if it is proved that $P' + (X^f P''/I^w) < 0$. We easily verify that $g' = 1/P'$ and $P'' = -g''/(g')^3$, for $p = P(Q/I^w)$ and $Q = I^w g(p)$. and $Q = I^w g(p)$. Thus, we have

$$P' + \frac{X^f P''}{I^w} = \frac{1}{(g')^2} [g' + (- \frac{X^f}{pg' I^w}) pg''] . $$

$$(4.10)$$

On the other hand, the fact that $1 - \varepsilon(p) > 0$ yields $g + pg' < 0$, so that

$$0 < - \frac{X^f}{I^{wpg'}} \leq \frac{X^f}{I^{wg}} = \frac{X^f}{Q} < 1 .$$

This, together with (4.10) and Assumption 1, assures $P' + (X^f P'' / I^w) < 0$. Q.E.D.

Therefore, the slope of the follower's reaction function is in between -1 and 0.[1]

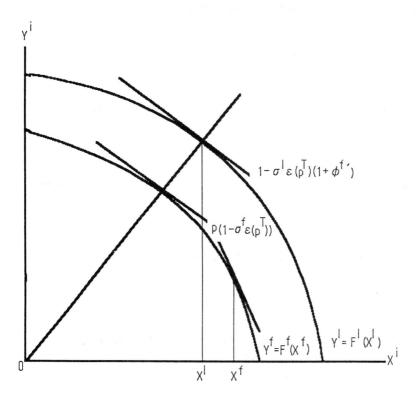

Figure 4.2 The proof of Theorem 1 by contradiction

Let us proceed to the leader's behaviour. The monopolist of country 1 incorporates the reaction of the monopolist of country f into his strategy. So the monopolist of country 1 as the leader of the duopolists considers

$$\underset{x^l}{\text{Max}} \ P(\frac{X^l + X^f}{I^l + I^f})X^l - C^l_X(X^l), \quad \text{s.t. } X^f = \phi^f(X^l).$$

The above optimization problem gives rise to the following equation as the producer's equilibrium condition in country 1:

$$p[1 - \sigma^l \varepsilon(p)(1 + \phi^f)] = -F'(X^l),$$ (4.11)

where $\sigma^l \equiv X^l / Q$.

In what follows, we analyse the Stackelberg trade equilibrium and compare it with the autarkic equilibria. Let p^T and X^{iT} be the trade equilibrium price and quantity of X in country i, respectively. First of all we present:

Theorem 1
In the Stackelberg trade equilibrium, the output of X in country l is greater than that of country f (when $\alpha > 1$).

Proof. Suppose that $X^{1T} \leq X^{fT}$. Then, in view of (4.8) and (4.11), it must hold from Figure 4.2 that

$$p^T[1 - \sigma^f \varepsilon(p^T)] \geq p^T \{1 - \sigma^l \varepsilon(p^T)[1 + \phi^{f'}(X^{lT})]\}.$$ (4.12)

On the other hand, Lemma 2 and the assumption that $\sigma^f \geq \sigma^l$ assure that

$$p^T[1 - \sigma^f \varepsilon(p^T)] < p^T\{1 - \sigma^l \varepsilon(p^T)[1 + \phi^{f'}(X^{lT})]\},$$

which contradicts (4.12). Thus, $X^{1T} > X^{fT}$. Q.E.D.

We can also prove

Theorem 2
The relative price of good X is lower at the trade equilibrium than at the autarkic equilibrium of each country.
Proof. Suppose that $p^T \geq p^A$. Then we have

$$p^A[1 - \varepsilon(p^A)] < p^T [1 - \sigma^f \varepsilon(p^T)],$$

and

$$p^A[1 - \varepsilon(p^A)] < p^T[1 - \sigma^l \varepsilon(p^T)(1 + \phi^{f'})].$$

Thus, by (4.8), (4.11) and (4.7), it follows that

$$\frac{D_X^{iA}}{D_Y^{iA}} = \frac{X^{iA}}{Y^{iA}} < \frac{X^{iT}}{Y^{iT}}, \quad i = l, f,$$

where D_j^{iT}, for $i = l,f$, and $j = X,Y$, is the trade equilibrium demand for good j in country i.

On the other hand, the supposition that $p^T \geq p^A$ implies

$$\frac{D_X^{iT}}{D_Y^{iT}} \leq \frac{D_X^{iA}}{D_Y^{iA}}, \quad i = l,f,$$

where D_j^{iA} for $i = l,f$, and $j = X,Y$, is the autarkic equilibrium demand for good j in country i.

Therefore, the world market clearing condition that

$$\frac{D_X^{lT} + D_X^{fT}}{D_Y^{lT} + D_Y^{fT}} = \frac{X^{lT} + X^{fT}}{Y^{lT} + Y^{fT}},$$

is not satisfied, a contradiction to the trade equilibrium. Thus, $p^T < p^A$. Q.E.D.

Moreover, Theorem 1 brings forth of the following theorem.

Theorem 3
At least one of the two countries expands the production of good X by trade.
Proof. Since $p^A < p^T$ by Theorem 2, we have

$$\frac{X^{iA}}{Y^{iA}} = \frac{D_X^{iA}}{D_Y^{iA}} = \frac{D_X^{fA} + D_X^{lA}}{D_Y^{fA} + D_Y^{lA}} < \frac{D_X^{fT} + D_X^{lT}}{D_Y^{fT} + D_Y^{lT}} = \frac{X^{fT} + X^{lT}}{Y^{fT} + Y^{lT}}, \quad i = l,f$$

Thus, either $X^{fA}/Y^{fA} < X^{fT}/Y^{fT}$ or $X^{lA}/Y^{lA} < X^{lT}/Y^{lT}$ must hold, which implies $X^{fA} < X^{fT}$ or $X^{lA} < X^{lT}$. Q.E.D.

Corollary 1
If two countries are the same in factor endowment, then, by trade, the supply of good X increases in the country where the firm of industry X acts as the leader of the Stackelberg duopoly.

Proof. Since two countries are identical in scale, it is obvious that $X^{lA} = X^{lT}$. This combined together with Theorems 1 and 2 brings forth the desired result. Q.E.D.

Now let us turn our attention to the analysis on the pattern of trade. We first present the following theorem.

Theorem 4
(i) Suppose that $[1+ \phi^{f'}(X^{fT})]X^{1T} < X^{fT}$. Then country 1 expands the supply of good X and contracts that of good Y by opening trade and the pattern of trade is that country 1(f) exports good X(Y) and imports good Y(X).
(ii) Suppose that $[1+ \phi^{f'}(X^{fT})]X^{1T} > X^{fT}$. Then country f expands the supply of good X and contracts that of good Y by opening trade and the pattern of trade is that country f(1) exports good X(Y) and imports good Y(X).
(iii) If $[1+ \phi^{f'}(X^{fT})]X^{1T} = X^{fT}$, then both countries expands the production scale of good X and contracts that of good Y after opening trade but there is no trade.

Proof. We prove first (i) and (ii). Under Assumption 1, we have

$$p^T[1 - \sigma^f \varepsilon(p^T)] < (>) \, p^T[1 - \sigma^l \varepsilon(p^T)(1 + \phi^f)] \, .$$

Hence $X^{fT}/Y^{fT} < (>) \, X^{1T}/Y^{1T}$, whence we have a desired result by Theorem 3. In order to show (iii), we notice that $X^{fT}/Y^{fT} = X^{1T}/Y^{1T}$. So there is no trade. Moreover, Theorem 3 assures $X^{iT}/Y^{iT} > X^{iA}/Y^{iA}$, for i = 1,f, implying both countries expand the production level of good X by trade. Q.E.D.

Corollary 2
If two countries are the same in scale, the country where the firm of industry X acts as the leader exports good X and the other country where the firm of industry X acts as the follower exports good Y.

Proof. Theorem 1 implies $X^{iT} > X^{fT}$, from which

$$p^T[1 - \sigma^f \varepsilon(p^T) < p^T[1 - \sigma^l \varepsilon(p^T)(1 + \phi^{f'})] \, .$$

Therefore, we have $(1+ \phi^{f'})X^{1T} < X^{fT}$. By Theorem 4, this implies that country 1 exports good X. Q.E.D.

Markusen showed that when the world market of good X is subject to the Cournot oligopoly, the smaller country necessarily increases the production scale of good X after the opening of trade and exports it. On the other hand, our two corollaries assert that, if two countries are identical in scale and the Stackelberg oligopoly prevails in the world market of good X, the country where the firm producing good X acts as the leader expands the production of good X and exports it. Therefore, if the leader country is larger than the other country in scale, then which country expands the production of good X and exports it depends on which element, the country size or the Stackelberg type of imperfect competition, is more dominant. This aspect is reflected in Theorem 4. If the country scale is more dominant, X^l is sufficiently large. So, (ii) of Theorem 4 can apply. Obviously, Markusen's conclusion carries over. If the Stackelberg duopoly is more influential, $1 + \phi^{f'}$ becomes close to zero. Then we have the case (i) in Theorem 4, which means that the country where the Stackelberg leader exists expands the supply of good X and exports it.

Up to here, we have supposed that the Stackelberg leader exists in the larger country. Here, we briefly discuss the converse case that the Stackelberg leader exists in the smaller country. Tracing the ways of the proofs, we can confirm that Theorems 2, 3 and 4 are still valid in this case. As for Theorem 1 asserting that the Stackelberg leader country produces good X more than the follower country, we cannot exclude the case that the follower country produces the good X more than the other country if the follower country is large enough. Thus, Theorem 1 is not always true. So $[1 + \phi^{f'}(X^{fT})]X^{lT} < X^{fT}$ in Theorem 4 does not always hold in this case. The following remark may be in order.

Remark
Theorem 1 holds when the Stackelberg leader country is larger in size than the other country. But Theorems 2, 3 and 4 hold irrespective of country size.

4. GAINS FROM TRADE

We are now in a position to investigate whether trade is gainful or not to each country.

A country production frontier is drawn in Figure 4.3. Point A is an autarkic equilibrium. We know that in any country the trade equilibrium price line is steeper than the tangent line of the production frontier at the trade equilibrium production point T. This is illustrated in Figure 4.3, where the line B is the trade equilibrium price line.

The national budget constraint after trade is expressed by the line B. The figure shows that the autarkic equilibrium point can be attained even after opening trade if the country expands the production of good X. Therefore, trade is gainful to the country which expands the production of good X. This enables us to reach the following theorem.

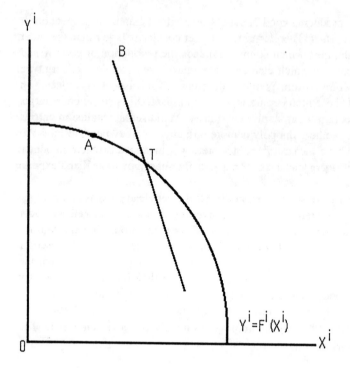

Figure 4.3 Autarky and gains from trade

Theorem 5

i)   If $[1+ \phi^{f'}(X^{fT})]X^{1T}<(>)X^{fT}$, then country 1 (f) receives a gain from trade.

(ii) If $[1+\phi^{f'}(X^{fT})]X^{1T}= X^{fT}$, then the possibility of trade makes both countries better off.

Both (i) and (ii) are true irrespective of the country size.

(iii) If two countries are the same in size, then trade is gainful to country 1 which acts as the leader of the Stackelberg duopoly in industry X.

5.   CONCLUDING REMARKS

We have examined the pattern of trade and the gains from trade under the Stackelberg type of imperfect competition and showed that the Stackelberg leader country tends to export the imperfect competition good and to obtain the gains from trade. The analysis of international trade with imperfect competition seems to become more realistic when regionalization proceeds in the world economy. A small country in the world economy may possibly become relatively large in the regionally configured economy. Moreover, the country may have a tighter relation and more information on countries in the same region after regionalization. Thus the analysis of international trade incorporating strategical aspects may be more meaningful when we consider the trade between countries within the same global region.

There are several problems we have not tackled in the present chapter. For instance, it is attractive to compare the trade equilibrium of the Stackelberg oligopoly with that of the Cournot oligopoly. As we have stated in the first section, this kind of analysis enables us to deal with the problem in a more game-theoretical framework. It may be also interesting to examine the factor price equalization theorem in the present framework by introducing two factors explicitly. Then we can apply the present analysis to the case where primary factors are internationally mobile. For instance, consider an economy where two primary factors, say labour and capital, exist and the imperfect competition good is more capital-intensive than the other good. In this economy, intuitively speaking, if

$$p^T[1 - \sigma^f \epsilon(p^T)] < (>) \ p^T\{1 - \sigma^l \epsilon)([1 + \phi^{f'}(X^{fT})]\}$$

the wage is lower and rental is higher in country l(f) than in country f(l) under the world equilibrium situation without international factor mobility. This is a simple deduction from the Stolper–Samuelson Theorem. Therefore, capital tends to move from country f(l) to the other and labor tends to move from country l(f) to the other, once factors are allowed to move internationally. As for a comparative static analysis, there is a problem of how the trade equilibrium is affected by a change in the size of each country. Furthermore, we may extend the analysis to the case of the conjectural variation type of imperfect competition. All these problems seem to be significant and possible to deal with.

Finally, we should notice one important argument that an oligopolistic firm may be able to manipulate not only the price of the commodity it produces but also the prices of other commodities and even the factor prices in a general equilibrium setting (see, for example, Gabszewicz and Vial 1972; Kemp and Shimomura 1995). Thus, we have to be careful about how the oligopolistic firms behave in the general equilibrium framework. If we take a full consideration on this problem, the general equilibrium analysis with oligopolistic competition becomes quite complicated.[2] For this reason, we have followed the traditional treatment in this aspect. That is, like Melvin and Warne (1973), Markusen (1981), Lahiri and Ono (1995), and so on, an oligopolistic firm is assumed to regard the national income and factor prices to be constant when he controls the price of his commodity. Although it seems to be difficult to relax this assumption, we need to pay much attention to this problem in future.

REFERENCES

Albaek, S. (1990), 'Stackelberg leadership as a national solution under cost uncertainty', *The Journal of Industrial Economics* **38**, pp. 335–47.

Collie, D.R. (1994), 'Endogenous timing in trade policy games: should governments use countervailing duties?', *Weltwirtschaftliches Archiv* **130**, pp. 191–209.

Gabszewicz, J.J. and J.-P. Vial (1972), 'Oligopoly "à la Cournot" in a general equilibrium analysis', *Journal of Economic Theory* **4**, pp. 381–400.

Hamilton, J.H. and S.M. Slutsky (1990), 'Endogenous timing in duopoly games: Stackelberg or Cournot equilibria', *Games and Economic Behavior* **2**, pp. 29–46.

Kemp, M.C. and K. Shimomura (1995), 'The apparently innocuous representative agent', *The Japanese Economic Review* **46**, pp. 247–56.

Kemp, M.C. and M. Okawa (1995), 'The gains from free trade under imperfect competition', in Chang, W. and S. Katayama (eds), *Imperfect Competition in International Trade*, Kluwer Academic Publishers, pp. 53-62.

Lahiri, S. and Y. Ono (1995), 'The role of free entry in an oligopolistic Heckscher–Ohlin model', *International Economic Review* **36**, pp. 609–24.

Markusen, J.R. (1981), 'Trade and the gains from trade with imperfect competition', *Journal of International Economics* **11**, pp. 531–51.

Melvin, J.R. and R. Warne (1973) 'Monopoly and the theory of international trade', *Journal of International Economics* **3**, pp. 117–34.

Quirk, J.P. and R. Saposnik (1966), 'Homogeneous production function and convexity of the production possibility set', *Metroeconomica* **18**, pp. 192–97.

NOTES

1. In a similar manner, the slope of the reaction function for country 1 can be shown to have the same property, so that, under the usual dynamic adjustment process in the Cournot-Nash behaviour, the stability of the equilibrium is assured. This aspect was not revealed in Markusen (1981). Therefore, the input adjustment process of the Stackelberg leader is dynamically stable, when the process is described as $dX^1/dt = d\pi^1[X^1, \phi^f(X^1)]/dX^1$, where π^1 is the profit of the leader.

2. See Kemp and Okawa (1995) who recently tackled this topic.

5. The Pattern of Industrialization of the South

Masamichi Kawano

1. INTRODUCTION

Krugman (1981) described the uneven development of North and South by means of a model with a Leontief-type production technology and the scale economy.

Dutt (1992) studied Indian economic development and showed that the development of the manufacturing sector increases the productivity of the agricultural sector. Taking into account this external effect, he showed the existence of a steady state in which the South is engaged in the production of manufactured goods. Kubo (1994) showed the possibility of a steady state where the South engages in the production of manufactured goods when the external economy from the developed region to the less-developed region is sufficiently strong in order to overcome the scale economies in the North.

The purpose of this chapter is to extend Krugman's model by introducing two manufactured goods in the framework of the Leontief-type technology with scale economy, and derive the takeoff of the South and the steady state where both North and South will produce at least one type of manufactured good.

In the modern economy, the less-developed countries such as NIEs are catching up with developed countries. We are interested in the pattern of the catching up process. Do they begin to produce labour-intensive goods? Does the production of manufactured goods in the South grow monotonically and gradually? To answer these questions, we present the model of the 'takeoff' of the less-developed region. The mechanism of the takeoff of the South is as follows. When there is enough labour in this economy, then Krugman's result, that is, the region which has the larger capital at the initial point will occupy the whole production of the manufactured goods, will also hold in this extended economy. We extend the model by introducing an external technical progress, that is, an improvement in productivity in the agricultural sector. It is clear that production technology has been improving throughout history, because knowhow accumulates. We derive that this technical progress causes the takeoff of the South. The income of the regions increases due to the technical progress and the consumption rate of manufactured goods also increases. Then the profit of the manufacturing sector of the North, where it is assumed that the manufacturing is concentrated, increases, and the demand for labour there increases. Labour, which is assumed to be withdrawn from the agricultural sector is finite and eventually the wage rate begins to increase. The North suffers from high labour costs, and at last it loses the comparative advantage in one of the two manufactured goods, even though it has the advantage in technology because of the scale economy.

In Krugman's model, where there is only one manufactured good, in the case of a labour shortage capital is assumed to flow out to foreign countries. This situation is called Lenin's 'second stage'. In our model, we do not assume the outflow of capital to foreign countries. Even if there is a labour shortage and abundant capital in the North, capital cannot flow out to foreign countries, that is, to the South, when there is no profitability there. If the wage rate in the North had risen sufficiently and there emerged the profitability to manufacture in the South, then capital could flow out. However, at this point, the South is able to begin manufacturing by themselves. Thus, there would be a difference in the speed of takeoff of the South when we prohibit free capital mobility, the characteristics of the model or the property of the steady state would not be much different.

The problem which we consider here is that in which one of the manufactured goods the South gets the comparative advantage, that is, which one they begin to produce. Without loss of generality, we assume that the consumption rate out of income for manufactured good 1 is less income elastic, then as the wage rates of both regions increase, the demand for good 1 decreases and that of good 2 increases. Because the amount of labour is constrained, in order to increase the production of good 2, that of good 1 has to be decreased. Due to the rise in the wage rate in the North, the first manufacturing sector loses and releases some amount of labour, and the second sector employs them. Under this adjustment process, the wage rate of the North increases faster than that of the South. This shows that the North is losing the comparative advantage in at least one of the manufactured goods.

The technological productivity of good 1 is decreasing and that of good 2 is increasing. It is not known, however, that the North loses the production of good 1, because it is not certain how this productivity differed at the initial point of the second state, where the wage rate of the North began to diverge from that of the South, that is, when labour in the agricultural sector vanished in the North. If, at this initial point of the second stage, the productivity of good 1 is lower, that is, it has a comparative disadvantage for good 2, then the North is surely losing the production of good 2. In other cases, it is not certain which one the North will lose. It depends on the global shapes of the functions of labour and capital coefficients and the consumption rates of the manufactured goods.

In fact, the definite difference between North and South is a gap in income levels. In the original Krugman model, the wages in both regions are equal. He did not pay attention to the difference in the wage rates between North and South. In our chapter, we derived endogenously the difference in the incomes between the two regions and this plays an important role in deriving our result.

The next section presents the basic model. Section 3 investigates the takeoff of the South. The last section gives concluding remarks.

2. THE MODEL

Let us summarize Krugman's model. There is one type of manufactured good and one type of agricultural good. The wage rates of the manufacturing sector and the agricultural sector of both regions are equal and assumed unity, since the marginal productivity of the agricultural sector is constant and labour is mobile within each region. The agricultural goods are produced by labour alone, while the manufactured goods are produced by labour and capital. Both manufactured goods and agricultural goods are mobile across the regions, while capital and labour are immobile.[1]

The profit of the manufacturing sector is totally accumulated as capital within each sector. As the result of the increasing returns to scale in the manufacturing sector, and the free trade of the products, either of the two regions which has the larger capital at the initial point of time takes the entire production of the manufactured goods in the long run.

Let us describe our model. Our model is an extension of Krugman's model in the sense that we introduce two manufactured goods denoted by the suffix i, where i = 1 or 2. We assume, for the sake of simplicity, that production of one type of manufactured good does not affect the production of the other.

As in the original Krugman model, the technologies, the preferences, and the labour endowment of the two regions are the same. The production technology of manufactured goods is expressed by the Leontief-type production function.

$$M_i^j = \min \left[\frac{1}{v_i(K_i^j)}, \frac{K_i^j}{c_i(K_i^j)} \right] , i = 1,2, j = N,S,$$

(5.1)

where M_i^j denotes the amount of manufactured good i of region $j = N$ or S, where N and S denote North and South, respectively. $v_i(\cdot)$ and $c_i(\cdot)$ denote the labour and capital coefficient, respectively, which satisfy

$$v_i'(K_i^j) < 0, c_i'(K_i^j) < 0,$$

(5.2)

where K_i^j denotes capital of manufacturing sector i of region j. This shows the increasing return to scale. For the sake of convenience in the following discussions, we assume $v_i / c_i = \gamma_i$ is constant for all K_i^j. This implies neutral technical progress. The demand for labour in each region does not exceed the existing labour supply, which is assumed unity, or

$$\sum_{i=1}^{2} v_i^j M_i^j = \sum_{i=1}^{2} \gamma_i K_i^j \le 1 .$$

(5.3)

We call this condition the 'labour constraint'. As in Krugman's model, the manufacturing sectors employ labour and the residual labour is absorbed by the agricultural sector. Production in the agricultural sector does not need capital. The production technology exhibits the constant return to scale, that is, the marginal productivity of the labour is constant and equal to w^0. When labour is employed in both sectors, the wage rates of these sectors are common, since the labour is mobile between the sectors. When the labour demand of the manufacturing sector exceeds the existing amount, the wage rate exceeds w^0.

Agricultural and manufactured goods are mobile across the borders of the regions. People of both regions can buy goods at the same international prices. As long as the wage rates of the two regions are the same, they spend the rate of μ_1 out of the income on the first manufactured good, and μ_2 on the second manufactured good, and the rest, that is, $1 - \mu_1 - \mu_2$, on agricultural products. These ratios are non-negative and $\mu_1 + \mu_2 < 1$ holds. These ratios, μ_i (i= 1,2), depend on income levels and are increasing with them. This implies the well known relationship that the rate of expenditure on food out of income decreases as income increases. That is, the consumption rate out of the income for the manufactured good of i-type is given by

$$\mu_i^j = \mu_i(w^j), 0 < \mu_i < 1, \mu_i' > 0 ,$$

(5.4)

where w^i is the wage rate of the region j. Let us begin with the case where there is enough labour in both regions, and capital is binding in the production of the manufacturing sector. The wage rates of the two regions are common and equal to w^0 and the production of good i is given by

$$M_i = \sum_{j \in R} M_i^j = \sum_{j \in R} \frac{K_i^j}{c_i(k_i^j)},$$

(5.5)

where R is the set of superscript, {N, S}, which denote the regions. The demand for good i of these two regions in sum is given by $2\mu_i w^0$ regardless of the price. Then the price is given by

$$p_i = \frac{2\mu_i w^0}{M_i}.$$

(5.6)

When we subtract the unit labour cost from the price, we have the profit per unit of production. Hence the total profit is given by

$$\Pi_i^j = (p_i - v_i^j w^0) M_i^j.$$

(5.7)

The profit is accumulated in the form of capital within its own manufacturing sector. Thus the dynamic equation of capital is given by

$$\dot{K}_i^j = \frac{K_i^j}{c_i^j} \left(\frac{2\mu_i w^0}{\sum_{r \in R} K_i^r / c_i^r} - w^0 v_i^j \right).$$

(5.8)

Following Krugman, we assume that $\partial \dot{K}_i^j / \partial K_i^j < 0$ around $\dot{K}_i^j = 0$ to guarantee the stability of the steady state. This implies

$$\frac{\partial \dot{K}_i^{j_r}}{\partial K_i^{j_r}} \bigg|_{\dot{K}_i^{j_r} = 0} = \frac{K_i^{j_r}}{c_i^{j_r}} \left\{ \frac{-2\mu_i (c_i^{j_r} - K_i^{j_r} c_i^{j_r})}{(c_i^{j_r} \sum_{r \in R} K_i^r / c_i^r)^2} - v_i^j \right\} w^0 < 0$$

(5.9)

for $j_r \neq j_s$ and j_r, $j_s \in R$. Also, for the same j_r, j_s it is evident that

$$\frac{\partial \dot{K}_i^{j_r}}{\partial K_i^{j_s}}\bigg|_{\dot{K}_i^{j_r}=0} = \frac{K_i^{j_r}}{c_i^{j_r}} \left\{ \frac{-2\mu_i(c_i^{j_s} - K_i^{j_s} c_i^{j_s\prime})}{(c_i^{j_r} \sum_{r \in R} K_i^r / c_i^r)^2} \right\} w^0 < 0$$

(5.10)

holds from $c_i^{j\prime} < 0$. This shows that when the rival's capital increases, (the supply of the goods increases), the profit and the capital formation deteriorate. It is also evident that the negative effect of the capital on its own profit rate is smaller in absolute value than the rival's, for, as capital accumulates, labour efficiency improves, or the labour coefficient decreases. This has a positive effect on its own profit rate.

From (5.9) and (5.10) we can easily derive

$$\frac{dK_i^N}{dK_i^S}\bigg|_{\dot{K}_i^N=0} < \frac{dK_i^N}{dK_i^S}\bigg|_{\dot{K}_i^S=0}$$

(5.11)

is crucial in deriving the stability of the steady state in Krugman-type equilibrium.

We assume that $K_i^N > K_i^S$ holds at the initial point of our dynamic process without loss of generality. When we assume that condition (5.3) is satisfied by strict inequality in all of this dynamic process, the steady state capitals are given by $K_i^{N*} > 0$, $K_i^{S*} = 0$, where * denotes the steady state level (see Figure 5.1).

Let us introduce the definition of the Krugman Equilibrium:

Definition: (Krugman Equilibrium) Krugman equilibrium is the steady state which satisfies

$$K_i^{j_r} > 0, \text{ and } K_i^{j_s} = 0, i = 1,2,$$

(5.12)

for $j_r \neq j_s$ and $j_r, j_s \in R$.

The positive amount of capital $K_i j^*$ at the Krugman equilibrium is given by

$$K_i^{j*} = \frac{2\mu_i}{\gamma_i} .$$

(5.13)

When the existing labour is not completely absorbed by the manufacturing sector, from (5.3) and (5.13), we have

$$\sum_{i=1}^{2} \mu_i < \frac{1}{2}.$$

(5.14)

That is, in order for the Krugman equilibrium to hold, the consumption rate for the manufactured good i should be less than a half.

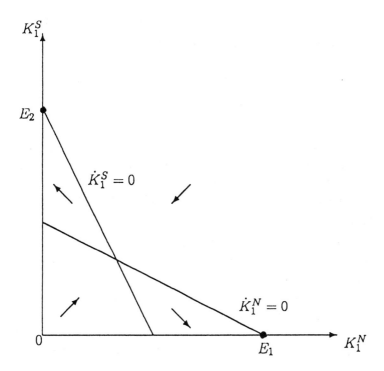

Figure 5.1 The Krugman equilibrium (E_1, E_2)

In this situation, assuming that technological progress occurs in the agricultural sector, we investigate the effect of the increase in income, that is, the agricultural wage rate. Thus, the consumption rate for manufactured goods increases up to $\Sigma_{i=1}^{2} \mu_i = 1/2$ as a result of the increase in the income of both regions. Then we assume that the condition (5.3) then becomes binding for the North, and

$$\sum_{i=1}^{2} \gamma_i K_i^N = 1 \tag{5.15}$$

holds. The wage rate in the North then begins to increase and exceeds w^0. Let it be w^N, while in the South, it still remains at w^0. In order to keep the symmetry of notations, we denote the wage rate of the South as w^S, which is equal to w^0.

Thus, the consumption rates of the two regions differ, and $\mu_i^N > \frac{S}{i}$ holds. Then the dynamic equation of capital (5.8) is modified to

$$\dot{K}_i^j = \frac{K_i^j}{c_i^j} \left(\frac{\sum\limits_{r \in R} \mu_i^r w^r}{\sum\limits_{r \in R} K_i^r / c_i^r} - w^j v_i^j \right) \tag{5.16}$$

Let us describe the mechanism for the determination of the wage rate of the North when the labour constraint is binding. Under the production technology of the Leontief type, the demand for labour by the manufacturing sector is determined by the level of capital. Let $K_i^N(t)$ be the level of capital at time t, then we have $K_i^N(t + dt) = K_i^N(t) + \dot{K}_i^N(t)$. $\dot{K}_i^N(t)$ is given by (5.16) as the function of $w^j(t)$, j = N and S, the wage rate of both regions. Labour input at time t + dt is given by $\Sigma_{i=1}^2 \gamma_i K_i^N(t + dt)$, which is given as the function of the wage rates at time t. The wage rates, $w^j(t)$, are the equilibrium wage rates which determine the dynamic path given by (5.16). Let us introduce the notional wage rate, which is called 'quoted wage rate' and which is not necessarily the equilibrium wage rate. When the notional wage rate is given by $\tilde{w}^j(t)$, then let the increment of the notional capital be $\tilde{K}_i^N(t)$. This is given as the function of $\tilde{w}^j(t)$ from (5.16), and is given by $\tilde{K}_i^N(t + dt) = \dot{\tilde{K}}_i^N(t)$. Then the labour demand of the North at time t + dt is given by

$$D_L^N = \sum_{i=1}^{2} \gamma_i \tilde{K}_i^N (t + dt) . \tag{5.17}$$

Then the demand for labour can be written as

$$D_L^N = D_L^N [\tilde{w}^N(t)] . \tag{5.18}$$

The disequilibrium of the labour market of the North is cleared by the adjustment of the quoted wage rate $\tilde{w}^N(t)$. Let us assume the existence of the equilibrium in the labour market.[2] The stability condition of the equilibrium under the Walrasian adjustment mechanism is

$$\frac{\partial D_L^N}{\partial \tilde{w}^N} = \sum_{i=1}^{2} \gamma_i \frac{\partial \tilde{K}_i^j(t+dt)}{\partial \tilde{w}^N(t)} = \sum_{i=1}^{2} \gamma_i (\mu_i^N + \mu_i^{N'} \tilde{w}^N - v_i^N M_i) < 0 .$$

(5.19)

We assume that this condition is satisfied. The equilibrium of the labour market at the period $t + dt$ is given by the equilibrium wage rate w^N at time t which satisfies

$$D_L^N(w^N(t)) = 1 ,$$

(5.20)

provided that the labour market equilibrium condition at time t, (5.15) holds. Hence, (5.15) and (5.20) give the equilibrium wage rate. Let us consider a Krugman equilibrium where manufacturing is concentrated in the North, that is, $K_i^{N*} > 0$, $K_i^{S*} = 0$. Around this steady state, the dynamic behaviour of the capital K_1^N and K_2^N is given by

$$\dot{K}_1^N = \Phi_1^N (K_1^N , w^N)$$

(5.21)

$$\dot{K}_2^N = \Phi_2^N (K_2^N, w^N)$$

(5.22)

$$\gamma_1 K_1^N + \gamma_2 K_2^N = 1 ,$$

(5.23)

where Φ_i^j denotes the RHS of (5.16). Totally differentiating and eliminating w^N and K_2^N, we have

$$dK_1^N = \frac{\gamma_1 \Phi_{1_{w^N}}^N \Phi_{2_{N2}}^N + \gamma_2 \Phi_{2_{w^N}}^N \Phi_{1_{N1}}^N}{X} dK_1^N$$

(5.24)

where

$$X = \gamma_1 \Phi_{1_{w^N}}^N + \gamma_2 \Phi_{2_{w^N}}^N, \text{ and } \Phi_{i_{rs}}^j = \partial \Phi_i^j / \partial K_s^r .$$

(5.19) implies X < 0.

$$\Phi^j_{i_{ji}} < 0$$

holds as we assumed in the above the same as in Krugman (1981). Thus, we can easily find that the Krugman equilibrium is stable when

$$\frac{\gamma_1 \Phi^N_{1_{wN}} \Phi^N_{2_{N2}} + \gamma_2 \Phi^N_{2_{wN}} \Phi^N_{1_{N1}}}{\gamma_1 \Phi^N_{1_{wN}} + \gamma_2 \Phi^N_{2_{\omega N}}} < 0 \tag{5.25}$$

holds. X < 0 does not necessarily imply that the numerator is positive. Hence we have to assume

$$\gamma_1 \Phi^N_{1_{wN}} \Phi^N_{2_{N2}} + \gamma_2 \Phi^N_{2_{wN}} \Phi^N_{1_{N1}} > 0 \tag{5.26}$$

and thus, (5.25) is satisfied.

3. THE TAKEOFF OF THE SOUTH

Assume that the economy is at the Krugman equilibrium, and that the labour constraint (5.3) is binding in the North. Let us explain the process of the emergence of manufacturing in the South as a result of technical progress in the agricultural sector.

3.1 The Effect of the Increase in the Agricultural Wage Rate on the Krugman Equilibrium

The steady state can be described by the following conditions:

$$\frac{K^j_i}{c^j_i} \left(\frac{\sum_{r \in R} \mu^r_i w^r}{\sum_{r \in R} K^r_i / c^r_i} - w^j v^j_i \right) = 0, \tag{5.27}$$

$$\sum_{i=1}^{2} \gamma_i K^j_i \leq 1 \quad \Longleftrightarrow \quad w^j \geq w^s \tag{5.28}$$

When the labour constraint is binding in the North, the first equation of (5.28) is satisfied with equality for $j = N$.

Here we examine the effect of the increase in labour productivity in the agricultural sector on the steady-state equilibrium where the labour constraint is binding. Differentiating the steady state conditions (5.27) and (5.28) for $j = N$, assuming $K_i^N \neq 0$ and $K_i^S = 0$, we have

$$\Phi_{1_{N1}}^N \frac{dK_1^N}{dw^S} + \Phi_{1_{wN}}^N \frac{dw^N}{dw^S} + \Phi_{1_{wS}}^N = 0 , \tag{5.29}$$

$$\Phi_{2_{N2}}^N \frac{dK_2^N}{dw^S} + \Phi_{2_{wN}}^N \frac{dw^N}{dw^S} + \Phi_{s_{wS}}^N = 0 , \tag{5.30}$$

$$\gamma_1 \frac{dK_1^N}{dw^S} + \gamma_2 \frac{dK_2^N}{dw^S} = 0 , \tag{5.31}$$

From (5.29)–(5.31), we obtain

$$\frac{dw^N}{dw^S} = - \frac{\gamma_1 \Phi_{1_{wS}}^N \Phi_{2_{N2}}^N + \gamma_2 \Phi_{2_{wS}}^N \Phi_{1_{N1}}^N}{\gamma_1 \Phi_{1_{wN}}^N \Phi_{2_{N2}}^N + \gamma_2 \Phi_{2_{wN}}^N \Phi_{1_{N1}}^N} \tag{5.32}$$

We show that (5.32) is positive and greater than 1. We have

$$\frac{dw^N}{dw^S} - \frac{w^N}{w^S} = - \frac{\gamma_1 \Phi_{2_{N2}}^N \left(\Phi_{1_{wS}}^N + \Phi_{1_{wN}} \right) + \gamma_2 \Phi_{1_{N1}}^N \left(\Phi_{2_{wS}}^N + \Phi_{2_{wN}} \right)}{\gamma_2 \Phi_{1_{N1}}^N \Phi_{2_{w}}^N + \gamma_1 \Phi_{2_{N2}}^N \Phi_{1_{wN}}^N} , \tag{5.33}$$

where

$$\Phi_{i_{wS}}^N + \Phi_{i_{wN}}^N = \frac{\mu_i^S (w^N - w^S)/w^N + \mu_i^{N*} w^N + \mu_i^{S*} w^S}{M_i} > 0 , \tag{5.34}$$

holds since $w^N > w^S$. The denominator of (5.33) is positive from (5.26). Thus, we obtain

$$\frac{dw^N}{dw^S} - \frac{w^N}{w^S} > 0 . \tag{5.35}$$

and (5.32) is positive. Thus, when the wage rate of the agricultural sector, w^S, increases, that of the manufacturing sector in the North, w^N, increases more rapidly.

Also, we can solve (5.29)–(5.31) for dK_1^N / dw^S and obtain

$$\frac{dk_1^N}{dw^S} = \gamma_2 \frac{\Phi^N_{1_{w^N}} \Phi^N_{2_{w^S}} - \Phi^N_{1_{w^S}} \Phi^N_{2_{w^N}}}{\gamma_1 \Phi^N_{1_{w^N}} \Phi^N_{2_{N2}} + \gamma_2 \Phi^N_{1_{N1}} \Phi^N_{2_{w^N}}} \tag{5.36}$$

The denominator of RHS is positive. Hence the sign of (5.36) is determined by that of the denominator, or,

$$\mathrm{sgn}\left(\frac{dK_1^N}{dw^0}\Big|_{K_1^N=0}\right) = \mathrm{sgn}\left(\Phi^N_{1_{w^N}} \Phi^N_{2_{w^S}} - \Phi^N_{2_{w^N}} \Phi^N_{1_{w^S}}\right). \tag{5.37}$$

Further, assuming that $\eta_1 < \eta_2^j$, which shows that the preferences of both regions are identical and the elasticities are constant, we derive

$$\Phi^N_{2_{w^S}} \Phi^N_{1_{w^N}} - \Phi^N_{1_{w^S}} \Phi^N_{2_{w^N}}$$

$$= \eta_2(\eta_1 + 1)(\pi_1 - \pi_2) + \pi_2(\eta_1 - \eta_2)(\pi_1 + 1). \tag{5.38}$$

In order to determine the sign of (5.38), without loss of generality, we introduce the next assumption.

Assumption 1: The income elasticity of the consumption ratio for the manufactured good 1 is less than that of good 2.

This assumption, $\eta_1 < \eta_2$, implies $\pi_1 > \pi_2$. In the following, we derive this. Let us introduce Z, that is,

$$Z = \frac{\mu_2^S}{\mu_2^N} \Big/ \frac{\mu_1^S}{\mu_1^N}. \tag{5.39}$$

Differentiating Z with respect to w^S, we obtain

$$\frac{\partial Z}{\partial w^S} = \left\{ \left[\frac{w^S \mu_2^{S'}}{\mu_2^S} - \frac{w^N \mu_2^{N'}}{\mu_2^N} + \left(\frac{dw^N}{dw^S} \middle/ \frac{w^N}{w^S} \right) \left(\frac{w^N \mu_1^{N'}}{\mu_1^N} - \frac{w^N \mu_2^{N'}}{\mu_2^N} \right) \right] \right\} Z$$

(5.40)

$$= \left\{ (\eta_1 - \eta_2) \left(\frac{dw^N}{dw^S} \middle/ \frac{w^N}{w^S} - 1 \right) \right\} Z < 0$$

from assumption 1 and (5.33). This shows that, since we have $Z = 1$ when $w^N = w^S$, we obtain $Z < 1$ when w^S increases and $w^N > w^S$ holds. Hence we have

$$\pi_1 - \pi_2 = \frac{w^S \mu_1^S}{w^N \mu_2^N} (1 - Z) > 0 .$$

(5.41)

Thus, we have proved (5.37) is negative, and we obtain

$$\frac{dK_1^N}{dw^S} < 0$$

(5.42)

Since K_1^N and K_2^N move to the opposite direction from (5.31), we obtain

$$\frac{dK_2^N}{dw^S} > 0 .$$

(5.43)

In the above, we have derived that when the labour productivity in the agricultural sector increases, the wage rate of the manufacturing sector of the North also increases more rapidly. As a result, the steady state capital of the first manufacturing sector decreases, while that of the second manufacturing sector increases under Assumption 1.

3.2 Takeoff

Here we begin to analyse the impact of the improvement of the production efficiency of the agricultural sector on the global behaviour of the system.

When the wage rate of the South exceeds some level, the South begins to produce manufactured goods. When the agricultural wage rate, that is, the wage rate of the South, increases, that of the North also increases and, moreover, more rapidly. As a result, even though there is an advantage for the North in the production efficiency of manufactured goods, it has a disadvantage in the labour cost. Thus, there is a possibility that the South will begin to produce one of the two types of manufactured goods. In order to examine this, we have to investigate how the phase diagram showing the movement of capitals of both regions shifts due to the increase in the agricultural wage rate. Our dynamic system is composed of four variables, K_1^N, K_2^N, K_2^S and K_2^S. Since we assumed that the labour market is binding, K_1^N and K_2^N are linked and are not independent. Also we assume that $K_1^S = 0$ for a while. This does not constrain our discussion as we will explain later. Thus we can illustrate the loci of $\dot{K}_1^j = 0$, $j = N$ and S in the two-dimensional space (K_1^N, K_1^S).

3.2.1   Derivation of the loci of $\dot{K}_i^N = 0$

The locus of $\dot{K}_1^N = 0$ is determined by K_1^N, K_1^S, and w^N from (5.16). Hence we have to take into consideration the equations to determine w^N. When (5.15) holds, (5.20) implies

$$\gamma_1 \Phi_1^N + \gamma_2 \Phi_2^N = 0 .$$

when $\dot{K}_1^N = 0$, then $\dot{K}_2^N = 0$ holds. Hence, the locus of $\dot{K}_1^N = 0$ is shown by the following three equations

$$\Phi_1^N = 0 , \tag{5.44}$$

$$\Phi_2^N = 0 , \tag{5.45}$$

$$\gamma_1 K_1^N + \gamma_2 K_2^N = 1 . \tag{5.46}$$

Totally differentiating with respect to K_1^S, we have

$$\Phi_{1_{N1}}^N \frac{dK_1^N}{dK_1^S} + \Phi_{1_{w^N}}^N \frac{dw^N}{dK_1^S} + \Phi_{1_{S1}}^N = 0 , \tag{5.47}$$

$$\Phi_{2_{N2}}^N \frac{dK_2^N}{dK_1^S} + \Phi_{2_{w^N}}^N \frac{dw^N}{dK_1^S} + \Phi_{2_{S1}}^N = 0 , \tag{5.48}$$

$$\gamma_1 \frac{dK_1^N}{dK_1^S} + \gamma_2 \frac{dK_2^N}{dK_1^S} = 0 \,. \tag{5.49}$$

Thus we obtain

$$\frac{dK_1^S}{dK_1^N}\Big|_{\dot{K}_1^N = 0} = - \frac{\gamma_1 \Phi_{1_{wN}}^N \Phi_{2_{N2}}^N + \gamma_2 \Phi_{2_{wN}}^N \Phi_{1_{N1}}^N}{\gamma_2 \Phi_{2_{wN}}^N \Phi_{1_{S1}}^N} < 0 \,. \tag{5.50}$$

We already have the sign conditions,

$$\Phi_{1_{wN}}^S > 0, \ \Phi_{1_{N1}}^N < 0 \text{ and } \Phi_{1_{S1}}^S < 0$$

and the numerator is positive from (5.25). Thus we can derive that the locus of $\dot{K}_1^N = 0$ in K_1^N, K_1^S plane is negatively (or positively) sloped when $\Phi_{2_{wN}}^N$ is negative (or positive). However, we can derive the global shape of the locus. When $K_1^S = 0$, $\dot{K}_1^N = 0$ is given by positive and finite K_1^N. When K_1^S is sufficiently large, p_1 is sufficiently low, and the profit π_1^N cannot be positive even for $K_1^N = 0$. Thus, both intercepts of the locus of $\dot{K}_1^N = 0$ in the plane K_1^N, K_1^S are positive.

3.2.2 Derivation of the locus of $\dot{K}_1^S = 0$

When the labour market is binding, this locus is given by

$$\Phi_1^S = 0 \,, \tag{5.51}$$

$$\gamma_1 \Phi_1^N + \gamma_2 \Phi_2^N = 0 \,, \tag{5.52}$$

$$\gamma_1 K_1^N + \gamma_2 K_2^N = 1 \,. \tag{5.53}$$

In discussing the locus of $\dot{K}_1^S = 0$, the condition $\dot{K}_i^N = 0$ is not necessary. Hence the labour market equilibrium condition is given by the two equations, (5.52) and (5.53). Totally differentiating (5.51)–(5.53), and arranging, we obtain

$$\Phi^S_{1_{N1}} dK^N_1 + \Phi^S_{1_{S1}} dK^S_1 + \Phi^S_{1_{wN}} dw^N = 0 \tag{5.54}$$

$$\gamma_1(\Phi^N_{1_{N1}} - \Phi^N_{2_{N2}}) dK^N_1 + \gamma_1 \Phi^N_{1_{S1}} dK^S_1$$
$$+ (\gamma_1 \Phi^N_{1_{wN}} + \gamma_2 \Phi^N_{2_{wN}}) dw^N = 0. \tag{5.55}$$

Eliminating d^N_w, we obtain

$$\frac{dK^S_1}{dK^N_1}\bigg|_{\dot{K}^S_1=0} = \frac{\Phi^S_{1_{N1}}(\gamma_1 \Phi^N_{1_{wN}} + \gamma_2 \Phi^N_{2_{wN}}) - \gamma_1 \Phi^S_{1_{wN}}(\Phi^N_{1_{N1}} - \Phi^N_{2_{N2}})}{\gamma_1 \Phi^N_{1_{s1}} \Phi^S_{1_{wN}} - \Phi^S_{1_{s1}}(\gamma_1 \Phi^N_{1_{wN}} + \gamma_2 \Phi^N_{2_{wN}})}. \tag{5.56}$$

The denominator is negative. On the other hand, the sign of the numerator is ambiguous, since the sign of

$$\Phi^N_{1_{N1}} - \Phi^N_{2_{N2}}$$

is not determined.[3] However, as shown in the above for the global shape of the locus $\dot{K}^N_1 = 0$, the locus $\dot{K}^S_1 = 0$ can also be derived. It has positive intercepts in (K^N_1, K^S_1).

In order to see the relative locations of the loci $\dot{K}^N_1 = 0$ and $\dot{K}^S_1 = 0$, we derive their intercepts in the plane of (K^N_1, K^S_1).

The locus of $\dot{K}^N_1 = 0$ is composed of $K^N_1 = 0$ and $p_1 - w^N_{v_1}(K^N_1 = 0)$. Let $\check{K}^N_1$ be the vertical intercept of $\dot{K}^N_1 = 0$, then $p_1 - w^N_{v_1}(\check{K}^N_1) = 0$ holds. At $(\check{K}^N_1, \varepsilon)$, for sufficiently small $\varepsilon > 0$, the value of $\dot{K}^S_1$ is given by

$$\dot{K}^S_1\bigg|_{K^N_1=\check{K}^N_1, K^S_1=\varepsilon} = \frac{\varepsilon}{c_1} - \left[w^N v_1(\check{K}^N_1) - w^S v_1(\varepsilon) \right] < 0, \tag{5.57}$$

when w^S and w^N are sufficiently close. When the labour market is not binding, (5.57) is evidently negative since $w^N = w^S$ and $v_1(0) > (\check{K}^N_1)$ hold. Even when the labour market is binding, if w^S is small enough and w^N, w^S are sufficiently close, (5.57) is still negative. This implies that the locus of

$\dot{K}_1^N = 0$ is on the right of $\dot{K}_1^S = 0$ in (K_1^N, K_1^S) in the neighbourhood of the horizontal axis.

Similarly, let $\check{K}_1^S$ be the horizontal intercept of $\dot{K}_1^S = 0$, then we have

$$\dot{K}_1^N \Big|_{K_1^N = \varepsilon, K_1^S = \check{K}^S} = \frac{\varepsilon}{c_1} - \left(w^S v_1(\check{K}_1^S) - w^N v_1(0) \right) < 0, \tag{5.58}$$

when w^S and w^N are sufficiently close. This implies that the locus of $K_1^S = 0$ is on the above of $\dot{K}_1^N = 0$ in the plane in the neighbourhood of the vertical axis. Hence, these loci intersect with each other at least once in the positive orthant of (K_1^N, K_1^S).[4]

3.2.3　The shift of the loci
From (5.57), we have

$$\dot{K}_1^S \Big|_{K_1^N = \check{K}_1^N, K_1^S = 0} = \frac{\varepsilon w^S v_1(\check{K}_1^N)}{c_1(\varepsilon)} \left| \frac{w^N}{w^S} - \frac{v_1(0)}{v_1(\check{K}_1^N)} \right| < 0. \tag{5.59}$$

As we have shown that w^N/w^S increases with w^S and $dK_1^N/dw^S < 0$, the direction of the change in the bracket is positive. That is, the loci of $\dot{K}_1^N = 0$ and $\dot{K}_1^S = 0$ come closer as w^S increases on the horizontal axis. However, as for the counterpart of the second manufacturing sector, that is,

$$\dot{K}_2^S \Big|_{K_2^N = \check{K}_2^N, K_2^S = \varepsilon} = w^S v_2(\check{K}_2^N) \left| \frac{w^N}{w^S} - \frac{v_2(\varepsilon)}{v_2(\check{K}_2^N)} \right| < 0. \tag{5.60}$$

it is not clear whether the value of the bracket increases or not. The possibilities of the relative locations of w^N/w^S, $v_1(0)/v_1(K_1^N)$ and $v_2(0)/v_2(K_2^N)$ are illustrated in Figure 5.2.

At the point where the labour constraint becomes binding, that is, $w^N = w^S$ still holds, and let the level of the wage rate be w^{0*}, then the equilibrium capital is as given by (5.13), that is, $\check{K}_1^N = 2\mu_1/\gamma_1$, $\check{K}_2^N = 2\mu_2/\gamma_2$, where $\mu_i = \mu_i^N = \mu_i^S$, where $\mu_i = \mu_i^N(w^{0*}) = \mu_i^S(w^{0*})$ holds. Case A in Figure 5.2 illustrates the case of

$$\frac{v_2(0)}{v_2(2\mu_2/\gamma_2)} > \frac{v_1(0)}{v_1(2\mu_1/\gamma_1)}.$$

(5.61)

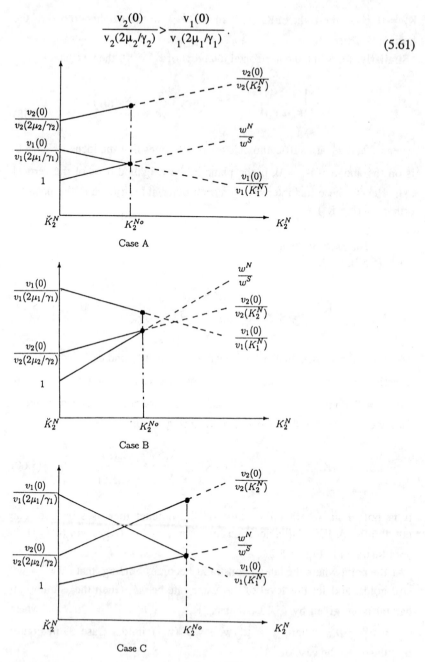

Case A

Case B

Case C

Figure 5.2 The south takes off at $K_2^N = K_2^{N0}$

In this case, as K_2^N increases (K_1^N decreases), $v_1(0)/v_1(\check{K}_1^N)$ intersects w^N/w^S first. This shows that the South obtains profitability in producing the first manufactured good. As we will show later, the South eventually takes off. On the other hand, when

$$\frac{v_2(0)}{v_2(2\mu_2/\gamma_2)} < \frac{v_1(0)}{v_1(2\mu_1/\gamma_1)} \ . \tag{5.62}$$

holds, there are two possibilities. One possibility is that before $v_1(0)/v_1(\check{K}_1^N)$ and $v_2(0)/v_2(\check{K}_2^N)$ intersect, $v_2(0)/v_2(\check{K}_2^N)$ and w^N/w^S intersect first. This is Case B. The other case is that w^N/w^S and $v_1(\check{K}_1^N)$ intersect first. This is called Case C. The second sector takes off in Case B, while the first sector takes off in Case C. It is not determined which of the cases is realized. In the following, we will show by numerical examples that it is not predetermined which case is realized.

Numerical example: let $v_i(\cdot)$s be given by

$$v_1 = 1 - K_1^N \ , \tag{5.63}$$

$$v_2 = 1 - K_2^N \ . \tag{5.64}$$

We examine whether w^N/w^S intersects $v_1(0)/v_1(\check{K}_1^N)$ or $v_2(0)/v_2(\check{K}_2^N)$ first. At first, let us derive the level of K_1^N, which satisfies

$$\frac{v_1(0)}{v_1(K_1^N)} = \frac{v_2(0)}{v_2(K_2^N)} \ . \tag{5.65}$$

From (5.15), we have

$$K_2^N = \frac{1 - \gamma_1 K_1^N}{\gamma_2} \ . \tag{5.66}$$

Substituting this into (5.65), we obtain

$$K_1^N = K_2^N = \frac{1}{\gamma_1 + \gamma_2} \ . \tag{5.67}$$

Here the value of $v_1(0)/v_1(K_1^N) = v_2(0)/v_2(K_2^N)$ is given by

$$\frac{\gamma_1 + \gamma_2}{\gamma_1 + \gamma_2 - 1} . \tag{5.68}$$

Next, let us derive the value of w^N/w^S when (5.65) holds. w^N/w^S is given by $\dot{K}_i^N = 0$ and $\dot{K}_i^S = 0$ by using (5.16), we have

$$\mu_1^N w^N + \mu_1^S w^S = w^N \gamma_1 K_1^N , \tag{5.69}$$

$$\mu_2^N w^N + \mu_2^S w^S = w^N \gamma_2 K_2^N \tag{5.70}$$

and from (5.15) we obtain

$$\frac{w^N}{w^S} = \frac{\mu_1^S + \mu_2^S}{1 - \mu_1^N - \mu_2^N} . \tag{5.71}$$

Since we have $w^N/w^S > 1$, $1 - \Sigma_i \mu_i^N - \Sigma_i \mu_i^S < 0$ holds. When we obtain the relative magnitude of (5.65) and 5.71), we can determine the relative locations. For the sake of simplicity in our discussion, let us assume that $\gamma_1 = \gamma_2 = \gamma$, $\mu^j = \Sigma_{i=1}^2 \mu_i^j$, ($j$ = N, S). Then we have

$$\frac{v_1(0)}{v_1[1/(\gamma_1 + \gamma_2)]} - \frac{w^N}{w^S} = \frac{2\gamma(1 - \mu^N - \mu^S) + \mu^S}{(2\gamma - 1)(1 - \mu^N)} . \tag{5.72}$$

From (5.67), we have $K_1^N = 1/2\gamma$, and since we have assumed (5.63) and (5.64), $2\gamma > 1$ necessarily holds from the positivity of K_i^N. Since we have $1 - \mu^N - \mu^S < 0$ and $1 - \mu^N > 0$, we obtain

$$\gamma \underset{<}{\overset{\geq}{}} \frac{\mu_S}{2(\mu^N + \mu^S - 1)} \iff \frac{v_1(0)}{v_1[1/(2\gamma)]} \underset{>}{\overset{\leq}{}} \frac{w^N}{w^S} \tag{5.73}$$

from (6.72). This implies that if γ is sufficiently large, since $v_1(0)/v_1(2\mu_1/\gamma_1) > v_2(0)/v_2(2\mu_2/\gamma_2)$ is assumed, the second manufacturing sector of the South takes off as shown in Case B. Otherwise, the first sector takes off as shown in Case C.

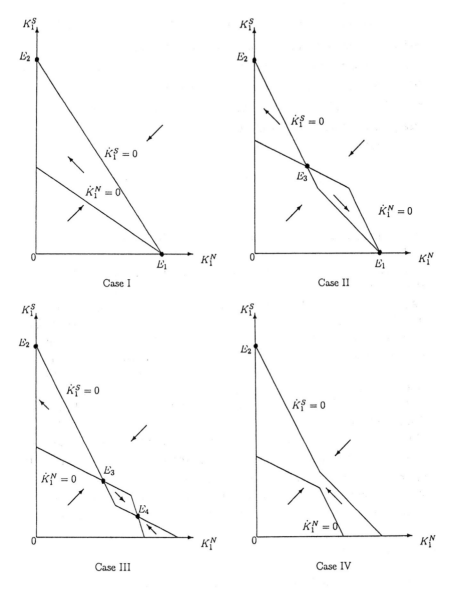

Figure 5.3 The pattern of takeoff

In the following we continue our discussion assuming that w^N/w^S and $v_1(0)/v_1(K_1^N)$ intersect first. When $w^N/w^S = v_1(0)/(K_1^N)$, the loci $\dot{K}_1^N = 0$ and

$\dot{K}_1^S = 0$ intersect on the horizontal axis of the (K_1^N, K_1^S) plane before $\dot{K}_2^N = 0$ and $\dot{K}_2^S = 0$ intersect on the horizontal axis of the (K_2^N, K_2^S) plane.

As we have mentioned above, we cannot exclude various types of steady states. In Figures 5.3, Case I shows the case where $\dot{K}_1^N = 0$ is completely below $\dot{K}_1^S = 0$ when these loci meet on the horizontal axis, and finally the steady state equilibrium E_2 is attained.

In Case II, on the horizontal axis,

$$\left. \frac{dK_1^S}{dK_1^N} \right|_{K_1^S = 0} > \left. \frac{dK_1^S}{dK_1^N} \right|_{K_1^N = 0} \tag{5.74}$$

holds. In this case, the South does not take off. The intersection of these loci on the horizontal axis E_1 is a stable steady state. As w^S keeps increasing, Case II is converted to Case III. It implies that the South takes off to a steady state E_2. However, the North does not lose the first manufacturing sector.

As the North loses the production of good 1, the labour employed in the manufacturing sector 1 is released. This decreases the demand for labour and, consequently, decreases the wage rate of the North. However, in Case III, $w^N > w^S$ must be satisfied. If $w^N = w^S$ holds, the equilibrium is only the original Krugman type, where the interior equilibrium is unstable. Hence, when there is a stable interior equilibrium as shown in Case III, it implies that the labour market is binding and the wage rate is endogenously determined as $w^N > w^S$.

In Case III, as the agricultural wage rate keeps increasing, it is easy to derive that the locus of $\dot{K}_1^S = 0$ moves to the right, and that of $\dot{K}_1^N = 0$ moves to the left and finally Case IV is obtained. Then the only stable steady state is given by E_2. In any case, the total production of manufactured good 1 is taken by the South eventually as the agricultural wage keeps increasing.

In the above discussion, $\dot{K}_2^S = 0$ was always assumed. This assumption is justified by the following proposition:

Proposition 1: *the South does not begin to produce good 2 even when the agricultural wage rate increases and she produces the good 1 on the steady state or off the steady state.*[5]

During this process, the labour market of the North might be unbinding from a certain point of time. However, even in that case, there is no possibility that the North regains the entire production of goods 1 and 2, since there is no wage rate which supports the Krugman equilibrium because the agricultural wage rate has increased sufficiently.

At the new steady state, it is ambiguous whether the labour market of the North is still binding or not. For example, assume that there is an operating agricultural sector in both regions, and the wage rate is common. When the consumption rate for good 1, μ_1 is 0.6, the demand for good 1 is 1.2 times as much as the income of each region. Then the region which occupies the production of good 1 receives 1.2w, but only w is distributed to the residents there. This is a contradiction.

Hence, there is no operating agricultural sector in the region which occupies the production of good 1 and the labour market is binding there. Assume that it is the South, as in our main discussion, that occupied the manufacturing sector of good 1, then the income level of the South should be greater than that of the North. This implies that there is a possibility in our model that the South passes the North.

4. CONCLUDING REMARKS

We have analysed the economic development in a North–South economy, where there are two manufacturing sectors. In Krugman's model, where there is only one manufacturing sector, one of the two regions, that is the North occupies the entire production of the manufacturing goods. By introducing another manufacturing sector, we showed that the South would be able to begin producing one of the two manufactured goods as the wage rate in the agricultural sector increased due to the technical progress. As the agricultural wage rate keeps increasing (this is a natural assumption, since people develop knowhow and it accumulates, in history), the South eventually gets the whole market.

For example, consider high-tech and textile industries. The income elasticity of the former is larger than of the latter. When the labour constraint is binding for manufacturing sectors in the North, as the wages of both regions increase due to the improvement of agricultural productivity, the North has to shift the labour from textile to high-tech goods.

As the economy of scale works, the efficiency in the high-tech sector increases, while that in the textile sector decreases. However, at the initial point, assume that there was a big gap between the regions in the efficiency of production in the textile industry, while in the high-tech industry the gap was small. For example, let us assume that the ratio of the labour coefficients in the production of high-tech between North and South was 1.5, while in textile, it was 4. When the North shifts labour from the textile industry to high-tech industry, the gap in the labour coefficients expands in high-tech and shrinks in textile to 2 and 3, respectively. During this process, the wage ratio between the regions also expands to 2, that is, the wage rate of the North is twice as large as that of the South. Then, the North loses the comparative advantage in high-tech to the South. The South begins to produce high-tech.

At the initial point, if the gap in technological efficiencies is bigger in the high-tech industry than in textile, then there is no possibility that the South will take the high-tech market.

Actually, in the new technologies such as telecommunications, there are some sectors where there are little technological gaps between North and South. There exists a possibility that the South can take the total market in this kind of high-tech field. Also, we have shown that there is a possibility of the outdevelopment of the South in the sense that the agricultural sector exists only in the North, and the South specializes in manufacturing, and the wage rate there is greater than that in the North.

REFERENCES

Dutt, A.K. (1992), 'The origin of uneven development: The rise of the west and the lag of the rest, the Indian subcontinent', *American Economic Review, Papers and Proceedings* **82**, pp. 146–50.

Krugman, P.R. (1981), 'Trade, accumulation and uneven development', *Journal of Development Economics* **8**, pp. 149–61.

Kubo, Y. (1994), 'On the possibility of uneven industrial development under economies of scale and free international trade', *Studies in Regional Science* **24** (1), pp. 65–78.

NOTES

1. Krugman derived the dynamic path of capital of both regions assuming immobility of capital across the regions. After the capital accumulated enough and there was no labour in the country to withdraw from the agricultural sector, then foreign direct investment was considered. He also discussed the case where the direct investment is freely admitted during the accumulation process, however, it is not an important part of this chapter.

2. We do not discuss the existence in detail here.

3. When $K_1^S = 0$, $\Phi_{1_{N1}}^N - \Phi_{2_{N2}}^N = (\gamma_1 - \gamma_2)w^N$ holds.

4.   From the above discussion, the essential relative locations of the loci when the wage rate is endogenously given is the same when the wage rate is exogenously given, provided that w^S is close to w^N.

5.   The proof can be obtained from the author upon request.

6. International Transaction Costs, Trade in Producer Services and FDI Agglomeration

Dapeng Hu

1. INTRODUCTION

Lucas (1990) raised a well-known question about international capital movement: Why doesn't capital flow from rich to poor countries? As a special form of capital flow, foreign direct investment (FDI) shows a strong agglomeration trend rather than simply flowing from rich to rich or from rich to poor. FDI had concentrated in developed countries for a long period before 1990, but the developing countries' share of total FDI has steadily increased in the 1990s (see Figure 6.1). Among developed countries, FDI flows intensively to the US, while only a little goes to Japan. In developing countries, FDI remains highly concentrated (World Bank, 1996). In 1993, for example, the Asia NIEs, ASEAN and China took 67 percent of all the FDI that flowed to developing countries. Further, within a country, FDI also frequently agglomerates in several regions. For example, in China more than 87 percent of FDI flowed to the coastal area in 1994 (Hu and Fujita 1996). So, besides Lucas's question, we need to ask: why does FDI agglomerate?

A distinguishing characteristic of FDI as compared with other forms of investment is that FDI transfers not only capital, but also producer services.[1] Along with the spread of 'flexible production methods', producer services have become increasingly important in manufacturing production. Because of the non-storable nature of services, trade in producer services usually involves high transaction costs. Like transportation costs, transaction costs can also have significant effects on the economic geography of international production. However, unlike transportation costs, transaction costs do not affect final products but only intermediates (producer services). So the effect of transaction costs can be different from that of transportation costs. The role of transportation costs in spatial agglomeration has been well studied in spatial monopolistic competition models since Krugman (1991). However,

102

the role of transaction costs on intermediate producer services has been less explored.[2] Applying the spatial monopolistic competition model, this chapter tries to give an explanation of the FDI agglomeration from the aspect of transaction costs and trade in producer services.

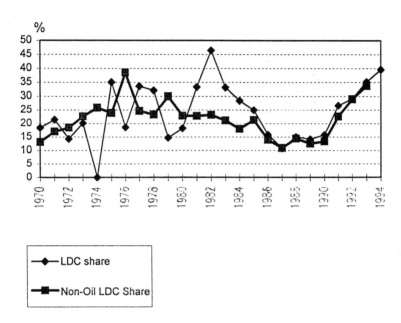

Source: IMF, Balance of Payments, various years.

Figure 6.1 Developing countries' (LDC) share of world FDI: the changing trend 1970–94

Transaction costs have been generally discussed in multinational firm theories by Caves (1982), Williamson (1986) and Ethier (1986, 1992). Transferring firm-specific assets (producer services) at arm's length usually involves high transaction costs. In order to avoid these transaction costs, firms would internalize these transfers by FDI. This 'internalization advantage' gives an incentive for a firm to go to multinational. The higher the transaction costs, the stronger this incentive, and hence the more likely for firms to use FDI to substitute trade of producer services at arm's length (Ethier 1986; Williamson 1986). This implies that the relationship of FDI and trade in producer services is substituted, and high transaction costs lead to a large FDI flow. In reality, however, the complementary relationship of FDI and trade in producer services is stronger. Figure 6.2 shows that over the past ten years, the trend of trade in producer services and the trend of FDI.

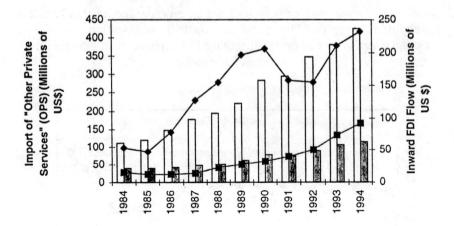

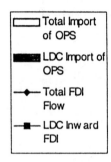

Source: MF, Balance of Payments, various years; UNCTAD, World Investment Report 1994.

Notes: The item 'other private service' (OPS) contains not only producer services, but these are the closest data we can get.

Figure 6.2 The complementary relation of FDI and trade in producer services

This chapter emphasizes the complementary relationship between the trade of producer services at arm's length and internal transfer through FDI. The strong complementary relationship between FDI and trade in producer services results from two reasons. First, technological progress in telecommunications and information processing make transfers of producer services easier. Transaction costs are reduced for both internalized (FDI) and market (trade) transfers. Second, producer services are essential intermediates to manufacturing production. The varieties of specialized producer services can make manufacturing more efficient because of the national or international increasing returns to scale, and hence can generate higher returns on investment. If more varieties of producer services are available at cheaper prices, higher productivity can be achieved in manufacturing, which will attract more FDI flows.

Considering this complementary relationship, a general equilibrium trade model is developed to explain the effects of transaction costs on FDI flow. Following Burgess (1990), Francois (1990) and Ethier and Horn (1991), the model characterizes producer services as intermediate input to manufacturing, with increasing returns to scale and monopolistic competition. In addition, the model allows producer services to be traded directly, adding transaction costs in the trade. The analysis shows that low transaction costs correspond to large investment flows. The model also emphasizes the knowledge-intensive character of producer services by introducing high-skilled (professional) labour into the production of producer services. This device allows us to analyse the important effect of a professional labour pool on manufacturing production and FDI. It shows that a country with a larger professional labour pool will attract more FDI.

Another contribution of this chapter is that it has introduced a symmetric equilibrium method to obtain analytical results for spatial general equilibrium models. Spatial general equilibrium models are known for the complexities in solving the equilibrium. Most papers, following Krugman (1991), used numerical simulation instead of analytical results. This chapter provides a way to obtain a symmetric equilibrium, and gives the proof to the existence of equilibrium. All the conclusions in this paper hence are based on comparative static analysis.

Section 2 of this chapter provides a brief discussion of the idea of international transaction costs and their role in the formation of FDI agglomeration, and Section 3 gives a formal spatial general equilibrium model. The symmetric equilibrium is derived in Section 4, and comparative static results are obtained in Section 5. Finally, policy implications of the model are given in the concluding section.

2. INTERNATIONAL TRANSACTION COSTS IN PRODUCER SERVICES

Transaction costs are associated with different organizational forms and institutional and contractual arrangements. Because services are non-storable and non-standard, transfers of services involve more complicated contacts, negotiations, and monitoring activities among different agencies, and hence higher transaction costs. These costs may include telecommunication and commuting costs, negotiation costs, controlling or monitoring costs, costs due to possible technology spillover of R&D assets, costs for transportation of key parts and tools, and uncertainties. The determinants of transaction costs are the nature of the services,[3] the differences between agencies, and the related technologies, especially telecommunication and information processing technologies.

When transactions occur across national borders, international transaction costs will be higher because of the larger differences among agencies from different countries. In addition to the factors we mentioned above, the following three factors may affect the international transaction costs: (1) geographical distance, (2) differences in culture, business customs and economic systems, and (3) government policies and possible political risks.[4]

Distance matters because telecommunication and commuting costs, to a certain extent, depend upon distance. Geographical proximity provides greater convenience for communication and transportation, which can create more business opportunities. Also geographical proximity can promote the convergence of culture and business customs.

Differences in cultural and economic aspects of geography are associated with gaps in culture, business custom, regulation, economic system and development level. We can call these differences the 'culture/business distance'. Language differences, for example, will definitely increase the transaction costs of management consulting, advertising and many other producer service activities. Geographical closeness matters partly because closeness implies a similar cultural background. For instance, East Asian countries have much in common in terms of culture, even language. Therefore, transaction costs are lower within this region.

Government effectiveness, attitudes and policies also affect international transaction costs. Tariffs, quotas and other ad hoc restrictions may increase the transaction costs greatly. Moreover, bureaucratic failure, usually a problem for developing countries, makes procedures for licensing, registration and other transaction activities very time-consuming. Lack of protection on intellectual property right can lead to serious losses of foreign firms' R&D assets. Political and business relationships, such as trade friction, can also influence international transaction costs.

If transaction costs are considered only in transfers of producer services at arm's length, the internalization incentive will promote more FDI to substitute market transfers of producer services when transaction costs are high. However, since FDI itself is also a kind of transfer of producer service (within a firm), international transaction costs can also block some of this internalized transfer. For example, while language differences can make negotiation for technology licensing more difficult, it can also make the technological instruction and monitoring more difficult for FDI. Hence, lower transaction costs can directly lead to more FDI.

One example is the composition of the inflow of FDI in China. FDI flows from four Chinese-speaking economies (Hong Kong, Macao, Singapore and Taiwan) account for 75 percent of the total inward FDI in China, while FDI flows from European countries account for a very small share (see Figure 6.3). International transaction costs play an important role here. In terms of language and cultural differences, the transaction costs among the four Chinese speaking economies and the Chinese market are much smaller.

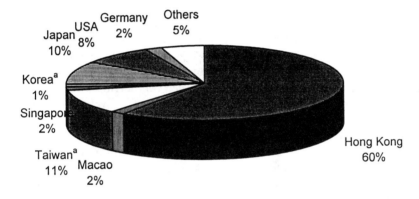

Note: a1992–1993 data.

Source: Almanac of China's Foreign Economics Relations and Trade, various years.

Figure 6.3 Home-country distribution of inward FDI in China: 1989–93 average

Another less obvious reason for the complementary relation of FDI and trade in producer services comes from the increasingly important role of producer services in manufacturing production. Since the late 1970s, the traditional mass production method, also known as Fordism or Taylorism, has encountered a crisis, and firms have become increasingly interested in flexible production methods (also known as Toyotaism) (see, for example, Piore and Sabel 1984). In contrast to mass production's big physical fixed capital input and large plant size, flexible production is a progressive externalization of production and a formation of network production structure, which emphasizes specialized producer services and business partnership. As a consequence, industrial analysts predict that global corporations of the future will develop a manufacturing network of decentralized plants, and each plant will be smaller and more flexible than is typical today (see Coffey 1992).

While mass production methods give firms the internal increasing returns to scale, they are also associated with greater risks. Flexible production, by emphasizing specialized producer services and the production network, can allow firms to enjoy the external increasing returns to scales caused by varieties of specialized producer services. Larger varieties of producer services and easier access to producer services can generate higher production efficiency and higher returns on investment. Therefore, lower international transaction costs can lead to more trade in producer services and more FDI flows.

The view of transaction costs can provide one explanation for the world FDI trends we mentioned earlier. Because of the *similarity* of developed countries in terms of economic systems, business culture, international standards and government regulations, and because of the lower trade barriers among developed countries, transaction costs between two developed countries are generally lower than those between a developed and a developing country. Hence developed countries receive a larger share of FDI (since most FDI flows from developed countries).

More innovations and more experiences in management make developed countries produce more producer services and key intermediate goods. FDI in developing countries usually requires the import of substantial producer services or key intermediate goods from developed countries. If the international transaction costs are high, then the prices of producer services will be higher, which can offset the attractiveness of lower wage rates in developing countries. To promote inward FDI, one strategy for developing countries is to reduce the international transaction costs in producer services.

Now the argument 'the lower transaction costs, the larger flows of FDI' seems quite straightforward given the importance of producer services. However, because reducing transaction costs makes all countries have larger varieties and lower priced producer services, who will get a larger FDI increase? Are the effects monotonic or not?[5] How will relative wages change? The answers are not obvious. So a formal model is needed.

3.   THE MODEL AND EQUILIBRIUM CONDITIONS

3.1 The Basic Setup of the Model

The economy has two sectors: manufacturing and producer services. The manufacturing sector produces a composite consumption good using capital, workers and producer services. The producer services sector produces differentiated intermediate goods using high-skilled (professional) labour only. Both workers and professionals are specific to each sector.

Two countries, home and foreign, are different with respect to endowments. Home (DC) is abundant in capital and high-skilled labour (professional labour), and foreign (LDC) is abundant in workers. There is no labour migration, however, capital is perfectly mobile.

Consumers in each country consume composites of the foreign and domestic goods, and the countries share common tastes by the same aggregate CES utility function. Home and foreign have the same form equations. An asterisk (*) is used to indicate foreign variables.

$$[U]\ U = \left[M_h^{(\sigma-1)/\sigma} + M_h^{*(\sigma-1)/\sigma} \right]^{\sigma/(\sigma-1)},$$

where M_h, M_h^* are home demands for home products and foreign products, respectively. Here we assume that M-goods are distinguished by country of production. It is observed that sometimes consumers have a preference for imported goods, while some consumers prefer domestic goods. The production location itself matters. σ is the substitution elasticity, and when $\sigma \to \infty$, there is no taste difference between domestic and imported goods.[6]

The budget constraint is

$$[Y]\ p_m M_h + p_m^* M_h^* = w_m L_m + w_s L_s + r K_e,$$

where p_m, pm^* are the prices of M-goods from home and abroad, w_m, w_s, L_m, L_s are the wage rates for workers, wage rate for highly-skilled labour, the endowment of worker, and endowment of highly-skilled labour, respectively. r is the interest rate for capital, and K_e is the endowment of capital at home.

The production of services uses only professional labour, and we assume a symmetric case. The representative production function is:

$$[S]\ L_{js} = b\, S_j + a$$

where S_j is the product quantity of a typical S-firm, L_{js} is the amount of professional labour hired in this firm, a is fixed cost, and b is marginal cost. The service sector is characterized by monopolistic competition.

Manufacturing production is of the Cobb–Douglas type, and the two countries have the same technology,

$$[\mathbf{M}]\ M = L_m^{1-\alpha-K^\beta} \left\{ \left[\sum_{i=1}^{N_s} S_i^{(\phi-1)/\phi} \right]^{\phi/(\phi-1)} \right\}^\alpha$$

where S_j is the amount of producer service j N_s, is the total number of S-firms (also the number of varieties of producer services) in the economy, and K is the capital used at home. The production function is homogenous and of degree one to L, K and S, but not to N_s. It implies external increasing returns to varieties of producer services (see Ethier 1982).

We have free trade for M-goods. Because of the non-storable and non-tangible character of services, the trade of producer services is subjected to an iceberg-type international transaction cost. When one unit of service is shipped, only a proportion t will arrive, $0 \leq t \leq 1$. t = 1 means all original shipments arrives, which implies no transaction cost. t=0 means none of the original shipments arrive, and this implies an infinite transaction cost. Hence a *larger t corresponds to a lower transaction cost*. The arrival price will be p/t, which is higher than the f.o.b. price p.[7]

3.2 Equilibrium Conditions

The equilibrium conditions are expressed in simultaneous equations. We will write the equations of the home country, and simply note that the same types of equations apply to the foreign country.

Because capital is perfectly mobile, in equilibrium the interest rate will be the same everywhere, that is, $r = r^*$, and is determined by the world total capital endowment $\bar{K}$. Capital usage allocation (K and K*) has no location effect on other variables. Because we are only concerned with the ratio of each variable for the two countries, for convenience, we can abstract K from the production function temporarily and discuss it later on. The production function [M] can then be simplified as

$$[\mathbf{M}']\ M = L_m^{1-\alpha} \left\{ \left[\sum_{i=1}^{N_s} S^{(\phi-1)/\psi} \right]^{\psi/(\psi-1)} \right\}^\alpha .$$

By maximizing utility, we can get the demand for M-goods produced in home,

$$M = \frac{w_m L_m + w_m L_s + w_m^* L_m^* + w_s^* L_s^*}{P_m^\sigma (p_m^{1-\sigma} + p_m^{*1-\sigma})} . \tag{6.1}$$

The demands for workers, home producer services and foreign producer services can be derived by minimizing the production cost of manufacturing,

$$L_m = \left(\frac{1-\alpha}{\alpha}\right)^\alpha w_m^{-\alpha} P^\alpha M,$$

(6.2)

$$S_j = \left(\frac{1-\alpha}{\alpha}\right)^{\alpha-1} w_m^{1-\alpha} P^{\alpha+\phi-1} p_s^{-\phi} M,$$

(6.3)

$$V_i = \left(\frac{1-\alpha}{\alpha}\right)^{\alpha-1} w_m^{1-\alpha} P^{\alpha+\phi-1} \left(\frac{p_s^*}{t}\right)^{-\phi} M$$

(6.4)

where S_j is the home demand for service j produced at home, V_i is the home demand for service i produced abroad,[8] p_s is the home price of services (S-goods) produced at home, p^* is the f.o.b. price of services (S-goods) produced abroad, and P is the price index of S-goods in the home market:

$$\text{[P] } P^{1-\phi} = n_s p_s^{1-\phi} + n_s^*(p_s^*/t)^{1-\phi}.$$

where, n_s and n_s^* are the numbers of S-firms at home and abroad.

Under the zero profit condition, the total wage bill should be equal to the proportion $1 - \alpha$ of the total sale value of M-goods.

$$w_m L_m = (1 - \alpha) p_m M.$$

(6.5)

Now look at the production of S-goods. Thanks to the iceberg form of transaction cost, the price elasticity to S-goods is always ϕ no matter where they are produced. By marginal revenue equalling marginal cost, we get

$$p_m \left(1 - \frac{1}{\phi}\right) = b w_s$$

(6.6)

The demand for each S-firm is the sum of home demand, foreign demand and loss during transaction, that is $S = S_j + S_j^* + S_j^*(1/t - 1)$. So the demand for S-labour by each firm is determined by

$$L_{js} = a + b(S_j + S_j^* / t),$$

(6.7)

where are S_j, S_j^* are S-goods produced in the home country and demanded by the home and foreign countries respectively.

Then the total number of S-firms can be determined by initial endowment,

$$n_s = L_s / L_{js} .$$

(6.8)

Finally, the zero profit condition of monopolistic competition will close our model,

$$P_s(S_j + S_j^* / t) = L_{js} w_s .$$

(6.9)

Given the initial endowments of the two countries, L_m, L_s, L_m^*, L_s^*, we have 18 unknowns and 18 equations: equations (6.1)–(6.9) and their counterpart equations for the foreign country.

4. SYMMETRIC EQUILIBRIUM

From (6.3) and (6.4), we get

$$S_j + S_j^* / t = \left(\frac{1-\alpha}{\alpha}\right)^{\alpha-1} p_s^{-\phi} \left(w_m^{1-\alpha} P^{\alpha+\phi-1} M + w_m^{*1-\alpha} P^{*\alpha+\phi-1} t^{\phi-1} M^* \right),$$

(6.10)

and

$$V_j / t + V_j^* = \left(\frac{1-\alpha}{\alpha}\right)^{\alpha-1} p_s^{*-\phi} \left(w_m^{1-\alpha} P^{\alpha+\phi-1} t^{\phi-1} M + w_m^{*1-\alpha} P^{*\alpha+\phi-1} M^* \right)$$

(6.10')

From (6.6)–(6.9) we know that under monopolistic competition, $S_j + S_j^* / t = V_i / t + V_i^*$. Then dividing (6.10) by (6.10') and simplifying, we have

$$1 = \rho_s^{-\phi} \frac{\omega_m^{1-\alpha} \rho^{\alpha+\phi-1} m + t^{\phi-1}}{\omega_m^{1-\alpha} \rho^{\alpha+\phi-1} mt^{\phi-1} + 1}$$

(6.11)

where

$$\omega_m \equiv \frac{w_m}{w_m^*}, \ \omega_s \equiv \frac{w_s}{w_s^*}, \ m \equiv \frac{M}{M^*}, \ \rho_s \equiv \frac{p_s}{p_s^*}, \text{ and } \rho \equiv \frac{P}{P^*} .$$

Further, we define

$$l_m \equiv \frac{L_m}{L_m^*}, \ l_s \equiv \frac{L_s}{L_s^*}, \ \rho_m \equiv \frac{P_m}{P_m^*} .$$

Then by (6.5) and (6.1), we have

$$\omega_m l_m = \rho_m m \tag{6.12}$$

and

$$m = \rho_m^{-\sigma} \tag{6.13}$$

Prices of M–goods are equal to their average costs, so from (6.2)-(6.4), we can have

$$\rho_m = \omega_m^{1-\alpha} \rho^\alpha . \tag{6.14}$$

Now by (6.12)–(6.14) we can get

$$\rho_m = l_m^{\frac{\alpha-1}{\alpha+\sigma-\alpha\sigma}} \rho^{\frac{\alpha}{\alpha-\sigma-\alpha\sigma}}, \tag{6.15}$$

$$\omega_m = \rho^{\frac{\alpha(1-\sigma)}{\alpha+\sigma-\alpha\sigma}} l^{\frac{-1}{\alpha+\sigma-\alpha\sigma}}, \tag{6.16}$$

and

$$m = \rho_m^{-\sigma} = l_m^{\frac{-(\alpha-1)\sigma}{\alpha+\sigma-\alpha\sigma}} \rho^{\frac{-\alpha\sigma}{\alpha+\sigma-\alpha\sigma}} . \tag{6.17}$$

Substituting (6.15)–(6.17) into (6.11) we have

$$1 = \rho_s^{-\phi} \frac{\rho^{\frac{\alpha\phi+\phi\sigma-\alpha\sigma\phi-\sigma}{\alpha+\sigma-\alpha\sigma}} l^{\frac{\alpha-1-\alpha\sigma+\sigma}{\alpha+\sigma-\alpha\sigma}} + t^{\phi-1}}{\rho^{\frac{\alpha\phi+\phi\sigma-\alpha\sigma\phi-\sigma}{\alpha+\sigma-\alpha\sigma}} l_m^{\frac{\alpha-1-\alpha\sigma+\sigma}{\alpha+\sigma-\alpha\sigma}} t^{\phi-1} + 1} . \tag{6.18}$$

Noting that $\rho_s = \omega_s$ from (6.6), and rearranging (6.18) we get

$$\frac{\omega_s^\phi t^{\phi-1} - 1}{\omega_s^\phi - t^{\phi-1}} = -\frac{1}{A} \rho^{e(\phi-1)}, \tag{6.19}$$

where

$$e = \frac{\alpha\phi + \phi\sigma - \alpha\phi\sigma - \sigma}{(1-\phi)(\alpha + \sigma - \alpha\sigma)} = \frac{\sigma\phi(1-\alpha) + \alpha\phi - \sigma}{(1-\phi)(\alpha + \sigma - \alpha\sigma)}$$

and

$$A = l_m^{\frac{\alpha-1-\alpha\sigma+\sigma}{\alpha+\sigma-\alpha\sigma}} < 1.$$

Noting that

$$\rho = \frac{p}{p^*} = \left[\frac{1 + l_s^{-1}\omega_s^{\phi-1} t^{\phi-1}}{t^{\phi-1} + l_s^{-1}\omega_s^{\phi-1}}\right]^{\frac{1}{1-\phi}}$$

by definition [P], we can rewrite (6.19) into

$$(A\omega_s^{\phi} t^{\phi-1} - A)(1 + l_s^{-1}\omega_s^{\phi-1}t^{\phi-1})^e + (\omega_s^{\phi} - t^{\phi-1})(t^{\phi-1} + l_s^{-1}\omega_s^{\phi-1})^e = 0. \quad (6.20)$$

Equation (6.20) is a reduced form of our simultaneous equation system, and we have only one unknown ω_s in it. Once we obtain a solution $\omega_s(t)$, we can plug it back into equations (6.11)–(6.19) to get an equilibrium solution set, including ω_s, m, w_m, ρ, ρ_m and ρ_s. In this equilibrium, $\omega_s(t)$, ω_s, m, w_m, ρ, ρ_m and ρ_s, and are all ratios of home to foreign variables. We therefore call the equilibrium determined by equation (6.20) a symmetric equilibrium.

Proposition 1 (Existence Proposition): The solution to equation (6.20) exists, which implies the existence of the equilibrium.

Proof. Let us define the LHS of equation (6.20) as f.

First we can check that at the two boundary points, $t = 0$ and $t = 1$, solutions exist:

$$\omega_s = (A_s^e)^{\frac{1}{\phi+\phi e-e}} \text{ at } t = 0.$$

and $\omega_s = 1$ at $t = 1$.

Now consider $0 < t < 1$. When $\omega_s = t^{(\phi-1)/\phi}$, we have $f < 0$, and when $\omega_s = t^{(1-\phi)/\phi}$ we have $f > 0$. So by Rolle's theorem, we know that there must exist at least one point at which $f = 0$. It finishes our proof. Further, we also know that

$$t^{\frac{\phi-1}{\phi}} < \omega_s < t^{\frac{1-\phi}{\phi}}. \qquad\qquad \text{Q.E.D.}$$

Proposition 2 (Uniqueness Proposition): the equilibrium of this model is unique.

Proof. The proof follows from Lemma 1 (which will be proved independently in the next section). From Lemma 1, we know that ω_s, the solution to the equation $f = 0$, is a monotone function of t. Hence given one t, we can have only one ω_s correspondingly, and one solution set to the equation system in Section 2. The equilibrium is unique. Q.E.D.

5. MODEL ANALYSIS

5.1 Assumptions

1. Endowment differences: $L_m / L_m^* \leq 1$, and $L_s / L_s^* \geq 1$. Because we have increasing returns to scale in the economy, the relative endowments of the two countries are important.

2. Substitute elasticity condition:

$$\phi \geq \frac{1}{1 - \alpha + \frac{\alpha}{\sigma}}.$$

This assumption implies that, given the technology of manufacturing production α, the substitution elasticity of various producer services should not be too small compared with the consumer's preference for final products. For example, given a neutral technology $\alpha = 0.5$, if $\sigma = 1$, then $\sigma \geq 1$ will satisfy the assumption; even if $\sigma = \infty$, the assumption only needs $\phi \geq 2$. This is just a sufficient condition that can make our analysis easier, but not a necessary one.[9]

5.2 Comparative Static Analysis

In this section we will prove several analytical results and explore how the manufacturing production pattern changes as the transaction cost changes.

Lemma 1: $\omega_s(t)$, the solution of the symmetric equilibrium defined by equation (6.20), is a monotonically increasing function of t, that is,

$$\frac{d\omega_s}{dt} > 0, \quad \forall t \in [0, 1]$$

Proof. Denote the LHS of equation (6.20) as f. Differentiating f with respect to t, we have

$$\frac{\partial f}{\partial t} = A(1 + l_s^{-1}\omega_s^{\phi-1} t^{\phi-1})^e \omega_s^{\phi}(\phi - 1)t^{\phi-2} +$$
$$+ Ae(\omega_s^{\phi} t^{\phi-1} - 1)(1 + l_s^{-1}\omega_s^{\phi-1} t^{\phi-1})^{e-1}(\phi - 1) t^{\phi-2} l_s^{-1} w_s^{\phi-1}$$
$$+ e(\omega_s^{\phi} - t^{\phi-1})(t^{\phi-1} + l_s^{-1}w_s^{\phi-1})^{e-1}(\phi - 1)t^{\phi-2}$$
$$+ l_s^{-1} w_s^{\phi-1})^e(\phi - 1)t^{\phi-2}$$

Substituting

$$(\omega_s^{\phi} - t^{\phi-1})(t^{\phi-1} + l_s^{-1} w_s^{\phi-1})^e \text{ with} - A(\omega_s^{\phi} t^{\phi-1} - 1)(1 + l_s^{-1} \omega_s^{\phi-1} t^{\phi-1})^e,$$

we have

$$\frac{df}{dt} = (\phi - 1)t^{\phi-2} G + e(\phi - 1)t^{\phi-2} A(\omega_s^{\phi} t^{\phi-1} - 1)(l_s^{-1}\omega_s^{\phi-1}t^{\phi-1})^e H,$$

where

$$G = \left[A\omega_s^{\phi}(l_s^{-1} \omega_s^{\phi-1} t^{\phi-1})^e - (l_s^{-1} \omega_s^{\phi-1} + t^{\phi-1})^e \right].$$

and

$$H = \left[(1 + l_s^{-1} \omega_s^{\phi-1} t^{\phi-1})^{-1} - (t^{\phi-1} + l_s^{-1} \omega_s^{\phi-1})^{-1} \right].$$

For the moment, let us assume $\omega_s \le 1$ (we will prove it later). Because $A < 1$, $l_s > 1$, $1 - \phi < 0$, $t \le 1$ and

$$e = \frac{\alpha\phi + \phi\sigma - \alpha\phi\sigma - \sigma}{(1 - \phi)(\alpha + \sigma - \alpha\sigma)} < 0$$

under assumption 2, we have

$$G < (1 + l_s^{-1}\omega_s^{\phi-1}t^{\phi-1})^e - (l_s^{-1}\omega_s^{\phi-1} + t^{\phi-1})^e$$

$$= ([1 + \frac{(1 - l_s^{-1}\omega_s^{\phi-1})(1 - t^{\phi-1})}{l_s^{-1}\omega_s^{\phi-1} + t^{\phi-1}}]^e - 1)(l_s^{-1}\omega_s^{\phi-1} + t^{\phi-1})^e$$

$$\leq 0,$$

and

$$H = \frac{(1 - t^{\phi-1})(l_s^{-1}w_s^{\phi-1} - 1)}{(l_s^{-1}\omega_s^{\phi-1} + t^{\phi-1})(l_s^{-1}\omega_s^{\phi-1}t^{\phi-1} + 1)} < 0$$

Now we have

$$\frac{\partial f}{\partial t} = (\phi - 1)t^{\phi-2}G + e(\phi - 1)t^{\phi-2}A(\omega_s^{\phi}t^{\phi-1} - 1)(1 + l_s^{-1}\omega_s^{\phi-1}t^{\phi-1})^e H$$

$$\leq 0 \,(\text{ and } = 0 \text{ iff } t=0) .$$

Next, let us check the sign of $\partial f / \partial \omega_s$.

$$\frac{\partial f}{\partial \omega_s} = A(1 + l_s^{-1}\omega_s^{\phi-1}t^{\phi-1})^e t^{\phi-1}\phi\omega_s^{\phi-1}$$

$$+ Ae(\omega^{\phi}t^{\phi-1} - 1)(1 + l_s^{-1}\omega_s^{\phi-1}t^{\phi-1})^{e-1}l_s^{-1}t^{\phi-1}(\phi - 1)\omega_s^{\phi-2}$$

$$+ e(\omega^{\phi} - t^{\phi-1})(t^{\phi-1} + l_s^{-1}\omega_s^{\phi-1})^{e-1}l_s^{-1}(\phi - 1)\omega_s^{\phi-2} + (t^{\phi-1} + l_s^{-1}\omega_s^{\phi-1})^e \phi\omega^{\phi-1}$$

$$= C + D$$

where

$$C = A(1 + l_s^{-1}\omega_s^{\phi-1}t^{\phi-1})^{e-1} \omega_s^{\phi-2}t^{\phi-1}\left[\phi\omega_s + l_s^{-1}\omega_s^{\phi}t^{\phi-1}(\phi + e\phi - e) - el_s^{-1}(\phi - 1)\right],$$

and

$$D = (t^{\phi-1} + l_s^{-1}\omega_s^{\phi-1})^{e-1} \omega_s^{\phi-2} [\phi\omega_s t^{\phi-1} + l_s^{-1}\omega_s^{\phi-1} (\phi + e\phi - e) - t^{\phi-1}el_s^{-1}(\phi - 1)] .$$

Because $e < 0$, and $x > 0$, it is easy to show that $C > 0$, and $D > 0$, and

$$\phi + e\phi - e = \frac{\sigma}{\alpha + \sigma - \alpha\sigma} > 0,$$

it is easy to show that $C > 0$, and $D > 0$, and hence $\partial f/\partial\omega_s > 0$. Now we have

$$\frac{d\omega_s}{dt} = -\frac{\dfrac{\partial f}{\partial t}}{\dfrac{\partial f}{\partial\omega_s}} > 0.$$

The last thing is to verify the earlier temporary assumption $\omega_3 \le \forall t \in [0,1]$. When $t = 1$, $\omega_s = 1$,

$$\frac{d\omega_s}{dt}\Bigg|_{t=1} -\frac{\dfrac{\partial f}{\partial t}}{\dfrac{\partial f}{\partial\omega_s}}\Bigg|_{t=1} = -\frac{A(l_s + 1)^e(\phi - 1) - (l_s + 1)^e(\phi - 1)}{A(l_s + 1)^e\phi + (l_s + 1)^e\phi} = -\frac{(\phi - 1)(A - 1)}{\phi(A + 1)} > 0$$

Since

$$\frac{d\omega_s}{dt}\Bigg|_{t=1} > 0,$$

a small change from $t = 1$ to $t' < 1$ will decrease ω_s from $\omega_s(t) = 1$ to $\omega_s(t')$ < 1. Then at t', the function is monotonically increasing, which generates a smaller ω_s for a smaller t. Along these lines, we can verify $\omega_s(t) \le 1$ $\forall t \in [0,1]$.

So, it is proved that the function $\omega_s = \omega_s(t)$ is a monotonically increasing function, that is:

$$\frac{d\omega_s}{dt} \ge 0, (= 0 \text{ iff } t = 0, \forall t \in [0,1].$$ Q.E.D.

Proposition 3: The price of S-goods in the foreign country (LDC) becomes relatively cheaper when the transaction cost decreases (t increases) , that is,

$$\frac{d(P/P^*)}{dt} > 0.$$

Proof. From Definition **[P]**, we have

$$\frac{P}{P^*} = \left[\frac{n_s\, p_s^{1-\phi} \neq n_s^*\, p_v^{1-\phi}\, t^{\phi-1}}{n_s p_s^{1-\phi} t^{\phi-1} + n_s^*\, p_v^{1-\phi}} \right]^{\frac{1}{1-\phi}} = \left[\frac{1 \neq \ell_s^{-1}\, \omega_s^{\phi-1}\, t^{\phi-1}}{t^{\phi-1} + \ell_s^{-1}\, \omega_s^{\phi-1}} \right]^{\frac{1}{1-\phi}}.$$

Then the proof can be obtained straightforwardly by totally differentiating
P/P* with respect to t.   Q.E.D.

Corollary 1: Wage rates in the manufacturing sector in DC become
relatively lower, hence the workers in DC are worse off, that is:

$$\frac{d(w_m / w_m^*)}{dt} < 0 .$$

Corollary 2: M-good prices in LDC become cheaper with the decrease of
transaction cost, that is:

$$\frac{d(p_m / p_m^*)}{dt} > 0 .$$

Proposition 4: The manufacturing production pattern (M-goods
production shares) will change with the change of the transaction cost. If the
international transaction cost decreases (t increases), more manufacturing
goods will be produced in the foreign country (the LDC), that is:

$$\frac{d(M / M^*)}{dt} < 0 .$$

Given Proposition 3, the proofs of Corollary 1, 2 and Proposition 4 are
straightforward by recalling equations (6.15)–(6.17).

Intuitively, because of free trade in the M-sector, the difference in market
size has no effect. The manufacturing production pattern will be determined
only by the production costs of the two countries. When the transaction cost
is very high, producer services will be relatively expensive in the LDC
(foreign) country, which offsets the advantage of its lower wage rate. As a
result, manufacturing production will concentrate in DC. When the
transaction cost decreases, that is, when t gets closer to 1, the lower wage
rate in manufacturing in LDC will become more and more attractive.
Consequently, the manufacturing share of LDC will increase.

Following the same procedures, we can also check the effect of the
professional labour pool on manufacturing production. Now consider t is

given, and $l_s = L_s/L_s^*$ is a control variable, we then have Propositions 5 and 6.

Proposition 5: Producer services in the foreign country (LDC) will be cheaper if LDC can increase its professional labour pool, that is:

$$\frac{d(P / P^*)}{d(L_s / L_s^*)} \leq 0 \, , (= 0, \text{ iff } t = 1) \, .$$

Corollary: The wage rate of professional labour in LDC will be lower if the professional labour pool increases in LDC, that is:

$$\frac{d(w_s / w_s^*)}{d(L_s / L_s^*)} \leq 0, (= 0, \text{ iff } t = 1) \, .$$

Proposition 6: If the foreign country (LDC) can increase its professional labour pool (high-skilled labour), its manufacturing production share will increase, that is,

$$\frac{d(M / M^*)}{d(L_s / L_s^*)} \geq 0 \, , (= 0, \text{ iff } t = 1) \, .$$

By combining Propositions 1 and 6, we can easily have

$$\frac{dl_s}{dt}\Big|_m \geq 0 \, , (= 0, \text{ iff } t = 1), \text{ and } \frac{dl_s}{dt}\Big|_m = \infty \text{ when } t = 1 \, , \tag{6.21}$$

and the relation can be shown in Figure 6.4.

In Figure 6.4, $m = M/M^*$, which represents the world manufacturing production pattern. m_1, m_2 and m_3 are three different levels of m, and $m_1 > m_2 > m_3$. Given the transaction cost, increasing the home–foreign high-skilled labour ratio (L_s/L_s^*) will have more M-goods produced at home. Given the relative endowment of high-skilled labour L_s/L_s^*, lowering the transaction cost (moving t from 0 to 1) will make more M-goods produced abroad (LDC).

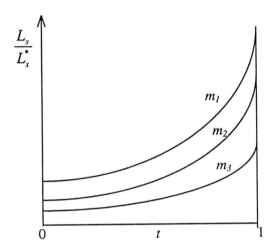

Notes: Transaction costs decrease as T increases. m = M/M*, m_1, m_2 and m_3 represent three different ratios and $m_1 > m_2 > m_3$.

Figure 6.4 Production pattern changes with changes in transaction costs and the professional labour ratio

5.3 International Investment

Since capital is perfectly mobile, without damaging the above analysis, we can add the capital back into the model and check the international capital movement. Because in this model the capital movement is directly linked with the trade of producer services and international transaction costs, we can name the capital movement as FDI.

From production function **[M]**, we can immediately have

$$\beta MP_m = rK \tag{6.22}$$

for home, and

$$\beta M^* P_m^* = rK^* \tag{6.22'}$$

for abroad. Then,

$$\frac{K}{K^*} = \frac{MP_m}{M^* P_m^*} \tag{6.23}$$

From (6.1) we know that

$$\frac{P_m}{P_m^*} = \left(\frac{M}{M^*}\right)^{-\frac{1}{\sigma}}.$$

(6.24)

Then

$$\frac{K}{K^*} = \left(\frac{M}{M^*}\right)^{1-\frac{1}{\sigma}}.$$

(6.25)

Since $\sigma = 1$, we have

$$\frac{d\left(\frac{K}{K^*}\right)}{d\left(\frac{M}{M^*}\right)} > 0.$$

(6.26)

(6.25) gives a positive relationship of capital allocation and the manufacturing production pattern. Recalling Proposition 4 and Proposition 6, we can have Propositions 7 and 8 immediately.

Proposition 7 (FDI and Transaction Cost): Lowering transaction cost (increasing t) will increase the flow of FDI from home to foreign, that is,

$$\frac{d(K / K^*)}{dt} < 0.$$

Proposition 7 gives one explanation of why LDC's share of FDI is small (Figure 6.1). According to the 'cultural/business distance' and the government policy criteria, transaction costs between DC and DC are generally lower than those between DC and LDC, hence we observe a larger share of FDI flowing to developed countries. Given the large amount of ad hoc barriers in Japan, it is also not surprising to see that little FDI flows into Japan. Along with trade liberalization in East Asian countries, transaction costs between these countries and developed countries are decreasing. Proposition 7 can explain the surge of FDI in East Asian economies in the last decade.

Proposition 8 (FDI and high-skilled labour): The more high-skilled labour endowment the foreign has, or the more similar the two countries are (in term of endowment), the larger the flow of FDI, that is,

$$\frac{d(K / K^*)}{d(L_s / L_s^*)} \geq 0 , \ (= 0 , \ \text{iff } t = 1) .$$

Proposition 8 implies that if the foreign country is more similar to home in terms of high-skilled labour endowment, there will be more FDI from home to the foreign country. This offers another reason why developed countries have a large share of world total inward FDI. Propositions 7 and 8 verify our general discussion at the beginning of this chapter. The two factors, transaction costs and the professional labour pool make manufacturing production, as well as FDI, agglomerate in those locations either with large professional labour pool or easy access to producer services.

6. CONCLUSION AND POLICY IMPLICATIONS

This chapter uses a general equilibrium model to analyse the international transaction costs in producer services and their relationship with international production patterns and FDI. The model characterizes the producer services sector as professional labour-intensive employment and increasing returns to scale under a monopolistic competition market structure. The model also includes transaction costs in the trade of producer services, and allows services to be traded directly. The comparative static analysis shows that reducing transaction costs can increase manufacturing productivity because of external increasing returns to scale, and hence can increase FDI flows. Also, increasing the professional labour pool can increase the availability of local producer services and increase FDI inflow. These two reasons make manufacturing production concentrate in developed countries where there is a large professional labour pool and easy access to producer services from other developed countries. This provides an explanation for the FDI agglomeration.

East Asia's experience can shed light on our conclusion. Whether the rapid growth in East Asia is a 'miracle' or not, we should ask a question 'why does FDI go to East Asia?'. Our theory about transaction costs and a highly-skilled labour pool can offer some explanations. Economic reform and liberalization integrate East Asia into the world economy rapidly, hence the cultural/business differences between East Asia and major developed countries, especially Japan, have become smaller than those between other developing countries and major FDI home countries. An emphasis on education is a tradition in East Asia, and education levels in East Asian countries are generally higher than average levels in other developing countries. Education not only improves labour's skills, but also helps East Asia to have a large professional labour pool. As our model shows, smaller transaction costs and a bigger professional labour pool make East Asia an attractive place for foreign direct investment.

For LDCs who take export extension as their development policy and attempt to attract more FDI, two policy implications can be derived from this analysis. One is to increase the quantity of highly-skilled labour in their countries. This can be achieved by promoting education. Empirical studies of FDI determinants have uncovered the importance of education in growth. Another is to reduce transaction costs or trade barriers in producer services, which can make their lower labour costs more attractive to FDI, and promote their manufacturing export. International transaction costs are mainly determined by government efficiency as well as culture/business differences with developed countries. Therefore, it will be important for LDCs to improve the business environment toward reducing differences with the international standard. For example, efforts such as reducing the tariffs and restrictions on intermediate service trade, improving the legal system to protect intellectual property rights, and correcting bureaucratic failure, will be helpful for encouraging export growth.

ACKNOWLEDGEMENT

I am grateful to Masahisa Fujita, Tony Smith, Wilfred Ethier, Patrick Kehole, Tomoya Mori and participants at the regional science theory workshop and the international economics workshop at the University of Pennsylvania. Thanks also go to Makoto Tawada, Mikoto Usui and an anonymous referee for their helpful comments. An earlier version of this paper appeared as Working Paper in Regional Science, No. 168, University of Pennsylvania.

REFERENCES

Armington, P. (1969), 'A theory of demand for products distinguished by place of production', *IMF Staff Paper* **16**, pp. 159–78.

Burgess, D.F. (1990), 'Services as Intermediate Goods', in Jones, R. and A. Krueger (eds), *The Political Economy of International Trade*, New York: Basil Blackwell.

Caves, R.E. (1982), *Multinational Enterprise and Economic Analysis*, Cambridge: Cambridge University Press.

Coffey, W.J. (1992), 'The role of producer services in systems of flexible production', in Ernste and Meier (eds), *Regional Development and Contemporary Industrial Response*, NewYork: Basic Books.

Ethier, W. (1982), 'National and international returns to scale in the modern theory of international trade', *American Economic Review* **72**, pp. 950–59.

Ethier, W. (1986), 'The multinational firm', *Quarterly Journal of Economics* **101**, pp. 805–33.

Ethier, W. (1992), 'Multinational firms in the theory of international trade', IERC Discussion Paper **30**.

Ethier, W.J. and H. Horn (1991), 'Service in international trade', in Helpman, E. and A. Razin (eds), *International Trade and Trade Policy*, Cambridge, MA, MIT Press.

Francois, J.F. (1990), 'Trade in producer services and returns due to specialization under monopolistic competition', *Canadian Journal of Economics* **23**, pp. 109–24.

Hu, D. and M. Fujita (1996), 'Regional disparity in China: effects of globalization and economic liberalization', *UNU/IAS Working Paper* **22**.

Krugman, P. (1991), 'Increasing returns and economic geography', *Journal of Political Economics* **99**, pp. 483–99.

Krugman, P. and A. Venables (1993), 'Integration, specialization and adjustment' mimeo, MIT.

Lucas, R.E. Jr. (1990), 'Why doesn't capital flow from rich to poor countries?, *American Economic Review* **80**, pp. 92–6.

Milgram, P. and J. Roberts (1992), *Economics, Organization and Management*, New York: Prentice-Hall.

Piore, M.J. and C.F. Sabel (1984), *The Second Industrial Divide*, New York: Basic Books.

Venables, A.J. (1993), 'International trade in vertically linked industries', CEPR discussion Paper.

Williamson, O.E. (1986), *Economic Organization*. New York: New York University Press.

World Bank (1996), *World Debt Tables 1996*, Washington DC: The World Bank.

NOTES

1. Producer services are intermediate inputs to manufacturing production, including management services, R&D, financial and accounting service, marketing, advertising, personnel and training, legal service, engineering and consulting services, trade services, and the design and trial production of key parts.

2. Several models on trade of intermediate goods, for example, Venables (1993) and Krugman and Venables (1993) add an identical transportation cost to both intermediates and final goods. This mixture cannot distinguish the role of transaction cost from transportation cost. Transaction cost is not just another name of transportation cost in services trade, but there are different determining factors. It is necessary to explore the role of transaction cost separately from transportation cost.

3. As suggested by Milgram and Roberts (1992), those characters may include: transaction-related specific assets, frequency and duration of transaction, uncertainty/complexity, difficulties for performance measurement and connection to other transactions.

4. Although generally it is difficult to measure the cultural differences and the effect of government policies, it is possible to use these three factors to measure the international transaction costs.

5. The effects of transportation costs have been shown non-monotonic, see Krugman (1991).

6. This device, so called differentiation by production location, is widely used in general equilibrium trade models since Armington (1969).

7. This 'Iceberg-type' device may be more suitable to transaction cost rather than to transportation cost. Suppose an American accountant spends totally 1 unit of time to do a project for a foreign client. She uses actually t time for accounting, and uses 1–t time to deal with language and accounting standard problems. If she charges domestic client p, she will have to charge foreign client p/t for the same accounting activities.

8. We reserve S_j^* *to stand for the foreign demand* for service j produced at home, so we use V_i and V_i^* to denote home and foreign demands for service produced in the foreign country.

9. Numerical result shows that, without changing the result, the parameter range of ϕ can be very wide beyond the assumption.

7. An Empirical Analysis of Agglomeration Effects and Locational Choice of Japanese Electronics Firms in East Asia

Suminori Tokunaga and Ryoichi Ishii

1. INTRODUCTION

Japanese Foreign Direct Investment (FDI) has been increasing for the last two decades, especially since the yen appreciation following the Plaza Accord in 1985. This process rapidly increased the globalization of Japanese firms. Prior to this, most Japanese FDI was located in the US and European Community, whereas subsequently Japanese FDI to East Asia grew rapidly.

While Japanese FDI has almost assuredly played an important role in the growth of many countries in the Asian region there are few empirical studies of the process using micro level data. This study uses micro level data on Japanese multinational firms (MNFs) in East Asia to assess the determinants of global plant location choice. The results presented here combine survey responses of Japanese firm managers with empirical estimation of location choice in the electronics industry since 1986. In particular we focus on the role that industry-level agglomeration plays in location decisions in line with the literature in Marshall (1920); Krugman (1991a, 1991b, 1995); Smith and Florida (1994); Head et al. (1995) and Fujita and Thisse (1995).

The organization of the chapter is as follows. In Section 2, from survey results we examine the location behaviour of nine Japanese firms in East Asia since 1986 and deductively develop hypotheses about the important determinants of location choices in East Asia. In Section 3, we develop a theoretical location choice model. Section 4 is an explanation of our data sources, the independent variables affecting location choices and the model specification. Section 5 presents the estimation results of the new plant location choice model in East Asia. We conclude with a summary of the study's major results in Section 6.

2. LOCATION BEHAVIOUR AND LOCATION DETERMINANTS OF JAPANESE ELECTRONICS FIRMS

The Japanese electronics industry began overseas production in the early 1960s, however, with the rise in the yen after the Plaza Accord in 1985 the amount of production abroad accelerated. Figure 7.1 shows the locations and changes in location for the nine Japanese electronics firms being studied (Hitachi, Matsushita Electric, Toshiba, NEC, Mitsubishi Electric, Fujitsu, Sanyo Electric, Sony and Sharp) from 1975. As can be seen, the number of domestic plants in Japan gradually increased from 211 (1975) to 354 (1994), but the number of overseas plants increased much more rapidly growing from 74 (1975) to 335 (1994). Furthermore, the destination of these plants has also changed substantially over the last 20 years. In the late 1980s the destination of choice shifts from the US/European Community to East Asia. Specifically, the number of plants in East Asia (especially in Singapore, Malaysia, China and Thailand) grew from 40 (1975) to 163 (1994) in order to make the global and regional production networks for these types of plants. Thus, we focus on the determinants of location choices in East Asia.

As an example of global and regional production networks, we consider the present relationship among plants for colour TV production by Toshiba. To develop an efficient production system worldwide, Toshiba has developed an integrated production system for TVs (from components to assembly) which spans the four major markets (that is, Japan, North America, Asia and EC). In this system each plant is specialized in the production of particular products. For example, the Research and Development of future TV technologies is conducted at the Consumer Electronics Laboratories in Yokohama near its headquarters. High-tech products such as HDTVs (high definition televisions), LCDs (liquid crystal displays), and large-screen TVs with multi-functions are developed and manufactured at Fukaya and Himeji plants in Japan. Middle-sized TVs are produced in Singapore and Thailand plants and shipped to the US and Asian markets. The colour TV tubes produced in Thailand are exported to either Fukaya and Singapore plants or other plants worldwide. Furthermore, all colour computer displays produced in the Singapore plant are exported to Japan. Finally, the US plant produces some large and medium TVs for sale in the US market. From these facts, it appears that Japanese firms seem to prefer high export-GDP ratio countries in East Asia. Thus, we propose the export–GDP ratio as the location determinant of plants.

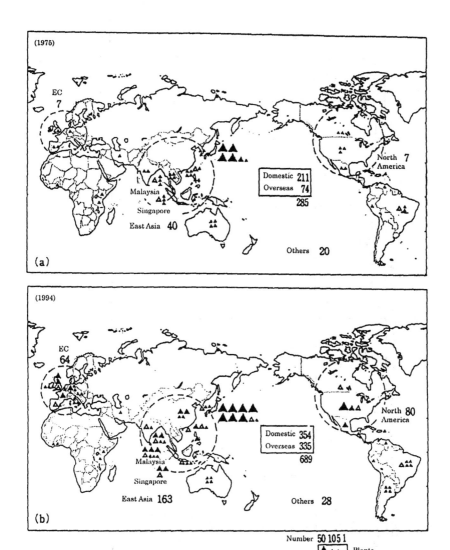

Figure 7.1 Location of new plants for Japanese electronics firms

Table 7.1 Location determinants of new overseas plants (by plant managers)

(a) The first stage: factors for choosing allocation in the US or East Asia

Location determinants (evaluation)
1: very important 2: important
3: less important 4: least important

Location determinants	Computers, communication (in the US) (1 Plant)				Industrial systems & others (in the US) (1 Plant)				Consumer electronics (in Asia) (4 Plants)				Electronic devices IC (in Asia) (2 Plants)			
	4	3	2	1	4	3	2	1	4	3	2	1	4	3	2	1
1 Cheaper labour cost	*						*					*				*
2 Availability of non-skilled labour	*						*				*			*		
3 Availability of skilled labour	*						*				*			*		
4 Weaker labour organization	*						*		*				*			
5 Cheaper land cost		*			*						*			*		
6 Saving in transportation cost				*			*				*		*			
7 Accessibility to new technologies	*						*				*		*			
8 Response to trade barriers		*					*				*					*
9 Being the major product market				*			*				*			*		
10 Diversification of production risks	*						*				*			*		
11 Existence of rival firms in region				*		*					*			*		
12 Response to yen appreciation			*			*					*			*		
13 Developing in communication network	*					*					*			*		

Table 7.1 (continued)

(b) The second stage: factors for choosing a location within the US/East Asia

Location determinants (evaluation)
1: very important 2: important
3: less important 4: least important

	Computers, communication (in the US) (1 Plant)				Industrial systems & others (in the US) (1 Plant)				Consumer electronics (in Asia) (4 Plants)				Electronic devices IC (in Asia) (2 Plants)			
	4	3	2	1	4	3	2	1	4	3	2	1	4	3	2	1
1 Cheaper labour cost	*						*			*						*
2 Availability of non-skilled labour	*						*			*				*		
3 Availability of skilled labour	*						*		*					*		
4 Weaker labour organization	*						*		*				*			
5 Cheaper land cost		*			*						*				*	
6 Availability of electricity and tel.		*				*				*					*	
7 High quality and quantity of water		*				*				*					*	
8 Saving in transportation cost							*			*						
9 Proximity to a large city	*						*				*			*		
10 Accessibility to highway		*					*			*				*		
11 Accessibility to airport		*								*					*	
12 Accessibility to port	*						*			*				*		
13 Proximity to major universities	*					*				*				*		
14 Good amenity	*					*				*			*			
15 Proximity to your other plants			*			*				*			*			
16 Accessibility to subcontractors	*					*				*				*		
17 Favourable treatment of corporate tax	*					*					*		*			
18 Existence of Free Trade Zone						*				*						
19 Other favourable actions of local gov		*				*				*					*	
20 Political stability										*				*		
21 English fluency										*				*		
22 Lower loan interest rate										*				*		
23 Favourable exchange rate vs yen and $										*						

Source: Ishii (1992), p. 266.

131

Table 7.2 Motivation for foreign direct investment (Export–Import Bank of Japan, 1991–93)

Region	NIEs			ASEAN			China		
Motivation for foreign direct investment	1991	1992	1993	1991	1992	1993	1991	1992	1993
Preservation and/or expansion of market share	59	50	60	47	46	50	22	39	33
Development of a new market	13	19	17	12	15	20	28	37	44
Reverse exports to Japan	10	6	1	8	10	21	8	8	19
Exports to a third country	11	8	26	16	12	32	8	6	15
Response to voluntary export restraints	1	0	0	2	3	1	3	3	1
Promotion of specialization with the firm	12	16	2	12	16	7	3	5	3
Diversification of production facilities overseas	18	11	8	23	18	20	3	6	15
Securing inexpensive labour forces	6	3	2	27	27	20	14	11	30
Supplying parts to an assembly manufacturer	2	0	3	6	8	17	40	3	12
Securing stable supply of raw materials	10	8	2	12	9	1	0	11	2
Request from the host country	4	0	1	4	5	2	5	11	2
Avoiding foreign exchange risk	1	1	3	1	4	10	14	16	6
Development of products adapted to the local market	1	1	3	2	2	2	0	5	6
							3	3	2
Number of responses	88	62	80	115	97	105	35	59	107

Note: The total figure of each column is more than 100 percent because of multiple answers for motivation.

Source: S. Tejima (1994), p. 72.

What are the location determinants for Japanese electronic plants like these? To look at these we review the results from Ishii (1992) and the Export–Import Bank of Japan (Tejima et al. 1994). Ishii conducted a questionnaire survey of location choice in 1991. His survey focused on the location determinants of plants and R&D laboratories of the nine Japanese firms listed above and looked at their choices to locate in Japan, East Asia and the US. Table 7.1 reviews the determinants of these choices for the new overseas plants. On the other hand, Table 7.2 presents results for Japanese FDI choices for 1991, 1992 and 1993 from annual surveys conducted by the Export–Import Bank of Japan.[1]

From Table 7.1 and Table 7.2, we can make the following observations about location determinants in East Asia (NIEs, ASEAN and China). At the regional level, important location factors are (1) labour cost, (2) the local market of their products (preservation and/or expansion of market share), (3) the yen appreciation, (4) exports potential to third countries (or re-exports to Japan), (5) availability of electricity and telephones.[2]

3.   A MODEL OF LOCATION CHOICE

Recent empirical studies of firm location in Asian include Tu (1990), Tsai (1991) and Alburo et al. (1992). Tu's work on Taiwan found that market growth, per capita income, the wage rate, the exchange rate appreciation and governmental policy were important for FDI inflow. Tsai's work on Taiwan also found that market growth and government policy were significant factors in FDI growth. Alburo et al. focused their work on the ASEAN nations. They found that an institutional capacity to absorb FDI as measured by the combination of R&D efforts and skill level was important.

A second set of more micro studies have looked at firm location behaviour based on discrete choice model. The first of these, which we review, was done by Carlton (1983) where he examined the location and employment choice of new branch plants in the US in a logit model. This model assumes that branch locations are chosen to maximize profits. He finds that energy costs are surprisingly important. However, the wage effect cannot be measured precisely while taxes and state incentive programmes do not seem to have major effects.

Bartik (1985) examined these same issues in the US using a conditional logit model. He assumes that the probability of a given state being chosen depends on the levels of variables affecting the firm's profits versus the levels of these same variables in other states. His results indicate that high levels of unionization and high state taxes discourage new manufacturing plants.

Schmenner et al. (1987) also examined the determinants of new manufacturing facilities assuming a two-stage process, using plant-specific characteristics. In the first stage the choice is narrowed to just a few of the 48 possible states, and in the second stage decision one state is chosen for the plant. Furthermore, McConnel and Schwab (1990) look at county and state characteristics and environmental regulations on the choice of locations of 50 new branch plants in the motor vehicle industry for the period 1973–82, using a conditional logit model. These empirical results indicate that agglomeration economies have very strong positive effects, and that state taxes have a strong negative effect, and no evidence that regional environmental policy plays an important role in the location decisions in the motor vehicle industry.

In the first published results focusing on Japanese-affiliated manufacturing investment, Woodward (1992) used US microdata on individual plant location choice for the period 1980–89. Separate conditional logit models were used to estimate probabilities of location at the state and county level. In the state model, independent variables include the market, the unionization rate, the wage rate, unemployment benefits, the climate, the corporate tax rate, the unitary tax, the state effort, Japanese office and land area. The county model shows that manufacturing agglomeration, population density, interstate connection and educational attainment variables are significant determinants.

Most recently David and Rosenbloom (1990); Krugman (1991a, 1991b); Smith and Florida (1994) and Head et al. (1995) have constructed formal theoretical models and obtained that industrial-level agglomeration benefits play an important role in location decisions.

These studies indicate the importance of a number of variables in location choice. We would like to extend these results by looking in more detail at Japanese-specific agglomeration effects (such as supplying parts to an assembler, including a Japanese overseas affiliate) in the location choice of Japanese firms.

We model the location decision of Japanese manufacturing plants as a conditional logit problem where the dependent variable is the region choice for each firm. Our approach builds on existing models of location choice by empirically modelling firm locations as a function of selected region characteristics. This method has been used in such earlier studies as Carlton (1983), Bartik (1985), Schmenner et al. (1987), McConnel and Schwab (1990) and Woodward (1992). We exploit McFadden's (1974) result that logit choice probabilities may be derived from individual maximization decisions if unobserved heterogeneity takes a suitable form. We assume that each multinational firm chooses the region that would yield the highest profit. However, the means to maximize profits may differ among branch plants. One firm may do this by maximizing profits and another by minimizing cost. These strategies will depend on location and the product location relationship. Each MNF will locate its branch plant where profits are expected to be highest in a region.

Suppose that profits, Π_{ij}, of a new branch plant i at location j are a function of a vector of observed characteristics, X_j, of the location and a disturbance term, e_{ij}. In a vector of X_j, we include firm/production specific characteristics which affect revenue and cost.

$$\Pi_{ij} = \beta' X_j + e_{ij} \tag{7.1}$$

McFadden (1974) demonstrated that if, and only if, e_{ij} is distributed as a Type I Extreme Value independent random variable, the probability of Japanese firm i selecting region j can be represented as

$$Pr(ij) = \exp(\beta' X_j) \left(\sum_k \exp(\beta' X_k) \right)^{-1}. \tag{7.2}$$

We use equation (7.2) to test many of the variables discussed above in the conditional logit formulation. The important location factors in the regional location choice model are (1) labour costs (the wage rate), (2) the size of the local market for the product of the plant (preservation and/or expansion of market share), (3) Japanese-specific agglomeration effect, (4) the yen (Yen/US$) appreciation, (5) exports potential to third countries (or re-export to Japan), (6) the availability of electricity and telephones.

4. DATA SOURCES AND MODEL SPECIFICATION

The data employed in this chapter come from a *Toyo Keizai Directory of Japanese Overseas Affiliates* and the survey data collected by Ishii (1992). We revised the data sets (Tokunaga and Ishii 1994).

Our estimation includes investments that began operations after the Plaza Accord in 1985, because the nine Japanese firms (Hitachi, Toshiba, Mitsubishi Electric, Matsushita Electric, Sony, Sanyo Electric, Sharp, NEC and Fujitsu) after the Plaza Accord increased their new production plants more rapidly in overseas countries than in Japan. That is, our estimation data is new plants location data established from 1986 to 1992 (74 observations).

In the location choice for plants we focus on East Asia, including nine alternative countries such as Singapore (choice 1), Hong Kong (choice 2), Taiwan (choice 3), Korea (choice 4), Malaysia (choice 5), Thailand (choice 6), Indonesia (choice 7), Philippines (choice 8) and China (choice 9) in Figure

7.1. The dependent variable in the model is the number of the nine Japanese electronics manufacturing establishments in each country.

Next, the independent variables are considered the following five variables in Table 7.3.

1. *Wage rate and Yen appreciation* In Asia, wage rate (WAGE) is consistently ranked at the top in Table 7.1. This shows that Japanese firms are more labour-intensive. As the wage rate is an important factor for opening plants of labour-intensive industries in East Asia, we assume that the relative real wage rate is an important determinant in the plant location level. This relative real wage (WAGE) is the real monthly wage in US$ in the manufacturing sector in country i ([nominal wage/GDP deflator]/[currency/US$]) divided by real monthly wage in US$ in manufacturing sector in Japan ([nominal wage/GDP deflator]/[Yen/US$]). Furthermore, we jointly adopt this relative exchange rate as a simple measure of the yen appreciation. Thus, we use the relative real wage in US$ as the labour cost and the yen appreciation.

2   *Market size* Market size is considered as an important determinant as shown in Table 7.1 and Table 7.2. Market size (MARKET) measures both demand potentials and economies of scale. As Woodward (1992) and Tu (1990) confirmed that market size is a significant determinant for plant location or FDI, we use the per capita real GDP of each country as the market variable.

3. *Japanese-specific agglomeration* Japanese firms often purchase competitors' electronic components such as ICs, TV tubes, motors and compressors in the same local area. The existence of those plants assures the assembly in an unfamiliar site using good quality Japanese standard components. In other words, if they locate close together in a foreign country, the local agglomeration helps to expand their sales and to save transportation costs and tariffs. Recent theories of economic geography suggest that firms in the same industry may be drawn to the same locations because proximity generates agglomeration effects (Marshall 1920; Head et al. 1995). Especially, Head et al. found that conditional logit estimates support the hypothesis that industry-level agglomeration benefits play an important role in location decisions in the United States. In this chapter we use the number of plants of the Japanese electronics and machine firms (industrial group member activity) in each country as an agglomeration (AGGLO) effect variable.

Table 7.3 Data summary

Variables	Definition	Expected sign	Source and Year
Location choice (CHOICE)	Number of investments in new establishments (nine Japanese electronics firms)		Toyo Keizai Directory of Japanese Overseas Affiliates (1986–92)
Wage rate (WAGE)	Real manufacturing monthly wage rate in country i divided by that of Japan (US$)	–	Statistical Yearbook for Asia and the Pacific, United Nations 1990
Market size (MARKET)	GDP per capita (US$)	+	International Financial Statistics, IMF 1990
Agglomeration (AGGLO)	Number of investment in establishments (Japanese electronics and machine firms)	+	Toyo Keizai Directory of Japanese Overseas Affiliates 1985–92
Export ratio (EXPORT)	Exports divided by GDP (percent)	+	International Financial Statistics, IMF 1990
Infrastructure (INFRA)	Government expenditure for economic development divided by GDP (percent)	+	Government Finance Statistics Yearbook, IMF 1990

4. *Export ratio* The factor of exports to a third country (or reverse exports to Japan) is ranked at the top in Table 7.2. As a lot of Japanese firms built new plants in order to make global and regional production networks, this factor is an important determinant of plants in East Asia. Thus, we utilize the export–GDP ratio (EXPORT) as a simple measure of exports to a third country.[3] We also utilize the export–GDP ratio as a simple measure of the effect of government export policy.[4]
5. *Infrastructure* Infrastructure factors such as the availability of electricity, telephones, water and the accessibility to airports and ports are ranked rather high. The level of infrastructure is measured by government expenditure to economic development against GDP (INFRA).[5]

5. EMPIRICAL RESULTS

The results of the conditional logit estimation are presented in Table 7.4 for the new plant location choice model. Table 7.4 presents the coefficients generated by the maximum likelihood estimation of equation (7.2).[6] Four variations of this model are estimated. Interestingly, the signs and magnitudes of the coefficient estimates were rather consistent across variations in Table 7.4. Thus, we consider the results for column (1) to column (4).

There are, several interesting findings which coincide with the empirical survey on Japanese FDI in Table 7.1 and Table 7.2 as follows.

The coefficient estimates for the manufacturing wages variable (WAGE) are all negative and statistically significant at the 0.05 level. This result confirms that, in terms of traditional location theory, Japanese firms will locate in low-wage regions (in East Asia) in order to minimize costs. One explanation is that Japanese electronics firms are not willing to pay higher wages in exchange for labour in Japan. Another possibility is as follows: if the yen appreciation occurs in Japan, then Japanese FDI inflow occurs in East Asia. The yen appreciation is an important factor in determining FDI. This result suggests that the yen appreciation plays an important role in determining Japanese FDI in East Asia, although in the survey the yen appreciation variable was not ranked particularly high in Table 7.1.

In the survey, product market (market share) was ranked high in determining FDI in East Asia. The coefficient estimates of market size (MARKET) are positive in all cases, statistically significant at the 0.05 level in two of the four cases.[7] This indicates that market size is a determinant for plant location as suggested by Woodward (1992) and Tu (1990).

Table 7.4   Results of the new plant location choice model in East Asia

	Dependent variable: location choice			
Variable	(1)	(2)	(3)	(4)
Wage rate	−0.1697**	−0.1650**	−0.1935**	−0.1739**
(WAGE)	(−4.01)	(−3.21)	(−3.92)	(−3.14)
Market size	0.0002**	0.0001	0.0003**	0.0001
(MARKET)	(2.59)	(0.76)	(2.92)	(0.86)
Agglomer-ation	0.0176**	0.0178**	0.0164**	0.0175**
(AGGLO)	(4.65)	(4.52)	(4.03)	(4.33)
Export ratio		0.0009**		0.0074*
(EXPORT)		(2.96)		(1.60)
Infrastruc-ture			0.0559**	0.0144
(INFRA)			(2.63)	(0.42)
log likelihood	−144.59	−139.92	−141.13	−139.84
no. of choice	666	666	666	666
no. of cases	74	74	74	74

Note: Conditional logit regression estimated by maximum likelihood using PC-TSP (Version 4.3), t-ratios are in parentheses under each coefficient. ** denotes significant at the 0.05 level, * denotes significant at the 0.10 level.

The coefficient estimates for Japanese-specific agglomeration effect variable (AGGLO) are all positive and are statistically significant at the 0.05 level in all of the four cases. This leads us to conclude that these estimates are robust and stable.[8] This finding indicates that the number of plants of the Japanese electronics and machine firms (includes the members of Japanese industrial groups) in the country is an important factor in the location of new Japanese plant in electronics industries. That is, we found that conditional logit estimates support the hypothesis that industry-level agglomeration benefits play an important role in location decisions in East Asia, like Head et al. (1995)

The coefficient estimates for the export–GDP ratio variable (EXPORT) are all positive and statistically significant at the 0.10 level in all cases. This result suggests that, if the government in East Asia considers tax incentives for export, favourable treatment of corporate tax and the existence of a Free Trade Zone in Table 7.1, then export–GDP ratio is higher, therefore, the export–GDP ratio is a very important factor in determining FDI in East Asia. Another possibility is that Japanese firms prefer to high export–GDP ratio country as Japanese firms have the motivation of exports to a third country or Japan in order to make regional production networks. Thus, the export–GDP ratio is a very important factor in determining FDI.

The coefficients for infrastructure variable (INFRA) are all positive and statistically significant at the 0.05 level in one of the two cases. This result suggests that, as infrastructure was regarded as a highly important factor by the survey, infrastructure plays a role for new Japanese plant establishments.[9]

6.   CONCLUSION

This chapter has presented the location behaviour of Japanese firms and the hypotheses of the location determinants from the survey results from Ishii (1992) and the Export–Import Bank of Japan, and the results of empirical estimation of the determinants of location choice using micro data (1986–92) after the Plaza Accord in 1985 on Japanese electronics investors who established new manufacturing plants in an international scale in East Asia. Especially we advanced the hypothesis that the industry-level agglomeration (AGGLO) plays an important role in location decisions. The empirical results strongly confirm this hypothesis. This finding indicates that the number of plants of the Japanese electronics and machine firms (includes the members of Japanese industrial groups) is a significant factor in the location of new Japanese plant in electronics industries. That is, this empirical result confirms the hypothesis that if Japanese firms locate close together in a local area, the local agglomeration helps to expand their sales and to save transportation costs and tariffs.

The most significant factors except agglomeration effect are wage rate (WAGE) and the yen appreciation, market size (MARKET) and the export–GDP ratio (EXPORT). The result regarding the wage rate (WAGE) confirms that in terms of traditional location theory Japanese firms will locate in low-wage regions (in East Asia) in order to minimize costs and that Japanese FDI inflow occurs in East Asia if the yen appreciation occurs in Japan. The empirical result of market size (MARKET) confirms that the Japanese firms prefer the country having both demand potentials and economies of scale. The result of the export–GDP ratio (EXPORT) confirms that Japanese firms prefer a high exports–GDP ratio country in East Asia.

A significant factor is the infrastructure (INFRA). The result of the infrastructure suggests that the infrastructure plays a role for new Japanese plant establishments.

In order to examine these issues in more detail, further studies are required. One of the possible future research directions is a further study of local agglomeration effects (Marshall 1920 and Fujita 1996). Another possible study is a comparative study of the Japanese electronics industry and semiconductor industry with a more skilled labour industry. Furthermore, in this chapter we have dropped the variables of the skilled labour level, education level, and political and economic instability as the location determinants. However, the education level and political and economic instability have an impact on the new plant location. Thus, we need further studies from these points.

ACKNOWLEDGEMENT

The first author is grateful to the Foundation of Reitaku University for financial support. We also acknowledge valuable comments by Masahisa Fujita, Takahiro Akita, William Wallace and anonymous referees.

REFERENCES

Alburo, R., Bautista, C. and M. Gochoco (1992), 'Pacific direct investment flow into ASEAN', *ASEAN Economic Bulletin* **8** (3), pp. 284–308.

Bartik, T.J. (1985), 'Business location decisions in the United States', *Journal of Business and Economic Statistics* **3** (1), pp. 14–22.

Carlton, D.W. (1983), 'The location and employment choices of new firms', *Review of Economics and Statistics* **65**, pp. 440–49.

David, P.A. and J.L. Rosenbloom (1990), 'Marshallian factor market externalities and the dynamics of industrial location', *Journal of Urban Economics* **28**, pp. 349–70.

Fujita, M. (1996), 'On the self-organization and evolution of economic geography', *The Japanese Economic Review* **47** (1), pp. 34–61.

Fujita, M. and J.F. Thisse (1995), 'Economics of agglomeration', paper presented at the Trilateral TCER/NBER/CEPR Conference on Economic Agglomeration, Tokyo.

Head, K., Ries, J. and D. Swenson (1995), 'Agglomeration benefits and location choice', *Journal of International Economics* **38**, pp. 223–47.

Ishii, R. (1992), 'Location behaviour and spatial organization of multinational firms and their impact on regional transformation in East Asia', PhD dissertation, University of Pennsylvania.

Krugman, P.R. (1991a), 'Increasing returns and economic geography', *Journal of Political Economy* **99**, pp. 483–99.

Krugman, P.R. (1991b), *Geography and Trade*, MA: The MIT Press.

Krugman, P.R. (1995), *Development, Geography, and Economic Theory*, Cambridge, MA: The MIT Press.

Marshall, A. (1920), *Principles of Economics* (Eighth Edition), Porcupine Press.

McConnel, V.D. and R.M. Schwab (1990), 'The impact of environmental regulation on industry location decision: the motor vehicle industry', *Land Economics* **66**, pp. 67–81.

McFadden, D. (1974), 'Conditional logit analysis of qualitative choice behaviour', in Zarembka, P. (ed.), *Frontiers in Econometrics*, New York: Academic Press, pp. 105–42.

Schmenner, R.W., Huber, J.C. and R.L. Cook (1987), 'Geographic differences and the location of new manufacturing facilities', *Journal of Urban Economics* **21**, pp. 83–104.

Smith, D.F. and R. Florida (1994), 'Agglomeration and industrial location', *Journal of Urban Economics* **36**, pp. 23–41.

Tejima, S. (1994), 'Prospects for Japanese foreign direct investment in the 1990s', in Ohno, K. and Y. Okamoto (eds), *Regional Integration and Foreign Direct Investment*, Tokyo: Institute of Developing Economics, pp. 49–83.

Tejima, S., Yazaka, T. and Y. Iwai (1994), 'The Outlook of Japanese Foreign Direct Investment Based on The EXIM JAPAN FY 1993 Survey', (in Japanese), *Journal of the Research Institute for International Investment and Development* **20** (1), pp. 4–73.

Tokunaga, S. and R. Ishii (1994), 'Empirical analysis of location choice of Japanese multinational firms', in Ohno, K. and Y. Okamoto (eds), *Regional Integration and Foreign Direct Investment*, Tokyo: Institute of Developing Economics, pp. 97–117.

Tokunaga, S. and R. Ishii (1995). 'Agglomeration and industrial location: empirical analysis of location choice of Japanese multinational firms in East Asia', paper presented at the annual meeting of the Japan Association of Economics and Econometrics.

Toyo-Keizai-shinpousya, annual, *Toyo Keizai Directory of Japanese Overseas Affiliates* (in Japanese), Tokyo.

Tsai, P.L. (1991), 'Determinants of foreign direct investment in Taiwan', *World Development* **19** (2–3), pp. 275–85.

Tu, J.H. (1990), *Direct Foreign Investment and Economic Growth* **48**, Institute of Economics, Academia Sinica.

Urata, S. (1996), 'Determinants of foreign direct investment in Japan and the effects of FDI towards LDCs', in Sekiguchi, T. and EXIM Bank (eds), *Foreign Direct Investment in Japan and Japanese Economy* (in Japanese), Tokyo: Toyo-keizai-shinpou-sya, pp. 61–79.

Woodward, D.P. (1992), 'Locational determinants of Japanese manufacturing startups in the United States', *Southern Economic Journal*, pp. 690–708.

NOTES

1. In the survey by Ishii (1991) the total number of plants mailed was 494 (Japan, 335; East Asia, 112; and US, 47). In the case of the 1993 survey of the Export–Import Bank of Japan, there were answers from 338 respondents which cover, approximately, more than 60 percent of total Japanese FDI in manufacturing sectors (see Tejima 1994, p. 50).

2. Although political stability is an important factor in the results from Ishii (1992), there were no big political instabilities for this period (1986–92) in East Asia. Thus, we drop this factor. We do not utilize the availability of skilled labour because there are no data on this variable for all the countries.

3. This point is mentioned by Prof. H. Yokoyama (Annual Conference of Japan Association of Economics and Econometrics at Gakusyuin in 1995). Prof. Urata also pointed out this factor (see Urata 1996).

4. We do not utilize the favourable actions of government because there are no data for all the countries. However, we have used the export–GDP ratio as an alternative.

5. We may employ the level of government education expenditure as a simple measure of the effect of government education policy instead of that of skilled labour. We tentatively tried to estimate the variable of adult literacy rate instead of that of skilled labour because there are no data on skilled labour for all the countries, but this was not statistically significant at the 0.05 level.

6. The estimation was done by PC–TSP version 4.3.

7. We also used the population size and GDP of each country as the market size, but the coefficient estimates are not statistically significant at the 0.05 level.

8. We used the number of plants of the nine Japanese electronics firms as an agglomeration effects variable, and obtained the welcome results that the coefficient estimates for agglomeration effect variable are all positive and are statistically significant at the 0.05 level in all of the ten cases in Tokunaga and Ishii (1995).

9. We used the number of the telephone mainlines as the level of infrastructure, but the coefficient estimates are not statistically significant at the 0.05 level.

PART THREE

Spatial Interaction and Competition

8. Regional Cosmopolitanization and the Rise of World Trade Regions

Jessie P.H. Poon

1. INTRODUCTION

Recent research on international trade has highlighted the role of location and geography in influencing trade interactions (Krugman 1991a; Krugman and Venables 1995; Frankel et al. 1995). This is perhaps most apparent in trade analysis associated with regionalization. With pan-European and pan-American integration visibly in progress, trade activities have become increasingly spread over multiple geographical regions. At the same time, a simultaneous trend of internationalization is also conspicuous as transnational commercial and capital networks increasingly drive the comparative advantage of global competitors. The two seemingly contradictory trends, one centripetal and the other centrifugal, have raised the suggestion that while regionalization appears to be on the rise, its prevailing form is different from that of the past.

The juxtaposition of regionalization and internationalization is being observed at a time when traditional explanations of international trade patterns are facing academic criticisms for their assumptions of a-spatiality, perfect competition and constant returns to scale. Newer trade theories argue that large-scale regional arrangements reflect two dominant forces: increasing returns to scale in production, and the costs of trade (for example, transportation costs). The operation of the two parameters has resulted in regionalization being viewed as a 'natural' process with supranational regions forming the spatial medium within which economic activities best thrive. This is especially true for global competitors whose continued growth depends on their ability to coordinate rationalized production and market networks across countries. However, the presence of international networks configured at the level of the region also implies that the economic health of a country is increasingly tied to its nodal position in the international production and distribution hierarchy, raising the need for conceptualization of the patterns of trade interactions on a global scale. Such a development is in line with recent concerns about the relevant scale in regional economic analysis (Bailly and Coffey 1994) that would reflect more accurately the spatial juncture of national and transnational activities.

While regionalization appears to be underway, there is a growing debate about the merits of such a trend. Traditional criticisms of regionalization arise from fears of countries retreating into isolated inward-oriented development. Such criticisms are being challenged as new instruments in trade analysis suggest higher growth potential for countries than had previously been envisaged. In addition, prevailing regionalization is occurring in an environment of stronger global interdependencies and thereby extraregional linkages, indicating that bloc traits may not be an automatic outcome. Instead, regions have become more extra-territorial with the result that the rise of world trade regions is also being accompanied by regional cosmopolitanization. In view of all this, the chapter has two major objectives: first, it ascertains the extent to which regionalization in world trade was occurring between 1965 and 1990, as well as its geography. Second, it examines the extraregional trends of trade regions in order to assess their extraterritorial orientation. In the next section, a summary of the literature on regionalization is provided. This is undertaken with a view to relating the logic of regionalization to economic efficiencies arising from scale economies as well as the microeconomic strategies of international corporations.

2.   THE NEW REGIONALIZATION

Regionalism, that is the governmental promotion of linkages between countries by the removal of barriers to mutual trade in the form of free trade areas, customs union and other preferential trading agreements, denotes a process of regional institution-building with the aim of greater economic or political integration. However, some scholars have argued that prevailing regionalization is occurring on the basis of market and industrial integration, without an explicit aim towards economic or political integration (Lorenz 1991, Oman 1994). The term 'regionalization', as opposed to regionalism, will thus be used here to cover *de jure* or *de facto* regional groupings, as well as the regional coalescence of countries driven by market forces such as significant transnational trade flows, even in the absence of *de jure* or *de facto* regional institutions.

In traditional neoclassical trade theory, regional coalitions are deemed to be a 'second-best' strategy when compared to global multilateral free trade that is premised upon comparative advantage. Viner's (1950) seminal paper on trade diversion and trade creation suggests that when trade diversion is greater than trade creation with regional integration, then overall global welfare decreases. Page (1991) has reported, for example,that with the formation of EC-12, the newly-industrializing countries (NICs) and middle income countries would lose considerably in terms of their manufactured exports to European firms. Davenport (1990) arrived at similar conclusions, reporting that any trade creation for developing countries with the EEC would be cancelled out by trade diversion. Apart from concerns on significant trade diversion, a free trading system is generally preferred because it is built on principles of cooperation between member countries. A cooperative trade regime presumes that there is no advantage in unilateral liberalization but there are advantages in multilateralism as long as all members 'play the game' (Hallett 1994).

In addition to potential costs and efficiency losses, supporters of free trade have raised the problem of uneven income distribution effects and economic bargaining power between weaker and stronger states (Bhagwati 1991; Malcolm 1995), and, the possible impediment of globalization (Palmer, 1991). More recently, even a moral case for free trade has been advanced. McGee (1995) argues that regional formation favours the rights of producers over the rights of consumers, concluding that free trade results in more winners than losers overall.

While support for free trade has remained strong among mainstream scholars (for example, Bhagwati 1991; Sapir 1993), a shift in thinking appears to be underway, with more and more academics writing on the merits of regionalization. A number of events recently may have prompted the reassessment of the impacts of regionalization on global welfare. First, there is the perception that regionalization is 'here to stay' (Bhagwati 1993) as the strongest supporter of postwar free trade, namely the United States, embraces regional initiatives such as NAFTA and a possible Western Hemispheric free trade area (FTA). Second, the emergence of new industrial epicentres such as Japan and the Asian NICs, has led to a more multicentric world economy. Third, the proclivity towards region-building with Europe 1992 and NAFTA has rejuvenated regionalist sentiments. Malaysia, for example, has attempted to counter region formation elsewhere in the world with its own Asian bloc, namely the East Asian Economic Caucus. Fourth, new formal instruments in analyzing regionalization impacts have challenged previous negative assessments of regionalization. This last point is particularly important and will be elaborated below.

3. THE NEW TRADE THEORY

Standard trade analyses based on the principle of comparative advantage have come under increasing attack since the 1980s for their assumptions of perfect competition and constant returns to scale. In a world where global trade is conducted more and more in the form of intra rather than inter-industry trade, and where multinational corporations (MNCs) have an important influence on the patterns of economic activities, the comparative advantage of countries is argued to be less relevant than the role of scale economies and imperfect competition.

Under the new trade theory, markets are shown to be imperfectly competitive to exhibit significant economies of scale in production. By providing proximity to several markets, regionalization permits access to multiple markets while decreasing the average costs in production as well as the market power of individual firms (Hallett and Braga 1994). For developing countries embarking on export-promoting development trajectories, this enhances growth in output which is not constrained by small domestic market size (Agosin and Tussie 1992). The gains from trade under such a situation are considerable because of increased competition due to the rationalization of the production process in order to take advantage of opportunities for specialization (Francois 1994). Building on the new growth theory which stresses endogenous growth, scholars reject traditional constant cost returns trade assessments of trade liberalization associated with regionalization (for example, Romer 1990; Kehoe 1994). By changing the global base over which external economies are generated and highlighting human capital accumulation and learning effects, it is maintained instead that regionalization induces positive growth effects (Francois 1994). The association between regionalization and growth is related to the nature of growth itself. An increase in economic output is due to the accumulation of factors of production. Regionalization affects growth by influencing the accumulation of factors (Baldwin 1994).

Clearly then, the literature now emphasizes dynamic gains as opposed to static gains from trade. In this respect, impressive economic gains with regional integration have been reported. Baldwin (1989; 1992) for example has estimated that the EC completion would likely raise the region's GDP growth rate by some 0.6 percent per year, with scale effects playing a prominent role. Similarly, Hufbauer and Schott (1994) estimate that regional formation with a western hemispheric FTA will likely result in some trade diversion, but the gains from trade associated with trade liberalization would more than offset this. They also show that Latin America's GDP would be 18 percent higher by the year 2002 with economic integration than without (p. 174). Their conclusion is supported by Anderson and Snape (1994) who expect the degree of trade diversion from NAFTA to be low. Finally, Nagaoka (1994) demonstrates that regional integration promotes global liberalization except when it is not accompanied by political integration.

The strengthening of comparative advantage through the effective use of productive factors with scale and induced investments are not the only arguments for the currently more positive thinking on regionalization. Political economy-related arguments have also pointed out that regionalization widens the market scope of countries which potentially weakens rent-seekers and special interest groups whose structural inertia has slowed down or even impeded an economy's capacity to reallocate resources in response to changing conditions (Oman 1994). By enlarging national economic and political networks to the supranational level, this encourages more cooperative behaviour amongst members because of the need to maintain several different targets and objectives simultaneously (Hallett and Braga 1994).

Regionalization is thus increasingly viewed as a building block for multilateral trade liberalization – that is, a sort of mini GATT coalescence of regions (Lawrence 1994). Additionally, greater attention is being paid to the impacts of overlapping linkages and interdependencies established from the forces of globalization. Globalization, thought to be driven by microeconomic behaviour related to firms' strategies to construct regional and international comparative advantage, now implies that economic inwardness that is associated with past patterns of region formation is less likely to occur. In particular, there is the perception that extraregional linkages are an important component of prevailing regionalization so that the world economic map is less likely to be composed of distended trading blocs (Palmer 1991). In this respect, the role of MNCs deserves some mention.

4. INTERNATIONAL PRODUCTION AND REGIONAL NETWORKS

The new trade theory's emphasis on scale economies and imperfect competition is precipitated by the observation that an increasing proportion of international trade is conducted by MNCs in the form of intra-firm and intra-industry trade. The transaction cost literature argues that the internationalization of production by MNCs is associated with hierarchy, vertical integration and the internalization of markets (Williamson 1975; Casson 1986; Hennart 1991). Such a process means that comparative advantage is dynamic and can be created as countries become absorbed as specialized locations for different segments of an industry. As Agosin and Tussie (1992) have observed, multinationalization has increased locational competition between countries as different countries become close locational substitutes. Hence, the economic health of a country is increasingly tied to its capacity to function as a node in the global–regional production system. Within the global reaches of MNCs, regions operate as a spatial medium within which the scale and dispersion of activities may be managed.

Japanese MNCs, for example, are reported to be pursuing globalization strategies through major regional networks. This is most conspicuous in the Asia-Pacific (Dobson 1993) where dense distribution and supplies networks are being constructed in order to refine the region's division of labour as well as to take advantage of the countries' varying levels of industrial development. An example may be given in the Mitsubishi Group, which sources automobile parts by means of a network of affiliates that spans East and Southeast Asia as well as North America (Phongpaichit 1990). Network theory suggests that networks increase interlinkages and flexibility (Hakansson 1987). When extrapolated to investment or production networks such as those being established in the Asia-Pacific by Japanese firms, increased linkages reduce transaction costs which facilitate regional integration.

The increase in scale in the activities of corporations, however, leads to a need for spatial coordination between geographically dispersed activities. In this respect, some scholars have related the conjunction of globalization and regionalization to the integration of production and markets by MNCs and related firms. Cantwell (1994) argues that while multinationalization permits the exploitation of scale through the local concentration of particular segments of the industry, it also requires considerable integration and rationalization. Thus, international production is being simultaneously accompanied by the regional integration of commercial affiliates that had previously served their own markets.

The integration of production networks by corporations on a worldwide basis suggests that economic activities are increasingly coalescing around a few major regions. This reflects the 'strategic positioning' of MNCs over multiple regions geographically. Supraregional content is increasingly fashioned by the intersections of international competition relationships. Hence the region has become the most efficient spatial unit to host concentrated, scale-efficient corporations thereby allowing firms to gain access to several markets at the same time.

However, there is also the problem of size with multinationalization. While global free trade is potentially attainable with one world region as Krugman (1991b) has shown, the reality of getting there is fraught with problems. This is because there are also diseconomies of scale associated with an increase in size (Hallett and Braga 1994). Given this, we would expect the world economic map to be dotted with a few trading regions in response to tradeoffs between scale advantages and size disadvantages. The literature speculates on a tripolar structure even though Krugman has shown this number to be suboptimal. Still, the hub and spoke model of integration (Hufbauer and Schott 1994) suggests that global trade will likely pivot around a few regional cores which form the magnets around which trade linkages intersect.

Overall, the discussion here indicates growing receptiveness among academics to a world economy operating on the basis of multiple centres. More recently, a new twist has been given to the argument for regionalization. Trade regions are also said to be 'natural' regions because economic neighbours tend to trade more with one another (Krugman 1993; Frankel et al. 1995). Hence, trade regions merely reflect the influence of geographical realities such as agglomeration advantages, cultural and historical affinities. This has been supported to some degree by Hufbauer and Schott (1994) who concluded that countries in Western Europe are the most natural neighbours from the vantage view of trade interactions.

The simultaneous trend of globalization and regionalization all point to a regionalization trend that is different from the past. Stronger global linkages indicate that prevailing regionalization is more market-driven with firms investing and integrating their production regionally in order to service both regional and global markets (UNCTC 1991; Lawrence 1994). The sources of comparative advantage are not only tied to locational attributes, but also to national policies and firm strategies.[1] However, since globalization involves interactions between the region and other spaces of production, it is apparent that regions are themselves becoming more cosmopolitan with strong trans- and extra-regional tendencies (Anderson and Norheim 1993). Hence 'open' regionalization, that is, when intraregionalization is not accompanied by a significant decline in extraregionalization, has been advanced as a mechanism to complement multilateralism.

5. THE INTRAMAX METHOD

The discussion in the previous section suggests that global trade is increasingly occurring between and within a few mega world regions. The idea of trade hubs is best explored in the context of functional regions. Functional regions are derived by analysing the interactions between countries or areas. Interconnectivities and linkages between spatial units are emphasized so that while such regions may be characterized by considerable internal diversity, the region is also at the same time homogenous because its spatial structure is unified in internal circulation. When applied to trade interactions, functional trade regions may be interpreted to be the realization of the absorption of space into a system of commodity production.

To examine the spatial structure of world trade regions, interrelated groups of countries with maximum trade interactions have been identified using a hierarchical clustering procedure. A number of aggregation techniques have been reviewed by Masser and Scheurwater (1980) as well as Fischer et al. (1993). They suggest that the intramax approach is most suitable when flow matrices are relatively sparse. This is the case here with a number of developing countries trading minimally with other countries in the world. In the intramax approach, an objective function is defined such that:

$$\text{Max } (I_{ij} - I_{ij'}) + (I_{ji} - I_{ji'}) \quad i, j = 1, ..., n$$

where,

I_{ij} = the observed value of (i, j) in the trade interaction matrix, and

$I_{ij'}$ = $(\Sigma_j I_{ij} \Sigma_i I_{ij}) / \Sigma_{ij} I_{ij}$ $i, j = 1, ..., n$

By applying the above objective function, a transformed matrix is derived which measures the largest total interactions between pairs of countries in excess of the total of the expected values derived from row and column totals. The transformed matrix is then used to cluster trade flows using the following grouping procedure. Pairs of countries with high levels of interactions are joined together, building up from small to large clusters. This is done by of an iterative process whereby at each stage, the objective function is applied to the matrix which is reduced as pairs of spatial units or countries become fused together. Such a process of transformation and comparison is repeated at subsequent stages in order to take into account the effects of previous fusions, the total number of iterations being (n–1).

With each step, two countries are joined together such that the interaction between the two countries becomes internal or intrazonal. With n–1 steps, all countries are grouped together into one region and all interaction is intrazonal. This procedure maximizes the proportion of the within-group interaction at each step of fusion, taking into account the variations in the row and column totals of the matrix (Masser and Brown 1975).

The intramax analysis is conducted for 120 countries and for the years 1965 and 1990. The data consist of export and import figures in US dollars between the countries from various issues of International Monetary Fund's *Direction of Trade Statistics*.

6. WORLD TRADE REGIONS

The intramax procedure yielded tree diagrams which capture clusters of countries that have been grouped together based on the strength of interactions calculated from the intramax algorithm. Recall that the intramax procedure involves an iterative process such that when two countries are joined together with each step or iteration, the interaction between the two countries becomes internal or intrazonal interaction for the new resulting area.

To identify well-defined clusters, breakpoints in the tree were examined. These are characterized by large increments in intrazonal interaction associated with a particular iterative step. Based on the largest breakpoints, eight regions may be identified for 1965, and five for 1990.[2] Following from previous reasoning of trade cores, the regions are named according to their core dominance based on the countries' trade to regional GDP ratios. The eight regional cores in 1965 are Brazil, Germany, Italy, Spain, Sweden, United Kingdom (UK), United States (US) and the former USSR. The five cores in 1990 are Germany, Japan, UK, US and the former USSR.

The regions are mapped in Figures 8.1 and 8.2.[3] The two figures clearly show that 1990 is marked by a fewer number of regions but each region has a larger membership. In other words the trade interactions in 1990 are far more regionalized than in 1965. In 1965, the regions in Sweden, Brazil and Spain have five to seven members each. Those of Italy, Spain and the UK consist of a coalescence of countries which are rather geographically dispersed. That is to say, the 1965 world trade map is more geographically fragmented. Trade regions tend to be smaller and generally, appear less naturally oriented to one another. Most of them reflect historical divisions of labour such as the colonial relationship between the UK and its ex colonies, or political affinities in the case of the former USSR/Eastern Europe and even South Asia.

On the other hand 1990 displays stronger spatial logic. With the exception of the UK region, the remaining four regions exhibit much more geographical coherence and contiguity. A western hemispheric trade region is discernible, as is an Asia–Pacific region. Similarly, the German region stretches over most of Europe as well as its neighbours in Africa. The pattern of regional membership in 1990 supports strongly the notion of natural trade regions. Increased regionalization is the most conspicuous for the three regions based on the US, Germany and Japan. The US and German regions comprised 25 and 20 members in 1965 respectively. This rose to 36 and 28 respectively in 1990. Similarly, the Japanese region was shared between the UK, US and USSR regions in 1965. By 1990, Asia–Pacific countries have become tied together functionally with Japan emerging as the region's major hub. It is interesting to note that the influence of this region extends beyond Asia into Africa as well.

At the same time that the three regions centred on Japan, Germany and the US expanded, 1990 also saw the evaporation of three of the 1965 regions, namely Brazil, Italy and Sweden. The Sweden region ceded most of its members to the UK region, the Italy region to the Japan and Germany regions, and the Spain region to the Germany and US regions. The UK region is especially interesting in that while its size remained relatively stable over the 25-year period, it is characterized by considerable change in regional membership: Australia and New Zealand for example have become more integrated into Asia, while many of its ex-African colonies have come under the trade sphere of Germany. On the other hand, the region gained several members from Scandinavia probably because of the consolidation of EFTA among the Nordic countries.

Clearly the regional configuration of 1990 can be explained in part by the number of regional pacts formed over the last four decades such as EEC, EFTA, LAIA, and so on But it is also true that many of the linkages reflect market-driven forces. For example, the countries of the Japan-oriented region are thought traditionally to possess little historical regional consciousness (Drysdale 1988). Japan, South Korea and Taiwan are not members of any preferential trade agreements. The region's emergence is attributed to the export-oriented platform which underscores the trade policies of many Asian countries here, as well as the rapid diffusion of modernization and industrialization throughout the region. The region alone accounts for a quarter of total world exports in 1990.

It is also interesting that while a tripolar pattern is apparent in 1990 with the three regions of US, Japan and Germany accounting for over 80 percent of total membership, the existence of the USSR and the UK regions suggests a more multicentric structure than is currently recognized. Overall, the geography of trade patterns and interactions indicate strongly the emergence of natural trade regions over the 25-year period examined, or, at least the tendency of world trade to gravitate around a few regions. Within each trade region, a country core dominates acting as the region's major market or industrial magnet (see also Poon and Pandit 1996).

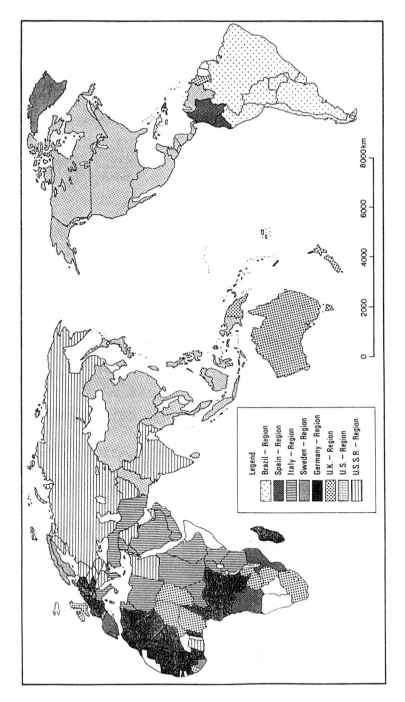

Figure 8.1 Major trade regions of the world in 1965

Legend

Brazil – Region
Spain – Region
Italy – Region
Sweden – Region
Germany – Region
U.K. – Region
U.S. – Region
U.S.S.R. – Region

8000km   6000   4000   2000   0

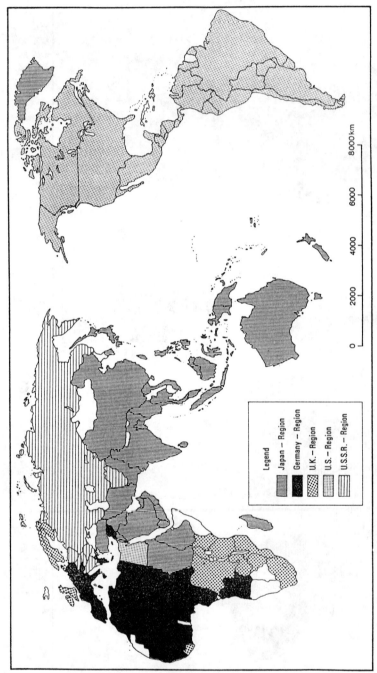

Note: The regions are named according to their regional cores (see text). Part of the data for the figures is replicated from Poon (1997).

Figure 8.2 Major trade regions of the world in 1990

7. EXTRAREGIONAL TRENDS

While the above intramax results indicate that regionalization has grown stronger in that international trade is increasingly concentrated in five major geographical regions, the literature reviewed earlier also suggests that globalization impacts may mitigate against the possibility of trade occurring in isolated distended blocs. Extraregional linkages imply that trade regions are becoming more interconnected, diluting the effects of closed, inward-looking blocs.

To ascertain extraregional patterns, the trade intensity index (I_{ij}) is used to examine the five regions' proclivity to trade with non-regional members, namely the rest of the world. The trade intensity index between a region (i) and the rest of the world (j) may be defined as:

$$I_{ij} = X_{ij} / \Sigma X_i \div [G_j/G_w / M_w G_w]$$

X_{ij} = exports of i to j,
M_j, M_w = imports of j, world, and
G_i, G_j, G_w = GDP of i, j, world.

Trade between two regions is influenced by factors such as tariff levels, factor endowments and distances. The significance of I_{ij} is that it represents a basis for measuring trade intensity by the omissions of these factors (Kunimoto 1977; Sautter 1974). I_{ij} is appropriate for comparing trade resistances but not the effects or causes of the resistance between the regions. If I_{ij} is greater than 1, then trade intensity between the two regions, i and j, is said to be above average. The opposite is true when I_{ij} is less than unity.

However, Anderson and Norheim (1993) have argued that Iij ignores the possibility that a region may be trading more or less with other regions because it has increased or decreased the share of its GDP that is traded extraregionally. So a propensity to trade index (P_{ij}) has been defined which takes into consideration both the effects of geographical bias as well as overall openness to trade. One important difference between the two indices is that unlike I_{ij}, P_{ij} is more useful for comparisons across time rather than across regions and will therefore be used here. Since P_{ij} highlights the share of GDP that is traded, ΣX_i in the above I_{ij} index is replaced by G_i.

Both the trading propensities I_{ij} and P_{ij} were calculated for the five world trade regions from 1965 to 1990. The results are presented on Table 8.1.

Table 8.1   Intensity and propensity to trade extraregionally by world regions

	Japan	US	Germany	UK	USSR
(A) Intensity to trade (I_{ij})					
1965	0.624	0.635	0.532	0.723	0.788
1970	0.692	0.682	0.560	0.759	0.402
1975	0.645	0.649	0.608	0.728	0.443
1980	0.673	0.660	0.587	0.843	0.418
1985	0.632	0.617	0.576	0.792	0.486
1990	0.656	0.611	0.541	0.784	0.430
(B) Propensity to trade (P_{ij})					
1965	0.058	0.035	0.076	0.113	0.012
1970	0.072	0.042	0.100	0.136	0.015
1975	0.108	0.055	0.129	0.155	0.026
1980	0.143	0.067	0.137	0.194	0.044
1985	0.112	0.050	0.149	0.205	0.053
1990	0.115	0.057	0.128	0.176	0.061

The I_{ij}s exhibit considerable fluctuations over the 25-year period. Except for the USSR and US-centred regions, the other three regions reveal higher I_{ij} values in 1990 than 1965: from 0.624 to 0.656, 0.532 to 0.541 and 0.723 to 0.784 for the Japan, Germany and UK regions respectively. Moreover, on a more disaggregated 5-yearly level, all three regions show generally increasing trends until 1980 before declining slightly. In the case of the USSR region, the lower I_{ij} value in 1990 is explained partly by a steep decline from 1965 to 1970. But this was subsequently followed by an upward trend from 0.402 in 1970 to 0.482 in 1990. As for the US region, I_{ij} rises to 0.660 in 1980 before falling.

The above suggests that for the majority of the trade regions, the intensity to trade extraregionally has not declined significantly although it should be noted that all of the I_{ij}s are below 1.0. The extraregional trends of the three regions of Japan, Germany and the UK are also interesting from the following vantage view: regionalization in the UK and Germany has derived much of its impetus from deeper institutional and policy integration within the European parts of the regions, yet the I_{ijs} here show no significant declines. In other words, these two regions fare no worse than the Asia–Pacific countries in the Japan-based region in terms of their trade intensities with the rest of the world. This is despite the fact that the Asia–Pacific has often been perceived to be far more open and outward-oriented than other regions such as those of 'fortress' Europe (Hallett and Braga 1994; Kirkpatrick 1994; Langhammer 1996).

The P_{ijs} display even stronger levels of extraregionalization in 1990 over 1965: from 0.058 to 0.115 (Japan region), 0.035 to 0.057 (US region), 0.076 to 0.128 (Germany region), 0.113 to 0.176 (UK region), and 0.012 to 0.061 (USSR region). That is to say, the shares of the five regions' GDP traded outside of the regions have risen over the 25 years examined. In fact, the indices have risen by as much as a ratio of 5 in the case of the USSR region. The P_{ijs} exhibit strongest upward trends between 1965 to 1985 for the three regions of Germany, UK and USSR, and between 1965 to 1980 for the remaining regions of Japan and the US. Except for the USSR region, all of the other four regions experienced a slight dip in the 1980s, although the P_{ijs} picked up again in 1990 for the Japan and US regions.

The reasons for the dips in the 1980s are not clear. The data suggest that exports contracted or grew only negligibly during this period. For instance, the total exports of the Japan region doubled between 1975 to 1980, but fell by 3 percent between 1980 to 1985. Moreover, the decline was generally greater for intraregional than for extra-regional markets. This could be due to recession and the rise of protectionism through the erection of non-tariff barriers (Tsoukalis 1993) in the early 1980s, which prompted countries to maintain interests in extraregional trade links. Thus, extraregionalization over the same period only registered small declines, or stabilized. Another plausible explanation is that foreign direct investments, which rose markedly during the 1980s, may have led to some trade-replacing activities. The steep declines in trade regionalization especially in the UK and Germany regions after 1985 would suggest this, due to the financial liberalization which followed the Single European Act.

Overall, the P_{ijs} indicate even stronger extraregional trends, exhibiting less variations at the disaggregated level. Thus, in spite of a trend towards increased regionalization, regions have continued to trade a larger share of their GDPs extra-territorially.

8. CONCLUSION

The increase in regionalization of world trade between 1965 to 1990 suggests that economic activities shape and are themselves shaped by the global space economy. On the one hand, new competitive relationships demand that global competitors increasingly draw their comparative advantage from international networks. On the other hand, problems of time–space coordination suggest that regions will continue to remain the dominant medium for efficient economic transactions. This chapter has attempted to analyse the spatial structure of regions by examining the organization of global trade flows.

Over the 25-year period, examined from 1965 to 1990, global trade interactions moved from a geographically fragmented pattern to a more geographically coherent pattern. In 1965, eight trade regions were identified. This gave way to five bigger regions in 1990 centred on the hubs of Japan, Germany, UK, former USSR and US. The greater spatial circumscription of trade flows in 1990 reflects the emergence of natural trade regions observed by Krugman and others.

While the content of some regions is clearly defined by postwar regional pacts and initiatives, many countries appear also to be concatenated on the basis of market integration. This is in line with the new regionalization and recent observations of the increased industrial networking between countries rather than institutional relationships. Not surprising, regional integration has been linked to growth because such spatial arrangements are thought to affect the accumulation of the factors of production positively.

Despite the generally more optimistic tone expressed by the literature on the growth contributions of regionalization, there remains the nagging fear that economic activities within trade regions will assume high levels of bloc traits thereby inhibiting the global multilateral liberalization of countries. Such a thesis was examined by exploring the extraregional proclivities of the trade regions. If countries were trading more and more intraregionally at the expense of the rest of the world, then extraregionalization trends should indicate consistent downward trends over the 1965–90 period. While such a decline was discernable, it occurred only briefly in the 1980s. Overall, the propensities to trade were generally positive and upwards, or at worst stable. Extraregionalization was surprisingly strong for the European regions despite the fact that many of the countries here conduct nearly two-thirds of their trade with one another.

The analysis here suggests that while global trade flows are becoming more directed spatially to a few trade regions, economic interlinkages from globalization forces may offset some of the centripetal forces. Trade regions are thus likely to become more cosmopolitan if the prevailing trend of economic globalism persists.

REFERENCES

Agosin, M.R. and D. Tussie (1992), 'Globalization, regionalization and dilemmas in trade policy for development', *World Competition* **15**, pp. 36–64.

Anderson, K. and H. Norheim (1993), 'From imperial to regional trade preferences: its effect on Europe's intra- and extra-regional trade', *Weltwirtschaftliches Archiv* **129**, pp. 78–102.

Anderson, K. and R. Snape (1994), 'European and American regionalism: effects on and options for Asia', *Journal of the Japanese and Developing Economies* **8**, pp. 454–77.

Bailly, A.S. and W.J. Coffey (1994), 'Regional science in crisis: a plea for a more open and relevant approach', *Papers in Regional Science* **73**, pp. 3–14.

Baldwin, R.E. (1989), 'On the growth effects of 1992', *Economic Policy* **9**, pp. 247–81.

Baldwin, R.E. (1992), 'Measurable dynamic gains from trade', *Journal of Political Economy* **100**, pp. 162–74.

Baldwin, R.E. (1994), *Towards an Integrated Europe*, Washington DC: Center for Economic Policy Research.

Bhagwati, J. (1991), *The World Trading System at Risk*, New York: Harvester Wheatsheaf.

Bhagwati, J. (1993), 'Regionalism and multilateralism: an overview', in De Melo, J. and A. Panagariya (eds), *New Dimensions in Regional Integration*, New York: Cambridge University Press.

Cantwell, J. (1994), 'The relationship between international trade and international production', in Greenaway, D. and A.L. Winters (eds), *Surveys in International Trade*, Oxford: Blackwell.

Casson, M. (1986), *Multinationals and World Trade: Vertical Integration and the Division of Labour in World Industries*, London: Allen and Unwin.

Davenport, M. (1990), 'The external policy of the Community and its effects on manufactured exports of the developing countries', *Journal of Common Market Studies* **29**, pp. 191–200.

Dobson, W. (1993), *Japan in East Asia: Trading and Investment Strategies*, Singapore: Institute of Southeast Asian Studies.

Drysdale, P. (1988), *International Economic Pluralism: Economic Policy in East Asia and the Pacific*, Winchester, Mass.:Allen and Unwin.

Fischer, M., Essletzbichler, J., Gassler, H. and G. Tricht (1993), 'Telephone communication patterns in Austria: A comparison of the IPFP-based graph-theoretic and the intramax approaches', *Geographical Analysis* **25**, pp. 224–33.

Francois, J.F. (1994), 'Global production and trade: factor migration and commercial policy with international scale economies', *International Economic Review* **35**, pp. 565–81.

Frankel, J., Stein, E. and S.J. Wei (1995), 'Trading blocs and the Americas: the natural, the unnatural, and the super-natural', *Journal of Development Economics* **47**, pp. 61–95.

Hakansson, H. (ed.) (1987), *Industrial Technological Development: Network Approach*, London: Croom Helm.

Hallett, A.J.H. (1994), 'The impact of EC-92 on trade in developing countries', *World Bank Research Observer* **9**, pp. 121–46.

Hallett, A.H. and C.A.P. Braga (1994), 'The new regionalism and the threat of protectionism', *Journal of the Japanese and International Economies* **8**, pp. 388–421.

Hennart, J.F. (1991), 'The transaction cost theory of the multinational enterprise' in Pitelis, C.N. and R. Sugden (eds), *The Nature of the Transnational Firm*, London: Routledge.

Hufbauer, G.C. and J.J. Schott (1994), *Western Hemisphere Economic Integration*, Washington, DC: Institute for International Economics.

Kehoe, T.J. (1994), 'Modeling the dynamic impact of North American free trade', in Francois, J. and C. Shields (eds), *Modelling Trade Policy: Applied General Equilibrium Analysis of a North American Free Trade Area*, Cambridge: Cambridge University Press.

Kirkpatrick, J. (1994), 'Regionalization, regionalism and East Asian economic cooperation', *World Economy* **17**, pp. 191–202.

Krugman, P. (1991a), *Geography and Trade*, Cambridge: MIT Press.

Krugman, P. (1991b), 'Is bilateralism bad?', in Helpman, E. and A. Razin (eds), *International Trade and Trade Policy*, Cambridge: MIT Press.

Krugman, P. (1993), 'Regionalism versus multilateralism: analytical notes', in De Melo, J. and A. Panagariya (eds), *New Dimensions in Regional Integration*, New York: Cambridge University Press:.

Krugman, P. (1994), 'Competitiveness: a dangerous obsession', *Foreign Affairs* **73**, pp. 28–44.

Krugman, P. and A.J. Venables (1995), 'Seamless World: A Spatial Model of International Specialization', National Bureau of Economic Research Working Paper No. 5220, Cambridge, Mass.: NBER.

Kunimoto, K. (1977), 'Typology of trade intensity indices', *Hitotsubashi Journal of Economics* **17**, pp. 15–32.

Langhammer, R.J. (1996), 'Regional integration in East Asia, from market-driven regionalization to institutionalized regionalism?', *Weltwirtschaftliches Archiv* **131**, pp. 167–201.

Lawrence, R.Z. (1994), 'Regionalism: an overview', *Journal of the Japanese and International Economies* **8**, pp. 365–87.

Lorenz, D. (1991), 'Regionalization versus regionalism: problems of change in the world economy', *Intereconomics* **26**, pp. 3–9.

Malcolm, N. (1995), 'The case against Europe', *Foreign Affairs* **74**, pp. 52–68.

Masser, I. and P.J. Brown (1975), 'Hierarchical aggregation procedures for interaction data', *Environment and Planning A* **7**, pp. 509–23.

Masser, I. and J. Scheurwater (1980), 'Functional regionalization of spatial interaction data: an evaluation of some suggested strategies', *Environment and Planning A* **12**, pp. 1357–82.

McGee, R.W. (1995), 'The moral case for free trade', *Journal of World Trade* **29**, pp. 68–77.

Nagaoka, S.N. (1994), 'Does regional integration promote global liberalization? A case of endogenous protection', *Journal of the Japanese and International Economies* **8**, pp. 551–64.

Oman, C. (1994), *Globalization and Regionalization: The Challenge for Developing Countries*, Paris: Organisation for Economic Cooperation and Development.

Page, S. (1991), 'Europe 1992: views of developing countries', *Economic Journal* **101**, pp. 155–66.

Palmer, H.D. (1991), *The New Regionalism in Asia and the Pacific*, Lexington, Mass.: Lexington Books.

Phongpaichit, P. (1990), *The New Wave of Japanese Investment in ASEAN*, Singapore: Institute of Southeast Asian Studies.

Poon, J.P.H. (1997) 'The cosmopolitanization of world trade regions', *Economic Geography* **73**, pp. 390–404.

Porter, M.E. (1990), *The Competitive Advantage of Nations*, New York: Free Press.

Romer, P.M. (1990), 'Endogenous technological change', *Journal of Political Economy* **98**, pp. s71–s102.

Sapir, A. (1993), 'Regionalism and the new theory on international trade: do the bells toll for the GATT? A European outlook', *World Economy* **16**, pp. 423–38.

Sautter, H. (1974), 'Tendencies of regionalization in world trade between 1938 and 1970', in Giersch, G. (ed.), *The International Division of Labor: Problems and Perspectives*, Tubingen: Mohr.

Tsoukalis, L. (1993), *The New European Economy*, Oxford: Oxford University Press.

UNCTC (1991), *World Investment Report 1991: the Triad in Foreign Direct Investment,* New York: United Nations.

Viner, J. (1950), *The Customs Union Issue,* New York: Carnegie Endowment for International Peace.

Warr, P.G. (1994), 'Comparative and competitive advantage', *Asia-Pacific Economic Literature* **8**, pp. 1–14.

Williamson, O.E. (1975), *Markets and Hierarchies: Analysis and Anti-Trust Implications*, New York: Free Press.

NOTES

1. An influential advocate of business organizations and strategies as the driving force behind current patterns of economic production is Porter (1990). In his competitive advantage concept, Porter suggests that locational and geographical advantages which dictate a country's comparative advantage are less important than created factors of production. Through technological innovations, firms can create favourable factors of production, potentially turning comparative disadvantage to comparative advantage. Competitive advantage, however, has been argued to draw from

the concept of comparative advantage because the scope for creating competitive advantage is still constrained by the national circumstances of a country. Hence, the fact that firms are internationally competitive does not directly imply that nations are also internationally competitive because the two do not operate under exactly the same conditions (Krugman 1994; Warr 1994).

2.   With each iteration, there is normally a small increment in intrazonal interaction of less than 2 percent. The breakpoints defining the eight and five clusters in 1965 and 1990, however, registered large increments of 6 and 11.5 percent respectively. These represented the largest increments of all iterations for the years under study.

3.   The regions are named after their core nations. Part of the data for the figures was replicated from Poon (1997).

9. Estimates of the Trade Flows between the EU and the East Asian Countries – a Panel Data Analysis on a Gravity-Type Model

Birgit Nahrstedt and Jie Zhang

1. INTRODUCTION

In this chapter we will describe the bilateral trade flows between the twelve member countries (1990) of the European Union (EU) and the ten East Asian (EA) countries,[1] and estimate the trade flows using a gravity-type model. The original gravity model was first used successfully in the field of international trade by Tinbergen (1962) and Pöyhönen (1963), later more comprehensively by Linnemann (1966). It has also been used frequently to understand the determinants and the estimation of trade flows between trading countries.

The EU's external trade with the EA countries has developed rapidly during the last 20 years. Japan's share of the EU's total external import rose from 3.4 percent in 1970 to 4.9 percent in 1980, and to 10.0 percent in both 1990 and 1993. The increase of the share of the nine EA developing countries of the EU's total external import was even greater. It increased from 3.6 percent in 1970 to 6.1 percent in 1980, and further to 10.6 percent in 1990 and 14.3 percent in 1993. The EU's total import from these ten EA countries accounted for nearly a quarter of its external imports in 1993; it was higher than the imports from the US, EFTA, and other areas of the world. The EU's export to the EA countries has also increased dramatically. In 1990 the share of the export to the EA countries in the EU's total external export was double of that of 1970 and reached 17.1 percent in 1993.[2]

At the same time, the trade structure also changed a lot from raw materials and basic manufactures to high value-added machinery and equipment. Taking an average of the years 1980 and 1990, the manufactured goods accounted for more than 90 percent of both import and export trade between the EU and the four Asian NIEs, around 85 percent between the EU and China, and accounted for 65 percent in the EU import from the four ASEAN countries, and 88 percent of its export to these countries.[3]

In the following the trade flows between the EU and the EA countries will be estimated for the different groups of import and export commodities, that is, Food and Live Animals (SITC 0),[4] Manufactures (SITC 5–8) and Total Trade.

The EU's foreign trade can be analysed either in terms of the individual EU member countries' trade with the non-EU countries, or as a single international unit exporting or importing to and from the non-EU countries. The first approach is applied here, meaning that the bilateral trade flows are estimated between the individual EU member countries and the individual East Asian countries.

The purpose of this chapter is to estimate the trade flows by using a gravity-type model and by applying panel data analysis. A gravity-type model is constructed in order to test the relevant variables, including the Linder Effect (Lindner 1961) on the trade flows. Linder maintained that the more similar the trading countries are in the demand structure, the more they will trade with each other, especially within the trade in manufactured goods. In Section 2, a gravity-type model of international trade will be explained and the determinants of bilateral trade flows will be discussed. The data, some of the panel data methods, and the estimations for the trade flows between the EU and the EA countries will be presented in Section 3, and the results and their interpretation will be discussed in Section 4. In Section 5 the conclusion will be given.

2.   GRAVITY-TYPE MODELS OF INTERNATIONAL TRADE

The basic feature of the gravity-type models is taken from physics in which the 'law' states that two bodies attract each other proportionally to the product of their masses divided by the square of the distance between them. The law was transferred to the social sciences by Stewart, an astronomer, and Zipf, a sociologist, who attempted to apply it to spatial interactions, such as commuting between cities, using the following specification:

$$I_{ij} = G(POP_i \, POP_j) / D_{ij}^{\alpha} \qquad (9.1)$$

where

$I_{ij} =$ the number of commuters between city i and city j
$POP_i =$ the population in city i

POP_j = the population in city j
D_{ij} = the distance between city i and city j
G = a parameter
α = a parameter

This formula was later generalized to:

$$I_{ij} = G(w_i \, POP_i^{\alpha 1} \, w_j \, POP_j^{\alpha 2}) / D_{ij}^{\alpha 3} \qquad (9.2)$$

where w_i and w_j are unspecified weights suited to specific applications of gravity-type models such as international trade, in which case, however, population is replaced by GDP as the counterpart of physical 'masses'. Since the early 1960s when gravity-type models were first applied in international trade, several different gravity-type models of international trade have been developed and estimated for different purposes, such as Pöyhönen (1963); Linnemann (1966); Aitken (1973), Bergstrand (1985, 1989); Brada and Méndez (1985); Thursby and Thursby (1987); Havrylyshyn and Pritchett (1991); and Zhang and Kristensen (1995).

In order to analyse the variables which determine the bilateral trade flows, a gravity-type model is constructed from the above-mentioned gravity-type models as follows:

$$TRADE_{ij} = \exp(\alpha_0) \, Y_i^{\alpha 1} \, Y_j^{\alpha 2} \, PCY_i^{\alpha 3} \, PCY_j^{\alpha 4} \, PCYD_{ij}^{\alpha 5} \, D_{ij}^{\alpha 6} \, ER_{ij}^{\alpha 7} \, e_{ij}^{\alpha 7}$$

$$\qquad (9.3)$$

where

$TRADE_{ij}$ = the value of exports or imports trade flows from country i to country j
Y_i = the national income of exporting country i
Y_j = the national income of importing country j
PCY_i = the per capita income of country i
PCY_j = the per capita income of country j
$PCYD_{ij}$ = the differences in the per capita income between country i and country j
D_{ij} = the distance between country i and country j
ER_{ij} = the bilateral exchange rate
e_{ij} = the multiplicate error term
$\alpha_1 - \alpha_7$ = the parameters of the respective variables
α_0 = a constant

In the following we will use the logarithm of the denoted variables as equation (9.4) since there is a strong conviction that this is the correct specification (Sanso et al. 1993). Furthermore, by using the logarithm of the variables the coefficients can be directly interpreted as elasticities. Now our model will be as follows:

$$LTRADE_{ij} = \alpha_0 + \alpha_1 LY_i + \alpha_2 LY_j + \alpha_3 LPCY_i + \alpha_4 LPCY_j + \alpha_5 LPCYD_{ij}$$
$$+ \alpha_6 LD_{ij} + \alpha_7 LER_{ij} + e_{ij} \qquad (9.4)$$

How the trade flow variables are expected to be influenced by the explanatory variables in equation (9.4) will now be discussed. The variables Y_i and Y_j, which indicate GDP in exporting and importing countries, are positively related to $TRADE_{ij}$, as they represent the potential economic capacities of both export supply from the exporting country and import demand from the importing country. In other words, the larger the economic capacities in both countries are, the greater the potential supply and demand will be, and the greater the bilateral trade will be between them.

As a measure of demand structure and taste of the consumers, the per capita income (PCY_i and PCY_j) is often used in gravity-type models. The per capita income can also be added in models as a linkage between gravity-type equations and factor endowment of the trading countries. Bergstrand (1989) used PCY_i and PCY_j in his model as proxies for capital per labour of an exporter or an importer. Thursby and Thursby (1987) and Havrylyshyn-Pritchett (1991) applied per capita income in gravity-type models as a measurement to test the Linder effect. They believe that it is better to use the absolute difference in the per capita incomes of trading countries when reflecting the Linder Effect than the per capita incomes of both countries separately.

Therefore, the trade flows between the two regions would be expected to be a negative function of the absolute difference in per capita income in the two regions (PCYD), as Linder hypothesized that 'the more similar the demand structures of two countries, the more intensive, potentially, is the trade between these two countries' (see Linder 1961, p. 94).

The distance (D) is expected to influence the bilateral trade in a negative way. In this investigation we use transportation time (measured in number of transportation days for containerized goods by ship from the main harbours of the exporting countries to the main harbours of the importing countries) as a proxy for transportation costs or distance.

The bilateral exchange rate between an EA country and an EU country is calculated by:

$$ER = (VALT / VAL) / (VALT_{1971} / VAL_{1971}) \qquad (9.5)$$

where VALT is the amount of the EA countries' currencies paid for one US dollar and VAL is the amount of the EU countries' currencies paid for one US dollar. In generally, we expect exchange rate (ER) to be negatively related to exports and positively related to imports.

After the examination of the relations between the dependent variables and the independent variables we will discuss the collection of the data and the estimation of our model.

3. DATA AND ESTIMATION

In our model we use data from 22 countries, that is, 10 EA countries and 12 EU countries. The 10 EA countries consist of the following: Japan, Hong Kong, Singapore, South Korea, Taiwan, Indonesia, Malaysia, the Philippines, Thailand and China. The EU countries include: Belgium, Luxembourg, The Netherlands, France, Germany, Italy, United Kingdom, Denmark, Ireland, Greece, Portugal and Spain, where Belgium and Luxembourg are taken as one country. This means that we are in a situation with 21 countries. The data cover a period of 20 years from 1971 to 1990 (both years included). The total number of observations is 2200.[5]

As mentioned above, the trade flows between the EU and the EA countries have been estimated for three groups of import and export commodities, that is, Export and Import of Food and Live Animals (EXF and IMF), Export and Import of Manufactures (EXM and IMM), and Total Export and Total Import (EXT and IMT).

The GDP data are extracted from the United Nations: *National Accounts Statistics*; the bilateral trade data from the OECD: *Foreign Trade by Commodities*; the GNP per capita from the World Bank: *World Trade* 1993; the exchange rate, the consumer price indexes,[6] and the producer price indexes or wholesale price indexes[7] are collected from the IMF: *International Financial Statistical Yearbook*. The consumer price indexes and the wholesale price indexes for Taiwan are collected from Directorate-General of Budget, Accounting and Statistics, ROC: *Commodity-Price Statistics Monthly in Taiwan Area of The Republic of China,* April 1996. The transportation data are obtained from three Danish transport companies.

The data for export, import and GDP are in millions of dollars, per capita income is in dollars, the distance is in number of transportation days, and the exchange rate is normalized as explained above. The data for export and import figures have been deflated by using the EU countries' wholesale price indexes and the EA countries' wholesale price indexes, respectively. Also, the data for GDP and GDP per capita used in this investigation are converted into constant price values by using consumer price indexes from the individual EU and EA countries. The variable LPCYD is the logarithm of the absolute differences in the deflated per capita income. The exchange rates are also converted into real exchange rates. The exchange rate for the export data is deflated as follows: the deflator is calculated as the EA's wholesale price indexes divided by the EA's wholesale price index in 1971. This ratio is divided by the ratio of the EU's wholesale price indexes to the EU's wholesale price index in 1971. The exchange rate for the import data is deflated in the same way, but by using the consumer price indexes in both the EA and the EU countries. All the price indexes have 1985 as a base year or are calculated to have 1985 as a base year.

The data we use have the following characteristics: on average the EU exported a small amount of food products to the EA, whereas the highest share of the total export from the EU to the EA concerns manufactured goods. The EU imported comparatively more food from the EA than the EU's export to the EA. Again, the highest share of the total import of the EU from the EA is also manufactured goods, especially from Japan. Statistics showed that on average the EU countries imported more from the EA countries than they exported.

On average, the GDP of the EA countries is nearly as high as that of the EU, the minimum of the GDP in the EA is only a little lower than that in the EU, and the maximum of GDP in the EA is almost the same as the maximum of that in the EU. But by studying the per capita income in the two regions, a large difference between the EU and the EA can easily be seen. The average per capita income of the EU countries is much higher than that of the EA, however, the maximum of the per capita income of the EA is higher than that of the EU, as the per capita income of Japan at the end of the period is higher than that of Denmark (the country with the highest per capita income in the EU). But the minimum of the per capita income is much lower in the EA compared to that of the EU. By studying the differences in the maximum and minimum values of the per capita income in the EU and in the EA, it can be seen that the biggest difference in the per capita income exists within the EA countries. The differences in the per capita income between the individual EU country and the individual EA country show a high distinction between the trading countries. Also, it can be seen that the maximum is very high compared to the minimum of the differences in the per capita income of the trading countries. Therefore, the difference between the maximum and minimum in this variable is greater than that of the per capita income in both the EU and the EA.

Finally, the distance shows that there is only a small difference between the maximum and the minimum of transportation days from the EU countries to the EA countries. Moreover, the standard deviation of the distance is small which might influence the estimation of the variables.

The model we estimate is:

$$LEXT = \alpha_0 + \alpha_1 LY + \alpha_2 LYT + \alpha_3 LPCY + \alpha_4 LPCYT$$

$$+ \alpha_5 LPCYD + \alpha_6 LD + \alpha_7 LER + e_{tij} \qquad (9.6)$$

where

LEXT =	the logarithm of the value of the total export from an EU country to an East-Asian country
LY =	the logarithm of the national income of an EU country
LYT =	the logarithm of the national income of an EA country
LPCY =	the logarithm of the per capita income in an EU country
LPCYT =	the logarithm of the per capita income in an EA country
LPCYD =	the logarithm of the absolute difference of PCY and PCYT
LD =	the logarithm of the distance between an EU country and an EA country
LER =	the logarithm of the bilateral exchange rate

A few remarks will be made here. The six equations are estimated by using the six different dependent variables, that is, LEXF, LEXM, LEXT, LIMF, LIMM and LIMT. In these estimations LY and LPCY always denote the national income and the per capita income of an EU country regardless of the export flows or the import flows. LYT and LPCYT are arranged in the same manner for an EA country. As mentioned above, LER is adjusted by using the wholesale price indexes (LERWHOL) for the export flows and by using the consumer price indexes (LERCON) for the import flows.

Before we show our estimated results, we will describe the models we used. We are in a situation where we have cross-section data combined with time-series data. The reason for our combining cross-section and time-series data is to obtain more efficient parameter estimates. But, when using the most restricted model, the Ordinary Least Squares Regression Model (by stacking all the data), there might arise problems like groupwise heteroscedasticity, groupwise autocorrelation and contemporaneous covariance (see Fomby 1984, p. 325). Therefore, we use the most common analytical methods within panel data models: the Fixed Effects Model or the Least Squares Dummy Variable (LSDV) Model and the Random Effects Model or the Error Components Model.

The idea behind these models is that all the structural changes, caused by pooling the cross-section and time-series data, are captured by the intercept.

The estimation procedure depends on whether the intercept varies in a fixed manner (the Fixed Effects Models) or in a random (the Random Effects Models) manner.

In the One Factor Fixed Effects Model and in the One Factor Random Effects Model, the intercept varies over countries (or units), and in models where the structural variations vary over countries *and* over time, we have the Two Factors Fixed Effects Model and the Two Factors Random Effects Model. Now, we consider the general model as follows:

$$y_{it} = \sum_{k=1}^{K} \beta_{kit} x_{kit} + \varepsilon_{it} \qquad i = 1, 2,..., N; \ \ t = 1, 2,..., T.$$

(9.7)

where y_{it} is the dependent variable, β_{kit} are the parameters, x_{kit} are the specific explanatory variables, ε_{it} is the error term, K is the number of parameters, N is the number of cross-section observations, and T is the number of time-series observations. Here, the parameters of this general model are indexed by both a cross-section index and a time-series index. This model can be estimated by using the Ordinary Least Squares Model, where the variation is contained in the error term. To use the Ordinary Least Squares Model, the usual assumptions have to be met. Unfortunately, these assumptions are not met in our analysis.

Now, we let the intercept term vary in a fixed manner over countries, but not over time, and obtain the *One Factor Fixed Effects Model*. We restrict equation (9.7), so that and β_{1it} may vary over countries. Only the intercept is allowed to vary, and the slope coefficients of this model are assumed to be constant for all cross-section countries.

The model to be estimated is as follows:

$$y_{it} = \beta_{1it} + \sum_{k=2}^{K} \beta_k x_{kit} + \varepsilon_{it} \qquad i = 1, 2,..., N; \ \ t = 1, 2,..., T.$$

(9.8)

Here, the parameter β_{1it} is composed of two components:

$$\beta_{1it} = \beta_1 + \mu_i \qquad i = 1, 2,..., N; \ \ t = 1, 2,..., T.$$

(9.9)

where μ_i represents a cross-section component: the difference between the country specific intercept parameter β_{1it} and the common intercept factor β_1.

In the *Two Factors Fixed Effects Model*, the intercept varies over countries and over time. Again, the slope coefficients of this model are assumed to be constant for all cross-section countries and time periods. The model we consider is:

$$y_{it} = \beta_{1it} + \sum_{k=2}^{K} \beta_k x_{kit} + \varepsilon_{it} \quad i = 1, 2,..., N; \quad t = 1, 2,..., T.$$

(9.10)

where β_{1it} is composed of three components:

$$\beta_{1it} = \beta_1 + \mu_i + \lambda_t \quad i = 1, 2,..., N; \quad t = 1, 2,..., T.$$

(9.11)

where μ_i represents the difference between the country specific parameter β_{1it} and the common factor β_1, and λ_t presents the difference attributable to a time-series factor.

The Fixed Effects Model can thus be used if the differences between the countries are caused by a parametric shift of the regression function.

In the *One Factor Random Effects Model*, the intercept β_{1i} may vary over countries in a random manner. We use the equation (9.8), but let the value of the intercept be random with mean β_1. The intercept can be formulated as:

$$\beta_{1i} = \beta_1 + u_i \quad i = 1, 2,..., N;$$

(9.12)

where β_1 is the mean intercept of the cross-section countries, and u_i is a random variable with $E[u_i] = 0$, $E[u_i^2] = \sigma_u^2$ and $E[u_iu_j] = 0$ for $i \neq j$, and the ε_{ij}s are not correlated with u_i. Only the intercept is allowed to vary, and the slope coefficients of this model are assumed to be constant for all cross-section countries. The model can be formulated as:

$$y_{it} = \beta_1 + \sum_{k=2}^{K} \beta_k x_{kit} + \varepsilon_{it} + u_i \quad i = 1, 2,..., N; \quad t = 1, 2,..., T.$$

(9.13)

In the *Two Factors Random Effects Model*, the intercept β_{1i} may vary over countries and over time in a random manner. We use the equation (9.9), but let the value of the intercept be random with the mean of β_1. The intercept can be formulated as:

$$\beta_{1i} = \beta_1 + u_i + v_t \quad i = 1, 2,..., N;$$

(9.14)

where β_1 is the mean intercept of the cross-section countries, and u_i and v_t are random variables. It is assumed that $E[u_i] = 0$, $E[u_i^2] = \sigma_i^2$, and $E[u_iu_j] = 0$ if $i \neq j$. It is also assumed that $E[v_i] = 0$, $E[v_i^2] = \sigma_v^2$, and $E[v_iv_j] = 0$ if $i \neq j$. Furthermore, it is assumed that neither u_i, v_t or ε_{ij} are correlated. Again, only the intercept is allowed to vary in a random manner, and the slope coefficients of this model are assumed to be constant for all cross-section countries. The model can be formulated as:

$$y_{it} = \beta_1 + \sum_{k=2}^{K} \beta_k \, x_{kit} + \varepsilon_{it} + u_i + v_t \quad i = 1, 2,..., N; \quad t = 1, 2,..., T.$$

(9.15)

The Random Effects Model differs from the Fixed Effects Model in adding random disturbances: a country-specific error component u_i, which is constant through time, and a time-specific error term v_t.

In this section we have described the different models[8] (except the Ordinary Least Squares Regression Model) which we have used to estimate our models. In Section 4 only the best model estimations will be presented.

4.   RESULTS AND INTERPRETATION

Since our dataset is a panel data set which combines cross-section and time-series data, we used the following estimation methods:[9] the Ordinary Least Squares Model, the One Factor Fixed Effects Model, the One Factor Random Effects Model, the Two Factors Fixed Effects Model and the Two Factors Random Effects Model. Unfortunately, since we used a fixed measurement for the distance between each of the EU countries and each of the EA countries we got multicollinearity when we used the One Factor Fixed Effects Model and the Two Factors Fixed Effects Model. We could then only choose between the Ordinary Least Squares Model, the One Factor Random Effects Model and the Two Factors Random Effects Model. In fact, we have chosen the Two Factors Random Effects Model for all our six models. The choice between the One Factor Random Effects Model and the Two Factors Random Effects Model was made by choosing the model with the highest R squared, because the Random Effects Models will not give any other best fit measurement.

For all the estimation methods it is assumed that we have neither time heteroscedasticity nor cross-sectional heteroscedasticity in our models. In all the models we have checked for multicollinearity, we found no multicollinearity problem in our estimations when we included all the mentioned variables. The estimation results for the six models are shown in Tables 9.1 to 9.6.

We will first discuss the estimated coefficients of the national incomes of both the exporting and importing countries. Then, we will discuss the per capita income for the both counterparts, together with the difference in the per capita income from the exporting and importing countries. The Linder effects will be explained here. Finally, the variables for distance and exchange rates will be discussed.

Table 9.1   Estimation of exporting food and live animals from the EU to EA (equation LEXF)

Variables	Coefficient	Std. Error	t-ratio	Prob-value
Constant	−26.867	3.968	−6.771	0.00000
LY	0.675	0.130	5.208	0.00000
LYT	0.554	0.106	5.247	0.00000
LPCY	−1.034	0.165	−6.257	0.00000
LPCYT	1.230	0.118	10.396	0.00000
LPCYD	0.00004	0.001	0.030	0.97641
LD	2.655	1.200	2.213	0.02690
LERWHOL	−0.574	0.063	−9.065	0.00000
R^2		0.3095		

Table 9.2 Estimation of exporting manufactures from the EU to EA (equation LEXM)

Variables	Coefficient	Std. Error	t-ratio	Prob-value
Constant	−24.447	2.642	−9.253	0.00000
LY	1.570	0.088	17.797	0.00000
LYT	0.423	0.073	5.815	0.00000
LPCY	−1.723	0.114	−15.122	0.00000
LPCYT	0.770	0.077	9.975	0.00000
LPCYD	0.00085	0.00076	1.116	0.26449
LD	3.046	0.801	3.802	0.00014
LERWHOL	−0.344	0.041	−8.458	0.00000
R^2		0.5845		

From Tables 9.1, 9.2, and 9.3 all the coefficients of LY, LYT, LPCY and LPCYT are highly significant in the estimations of the export flows of the three commodity categories from the EU to the EA countries. Except for LPCY the other three coefficients are positive as expected. Actually, the coefficients of LY in all the six estimations are quite high, higher than numerical one except the coefficient of LY in the equation LEXF. This result shows that the national income elasticity of the EU countries for the export is quite high. For example, if the value of the national income of the exporting EU countries increases by 1 percent, the manufacturing export will increase by 1.57 percent (Table 9.2), and the total export will increase by 1.37 percent (Table 9.3). The national income elasticity of the EU countries for the import is also high, the coefficients of LY for the import of the three commodity categories are all higher than one (Tables 9.4, 9.5 and 9.6).

Table 9.3   Estimation of the total export from the EU to EA (equation LEXT)

Variables	Coefficient	Std. Error	t-ratio	Prob-value
Constant	−23.237	2.119	−10.965	0.00000
LY	1.365	0.071	19.280	0.00000
LYT	0.411	0.059	6.936	0.00000
LPCY	−1.345	0.094	−14.379	0.00000
LPCYT	0.704	0.062	11.326	0.00000
LPCYD	0.00085	0.00064	1.326	0.18489
LD	2.679	0.643	4.169	0.00000
LERWHOL	−0.348	0.034	−10.317	0.00000
R^2		0.6372		

Table 9.4   Estimation of the exporting food and live animals from EA to the EU (equation LIMF)

Variables	Coefficient	Std. Error	t-ratio	Prob-value
Constant	−13.468	3.592	−3.750	0.00018
LY	1.292	0.116	11.125	0.00000
LYT	0.619	0.102	6.096	0.00000
LPCY	−1.341	0.171	−7.846	0.00000
LPCYT	−0.403	0.103	−3.932	0.00008
LPCYD	−0.0021	0.00013	−1.631	0.10290
LD	0.977	1.071	0.913	0.36120
LERCON	0.135	0.072	1.886	0.0594
R^2		0.3235		

The coefficients of LYT are not very high with an average of 0.46. The coefficients of LYT in Tables 9.1, 9.2 and 9.3 are explained as the national income elasticity of the EA countries for the import from the EU. The estimated results show that if the value of the national income of the importing EA countries increases by 1 percent, the food imports, the manufacturing imports, and the total imports from the EU will increase by 0.55, 0.42 and 0.41 percent respectively. However, the national income elasticity of the EA countries for the export to the EU countries is different in the different commodity categories, as shown in Tables 9.4, 9.5 and 9.6. The coefficient of LYT for the food exports of the EA is 0.62, which is much higher than that for the manufacturing exports (0.25). This means that the national income elasticity is more sensitive for the food exports than for the manufacturing exports in most EA countries.

Table 9.5 Estimation of the exporting manufactures from EA to the EU (equation LIMM)

Variables	Coefficient	Std. Error	t-ratio	Prob-value
Constant	−29.302	2.572	−11.393	0.00000
LY	1.484	0.082	18.211	0.00000
LYT	0.252	0.077	3.261	0.00111
LPCY	−2.029	0.139	−14.585	0.00000
LPCYT	0.945	0.072	13.185	0.00000
LPCYD	−0.00035	0.0011	−0.322	0.74779
LD	5.866	0.761	7.714	0.00000
LERCON	−0.148	0.058	−2.554	0.01064
R^2		0.6459		

Table 9.6 Estimation of the total export from EA to the EU (equation LIMT)

Variables	Coefficient	Std. Error	t-ratio	Prob-value
Constant	−23.974	2.001	−11.979	0.00000
LY	1.238	0.064	19.401	0.00000
LYT	0.499	0.059	8.431	0.00000
LPCY	−1.195	0.105	−11.438	0.00000
LPCYT	0.650	0.056	11.549	0.00000
LPCYD	0.00028	0.00083	0.336	0.73723
LD	2.902	0.593	4.894	0.00000
LERCON	0.073	0.044	1.665	0.09595
R^2		0.6249		

Now we come to the point of explaining the coefficients of the per capita income, the differences in the per capita income, and the Linder effects. The coefficients of LPCY in all the six estimations are negative, as we expected. In the EU countries the average per capita income is much higher than the average per capita income of the EA countries. If the per capita income in the EU countries increases, the EU countries will be more dissimilar to the EA countries, then the trade flows will decrease between the EU and the EA countries according to the Linder hypothesis. The coefficients of LPCYT in all the six estimations are positive as expected. When the per capita income in the EA countries increase, they become more similar to the per capita income of the EU countries, and then the trade flows will increase between the EU and the EA countries. From Table 9.5 it can be seen that the coefficient of LPCYT is 0.95. It is shown that when the per capita income of the EA countries increases by 1 percent, the manufacturing exports of the EA countries to the EU will increase by 0.95 percent.

All the coefficients of LPCYD are very insignificant, some of them are positive and some are negative. The Linder hypothesis, which says that the difference in the per capita income of trading countries is negatively correlated with the trade flows in manufactures, was tested by several researchers, such as Arad and Hirsch (1981), Ellis (1983), and Kleiman and Kop (1984). Most tests proved their success in the empirical tests in the case of the EU countries, but they were not as successful in the case of the United States (see Fortune 1979; Sailors et al. 1973; Arad and Hirwsch 1981). Arad and Hirsch (1981) explained: 'The case of the United States is the only country with the highest per capita income'.[10] Kleiman and Kop (1984, p. 518) claimed: 'The income effect can be expected to be stronger in the trade between industrialized countries than elsewhere ... . They show the Linder Effect to be mainly, if not even exclusively, a rich country phenomenon'.[11]

The coefficients of distance are significant except in equation LIMF (Table 9.4). The estimated coefficients are all positive in the six estimations, actually not as we expected. The reason for this may be that the trade flows between the EU and the EA countries are more like the flows between the two clusters and the differences between the distances of pairs of trading countries are small. Another reason is what we will call the *Japan factor*. Japan's location is comparatively farther away from the EU countries than the other EA countries as measured by ship transport days, but there are larger trade flows between Japan and the EU countries than between the other EA countries and the EU countries. According to the Linder theory, there are intensive trade flows between the countries which are more similar in per capita income, and Japan's per capita income is in the same spectrum as the EU countries.

Finally, we shall interpret the coefficients of LERWHOL and LERCON. As the exchange rates are transformed into the real exchange rates, they will show the effects of real exchange rate on trade flows. We found that the coefficients of LERWHOL are negative and highly significant (Tables 9.1, 9.2 and 9.3). The calculation based on formula (9.5) will show the appreciation of the currencies of the EU countries and depreciation of the currencies of the EA countries when ER has an upward trend. Altogether the negative correlation between the LERWHOL and the EU export flows shows that the EU countries faced the appreciation of their own currencies and the depreciation of the EA's currencies in the investigation period. Therefore the real exchange rates did not favour the EU export to the EA.

On the other hand the effects of the real exchange rates should be positively related to the EU import from the EA. We found the positive coefficients of LERCON in the equations of LIMF and LIMT (Tables 9.4 and 9.6), but the coefficients are numerically small and significant at 5 percent and 10 percent respectively. It is interesting to find that the coefficient of LERCON is negative and significant for the EU manufacturing imports (Table 9.5). The coefficient of LERCON in the equation of LIMM is −0.15, and it shows that the real exchange rate did not favour the EU manufacturing import from EA countries. The results have proved that the real exchange rates in the long run have negative effects on the EU manufacturing import from the EA countries.

5. CONCLUSION

The purpose of this study was to estimate the bilateral trade flows between the member countries of the European Union and the East Asian countries by using a gravity-type model and to test the Linder effect. We have now estimated a gravity-type model in which our dependent variable is the value of export and import (for Food, Manufactures and Total) from an EU country to an EA country. The dependent variables were explained by the national incomes in the EU countries, and the EA countries, per capita income in the mentioned countries, distance between them, and the bilateral exchange rate.

We used data from 22 countries altogether, that is, 10 East Asian countries and 12 EU countries over a period of 20 years from 1971 to 1990. This means that the data combine cross-section and time-series data, therefore, we estimated the equations by the following panel data estimation methods: the Ordinary Least Squares, the One Factor Fixed Effects Model, the One Factor Random Effects Model, the Two Factors Fixed Effects Model, and the Two Factors Random Effects Model. We found in all our six estimations that the Two Factors Random Effects Model gave us the best results.

The results, which we obtained from the estimations, show that the variables for the national income of both exporting and importing countries are significant factors in our models. The coefficients for the per capita incomes of both exporting and importing countries give the results as we expected. The estimation of the real exchange rate coefficients gave us rather good results as expected.

The main result has proved the Linder theory: when the per capita income of the two trading countries are more equal, the demand structure is more similar, and the trade flows between them are more intensive. When the per capita income of the richer partner increases, the bilateral trade will decrease, and when the per capita income of the poorer partner increases, the bilateral trade will increase. Also, our main conclusion is that the Linder effect is stronger than the effect of the distance variable in the gravity model, which can explain our positive coefficients for the distance variable.

This study surely has some shortcomings. We have estimated the trade flows between the EU countries and the EA countries, but it will be interesting to estimate the trade flows among the EU member countries, and among the EA countries as well. The influence of other variables, such as direct price influences, tariffs, business risks, and other trade barriers on trade flows are still unknown. Some interesting results might also be obtained by including these variables in the trade flows between the EA countries and the EU countries. As a measurement to calculate the income inequality, the Gini coefficient could be included as an explanatory variable.

It could be interesting to include groupwise heteroscedasticity in our panel data estimations, but as far as we know these models have not yet been built. The model could also be estimated by using Seemingly Unrelated Regression Estimation and hereby to incorporate heteroscedasticity, groupwise heteroscedasticity, autocorrelation and cross-section autocorrelation.

ACKNOWLEDGEMENT

We would like to thank the anonymous referees for their comments.

REFERENCES

Aitken, N.D. (1973), 'The effect of EEC and EFTA on European trade: a temporal cross-section analysis', *American Economic Review* **63**, pp. 881–92.

Arad, R.W. and S. Hirsch (1981), 'Determination of trade flows and the choices of trade partners: reconciling the H-O and the Burenstam-Linder models of international trade', *Weltwirtschaftliches Archiv* **117** (2), pp. 276–97.

Bergstrand, J.H. (1985), 'The gravity equation in international trade: some microeconomic foundations and empirical evidence', *The Review of Economics and Statistics* **67**, pp. 474–81.

Bergstrand, J.H. (1989), 'The generalized gravity equation, monopolistic competition, and the factor-proportions theory in international trade', *The Review of Economics and Statistics* **71**, pp. 143–53.

Brada, J.C. and J.A. Méndez (1985), 'Economic integration among developed, developing and centrally planned economies: a comparative analysis', *The Review of Economics and Statistics* **67**, pp. 54–56.

Directorate-General of Budget, Accounting, and Statistics, ROC (1996), *Commodity Price Statistics Monthly in Taiwan Area of The Republic of China*, April.

Ellis, C.M. (1983), 'An alternative interpretation and empirical test of the Linder Hypothesis', *Quarterly Journal of Business and Economics* **24** (4), pp. 53–62.

Eurostat, *External Trade Statistical Yearbook*, various years.

Fomby, T.B. (1984), *Advanced Econometric Methods*, New York: Springer-Verlag.

Fortune, J.N. (1979), 'Income distribution and Linder's Trade Thesis', *Southern Economic Journal* **46**, pp. 158–67.

Havrylyshyn, O. and L. Pritchett (1991), 'European trade patterns after the transition', World Bank, Working Papers, *Trade Policy*.

IMF (1992), *International Financial Statistical Yearbook.*

IMF (1993), *International Financial Statistical Yearbook.*

Kleiman, E. and Y. Kop (1984), 'Who trades with whom – the income pattern of international trade, *Weltwirtschaftliches Archiv* **117** (2), pp. 276–97.

Linder, S.B. (1961), *An Essay on Trade and Transformation*, Uppsala: Almqvist and Wiksells.

Linnemann, H. (1966), *An Econometric Study of International Trade Flows,* Contributions to Economic Analysis **42**, Amsterdam: North Holland.

Pöyhönen, P. (1963), 'Toward a general theory of international trade', *Ekonomiska, Samfundets Tidskrift, Tredje Serien* **16**, pp. 69–77.

OECD, *Foreign Trade by Commodities,* The Europe World Year Book, London: Europe Publications Limited, various years.

Sailors, J.W., Qureshi, U.A. and E.M. Cross (1973), 'Empirical verification of Linder's Trade Thesis', *Southern Economic Journal* **40**, pp. 262–8.

Sanso, M., Cuairan, R. and F. Sanz (1993), 'Bilateral trade flows, the gravity equation, and functional form', *The Review of Economics and Statistics* **75**, pp. 266–75.

Tinbergen, J. (1962), *Shaping the World Economy: Suggestion for an International Economic Policy*, New York: The Twentieth Century Fund.

Thursby, J.G. and M.C. Thursby (1987), 'Bilateral trade flows, the Linder Hypothesis, and exchange risk', *The Review of Economics and Statistics* **69**, pp. 488–95.

United Nations, *National Accounts Statistics,* various years.

World Bank (1993), *World Tables.*

Zhang, J. and G. Kristensen (1995), 'A gravity model with variable coefficients: the EEC trade with third countries', *Geographical Analysis* **27**, pp. 307–20.

NOTES

1. The East Asian countries mentioned here are Japan, China, four NIEs (newly industrialized economies, that is, Hong Kong, Singapore, South Korea and Taiwan), and four ASEAN countries (Association of South and East Asian Nations, that is, Indonesia, Malaysia, the Philippines and Thailand).

2. The shares are calculated based on the data from Eurostat: *External Trade Statistics Yearbook*, various years.

3.   The shares for trade structure are calculated based on data from OECD: *Statistics of Foreign Trade.*

4.   SITC stands for the Standard International Trade Classification.

5.   We are in a situation with 11 EU countries of which each trade with 10 EA countries over a period of 20 years. This means that we have altogether 2200 observations (11x10x20 observations); export flows from the EU to EA are estimated separately from those from EA to the EU.

6.   The consumer prices reflect changes in the cost of acquiring a fixed basket of goods and services by the average consumer. The Laspeyres formula is used in this investigation. The price indexes for Luxembourg and Belgium only consist of the price indexes of Belgium, because the trade from and to Luxembourg is relatively small compared with that of Belgium.

7.   The producer price indexes are in practice limited to the domestic agricultural and industrial sectors. The wholesale price indexes include prices of agricultural and industrial goods, and are inclusive of imports and import duties. The price indexes are calculated by using the Laspeyres formula. As far as possible we use the producer price index or wholesale price index, otherwise we have used: Producer price indexes (Belgium), Prices: Home Goods (Denmark, Portugal), Prices: Final Products price indexes (Netherlands), Prices: Industrial Products (Germany, Spain), Prices: Industrial Goods, Tax incl. (France), Prices: Manufacturing Output (United Kingdom). For Malaysia and China we only used consumer price indexes.

8.   For a study in depth, see Fomby (1984), pp. 324–38.

9.   All regression estimations are carried out in LIMDEP 6, version 386.

10. The data, which they mentioned, are from the year of 1975 (see Arad and Hirsch 1981, pp. 290–92).

11. See Kleiman and Kop (1984), p. 518.

10. Links between Emigrants and the Home Country: the Case of Trade between Taiwan and Canada

Hsianghoo S. Ching and Li-Lu Chen

1. INTRODUCTION

Since 1985 Asia has been a major and growing source of immigrants to Canada. In 1994, the number of Asian immigrants landed in Canada was 138,297 persons, which accounted for 63.5 percent of Canadian total immigrants landed in that year.[1] Of that total, 63,229 persons or 45.7 percent were Chinese immigrants, and 50,979 persons or 36.9 percent were from Hong Kong and Taiwan. The majority of immigrants from Hong Kong and Taiwan were in the business immigrant and independent classes.[2] The major causes of the high inflow of Hong Kong immigrants to Canada were the uncertain future of Hong Kong after annexation to China in 1997 and, to a lesser degree, the inflow of Hong Kong independent worker immigrants seeking better career opportunities in Canada. The immigrating family members of previously landed immigrants have also been adding to the total volume of migrants coming to Canada from Hong Kong. Taiwanese emigrants are responding to the pull of the allure of having a higher quality of life in Canada and the push caused by the perception of a diminishing quality of life in Taiwan caused by events such as increasing environmental pollution, increasing land prices, higher population congestion, the potential threat from Mainland China, and the stressful competitive nature of Taiwan's educational system. The type of contemporary Chinese immigrants to Canada are different from previous generations which were mainly from mainland China and were primarily family-class immigrants who were lower skilled workers. The contemporary Chinese immigrants are generally better educated and monied than the previous generations and have a higher representation of entrepreneurs and investors. The newest generation of Chinese immigrants have been described as being 'at the top of the feeding ladder' by Canadian journalists.

185

In the form of language, culture, preference, education, or entrepreneurial talent, the different generations of immigrants may possess differential endowments of human capital relative to the population of the receiving country. In addition to their human capital, immigrants may own financial capital that they bring with them to the receiving country. In general, there are three ways that international migration may stimulate the economic development of the receiving country: (1) A larger population will increase demand for employees to provide goods and services for the local population. If immigrants do not join the labour force, such as investors and retired persons, the demand for labour may increase more rapidly than supply. Immigrants may influence the price and profitability of locally provided goods and services due to the increased demand. (2) Immigrants may contribute to greater economic activity and to the achievement of economic scale and agglomeration economies. (3) The imposition of restrictive entry regulations may result in the local economy attracting more productive and enterprising individuals from overseas (Greenwood 1994).

International migration issues were mainly concerned with the flow of high level manpower from poor to rich countries. Among the most disputed issues was the effect of immigration on the labour market and public sector. However, these issues ignore other important aspects in describing the effect of immigration. The economic impact of immigrants are exerted through many channels. One of the possible channels is international trade. Since international immigrants may have knowledge of access to lower costs with foreign trade than non-immigrants or may have superior information on market opportunities than non-immigrants, they may serve a role as trade stimulator between the receiving and home countries. This gives rise to some concerns: what are the contemporary Chinese immigrants' contributions to the economy of their home country as compared to the earlier generations which provided their labour (such as building the inter-continental railroad) in the receiving country and transferred part of their income to dependents in the home country. Can they intensify bilateral trading flows between the receiving and home countries? This study is to investigate how contemporary Taiwanese emigrants might increase bilateral trade with their home country. This is done by applying the gravity equation derived by Gould (1994) to the case of Taiwan–Canada trade patterns as the basis of analysis. A major change in Canada's immigration regulations occurred in 1978 by creating the business immigration classes. The new regulations gave more weight to the economic contribution of immigrants and this was the main factor for admissibility. These immigrants might stimulate the bilateral trade with their home country more than the immigrants in other classes did. This study will also examine how different categories of immigrants may influence the trade patterns of their home country.

2. THE MODEL AND PROCEDURE

The analytical model is based on the model derived by Gould (1994), which is a modification of Bergstrand's (1985) model. The model consists of N countries. In each country j, consumers are assumed to share the constant elasticity of substitution (hereinafter called 'CES') utility function:

$$U_j = \left\{ \left[\left(\sum_{k=1}^{N} X_{kj}^{\theta_j} \right)^{1/\theta_j} \right]^{\psi_j} + X_{jj}^{\psi_j} \right\}^{1/\psi_j} \quad , \quad j = 1,..., N \text{ and } k \neq j$$

(10.1)

where X_{kj} is country k's good demanded by country j's consumers, X_{jj} is country j's good demanded domestically, $\psi_j = (\mu_j - 1) / \mu_j$ where μ_j is the CES between domestic and imported goods in country j, $(0 \leq \mu_j \leq \infty)$, and $\theta_j = (\sigma_j - 1)/\sigma_j$ where σ_j is the CES among importable goods $(0 \leq \sigma_j \leq \infty)$. Expenditures in j are subject to income.

$$Y_j = \sum_{k=1}^{N} \bar{P}_{kj} X_{kj} \, ,$$

(10.2)

and

$$\bar{P}_{kj} = P_{kj}(T_{kj}^{\beta_1} C_{kj}^{\beta_2} Z_{kj}^{-\beta_3}), \text{ where } \beta_1 > 0, \beta_2 > 0, \text{ and } \beta_3 > 0$$

$\bar{P}_{kj}$ is the price of k's product sold in j's market, P_{kj} is the price received for selling k's product in j's market, P_{jj} is its own domestic product price, T_{kj} is j's tariff rate on k's product $(T_{kj} \geq 1)$, C_{kj} is the transport cost factor to ship k's product to country j $(C_{kj} \geq 1)$ and Z_{kj} is the benefit factor to trade associated with gaining foreign market information about country k in country j $(Z_{kj} \geq 1)$. The benefit factor to trade is assumed to be a function of emigrants, that is, $Z_{kj} = f(EMI_{kj})$. Emigrants possess more foreign market information and access to foreign contacts than residents in their home country. They may play a role of reducing information barriers and transaction costs that affect bilateral trade. An important hypothesis is that emigrants provide foreign market information and contacts that increase the benefits to trade at a decreasing rate. We assume $Z_{kj} = \ln(EMI_{kj})$, that is,

$dZ_{kj}/dEHI_{kj} > 0$ and $d^2Z_{kj}/dEMI_{kj}^2 < 0$. Maximizing utility subject to income constraints gives $N(N + 1)$ first-order conditions and generates $N(N - 1)$ bilateral import demand equations (N_{ij}^D) and N domestic demand equations (X_{ij}^D). In each country i, firms maximize the profit function:

$$\Pi_i = \sum_{k=1}^{N} P_{ik} X_{ik} - W_i L_i, \quad i = 1,..., N \tag{10.3}$$

where L_i is a single, internationally immobile factor of production available to country i and W_i is the i-currency return of a unit of L_i. L_i is allocated across industries for every country according to the constant-elasticity-of-transformation (hereinafter called 'CET') joint production surface:

$$L_i \left\{ \left[\left(\sum_{k=1}^{B} X_{ik}^{1/\phi_i} \right)^{1/\phi_i} \right]^{\delta_i} + X_i^{\delta_i} \right\}^{1/\delta_i}, i = 1, \ldots, N \text{ and } k \neq 1 \tag{10.4}$$

where $\delta_j = (1 + \eta_j)/\eta_j$ where η_j is i's CET between any two goods for home and foreign markets ($0 \leq \eta_j \leq \infty$) and $\phi = (1 + \gamma_j)/\gamma_j$ where γ_j is i's CET among exportable goods ($0 \leq \gamma_j \leq \infty$). National income in i is constrained by

$$Y_i = W_i L_i, \quad i = 1,..., N \tag{10.5}$$

Maximizing profit subject to the CET function gives N^2 first order conditions and generates $N(N - 1)$ bilateral export supply equations (X_{ij}^s) and N domestic supply equation (X_{ij}^s). Assume N^2 equilibrium conditions:

$$X_{ij}^D = X_{ij} = X_{ij}^S, \quad i, j = 1,..., N \tag{10.6}$$

where X_{ij} is the actual trade flow volume from i to j as a function of the exogenous variables T_{ij}, C_{ij}, Z_{ij} and L_{ij}. The model can be simplified by assuming that changes in X_{ij} and P_{ij} to equilibrate X_{ij}^D and X_{ij}^S have a negligible impact on incomes and prices in other markets. Combining the above equations and assumptions yields bilateral prices:

$$P_{ij} = \left\{ \begin{array}{l} Y_i^{-1} Y_j C_j^{-\beta_1 \sigma_j} T_j^{-\beta_2 \sigma_j} Z_j^{\beta_3 \sigma_j} \times \left(\Sigma'_{\underset{ik}{P}} \frac{1+\gamma_i}{P} \right)^{(\gamma_i - \eta_i)/(1+\gamma_i)} \times \left(\Sigma''_{\underset{kj}{p}} \frac{1-\sigma_j}{p} \right)^{(\sigma_j - \mu_j)/(1-\sigma_j)} \\[2mm] \times \left[\left(\Sigma'_{\underset{ik}{P}} \frac{1+\gamma_i}{P} \right)^{(1+\eta_i)/(1+\gamma_i)} + P_i^{1+\eta_i} \right] \times \left[\left(\Sigma''_{\underset{kj}{p}} \frac{1-\sigma_j}{p} \right)^{(1-\mu_j)/(1-\sigma_j)} + P_j^{1-\mu_j} \right]^{-1} \end{array} \right\}^{1(\gamma_i + \sigma_i)} \tag{10.7}$$

and trade flows:

$$X_{ij} = \left\{ \begin{array}{l} Y_i^{\sigma_i} Y_j^{\gamma_i} C_j^{-\beta_1 \gamma_i \sigma_j} T_j^{-\beta_2 \gamma_i \sigma_j} Z_j^{\beta_3 \gamma_i \sigma_j} \times \left(\Sigma'_{\underset{ik}{P}} \frac{1+\gamma_i}{P} \right)^{-\sigma_i (\gamma_i - \eta_i)/(1+\gamma_i)} \times \left(\Sigma''_{\underset{kj}{p}} \frac{1-\sigma_j}{p} \right)^{\gamma_i (\sigma_j - \mu_j)/(1-\sigma_j)} \\[2mm] \times \left[\left(\Sigma'_{\underset{ik}{P}} \frac{1+\gamma_i}{P} \right)^{(1+\eta_i)/(1+\gamma_i)} + P_{ii}^{1+\eta_i} \right]^{-\sigma_j} \times \left[\left(\Sigma''_{\underset{kj}{p}} \frac{1-\sigma_j}{p} \right)^{(1-\mu_j)/(1-\sigma_j)} + P_j^{1-\mu_j} \right]^{-\gamma} \end{array} \right\}^{1/(\gamma_i + \sigma_i)} \tag{10.8}$$

where i, j = 1,.., N and i ≠ j, Σ' denotes summation over k = 1,..,N and k ≠ i, Σ'' denotes summation over k=1,..,N and k ≠ j. Assume identical utility and production functions across countries to ensure that parameters in (10.7) and (10.8) are constant. Combining (10.7), (10.8) and this assumption yields the value of trade flows:

$$P_{ij} X_{ij} = Y_j^{(\sigma_j - 1)/(\gamma_i + \sigma_j)} Y_i^{(\gamma_i + 1)/(\gamma_i + \sigma_j)} C_{ij}^{-\beta_1 \sigma_j (\gamma_i + 1)/(\gamma_i + \sigma_j)} T_{ij}^{-\beta_2 \sigma_j (\gamma_i + \sigma_j)} Z_{ij}^{\beta_3 \sigma_j (\gamma_i + 1)/(\gamma_i + \sigma_j)}$$

$$\times \left(\Sigma'_{\underset{ik}{P}} \frac{1+\gamma_i}{P} \right)^{-(\sigma_j - 1)(\gamma_i - \eta_i)/(1+\gamma_i)(\gamma_i + \sigma_j)} \times \left(\Sigma''_{\underset{kj}{p}} \frac{1-\sigma_j}{p} \right)^{(\gamma_i + 1)(\sigma_j - \mu_j)/(1-\sigma_j)(\gamma_i + \sigma_j)}$$

$$\times \left[\left(\Sigma'_{\underset{ik}{P}} \frac{1+\gamma_i}{P} \right)^{(1+\eta_i)/(1+\gamma_i)} + P_i^{1+\eta_i} \right]^{-(\sigma_j - 1)/(\gamma_i + \sigma_j)} \tag{10.9}$$

$$\times \left[\left(\Sigma''_{\underset{kj}{p}} \frac{1-\sigma_j}{p} \right)^{(1-\mu_j)/(1-\sigma)} + P_j^{1-\mu} \right]^{-(\gamma_i + 1)/(\gamma_i + \sigma_j)}$$

Equation (10.9) presents a preliminary version of the theoretical model as applied in our study. If we take the logarithm of equation (10.9), the value of bilateral trade flows is a linear function of income in the two countries, transportation costs, tariffs, benefit factor to trade associated with gaining foreign market information, an export price index for the exporting country, an import price index for the importing country, and domestic prices indices in the two countries.

The main focus of this study is to investigate the impact of contemporary Taiwanese emigrants on bilateral trade flows with their home country, so the study uses bilateral exports and imports between Taiwan and Canada as the dependent variable. The first two variables on the right side of our estimated equation attempt to capture the potential supply and demand, which are the

Taiwan and Canadian nominal GDPs. Because the distance between Taiwan and Canada is fixed, the transportation costs cannot be included in the time series analysis. The third variable is OPEN, which is a country's total trade divided by its GDP to capture openness to trade in the importing country j. This variable is included as a proxy for tariff rates T_{kj} In attempting to measure the impact of emigrants on bilateral trade flows, the cumulative sum of Taiwanese emigrants to Canada, EMI, is a proxy for the benefit factor to trade which decreases with the number of emigrants. Statistical information on emigration is not collected directly in Taiwan, but immigration figures from Taiwan are maintained by the Department of Citizenship & Immigration, Government of Canada. Four price terms in equation (10.9) are proxied by the export unit value index of the exporting country i (PX), the import unit value index of the importing country j (PM) and Taiwan and Canadian GDP deflators (P) to capture the substitution effect. All variables enter the models in the log form. Using our preferred measure of the variables, our investigation of possible contemporary Taiwanese emigrants' effects on Taiwan's export and import trade flows entailed econometrically estimating the following equations:

$$\ln EX_{T,C,t} = a_0 + \alpha_1 \ln Y_{T,t} + \alpha_2 \ln Y_{C,t} + \alpha_3 \ln OPEN_{C,t} + \alpha_4 \ln(\ln EMI_{T,C,t})$$
$$+ \alpha_5 \ln PX_{T,t} + \alpha_6 \ln PM_{C,t} + \alpha_7 \ln P_{T,t} + \alpha_8 \ln P_{C,t} + \mu_t \qquad (10.10)$$

$$\ln IM_{C,T,t} = b_0 + \beta_1 \ln Y_{T,t} + \beta_2 \ln Y_{C,t} + \beta_3 \ln OPEN_{T,t} + \beta_4 \ln(\ln EMI_{T,C,t})$$
$$+ \beta_5 \ln PX_{C,i} + \beta_6 \ln PM_{T,i} + \beta_7 \ln P_{T,t} + \beta_8 \ln P_{C,t} + v_t \qquad (10.11)$$

where:

$EX_{T,C,t}$ =   exports of goods from Taiwan to Canada in US\$ at time t;

$IM_{C,T,t}$ =   imports of goods from Canada into Taiwan in US\$ at time t;

$Y_{T,t}$ and $Y_{C,t}$ = Taiwan and Canada nominal GDP in US\$ at time t;

$OPEN_{T,t}$ and $OPEN_{C,t}$ = openness to trade for Taiwan and Canada at time t;

$EMI_{T,C,t}$ = cumulative sum of Taiwanese emigrants to Canada at time t;

$PX_{T,t}$ and $PX_{C,t}$ = Taiwan and Canada export unit value indices at time t;

$PM_{T,t}$ and $PM_{C,t}$ = Taiwan and Canada import unit value indices at time t;

$P_{T,t}$ and $P_{C,t}$ = Taiwan and Canada GDP deflators at time t;

μ and v_t = i.i.d. error terms and corr $(\mu_t, v_t) = 0$.

Bilateral trade flows and trade price indices are available on a monthly basis; GDP and immigration data are released on a quarterly basis. We decided to use quarterly data by aggregating monthly trade flows and averaging monthly trade price indices for the period 1980:1–1995:1. Sixty-one observations were used. Our choice of 1980 as an initiation date for our sample was dictated by the desire to capture the impact of immigrants in business class on the bilateral trade flows. In 1978, the new Canada Immigration Act became law and attempted to coordinate immigration with manpower requirements and other economic and social policies. The immigrants in the new business classes did not start arriving for at least one year, so we used data starting at 1980.

Immigrants to Canada are classified in three primary categories: (1) Family Class, (2) Humanitarian and compassionate admissions which includes refugee and Designated classes, and (3) Independent classes including those classes of immigrants who do not require sponsorship in Canada, such as the Assisted Relatives Class, Other Independents, Retired Class, and the business classes which consist of the Entrepreneur Class, Self-employed Class and Investor Class (see Appendix for details). The Retired Class was eliminated in August 1991. Taiwanese immigrants to Canada were mainly in one of six classes: Investor, Entrepreneur, Self-employed, Other independent, Family Class, and Assisted Relative Class. The Family Class of immigrants is not subject to the federal points system,[3] while the remaining five classes are subject to this system. The Other Independent and the Assisted Relatives Classes are assessed against economic selection criteria based on the prospective immigrants ability to settle and work in Canada. Business immigrants (Investors, Entrepreneurs and Self-employed) are expected to either make at least a CAD$250,000 investment in a government approved business activity, or to establish a business in Canada.[4] Presently, the Taiwanese immigrants to Canada are comprised mostly from the Investor and Entrepreneur Classes since the new regulations creating the business classes allowed the Taiwanese easier access to Canada. These immigrants tend to possess more market knowledge and connections in their home country than immigrants in other classes. Obviously emigrants will have different effects on bilateral trade flows across these classes. It seems likely that business emigrants will make a greater contribution to bilateral trade with their home country. To test for trade contributions across different categories of immigrants we adopt the approach of Head and Ries (1995) and disaggregate the emigration elasticity of trade to a linear function of the class composition. We define the emigration elasticities of export and import as

$$\varepsilon_{EMI}^{EX} = \frac{\partial \ln EX_{T,C,t}}{\partial \ln EMI_{T,C,t}} = \frac{\partial \ln EX_{T,C,t}}{\partial \ln Z_{T,C,t}} \div \frac{\partial \ln Z_{T,C,t}}{\partial \ln EMI_{T,C,t}} = \alpha_4 \times \frac{1}{\ln EMI_{T,C,t}};$$

(10.12)

$$\varepsilon_{EMI}^{IM} = \frac{\partial \ln IM_{T,C,t}}{\partial \ln EMI_{T,C,t}} = \frac{\partial \ln IM_{T,C,t}}{\partial \ln Z_{T,C,t}} \div \frac{\partial \ln Z_{T,C,t}}{\partial \ln EMI_{T,C,t}} = \beta_4 \times \frac{1}{\ln EMI_{T,C,t}}; \tag{10.13}$$

and disaggregate Taiwanese immigrants to Canada into four categories: (1) Investor Class immigrants; (2) Entrepreneur Class immigrants; (3) Self-employed Class immigrants; (4) Immigrants in other classes excluding business immigrants. The assumption that the emigration elasticities of export and import above are different for four categories is specified as

$$\varepsilon_{EMI}^{EX} = \varepsilon_0^{EX} + \varepsilon_1^{EX} S_I + \varepsilon_E^{EX} S_E + \varepsilon_S^{EX} S_S; \tag{10.14}$$

$$\varepsilon_{EMI}^{IM} = \varepsilon_0^{IM} + \varepsilon_1^{IM} S_I + \varepsilon_E^{IM} S_E + \varepsilon_S^{IM} S_S; \tag{10.15}$$

where:

S_I = the share of Taiwanese Investor Class immigrants to Canada;
S_E = the share of Taiwanese Entrepreneurs Class immigrants to Canada;
S_S = the share of Taiwanese Self-employed Class immigrants to Canada.

We do not define the share of Taiwanese immigrants in other classes in order to avoid perfect collinearity. The emigration elasticities for the four categories (Investor, Entrepreneurs, Self-employed, and other classes), would be $\varepsilon_0 + \varepsilon_1$, $\varepsilon_0 + \varepsilon_E$, $\varepsilon_0 + \varepsilon_S$, and ε_0, if all immigrants from Taiwan were from a particular class. If the source of emigrants from Taiwan are Family Class, Refugee, Designated Class, Assisted Relatives Class, and Other Independents only, the emigration elasticity of trade will be ε_0. If all emigrants from Taiwan are investors, S_I will be 1 and the emigration elasticity of trade will be $\varepsilon_0 + \varepsilon_1$, and similarly for others. We then tested for trade contributions of heterogeneous emigrants by adding three explanatory variables, $S_I \ln[\ln(EMI_{T,C,t})]$, $S_E \ln[\ln(EMI_{T,C,t})]$, and $S_S \ln[\ln(EMI_{T,C,t})]$ in the equations (10.10) and (10.11).

3. EMPIRICAL RESULTS

The analysis in this subsection is designed to (1) examine the roles that emigrants play in the trade-creation effects, and (2) calculate how much bilateral trade heterogeneous emigrants will generate as a result of emigrant-link effects.

3.1 Emigrants' Links to the Home Country

Table 10.1 shows the estimation results for Taiwan–Canada bilateral trade flow equations. Initial ordinary least squares (OLS) estimation of (10.10) and (10.11) indicated that the assumption of constant error variance was violated.

Table 10.1 Estimates of Taiwan–Canada bilateral trade flow equation

	Exports from Taiwan to Canada	Imports from Canada to Taiwan
Taiwan GDP	1.004*	0.658*
	(3.188)	(2.694)
Canada GDP	−0.534	0.007
	(−1.252)	(0.148)
Taiwan openness to trade		1.016*
		(2.729)
Canada openness to trade	0.371*	
	(1.927)	
Emigrants from Taiwan to Canada	3.131*	−0.680
	(2.272)	(−0.369)
Taiwan export unit value price index	−0.341	
	(−0.389)	
Canada export unit value price index		0.779
		(0.866)
Canada import unit value price index	−1.529*	
	(−3.189)	
Taiwan GDP deflator	−0.983	0.315
	(−1.286)	(0.232)
Canada GDP deflator	−0.733	0.906
	(−0.500)	(0.595)
Constant	15.123	−3.557
	(1.649)	(−0.333)
RHO	0.98	0.31
Adjusted R^2	0.96	0.95

Notes:
* indicates significance at the 5 percent levels.
Standard error in parentheses.

The Lagrange multiplier test was applied to check for first to eighth order serial correlation. In the process of estimating these models, the first-order autocorrelation coefficient ρ turned out to be high for both models. Models with autocorrelated errors were estimated so as to correct for the problem. The results suggest that Taiwanese emigrants to Canada have a positive and highly significant effect on Taiwan's exports to Canada but not a significant effect on Taiwan's imports from Canada. The emigration elasticity for exports from Taiwan to Canada in the second quarter of 1993 is approximately 0.3, that is,

$$\varepsilon_{EMI}^{EX} = \alpha_4 \times \frac{1}{\ln(EMI_{T,C,1993:2})} = 3.131 \times \frac{1}{\ln(31,785)} = 0.$$

A 10 percent increase in the stock of Taiwanese emigrants to Canada increases Taiwan's exports to Canada by 3 percent. What is surprising is how significant the estimated elasticity is for exports. If the emigrants' transaction costs are equal for both imports and exports, a comparison of the elasticities indicates that it is easier for Taiwanese emigrants in Canada to set up an importing business in Canada than an exporting business. Taiwan is generally an exporting country more than an importing country and has trade surpluses; Taiwanese business emigrants in Canada already have trade connections with their home country and are quite accustomed to the export of Taiwanese products to other countries and, therefore, the importing of Taiwanese goods to Canada may be just another part of their exporting of knowledge. The Taiwanese immigrants to Canada may require more time in order to establish their trade connections in order to export Canadian goods to Taiwan. Another possible explanation for the significance of elasticity for exports and not for imports is that Taiwanese immigrants in Canada have a greater preference for their home-country products. The positive, significant coefficient on Taiwan GDP in the import regression indicates that Taiwan's national income growth contributes more to imports than other variables.

3.2 Emigrants' Homogeneity

Contemporary Taiwanese emigrants to Canada can be divided into four categories: Investor, Entrepreneurs, Self-employed, and other classes. We allow the coefficient of the emigrant variable ($EMI_{T,C}$) in the original model to interact with three terms (S_I, S_E and S_S) in order to test for class differences. The LM test statistic was applied to check for serial correlation. Again, application of this test found evidence of first order autocorrelation, and the first order autoregressive error was chosen for application. Table 10.2 shows the result of the export regression when the class interaction variables are added. The resulting coefficients should be added to the other classes coefficient to obtain the trade elasticities, respectively. The negative coefficients estimated for Investor Class immigrants suggest that they have a smaller influence on both exports and imports than all other classes of immigrants. If all Taiwanese emigrants were Family Class emigrants, the export elasticity would have been only 0.233 as compared to 0.996 for Self-employed Class emigrants.

Table 10.2 Estimate of export elasticities for emigration by class

	Estimates of Taiwan–Canada export equation	Emigration elasticities for exports in 2nd Quarter of 1993
Taiwan GDP	1.077*	
	(4.730)	
Canada GDP	−0.345	
	(−0.767)	
Canada openness to trade	1.016*	
	(3.006)	
Other classes immigrants	3.174*	0.306
	(2.432)	
Taiwan export unit value price index	−1.101	
	(−1.710)	
Canada import unit value price index	−1.481*	
	(−3.372)	
Taiwan GDP deflator	−0.257	
	(−0.326)	
Canada GDP deflator	−1.382	
	(−0.986)	
Investor class immigrants[a]	−1.043*	−0.206
	(−2.745)	
Entrepreneur class immigrants	0.425	0.347
	(0.119)	
Self-employed class immigrants	8.377*	1.114
	(3.804)	
Constant	12.96	
	(1.167)	
RHO1	0.41	
Adjusted R^2	0.97	

Notes:
a The coefficient should be added to the Other Classes coefficient to obtain the appropriate elasticity.
* indicate significance at the 5 percent levels.

The results support the hypothesis that business immigrants who do intend to establish business in Canada (such as Self-employed and Entrepreneur immigrants) make a greater contribution to bilateral trade due to trade facilitating links to their home country, but the hypothesis is invalid for Investor Class immigrants. One possible explanation for the result is that the major criterion for Taiwanese Investor Class immigrants admitted to Canada was primarily based on the value of their capital assets, and not the significance of their business experience.[5] These Investor Class immigrants therefore did not bring strong trade connections to Canada. The bulk of these Investor Class immigrants to Canada achieved their wealth via capital gain from land or capital stock which dramatically increased in value due to the economic boom in Taiwan. For these persons, $250,000 was not a great deal of money to invest to try to obtain a Canadian passport. A second possible explanation is that the Investor Class immigrants may have retained their business interest in Taiwan and did not bother to expand their business interests to Canada. Asian business emigrants are accustomed to a totally different business environment and a different business 'culture' than that in Canada and they obtain much higher returns per unit of their effort in Asia than in Canada. The Asians are not accustomed to the very high degree of regulation by the government in businesses in Canada and are not accustomed to the high rates of taxation in Canada. It is far easier for them to earn money in Asia than in Canada and they logically would prefer to concentrate their business efforts in their home country rather than Canada. Other Taiwanese immigrants in the Self-employed and Entrepreneur Classes were expected to establish businesses and create jobs for the purpose of removing their terms and conditions of landing and therefore seek to make more significant and serious efforts in Canada. Investor Class immigrants did not have to make this commitment and essentially 'parked' their money for three years in the required investment funds. In other words for this Investor Class, Canada failed to attract the 'real' business people or people prepared to devote their skills to developing business with Canada.

4. CONCLUSION

In the area of immigration, Canada has always played a major role as host to immigrants from all over the world. Canada receives thousands of Taiwanese each year. According to our estimates, the result that Taiwan–Canada bilateral trade is positively influenced by Taiwanese Canadians – with exports from Taiwan being more strongly affected than Canadian imports in Taiwan – suggests that it is easier for new immigrants to set up importing businesses in the receiving country (Canada) than an exporting business to export Canadian goods abroad. Preferences for home country goods also play an important role. In the empirical results we find that the elasticity of Taiwan exports with respect to the stock of Taiwan's emigrants to Canada was roughly 0.3. This finding confirms the hypothesis that immigrant's knowledge and connections can lower the transaction costs associated with international trade. Our results also indicate that Taiwan's out-migration has the potential to exert a significant influence on Taiwan's trade patterns, and contributes more to Taiwan's exports to Canada than imports from Canada. The effect of out-migration on trade varies with the class of immigrant. Self-employed Class immigrants are estimated to have the largest influence on trade, and Investor Class immigrants the least. Investor Class immigrants did not have as large an influence on trade as the other business classes immigrants. From a policy perspective our results suggest that Taiwanese Investor Class emigrants are more difficult than expected to integrate into both Canadian society and the Canadian business environment. The Canadian government must reevaluate whether its business immigration class, as it is now defined, is effective creating Canadian opportunities and what services provided by both governments are most effective in assisting with the settlement and integration process of Taiwanese immigrants to Canada. These are very important questions which can only be addressed through further research.

APPENDIX

Family Class – includes parents, spouses, fiances, and unmarried children of current residents in the country, and their dependents.

Assisted Relatives Class – includes relatives (distant) who, like all independent immigrants, are assessed against economic selection criteria, but also receive 'points' because family members already in Canada are willing to help them to become established.

Convention Refugees – includes those persons who meet the definition specified by the United Nations Refugee Convention.

Designated Class – persons assessed under relaxed immigrant selection criteria for policy reasons.

Investor Class – those persons (and dependents) with a proven track record and substantial net worth who are willing to make a large investment for at least three years in specified government approved investments that will contribute to the creation or continuation of employment opportunities in Canada.

Entrepreneur Class – includes those persons (and dependents) who intend to actively establish or purchase a substantial interest in a business in Canada creating or maintaining employment for more than one Canadian citizen.

Self-employed Class – includes those persons (and dependents) who intend to establish business in Canada that will employ him/herself, and will make a significant contribution to the economy.

Other Independents – includes those persons selected on the basis of the 'point system' which measures the potential for successful establishment in Canada.

Retired Class – For immigration purposes a retiree is an independent immigrant (that is, without sponsorship) 55 years or older with sufficient funds to maintain an adequate life without government aid while living in Canada. This class has been eliminated in August 1991. Current landings in this class were immigrants who started the application prior to the removal of this class.

Business Immigrants – Immigrants in the Entrepreneur, Investor, or Self-employed Class.

Independent Classes – include those classes of immigrants who do not require sponsorship in Canada.

REFERENCES

Bergstrand, J.H. (1985), 'The Gravity equation in international trade: some microeconomic foundations and empirical evidence', *The Review of Economics and Statistics* **67**, pp. 474–81.

Gould, D.M. (1994), 'Immigration link to the home country: empirical implications for U.S. bilateral trade flows', *The Review of Economics and Statistics*, pp. 302–16.

Greenwood, M.J. (1994), 'Potential channels of immigrant influence on the economy of the receiving country', *Papers in Regional Science: The Journal of the RSAI* **73**, pp. 211–40.

Head, K. and J. Ries (1995), 'Immigration and trade creation: econometric evidence from Canada', Working Paper, College of Commerce, University of British Columbia.

NOTES

1. Source: Immigration Statistics Division, Department of Citizenship & Immigration, Government of Canada.

2. Business immigrants consist of immigrants in the Entrepreneur, Investor, and Self-employed Class. Independent classes include those classes of immigrants which do not require sponsorship.

3. The point system assesses a potential immigrant's ability to become successfully established in Canada. The criteria used include educational level, vocational preparation, occupational status, arranged employment, knowledge of an official language, age and other factors.

4. The purpose of the Investment Class was to obtain foreign funds in government approved business schemes that local Canadians were not interested in because of the risk or the low returns.

5. The criteria are set out in the Canada Immigration guidelines.

11. Monopolistic Competition Estimates of Interregional Trade Flows in Services

Frederick Treyz and Jim Bumgardner

1. INTRODUCTION

Regional scientists have often seen localities as the basic units of trade, and have long recognized the important role that service industries play in developing vital economic centres. This perspective on commerce has become increasingly relevant as the trend towards a borderless, post-industrial economy continues. With governments less able to exert control over the movement of labour and capital, fundamental location and transportation issues are more evident in their effects on trade. Even the nature of trade is changing as a result of the rising information economy. In this environment, growth is increasingly dependent on access to specialized knowledge that is most often provided by the service sector.

This study uses a model of monopolistic competition to calculate interregional trade flows in services for counties in Michigan. The monopolistic competition model provides a framework for describing interregional trade in terms of scale economies, preference for variety, transportation costs, and land scarcity at any given location (Krugman 1993; Fujita et al. 1995). Although various formulations of this model emphasize different results, the monopolistic competition models have similar structures. Economies of scale, in combination with preference for variety and transportation costs, result in a large number of specialized firms in the economy. Demand for a variety of products and transportation costs tend to concentrate economic activity while demand for land tends to disperse the location of firms and households; urban systems are in equilibrium when these centripetal and centrifugal forces are in balance. Demand for differentiated output results in trade across locations, as transportation costs are incurred in order to obtain a variety of products.

Urban and regional economics place an emphasis on the agglomeration economies that can be achieved from access to specialized products, both by firms and consumers. The monopolistic competition framework has been employed to explain positive externalities that can be obtained from the use of a variety of differentiated producer service inputs by firms (Rivera-Batiz 1988; Abdel-Rahman and Fujita 1990). Similar approaches have also been taken to explain agglomeration as the result of consumer preference for a variety of good and services (Abdel-Rahman 1988; Fujita 1988; Fujita and Krugman 1995). Ciccone and Hall (1996) use these theoretical approaches as the basis for evaluating large productivity differences in US states. Although their analysis does not directly calculate interregional trade, the authors are able to link high levels of density in the most productive states to increasing returns due to a greater variety of intermediate products.

Despite the apparent relevance of the monopolistic competition approach, this model has not yet been applied to interregional trade in producer services. Although the differentiated product approach has been used to explain international trade, case studies primarily concentrate on manufactured goods (Harris 1984; Deardorff and Stern 1986; and Stern and Brown 1987). In regional analysis, estimation of trade flows can be categorized into survey and non- survey approaches. Surveys provide an important tool to directly measure trade, yet those conducted for producer service industries lack comprehensive detail (Goe 1994; Beyers and Alvine 1985). Non-survey techniques provide for a more thorough characterization of interregional trade since they are based on readily available supply and demand data (Stull and Madden 1990; Treyz and Stevens 1984). These non-survey methods incorporate information on local specialization in production using an accounting framework. However, they do not provide an explicit characterization of underlying economic behaviours and structures.

The approach taken in this chapter is to generate inter-county trade flows in producer services using the monopolistic competition model, assuming fixed supply and demand locations. Assumptions concerning transportation costs and the market structure allow trade flows to be estimated in the absence of survey data. The data required for this method are expenditures and output for the counties in the sample, the distance between counties, the transportation cost per unit of distance, and the elasticity of demand. The elasticity parameter is obtained from a production function estimate for the producer service sector and the observed size of firms in this industry. The system of trade equations is solved by estimating the transportation cost per unit of distance that is most consistent with equilibrium conditions.

The remainder of the chapter proceeds as follows. Section 2 describes the monopolistic competition model of trade. In Section 3, the data sources and methodology used to calculate trade flows are described. Section 4 contains summary calculations of county trade flows in Michigan, and conclusions are presented in Section 5.

2. THE MODEL

The framework of model construction and assumptions is monopolistic competition. Industry shares of local and external markets are based on increasing returns to scale, preference for variety and transportation costs. We provide a summary of this approach only, since it has been described elsewhere (Krugman 1995; Abdel-Rahman 1996).

Model assumptions include the concept that a large number of services are at least potentially available in the economy. Demand agents include consumers and final goods producers. For simplicity, consumer preferences are embodied by a representative consumer and the preferences of the producers of final goods are given by a representative manufacturer. The representative consumer derives utility from the quantity and variety of services consumed, while the representative manufacturer produces using a variety of intermediate service inputs. On the supply side, service firms operate under a monopolistically competitive market structure. Each firm produces one variety using an increasing returns to scale technology. Transportation costs are borne by the consumer as a multiplicative increase in price across locations.

The consumer is assumed to spend a fixed proportion of her budget on the service, which is consistent with a two-stage budgeting procedure with Cobb–Douglas substitutability between the service and a composite commodity. Although preference for a variety of services could be seen as resulting from a diversity of individual tastes, we equivalently show these preferences in a Dixit–Stiglitz (1977) utility function for a representative consumer as follows:

$$U = \left(\sum_h x_h^{(\sigma-1)/\sigma} \right)^{\sigma/(\sigma-1)} \tag{11.1}$$

where x_h is consumption of x units of variety h. The consumer budget constraint is shown as

$$Y = \sum_h p_h x_h \tag{11.2}$$

where Y is the expenditure on the differentiated service, and p_h is the price of x units of each variety h that is consumed.

In a similar fashion, the use of differentiated producer service inputs are assumed to account for a fixed proportion of total expenditures by manufacturing firms, as in a production function with Cobb–Douglas substitution between a composite input and differentiated inputs. Manufacturing technology is assumed to have the constant elasticity of substitution (CES). form with the same elasticity of demand as that for consumers. The profit maximization problem of the representative manufacturer can then be stated as

$$\max \pi = \left(\sum_h x_h^{(\sigma-1)/\sigma} \right)^{\sigma/(\sigma-1)} - \sum_h p_h x_h .$$
(11.3)

Maximization of utility subject to the budget constraint, and profit maximization of manufacturing firms yields the integrated demand function

$$x_h = \frac{Y + Z}{p_h^\sigma \sum_h p_h^{(1-\sigma)}} .$$
(11.4)

where Z is the expenditure by manufacturers on differentiated service inputs.

The supply of services is provided by service firms operating in a market characterized by monopolistic competition. A large number of differentiated services, each of which can be produced by an individual firm, are assumed to exist. Firms enter freely into the market, and ignore the reaction of others. Each variety that is produced employs an increasing returns to scale technology, represented by the following inverse production function,

$$l_h = \alpha + \beta \, x_h .$$
(11.5)

Equation (11.5) shows that a fixed (α) and marginal (β) amount of the total labour (l) is used to produce a unit of output (x).

Transportation costs in service industries include non-monetary transaction costs of distance such as disparities in access to information and the time cost of travel. Various modes of interaction, including telecommunications, parcel post, and face-to-face discussion, may be employed to transport the output of service industries from the supplier to the consumer. For simplicity, we assume that transportation costs increase linearly with distance, and that these costs are paid by the consumer. They are represented in the price difference between locations, shown by:

$$p_{ij} = (1 + \gamma d_{ij}) p_{ii} ,$$
(11.6)

where p_{ij} is the price of a service produced in location i that is consumed in location j, p_{ii} is the f.o.b. price of service i, and d_{ij} is the distance between locations i and j.

The formulation of consumer utility and the manufacturing production function, in combination with multiplicative transportation costs, results in a constant elasticity of demand for service output of F, regardless of the location of production by firms. Service firms face a downward-sloping demand for services, and each firm maximizes profits by choosing the output and price level such that marginal costs are equal to marginal revenues. The f.o.b. price of the service is therefore set at a fixed markup over marginal costs, given by:

$$p_{ii} = \beta \, w_i \left(\frac{\sigma}{\sigma - 1}\right).$$

(11.7)

where w_i is the wage rate in location i.

Free entry of service firms into the market drives profits to zero. Optimal output for each variety can then be shown as:

$$x_h^* = \frac{\alpha}{\beta} (\sigma - 1).$$

(11.8)

Since all service firms produce at the same scale, the number of varieties h at any location is proportional to total output as follows:

$$n_i = \frac{X_i}{x_{hi}}$$

(11.9)

where, in location i, n_i is the number of firms, X_i is total output, and x_{hi} is the optimal production of any one variety as shown in (11.8). We introduce λ_i, the proportion of varieties produced in a given location, as:

$$\lambda_i = \frac{n_i}{\sum_i n_i}.$$

(11.10)

The demand function (11.4) can then be shown as

$$x_{ij} = \frac{\lambda_i (Y_j + Z_j)}{p_{ij}^\sigma \sum_i \lambda_i \, p_{ij}^{(1-\sigma)}}$$

(11.11)

in which x_{ij} is demand for the output produced in location i by consumers in location j, and Y_j and Z_j are, respectively, total consumer and producer expenditure.

3. DATA AND METHODOLOGY

Since comprehensive survey data on service industry trade are not available, this study uses a model calibration approach to estimate trade flows in the service sector. The method allows the determination of shares of local and external markets based on available data relating to supply, expenditure, distances and firm-level technology. Trade is calculated from the demand function derived from the monopolistic competition model shown as equation (11.11) above. Market clearing conditions are imposed by adjusting f.o.b. prices so that supply is equated with demand in all locations.

County-level market shares in the service sector are calculated for the state of Michigan. This industry includes hotels, personal services, business services, auto and miscellaneous repair services, motion pictures, and amusement and recreation services. Trade is calculated using expenditures of firms and households, since both use this category of services. For simplicity, Michigan is represented as a closed economy with respect to the service industry. Key variables and parameters in the demand function are the elasticity of demand (σ), supply proportions (λ_i for all i), total demand (D_i), transportation costs per unit of distance (γ), and the f.o.b. price of output (p_{ii}).

The elasticity of demand is calculated on the basis of the production function estimate and the scale of production of service firms. The inverse production function coefficient estimates are obtained using *1992 Census of Service Industries* observations for all US counties on receipts and paid employees, as follows:

$$l \;=\; 2.98 \quad + \quad 0.0121\, x$$
$$\quad (0.0532) \qquad (0.000102) \qquad\qquad (11.12)$$
$$N = 40$$
$$R^2 = 0.60$$

By rearranging equation (11.8), the elasticity of demand (σ) can be shown as

$$\sigma = \hat{\beta}/\hat{\alpha}\, x_h^* + 1 \qquad\qquad (11.13)$$

where $\hat{\alpha}$ and $\hat{\beta}$ are estimated fixed and marginal labour requirements, respectively, and x_h^* is the optimal level of output for any one firm, which is assumed to be represented by the observed scale of production for firms in Michigan. The median company size in services in the sample is 11.68 employees, and the median output per employee is 48,470 dollars. These values are used to calculate x_h^*, the output for the typical service firm, as 566,000 dollars per year. Substituting this value and the estimated production function parameters into equation (11.13), the elasticity of demand (σ) is calculated to equal 3.31.

Expenditure ($Y_j + Z_j$) takes the form of final demand and intermediate demand. Intermediate demand is calculated from the Bureau of Labor Statistics national input–output table and the regional output of industries. Final demand is obtained from final demand coefficients for the industry times the total demand from income, construction, federal government, and state and local government (see Regional Economic Models, Inc. 1996, for details).

Since all firms are assumed to produce on the same scale, the proportion of varieties available at any given location (λ_i) is equal to the fraction of total service output in that location. United States *1992 Census of Service Industries* data on receipts is used to estimate supply proportions for all counties in Michigan. The supply proportion is then calculated as

$$\lambda_i = \frac{S_i}{\sum_i S_i} \in [0,1] .$$

(11.14)

where S_i is the observed supply of services in county i.

The supply value proportions that are obtained from the demand equation (11.11) are called estimated proportions, shown in:

$$\lambda_i = \frac{\sum_j x_{ij}}{\sum_i \sum_j x_{ij}} \in [0,1]$$

(11.15)

By choice of units, and given our assumption of complete labour mobility, the price of output in (11.7) can be set equal to unity. The location of county supply and demand is represented by a point at the centre of each county. Distances between counties are assumed to be represented by a straight line between the central points. Including transportation costs and a multiplicative adjustment, M_i , the price of j of output produced in i is given by:

$$P_{ij} = M_i(1 + \gamma d_{ij}) .$$

(11.16)

The demand equations can then be shown in (11.17) and (11.18) as

$$x_{ij} = \frac{\lambda_i D_j}{p_{ij}^{\sigma} \sum_i \lambda_i p_{ij}^{1-\sigma}} ,$$

(11.17)

and

$$D_j = \sum_i P_{ij} x_{ij} .$$

(11.18)

In equations (11.15)–(11.18), γ is unknown. For every γ, however, we can find a unique set of Ms such that

$$\hat{\lambda}_i = f_i(M_1, M_2, ..., M_n \mid \gamma) = \lambda_i \; \forall \; i .$$

(11.19)

Then, we have sets of Ms conditioned on each γ that we evaluate. The difference in the Ms from unity is caused by data error, unobserved productivity differences, and disequilibrium in the economy. Since we have no further information on data or productivity differences, we select the most reasonable set of Ms based on the criterion of equilibrium. With no a priori reason to suggest that the economy is in disequilibrium, we assume that the most plausible set of Ms is the one in which the economy is most closely in equilibrium. Therefore, the value of γ that minimizes the variance in the supply weighted variance of the Ms is used to calibrate the model. This γ is

$$\underset{\gamma}{\arg \min} \sum_{i=1}^{n} [M_i(\gamma) - 1]^2 \left(\frac{S_i}{S}\right) .$$

(11.20)

The assumptions of uniform production costs and fixed supply and demand imply a trivial solution to equations (11.17) and (11.18) of γ equal to zero. Therefore the estimated transportation cost used to calculate trade flows for service industries represents a local solution to (11.20) that is in accordance with positive and not insignificant transportation costs. For the service sector, the transportation cost parameter γ is estimated to be 0.11 per mile of distance d_{ij}. This can be interpreted as an 11 percent increase in the effective price of services for every mile of distance travelled. For example, the cost of attending a motion picture in a cinema located next to the residence of a consumer would be one half of the total cost of attending the same film ten miles distant. Summary results of the estimation are presented in the following section.

4. RESULTS

This section presents estimates of trade flows for the service sector in Michigan. Using data and estimated parameters described in Section 3, an 83 × 83 county trade flow matrix is calculated for the state. Summary results are presented for major regions of Michigan, for counties in the Detroit–Ann Arbor Consolidated Metropolitan Statistical Area (*CMSA*), and for the proportion of local demand supplied locally for all counties in Michigan.

For the purpose of summarizing the results, the state is divided into six major regions, shown in Figure 11.1. These regions are: (1) the Detroit–Ann Arbor *CMSA*, (2) the rest of southeastern Michigan, (3) the Central/Capitol region, (4) the Southwest/Grand Rapids region, (5) the north Lower Peninsula, and (6) the Upper Peninsula. All of southern Michigan is industrialized and densely populated. Region 1, the Detroit metropolitan area, represents one of the largest urban agglomerations in the US, and is synonymous with the American automobile industry. The rest of southeastern Michigan (Region 2) is also dependent on this industry. The Central/Capitol region (Region 3) includes the state capitol, Lansing, in Ingham county. Grand Rapids, a large industrial city in Kent county, forms the core of the Southwestern region (Region 4). Both the northern Lower Peninsula (Region 5) and the Upper Peninsula (Region 6) are more sparsely populated and rural.

Table 11.1 presents summary trade flows for the major regions of Michigan. The summary results are obtained by aggregating trade flows that are calculated for 83 × 83 counties to six major regions. The row and column sums illustrate the relative magnitude of the regions, and the dominance of the Detroit *CMSA* in particular. Since services are supplied locally even on a sub-county basis, almost all deliveries occur within major regions. Thus, on an aggregate level, the model estimation illustrates the limited nature of trade across large distances in the service industry.

The asymmetrical trade relationships among the regions in Table 11.1 demonstrates the ability of the monopolistic competition model to represent the hierarchical structure of trade. Region 1 produces almost two-thirds of total service output in Michigan and supplies the greatest quantity of differentiated services available in the state. Therefore, Detroit area consumers and manufacturing firms do not need to purchase many services from outside of this region, since sufficiently specialized services are available internally. Additionally, other purchasing regions may be willing to pay high transportation costs in order to have access to distinct services produced in the Detroit area. Thus, Region 1 supplies more than ten times the value of services to each of the other regions than it purchases from them.

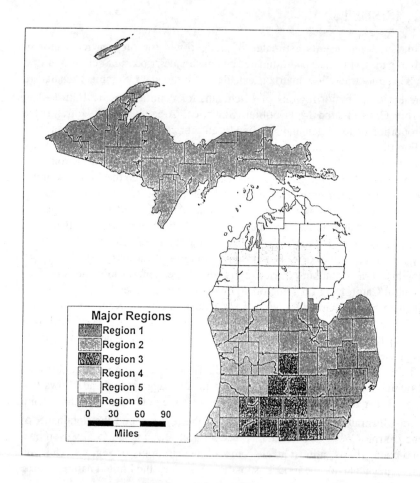

Figure 11.1 Major regions in Michigan

Trade flow estimations are presented for the eight counties of the Detroit–Ann Arbor *CMSA,* a subset of the 83-county interregional matrix, in Table 11.2. By far the largest share of trade occurs within, rather than among, counties. This is in part a result of the representation of counties as a single point, so that inter-county trade between neighbouring locations on the border of counties is not fully captured. Urban and suburban trade patterns are more fully accounted for in the trade matrix. An example of this is the trade pattern between Lapeer county, on the edge of the metropolitan area, and the much more urban Oakland county. While Oakland supplies over 99 percent of the services it uses within the metropolitan area to itself, Lapeer self-supplies less than half of its own purchases. Also, the trade pattern between the two counties is uneven, reflecting the greater variety of services offered by Oakland county. Thus, the use of services produced in Oakland by Lapeer are much greater than trade in the opposite direction.

Table 11.1   Trade flows within Detroit–Ann Arbor consolidated metropolitan statistical area (CMSA)

Region Selling	Region Purchasing						
	1	2	3	4	5	6	Total
1	23.61117	0.45114	0.23023	0.06322	0.04621	0.01360	24.41556
2	0.04099	2.72490	0.02834	0.01888	0.02407	0.00226	2.83943
3	0.02391	0.02968	3.50308	0.07939	0.00599	0.00197	3.64402
4	0.00146	0.00904	0.03100	4.32270	0.01440	0.00284	4.38143
5	0.00095	0.01127	0.00214	0.01328	1.27435	0.00806	1.31005
6	0.00003	0.00011	0.00007	0.00023	0.00244	0.65559	0.65847
Total	23.67852	3.22613	3.79486	4.49771	1.36746	0.68431	37.24899

The estimated proportion of local demand supplied locally for all counties in Michigan is shown in Figure 11.2. This statistic, also called the regional purchase coefficient (RPC), is computed as follows:

$$RPC_j = \frac{x_{jj}}{\sum_i x_{ij}}$$

(11.21)

where the numerator is the value of services supplied locally to county j and the denominator is the total value of services shipped from all locations to j. The map shows regional purchase coefficients ranging from 0.44 in Lapeer County to 0.99 in Oakland County. The RPCs are highest in isolated counties, where demand stays in the locality due to high transportation costs, and in cities, where specialized services are readily available. Rural counties surrounding cities, such as the areas around Grand Rapids or the edge of Detroit, have the lowest regional purchase coefficients. These counties have relatively fewer varieties available, and transportation costs to urban areas with an abundance of differentiated services are comparatively low.

Table 11.2 Trade flows for major regions of Michigan

Region Selling	Region Purchasing									
	Lapeer	Livingston	Macomb	Monroe	Oakland	St. Clair	Washtenaw	Wayne	Rest of State	Total
Lapeer	0.07154	0.00027	0.00335	0.00013	0.00160	0.00139	0.00027	0.00135	0.00979	0.089703
Livingston	0.00038	0.22341	0.00106	0.00090	0.00224	0.0032	0.00853	0.00404	0.03403	0.274902
Macomb	0.00585	0.00135	2.83312	0.00193	0.01164	0.03513	0.00220	0.02867	0.02845	2.94834
Monroe	0.00009	0.00045	0.00076	0.21771	0.00060	0.00019	0.00306	0.00913	0.00671	0.238688
Oakland	0.06659	0.06783	0.27713	0.03626	9.38893	0.04625	0.08289	0.63545	0.56730	11.16863
St. Clair	0.00053	0.00009	0.00763	0.00011	0.00042	0.26024	0.00013	0.00101	0.00420	0.274349
Washtenaw	0.00084	0.01967	0.00400	0.01420	0.00633	0.00108	1.55143	0.03045	0.09128	1.719282
Wayne	0.00323	0.00705	0.03944	0.03202	0.03671	0.00639	0.02303	7.49117	0.06264	7.701675
Rest of State	0.00530	0.01511	0.00698	0.00340	0.00901	0.00343	0.01230	0.01182		
Total	0.15435	0.33522	3.17347	0.30666	9.45747	0.35443	1.68383	8.21307		

Region 1: Detroit–Ann Arbor *CMSA* (Lapeer, St. Clair, Macomb, Oakland, Livingston, Washtenaw, Wayne, Monroe)
Region 2: Rest of southeastern Michigan (Sanilac, Huron, Tuscola, Genesee, Saginaw, Bay, Shiawassee, Gratiot, Midland, Isabella)
Region 3: Central/Capital Region (Lenawee, Hillsdale, Branch, St. Joseph, Kalamazoo, Calhoun, Jackson, Ingham, Eaton, Clinton)
Region 4: Southwest/Grand Rapids Regions (Cass, Berrien, Van Buren, Allegan, Barry, Ottawa, Kent, Ionia, Montcalm, Mecosta, Newaygo, Muskegon, Oceana)
Region 5: Northern Lower Peninsula (Mason, Lake, Osecola, Clare, Gladwin, Arenac, Iosco, Ogemaw, Roscommon, Missaukee, Lexford, Manistee, Benzie, Grand Traverse, Kalkaska, Crawford, Oscoda, Alcona, Alpena, Montmorency, Otsego, Antrim, Leelanau, Charlevoix, Emmet, Cheboygan, Presque Isle)
Region 6: Upper Peninsulka (Gogebic, Ontonagon, Keweenaw, Houghton, Baraga, Iron, Dickinson, Menominee, Marquette Alger, Delta, Schoolcraft, Luce, Mackinac, Chippewa)

Source: Regional Economic Models, Inc., September 1996

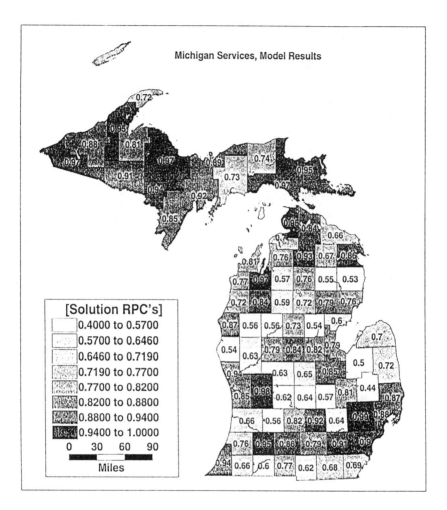

Figure 11.2 Proportion of local demand supplied locally

5. CONCLUSION

Product differentiation is the basis of agglomeration economies and trade in many theoretical regional and urban models. Additionally, access to a variety of specialized services and a strong service sector is seen as particularly important to the future viability of nations, regions and cities. Within this context, the monopolistic competition framework has been suggested as a way in which trade in differentiated products can be modelled. This chapter demonstrates the feasibility of this approach by developing monopolistic competition model estimates for service sector trade in small, open economies.

Results for the monopolistic competition model case study are presented for the total service sector for all Michigan counties. Summary measures shown in this chapter are consistent with acceptable values for regional purchase coefficients and interregional trade. The trade flow estimates also demonstrate the ability of the monopolistic competition model to represent the hierarchical nature of interregional trade. Thus, urban counties that provide a large variety of specialized services are shown to export a relatively high proportion of output, while satisfying their internal demand locally. Based on these results, the monopolistic competition model appears to be a very promising direction for applied structural modelling. This empirical demonstration is especially significant because the monopolistic competition framework provides the foundation of many theoretical urban and regional models.

A method to calibrate the monopolistic competition model is illustrated for the total service sector. This calibration represents a test case taken from a larger set of estimations conducted for other and more detailed industries. Although the technique performs well for the aggregate sector, it is possible to evaluate more detailed trade relationships at disaggregate levels. Within the general service sector, for example, coin-operated laundries may be much more locally oriented than colleges and universities. The price elasticities and transportation costs for these disaggregate industries may be quite different. In particular, trade flow estimates carried out for legal services and for engineering services each showed much greater interregional exports and imports than the total service sector.

Research directions include comparison of model results with surveys, extension of the model to include a full general equilibrium system, investigation into the dynamic response of the monopolistic competition model, and evaluation of the connection between access to specialized services and regional amenities and productivity. Although the lack of comprehensive survey data limits the types of statistical approaches that can be taken to estimate trade flows, some survey information is available. This information can provide a basis for evaluation of the results presented in this chapter. The partial equilibrium model presented in this chapter can be extended to include additional elements of full general equilibrium constructions. It is also possible to simulate the effects of parameter changes in either a partial or general equilibrium system.

The importance of the monopolistic competition model as an explanation for agglomeration economies suggests that the connection between access to specialized products and regional productivity and amenities should be more fully explored. In this chapter, estimates of trade in services, in combination with underlying consumption and production functions, imply differing utility and productivity levels across locations. These relationships can be made more explicit, and evaluated in comparison with observed levels of productivity.

REFERENCES

Abdel-Rahman, H.M. (1988), 'Product differentiation, monopolistic competition, and city size', *Regional Science and Urban Economics* **18**, pp. 69–86.

Abdel-Rahman, H.M. (1996), 'When do cities specialize in production?, *Regional Science and Urban Economics* **26**, pp. 1–21.

Abdel-Rahman, H.M. and M. Fujita (1990), 'Product variety, Marshallian externalities, and city sizes', *Journal of Regional Science* **30**, pp. 165–83.

Beyers, W.B. and M.J. Alvine (1985), 'Export services in postindustrial society', *Papers of the Regional Science Association* **57**, pp. 33–45.

Brown, D.K. and R.M. Stern (1987), 'A modelling perspective', in Stern, R.M., Trezise, P.H. and J. Whalley (eds), *Perspectives on a U.S.–Canadian Free Trade Agreement*, Washington: The Brookings Institution.

Ciccone, A. and R.E. Hall (1996), 'Productivity and the density of economic activity', *American Economic Review* **86**, pp. 54–70.

Deardorff, A.V. and R.M. Stern (1986), *The Michigan Model of World Production and Trade*, Cambridge, Massachusetts: MIT Press.

Dixit, A.K. and J.E. Stiglitz (1977), 'Monopolistic competition and optimum product diversity', *American Economic Review* **67**, pp. 297–308.

Fujita, M. (1988), 'A monopolistic competition model of spatial agglomeration: differentiated product approach', *Regional Science and Urban Economics* **18**, pp. 87–124.

Fujita, M. and P. Krugman (1995), 'When is the economy monocentric?: von Thünen and Chamberlin unified', *Regional Science and Urban Economics* **25**, pp. 505–28.

Fujita, M., Krugman P. and T. Mori (1995), *On the Evolution of Hierarchical Urban Systems*, manuscript.

Goe, W.R. (1994), 'The producer services sector and development within the deindustrializing urban community', *Social Forces* **72**, pp. 971–1009.

Harris, R.G. (1984), 'Applied general equilibrium analysis of small open economies with scale economies and imperfect competition', *American Economic Review* **74**, pp. 1016–32.

Krugman, P. (1993), 'First nature, second nature, and metropolitan location', *Journal of Regional Science* **33**, pp. 129–44.

Krugman, P. (1995), *Development, Geography, and Economic Theory*, Cambridge, Massachusetts: The MIT Press.

Regional Economic Models, Inc. (REMI) (1996), 'Model documentation for the REMI EDFS-53 forecasting and simulation model 1', REMI Reference Set.

Rivera-Batiz, F.L. (1988), 'Increasing returns, monopolistic competition, and agglomeration economies', *Regional Science and Urban Economics* **18**, pp. 125–53.

Stull, W.J. and J.F. Madden (1990), 'The emergence of a producer service economy in the Philadelphia PMSA', *Post-Industrial Philadelphia: Structural Changes in the Metropolitan Economy*, Philadelphia: University of Pennsylvania Press, pp. 44–66.

Treyz, G.I. and B.H. Stevens (1984), 'The TFS regional modelling methodology, *Regional Studies* **19**, pp. 547–62.

U.S. Bureau of the Census (1992), *Census of Service Industries*, Washington, D.C.

12. The Region Versus the Rest of the Economy: the Extraction Method

Michael Sonis, Geoffrey J.D. Hewings and Eduardo Haddad

1. INTRODUCTION

In recent years, there has been a renewed interest in the notion of key sectors and the elaboration of these ideas through the *extraction method*. Initial interest was stimulated by Strassert (1968a, b) and continued by Schultz (1973, 1976, 1977). Interpretation in the form of attention to backward and forward linkages may be found in the work of Cella (1984, 1986); Milana (1985); Clements (1990); Clements and Rossi (1991, 1992); Guccione (1986); Heimler (1991); Dietzenbacher (1992); Dietzenbacher et al. (1993) and Guilhoto et al. (1994, 1995). In this chapter, this work will be revisited from the viewpoint of partitioned input–output analysis; the perspective is different in that the focus of attention is not on the extraction of a sector (or region, in the case of a multiregional system) but on the consideration of the hierarchy of sectors (regions) and the rest of the economy and their synergetic interactions. This method may prove to be more flexible, especially in cases where interest is directed to several sectors or regions. In the next section, the approaches proposed by Cella (1984, 1986) and Dietzenbacher (1992) will be reviewed. The link with Miyazawa's (1976) formulations and some further extensions by Sonis and Hewings (1993, 1995) will be presented in Section 3. In Section 4, a hierarchical decomposition for a region versus the rest of the economy will be outlined. Using countries as regions, Section 5 will focus on the nature of these hierarchies for the European Union. The chapter will conclude with some evaluation in the final section.

2. THE CELLA AND DIETZENBACHER APPROACHES

Consider the multiregional, multisectoral input–output system given by the block matrix of direct inputs:

$$A = \| A_{ij} \|,$$

$$(12.1)$$

where each block, A_{ij}, represents the direct inputs of products from region i per unit of output in region j. The familiar input–output model is given by the system of equations:

$$x = Ax + f; \quad x = (I - A)^{-1} f = Bf,$$

$$(12.2)$$

where the matrix $B = \| B_{ij} \|$ is the Leontief inverse and x and f vectors of total outputs and final demands, respectively. For each region, j, one can write:

$$A = \begin{pmatrix} A_{jj} & A_{jR} \\ A_{Rj} & A_{RR} \end{pmatrix}; B = \begin{pmatrix} B_{jj} & B_{jR} \\ B_{Rj} & B_{RR} \end{pmatrix}; f = \begin{pmatrix} f_j \\ f_R \end{pmatrix}; x = \begin{pmatrix} x_j \\ x_R \end{pmatrix},$$

$$(12.3)$$

where, in this case, the index j corresponds to the region and R to the rest of the economy.

Cella (1984) and Dietzenbacher (1992) used the following decomposition of (12.3):

$$A = \begin{pmatrix} A_{jj} & A_{jR} \\ A_{Rj} & A_{RR} \end{pmatrix} = \begin{pmatrix} A_{jj} & 0 \\ 0 & A_{RR} \end{pmatrix} + \begin{pmatrix} 0 & A_{jR} \\ A_{Rj} & 0 \end{pmatrix} = A_1 + A_2,$$

$$(12.4)$$

where the block diagonal matrix, A_1, includes only the intraregional linkages for region j and for the rest of the economy, R. Matrix A_2, on the other hand, records the linkages between the two economies. Further,

$$B_1 = (I - A_1)^{-1} = \begin{pmatrix} B_j & 0 \\ 0 & B_R \end{pmatrix}; x_1 = B_1 f = \begin{pmatrix} B_j f_j \\ B_R f_R \end{pmatrix},$$

$$(12.5)$$

where,

$$B_j = (I - A_{jj})^{-1}, B_R = (I - A_{RR})^{-1}$$

$$(12.6)$$

are the internal Miyazawa (1976) multipliers for region j and the rest of the economy, R. The total linkage effect is measured by:

$$X - X_1 = Bf - B_1 f = \begin{pmatrix} B_{jj} - B_j & B_{jR} \\ B_{Rj} & B_{RR} - B_R \end{pmatrix} \begin{pmatrix} f_j \\ f_R \end{pmatrix} . \tag{12.7}$$

It is interesting to note here that the decompositions (12.4) and (12.7) were used in a different context by Goodwin (1980) and Stone (1985).

Cella (1984), however, measured the total linkage effect, TL, as a sum of components of the vector $x - x_1$:

$$TL = (1, 1, ..., 1)(x - x_1) \tag{12.8}$$

Further, he suggested that the following decomposition of total linkages could be made into their backward and forward parts:

$$TL = (1,1,...,1)(B_{jj} - B_j + B_{Rj}) f_j + (1,1,...,1)(B_{jR} + B_{RR} - B_R)f_R = BL + FL \tag{12.9}$$

This presentation is associated with the following matrix decompositions:

$$x - x_1 = \begin{pmatrix} B_{jj} - B_j & 0 \\ B_{Rj} & 0 \end{pmatrix} \begin{pmatrix} f_j \\ f_R \end{pmatrix} + \begin{pmatrix} 0 & B_{jR} \\ 0 & B_{RR} - B_R \end{pmatrix} \begin{pmatrix} f_j \\ f_R \end{pmatrix} \tag{12.10}$$

$$x - x_1 = \begin{pmatrix} B_{jj} - B_R & B_{jR} \\ B_{Rj} & B_{RR} - B_R \end{pmatrix} \begin{pmatrix} f_j \\ 0 \end{pmatrix} + \begin{pmatrix} B_{jj} - B_R & B_{jR} \\ B_{Rj} & B_{RR} - B_R \end{pmatrix} \begin{pmatrix} 0 \\ f_R \end{pmatrix} \tag{12.11}$$

Both decompositions (12.10) and (12.11), after the summation of suitable vector components, will provide the result shown in (12.9). Thus, there exist at least two different mechanisms for the derivation of backward and forward linkages.

Dietzenbacher et al. (1993) used the same formulation as (12.9) but interpreted this as the backward dependence of region j on the rest of the economy as well as the backward dependence of the rest of the economy on j. For the measurement of forward linkages, Dietzenbacher et al. (1993) used the dual supply-driven Ghosh–Augustinovics input–output model with its allocation coefficients and associated inverse. In this case, the backward and forward linkages are derived from different input–output models.

3. INTERPRETATION OF THE FINE STRUCTURE OF REGIONAL BACKWARD AND FORWARD LINKAGES THROUGH THE MIYAZAWA MATRIX MULTIPLIERS

In this section, the analysis will focus on the fine structure of the backward and forward linkages, drawing on some of the ideas initially developed by Miyazawa (1976) and extended by Sonis and Hewings (1993). Let matrix A be defined as the sum of two matrices:

$$A = A_1 + A_2 .$$

Then:

$$(I - A)^{-1} = (I - A_1 - A_2)^{-1} = G_2 G_1 = G_1 - (G_2 - I) G_1 , \qquad (12.12)$$

where:

$$G_1 = (I - A_1)^{-1} ,$$

$$G_2 = (I - G_1 A_2)^{-1} \qquad (12.13)$$

Using these definitions, the following decomposition may be revealed:

$$A = \begin{pmatrix} A_{jj} & A_{jR} \\ A_{Rj} & A_{RR} \end{pmatrix} = \begin{pmatrix} A_{jj} & 0 \\ A_{Rj} & 0 \end{pmatrix} + \begin{pmatrix} 0 & A_{jR} \\ 0 & A_{RR} \end{pmatrix} = A_1 + A_2 \qquad (12.14)$$

and from (12.14) the factorization expression of the Leontief inverse may now be presented (see Sonis and Hewings 1993):

$$B = (I - A)^{-1} = \begin{pmatrix} B_{jj} & B_{jR} \\ B_{Rj} & B_{RR} \end{pmatrix} = \begin{pmatrix} \Delta_{jj} & 0 \\ 0 & \Delta_{RR} \end{pmatrix} \begin{pmatrix} I & B_j A_{jR} \\ B_R A_{Rj} & I \end{pmatrix} \begin{pmatrix} B_j & 0 \\ 0 & B_R \end{pmatrix} , \qquad (12.15)$$

where:

$$B_j = (I - A_{jj})^{-1} ; B_R = (I - A_{RR})^{-1} \qquad (12.16)$$

are the Miyazawa internal multipliers for the region j and the rest of the economy, R, and:

$$\Delta_{jj} = (I - B_j A_{jR} B_R A_{Rj})^{-1} ; \Delta_{RR} = (I - B_R A_{Rj} B_j A_{jR})^{-1} \qquad (12.17)$$

are the external multipliers for region j influenced by the rest of the economy, R, and the rest of the economy influenced by region j.

Solving the RHS of (12.15) will yield the Schur–Miyazawa formula (see Miyazawa 1976):

$$
B = \begin{pmatrix} \Delta_{jj}B_{jj} & \Delta_{jj}B_{j}A_{jR}B_{R} \\ \Delta_{RR}B_{R}A_{Rj}B_{j} & \Delta_{RR}B_{R} \end{pmatrix} = \begin{pmatrix} \Delta_{j} & \Delta_{j}A_{jR}B_{R} \\ \Delta_{R}A_{Rj}B_{j} & \Delta_{R} \end{pmatrix} ,
\tag{12.18}
$$

where:

$$
\Delta_{j} = \Delta_{jj}B_{j} = (I - A_{jj} - A_{jR}B_{R}A_{Rj})^{-1} ,
$$

$$
\Delta_{R} = \Delta_{RR}B_{R} = (I - A_{RR} - A_{Rj}B_{j}A_{jR})^{-1}
\tag{12.19}
$$

are the internal multipliers of regions j and R, respectively, influenced by actions in the other region. Moreover:

$$
B_{j}A_{jR}\Delta_{R} = \Delta_{j}A_{jR}B_{R} ,
$$

$$
B_{R}A_{Rj}\Delta_{j} = \Delta_{R}A_{Rj}B_{j} .
\tag{12.20}
$$

Thus, the inner structure of the row multipliers of the Leontief inverse, B, are defined by the summation of the components of the block row:

$$
(\Delta_{j} \quad \Delta_{j}A_{jR}B_{R})
\tag{12.21}
$$

and the inner structure of the column multipliers are defined by the summation of the components of the block column:

$$
\begin{pmatrix} \Delta_{j} \\ B_{R}A_{Rj}\Delta_{j} \end{pmatrix} .
\tag{12.22}
$$

Since the row and column multipliers represent the sectoral backward and forward linkages, (12.21) and (12.22) provide the fine structure of these linkages, interpreted with the help of the Miyazawa multipliers. Note that both the backward and forward linkages are defined using the Leontief coefficient system. Further, the summation of the rows and columns of the Miyazawa multiplier, Δ_{j}, will reveal the sectoral intraregional forward and backward linkages while the summation of the rows of the matrix, $\Delta_{j}A_{jR}B_{R}$, will provide the sectoral interregional forward linkages for region j. Similarly, the summation of the columns of the matrix, $B_R A_{Rj} \Delta_j$, reveals the sectoral interregional backward linkages. Obviously, one could aggregate all the sectors in region j; in this case, the summations of the matrix, Δ_j, will give the aggregate intraregional linkages while the summation of elements of the matrices, $\Delta_j A_{jR} B_R$ and $B_R A_{Rj} \Delta_j$, will yield the aggregate interregional forward and backward linkages. This aggregation might be useful in attempting to gauge the degree of internal versus external dependence that might exist in a multiregional system of economies. In this case, there are some strong parallels with the extraction of complete feedback loops in the process of determining the degree of self-influence that might exist within a set of economies (see Sonis et al. 1993, 1995).

4.   THE REGION VERSUS THE REST OF THE ECONOMY: HIERARCHICAL DECOMPOSITIONS

It is important to stress that in the block matrix of direct inputs, $A = \|A_{ij}\|$, all information about the region j lies in the following matrix cross:

$$
C_j = \begin{pmatrix}
0 & \cdots & 0 & A_{1j} & 0 & \cdots & 0 \\
0 & \cdots & 0 & A_{2j} & 0 & \cdots & 0 \\
\vdots & \cdots & \vdots & \vdots & \vdots & \cdots & \vdots \\
A_{j1} & \cdots & A_{jj-1} & A_{jj} & A_{jj+1} & \cdots & A_{jn} \\
\vdots & \cdots & \vdots & \vdots & \vdots & \cdots & \vdots \\
0 & \cdots & 0 & A_{nj} & 0 & \cdots & 0
\end{pmatrix} \qquad (12.23)
$$

Thus, the extraction of region j from the economy that was given previously in the form,

$$
A = \begin{pmatrix}
A_{jj} & A_{jR} \\
A_{Rj} & A_{RR}
\end{pmatrix}
$$

can now be connected with the construction of the cross:

$$C_j = \begin{pmatrix} A_{jj} & A_{jR} \\ A_{Rj} & 0 \end{pmatrix}$$

(12.24)

It is important to stress that the analysis is essentially dependent upon the hierarchical viewpoint; there are two possible hierarchies, (1) *region versus the rest of the economy* in which region j is placed at the top of the hierarchy and (2) *the rest of the economy versus the region*, in which the order is reversed. Thus, there exist two identical additive decompositions:

$$A = \begin{pmatrix} A_{jj} & A_{jR} \\ A_{Rj} & A_{RR} \end{pmatrix} = \begin{pmatrix} A_{jj} & A_{jR} \\ A_{Rj} & 0 \end{pmatrix} + \begin{pmatrix} 0 & 0 \\ 0 & A_{RR} \end{pmatrix} = C_j + A_R,$$

(12.25)

$$A = \begin{pmatrix} A_{jj} & A_{jR} \\ A_{Rj} & A_{RR} \end{pmatrix} = \begin{pmatrix} 0 & 0 \\ 0 & A_{RR} \end{pmatrix} + \begin{pmatrix} A_{jj} & A_{jR} \\ A_{Rj} & 0 \end{pmatrix} = A_R + C_j$$

(12.26)

However, the corresponding multiplicative decompositions of the Leontief inverse for the two hierarchies (12.25) and (12.26) are very different. The methodology illustrated here represents but one of several approaches (see Sonis et al. 1997b for a typology of decompositions); one of the major contributions of the methodology is that it introduces, explicitly, the notion of an hierarchy of economic subsystems in the consideration of the influences of changes in a multi-economy system. The particular hierarchy that was chosen focuses on the viewpoint of the region in the context of a broader economic system while the other hierarchy takes an alternative perspective, placing primary emphasis on the viewpoint of the rest of the economy and its interaction with a particular region.

4.1 Decomposition of the Leontief Inverse Matrix and Gross Output Associated with the Hierarchy: Region Versus the Rest of the Economy

First of all, consider the regional cross (12.24) and calculate its Leontief inverse, $B(C_j) = (I - C_j)^{-1}$. As noted in Sonis and Hewings (1993), this Leontief inverse can be presented as a product:

$$B(C_j) = \begin{pmatrix} B_{jj}(C_j) & B_{jR}(C_j) \\ B_{Rj}(C_j) & B_{RR}(C_j) \end{pmatrix} = \begin{pmatrix} I & 0 \\ A_{Rj} & I \end{pmatrix} \begin{pmatrix} \Delta(C_j) & \Delta(C_j)A_{jR} \\ A_{Rj}\Delta(C_j) & 1 + A_{Rj}\Delta(C_j)A_{jR} \end{pmatrix} \begin{pmatrix} 1 & A_{jR} \\ 0 & I \end{pmatrix} =$$

$$= \begin{pmatrix} \Delta(C_j) & \Delta(C_j)A_{jR} \\ A_{Rj}\Delta(C_j) & 1 + A_{Rj}(C_j)A_{jR} \end{pmatrix} \tag{12.27}$$

where the enlarged regional Leontief inverse is:

$$\Delta_j(C_j) = (I - A_{jj} - A_{jR}A_{Rj})^{-1} \tag{12.28}$$

Comparing (12.27) with (12.18) and (12.20) provides:

$$B_{jR}(C_j) = \Delta_j(C_j)A_{jR} = B_jA_{jR}B_{RR}(C_j) \tag{12.29}$$

In this triple decomposition, the block matrices:

$$\begin{pmatrix} I & 0 \\ A_{Rj} & I \end{pmatrix} \text{ and } \begin{pmatrix} I & A_{jR} \\ 0 & 1 \end{pmatrix}$$

reflect the direct backward and forward interregional linkages for region j and the block diagonal matrix

$$\begin{pmatrix} \Delta(C_j) & 0 \\ 0 & I \end{pmatrix}$$

represents the intraregional economic linkages under the influence of the external interregional backward and forward linkages.

Further, if the decomposition (12.12) is applied to the hierarchy (12.25), the following is obtained:

$$A = C_j + A_R,$$

where

$$A_R = \begin{pmatrix} 0 & 0 \\ 0 & A_{RR} \end{pmatrix},$$

and

$$B = (I - A)^{-1} = (I - C_j - A_R)^{-1} = G_2^* G_1^* = G_1^* + (G_2^* - I)G_1^* \; , \quad (12.30)$$

where:

$$G_1^* = B(C_j) + (I - C_j)^{-1} \; ,$$

and

$$G_2^* = (I - G_1^* A_R)^{-1} = \left[I - \begin{pmatrix} B_{jj}(C_j) & B_{jR}(C_j) \\ B_{Rj}(C_j) & B_{RR}(C_j) \end{pmatrix} \begin{pmatrix} 0 & 0 \\ 0 & A_{RR} \end{pmatrix} \right]^{-1}$$

$$\qquad\qquad\qquad\qquad\qquad\qquad\qquad (12.31)$$

$$= \left[I - \begin{pmatrix} 0 & B_{jR}(C_j)A_{RR} \\ 0 & B_{RR}(C_j)A_{RR} \end{pmatrix} \right]^{-1} = \begin{pmatrix} I & -B_{jR}(C_j)A_{RR} \\ 0 & I - B_{RR}(C_j)A_{RR} \end{pmatrix}^{-1} = \begin{pmatrix} I & B_{jR}(C_j)A_{RR}\Delta_R^* \\ 0 & \Delta_R^* \end{pmatrix} ,$$

where

$$\Delta_R^* = (I - B_{RR}(C_j)A_{RR})^{-1} = (I - A_{RR} - A_{Rj}\Delta(C_j)A_{jR}A_{RR})^{-1} \quad (12.32)$$

Using the equality:

$$\Delta_R^* - I = B_{RR}(C_j)A_{RR}\Delta_R^* \qquad\qquad\qquad (12.33)$$

one obtains:

$$(G_2^* - I)G_1^* = \begin{pmatrix} 0 & B_{jR}(C_j)A_{RR}\Delta_R^* \\ 0 & B_{RR}(C_j)A_{RR}\Delta_R^* \end{pmatrix} \begin{pmatrix} B_{jj}(C_j) & B_{jR}(C_j) \\ B_{Rj}(C_j) & B_{RR}(C_j) \end{pmatrix}$$

$$= \begin{pmatrix} B_{jR}(C_j)A_{RR}\Delta_R^* B_{Rj}(C_j) & B_{jR}(C_j)A_{RR}\Delta_R^* B_{RR}(C_j) \\ B_{RR}(C_j)A_{RR}\Delta_R^* B_{Rj}(C_j) & B_{RR}(C_j)A_{RR}\Delta_R^* B_{RR}(C_j) \end{pmatrix}$$

$$= \begin{pmatrix} B_{jR}(C_j) \\ B_{RR}(C_j) \end{pmatrix} A_{RR}\Delta_R^* [B_{Rj}(C_j)B_{RR}(C_j)]$$

$$\qquad\qquad\qquad\qquad\qquad\qquad\qquad (12.34)$$

From this presentation, the following decomposition of the Leontief inverse may be obtained:

$$B = (I - A)^{-1} = B(C_j) + \begin{pmatrix} B_{jR}(C_j) \\ B_{RR}(C_j) \end{pmatrix} A_{RR} \Delta_R^* [B_{Rj}(C_j) B_{RR}(C_j)] \,.$$

$$(12.35)$$

This decomposition includes the Leontief inverse of the regional cross and the matrix representing the influence of this cross on the rest of the economy. Consider now, the gross output produced by region j:

$$x\,(C_j) = B(C_j)f = \begin{pmatrix} x_j^* \\ x_R^* \end{pmatrix},$$

$$(12.36)$$

where

$$x_j^* = B_{jj}(C_j)f_j + B_{jR}(C_j)f_R \,,$$

$$x_R^* = B_{Rj}(C_j)f_j + B_{RR}(C_j)f_R \,.$$

$$(12.37)$$

Further, consider the difference vector between the global (total economy) gross output

$$\begin{pmatrix} x_j \\ x_R \end{pmatrix}$$

and gross output produced by region j:

$$x - x\,(C_j) = \begin{pmatrix} \Delta^* x_j \\ \Delta^* x_R \end{pmatrix}.$$

$$(12.38)$$

The application of (12.34) and (12.37) provides:

$$\begin{cases} \Delta^* x_j = B_{jR}\,(C_j)\, A_{RR}\, \Delta_R^*\, x_R^* \\ \Delta^* x_R = B_{RR}\,(C_j)\, A_{RR}\, \Delta_R^*\, x_R^* \end{cases}.$$

$$(12.39)$$

After use of (12.32) and (12.36), one obtains:

$$\begin{cases} \Delta^* \ x_j \ = \ B_j \ A_R \ \Delta_R^* \ x_R^* \\ \Delta^* \ x_R \ = \ (\Delta_R^* \ - \ 1) \ x_R^* \end{cases}$$ (12.40)

Hence, the difference in (12.38) depends on the influence of the region on the rest of the economy.

4.2 Empirical Analysis of Gross Output in the European Union, 1975, 1985

4.2.1 The European Input–Output System The analysis of the propagation of structural changes in the EU is based on the 1975 and 1985 input–output tables for the European countries (Schinderinck 1984; Oosterhaven 1989; Boomsma et al. 1991). Considerable effort has been made to ensure that these tables are consistent, both internally and in terms of bilateral trading relationships.

4.2.2 Methodology for the Empirical Analysis For each European country,[1] (j = 1 ,2, ..., 8), in 1975 and 1985, the following input–output block matrices were constructed:

$$A^t = \begin{pmatrix} A_{jj}^t & A_{jR}^t \\ A_{Rj}^t & A_{RR}^t \end{pmatrix}, \quad t = 1975, \ 1985 \ ,$$ (12.41)

with the following crosses representing each country:

$$C_j^t = \begin{pmatrix} A_{jj}^t & A_{jR}^t \\ A_{Rj}^t & 0 \end{pmatrix}, \quad t = 1975, \ 1985 \ .$$ (12.42)

Further, the following additive decompositions of the Leontief inverses were calculated (see (12.35)):

$$B^t = (I - A^t)^{-1} = B(C_j^t) + \Delta^t, \quad t = 1975, \ 1985 \ .$$ (12.43)

Final demand and gross output vectors were presented in the form reflecting the hierarchy, namely, the region j versus the rest of the economy, R

$$f^t = \begin{pmatrix} f_j^t \\ f_R^t \end{pmatrix} x^t = \begin{pmatrix} x_j^t \\ x_R^t \end{pmatrix}. \tag{12.44}$$

From (12.43), the following decompositions of gross output can be obtained for each of the two years:

$$x^t = B^t f^t = B(C_j^t) f^t + \Delta^t f^t. \tag{12.45}$$

By introducing the following block-decompositions of each component of (12.44), (1) the impact of the regional subsystems, C_j^t on the final demands (regional and the rest of the economy) will be:

$$B(C_j^t) = \begin{pmatrix} f_j^t \\ f_R^t \end{pmatrix} = \begin{pmatrix} x_j^{*t} \\ x_R^{*t} \end{pmatrix} \tag{12.46}$$

and (2) the action of the rest of the economy, on overall final demand will be:

$$\Delta^t \begin{pmatrix} f_j^t \\ f_R^t \end{pmatrix} = \begin{pmatrix} \Delta x_j^{*t} \\ \Delta x_R^{*t} \end{pmatrix}, \tag{12.47}$$

yielding the following decompositions of gross outputs:

$$\begin{pmatrix} x_j^t \\ x_R^t \end{pmatrix} = \begin{pmatrix} x_j^{*t} \\ x_R^{*t} \end{pmatrix} + \begin{pmatrix} \Delta x_j^t \\ x_R^t \end{pmatrix}. \tag{12.48}$$

It is important to note that (12.39) implies that all the vectors from the expression (12.47) have only positive components; thus, the rank-size hierarchies of these components can be easily organized.

4.2.3 Preliminary Analysis The analysis will begin with the derivation of the rank-size hierarchy of inputs of the different sectors into the gross outputs vectors for both regions (the region and the rest of the EU) for both years. For example, the relative shares of the 1975 self-generated part of the gross output of Germany and the rankings of the sectoral inputs,

$$\frac{x_{sj}^{\bullet}}{x_{sj}}, x \frac{x_{sR}^{\bullet}}{x_{sR}},$$

where s indicates the sector, into the self-generated inputs are presented in Table 12.1.

Table 12.1 Rank–size hierarchy of relative sectoral inputs into self-generated gross output Germany, 1975

	Sector	x^*_{sj}/x_{sj}	Rank	x^*_{sr}/x_{SR}	Rank
1	Agriculture	0.95	6	0.26	15
2	Mining	0.89	14	0.38	10
3	Food	0.96	4	0.69	4
4	Textiles	0.94	7	0.63	6
5	Wood & Furniture	0.96	5	0.47	7
6	Energy	0.93	9	0.38	12
7	Chemical	0.82	16	0.39	11
8	Building Materials	0.92	12	0.14	16
9	Metal Manufacturing	0.85	15	0.29	14
10	Machinery	0.92	11	0.68	5
11	Industries, n.e.c	0.78	13	0.29	13
12	Construction	0.99	2	0.82	2
13	Trans. & Communications	0.99	10	0.42	9
14	Commerce & Restaurants	0.94	8	0.75	3
15	Public Service	0.99	1	0.88	1
16	Finance & Insurance	0.96	3	0.46	8

Similar tables could be constructed for all countries in the EU. The analysis of the inner structure of the components of vectors $x^*_j x^*_R$, Δx_j, and Δx_R can be accomplished in the following fashion: for each sector, the relative inputs can be calculated for x^*_j and Δx_j into x_j the similar components x^*_R, Δx_R into x_R. Furthermore, for each vector, the sum of all components can be obtained as expressed as a percentage, S; this would represent the average distribution of gross output between the region and the rest of the economy.

4.2.4 Empirical Analysis Prior to a discussion of the individual country patterns, reference should be made to Tables 12.2 and 12.3 where summary measures are provided. Table 12.2 contains the average distributions of inputs into the gross output of each country, divided into internal and rest-of-Europe sources. There are distinct patterns. First, the larger countries are heavily dependent on their internal sources and there is little variation in the standard deviation across sectors. For the smaller economies, Belgium, Ireland and the Netherlands, the internal dependence is smaller and the standard deviation (indicating sectoral variability) is larger. Denmark is unusual in that it is a small economy yet the averages and standard deviations would place it in the same category as the larger countries. The patterns in 1985 are very similar to those in 1975 but with a slight increase in variability across sectors.

Obviously, the changing composition of the EU will create some disturbances to any patterns; since three of the countries under consideration joined only in 1973, the impacts by 1975 are likely to be much smaller than those of the older members.

Table 12.2 Average inputs for the region and the rest of the economy as a percentage of gross output for the EU countries, 1975, 1985

	Average %		Average %		Average %		Average %	
	S^*_j 1975	Standard deviation	S^*_R 1975	Standard deviation	S^*_j 1985	Standard deviation	S^*_R 1985	Standard deviation
Bel-gium	81.9	14.7	56.6	23.6	79.2	15.8	56.6	21.4
Den-mark	93.6	7.9	56.3	23.7	93.9	5.6	56.3	21.5
France	94.6	7.8	56.3	22.9	93.5	5.91	56.6	20.5
Ger-many	93.7	4.6	59.5	21.9	92.9	5.9	59.2	21.1
Ireland	85.7	11.9	56.4	23.7	87.3	11.4	56.4	21.5
Italy	95.3	3.6	56.6	23.7	96.1	2.9	63.8	20.3
Holland	83.0	12.6	56.7	23.6	81.2	14.4	57.0	21.5
UK	95.8	3.3	57.1	24.7	92.3	8.1	57.1	21.2

Note: The averages and standard deviations are calculated across all sectors within a country.

The average dependence of the Rest-of-the-EU on itself is much lower and exhibits high variability; this variability is lower in 1985 than 1975 reflecting the mirror image of the trends in the intra-country dependencies.

Table 12.3 reveals the rank–size positions for individual sectors with the averages being obtained by summing across countries or the Rest-of-the-EU.[2] Here, there seems to be a sharp distinction between the manufacturing and non-manufacturing sectors with the latter tending to rank higher in terms of intraregional dependence. There have been few significant changes in the rankings. However, even small changes in intraregional dependency can generate important indirect effects on the rest of the region's economy (see Sonis et al. 1996 for a more detailed companion analysis of the impacts of the changes).

The analysis for individual countries is presented in a series of eight figures representing various components of the gross outputs for 1975 and 1985. The results in these figures confirm the findings noted from the inspection of

Table 12.2, namely, the variations across countries are smaller than the variations across sectors. In other words, it would appear that the differences in self/non-self dependencies are far more a reflection of the variations in the structure of the economy than merely a function of the size of the economy. Size does play a role in that the variations across sectors tend to be smaller in the larger countries.

Table 12.3 The average rank–size hierarchy of the sectoral inputs into self-generated gross output: EU countries, 1975, 1985

x^*_{sj}/x_{sj} 1975		x^*_{sj}/x_{sj} 1985		x^*_{sR}/x_{sR} 1975		x^*_{sR}/x_{sR} 1985	
Average Rank	Sector	Average Rank	Sector	Average Rank	Sector	Average Rank	Sector
1.2	Public Service	1.2	Public Service	1	Public Service	1	Public Service
1.7	Construction	1.8	Construction	2	Construction	2	Construction
3.4	Fin & Insurance	4.4	Com. & Rest.	3	Com. & Rest.	3	Com. & Rest.
5.3	Food	4.4	Fin & Insur	4	Food	4.3	Food
5.6	Com. & Rest.	5.9	Wood/Furniture	5	Machinery	4.8	Machinery
6	Wood/Furniture	6.4	Food	6	Textiles	6	Textiles
6.8	Energy	6.5	Energy	7	Wood/Furniture	7	Wood/Furniture
9.4	Machinery	7.8	Trans./Comm	8.1	Fin & Insur	8.4	Trans./Comm
9.6	Agriculture	10.5	Textiles	8.9	Trans./Comm	9.8	Fin & Insurance
9.6	Textiles	10.6	Agriculture	10.1	Mining	10.3	Energy
10.6	Building Mats.	10.9	Mining	11.1	Chemical	10.6	Chemical
11	Mining	10.9	Machinery	11.9	Energy	11	Mining
12.4	Indus. n.e.c.	11.8	Building Mats.	12.9	Indus n.e.c.	13	Indus n.e.c.
12.8	Trans./Comm	12.6	Indus. n.e.c.	14.4	Agriculture	14	Metal Manuf.
14.9	Metal Manuf.	14.6	Metal Manuf.	14.6	Metal Manuf.	15	Agriculture
15.8	Chemical	15.9	Chemical	16	Building Mats.	16	Building Mats.

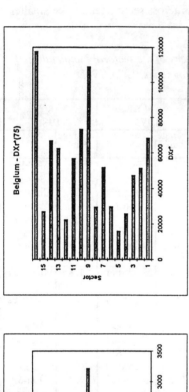
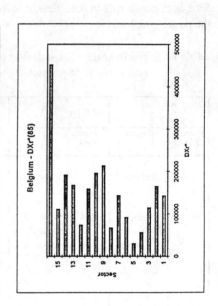
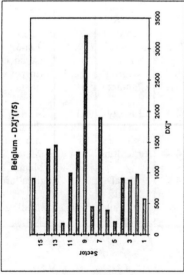
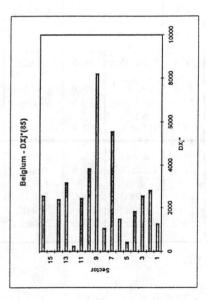

Figure 12.1 Decomposition of gross output for Belgium, 1975, 1985

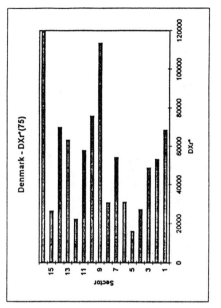

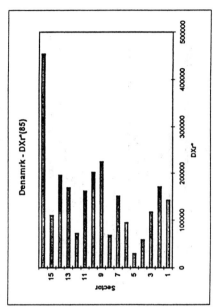

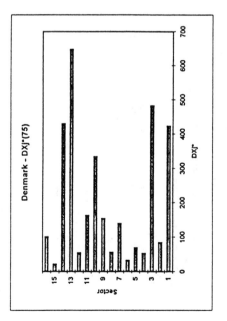

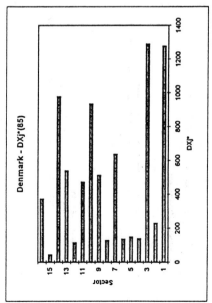

Figure 12.2 Decomposition of gross output for Denmark, 1975, 1985

231

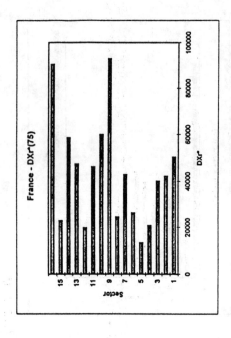

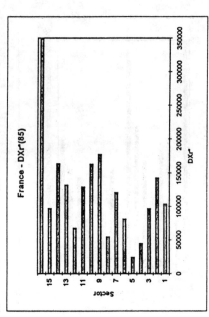

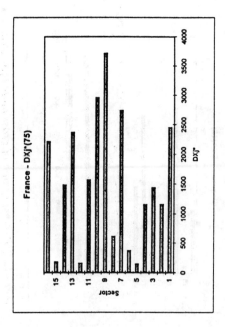

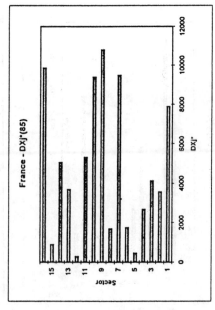

Figure 12.3 Decomposition of gross output for France, 1975, 1985

232

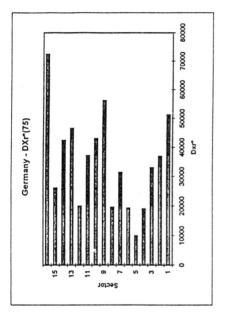

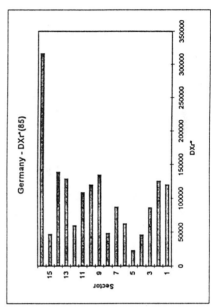

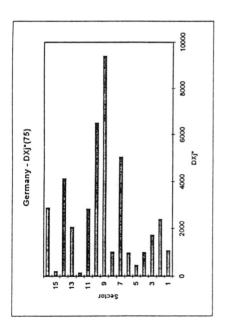

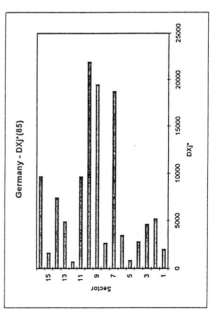

Figure 12.4 Decomposition of gross output for Germany, 1975, 1985

233

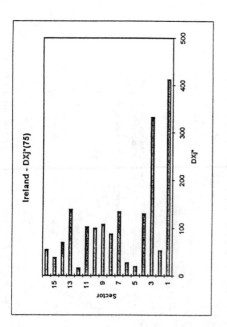

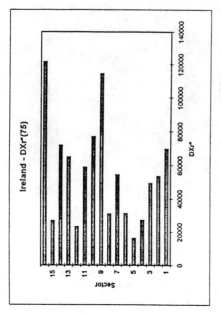

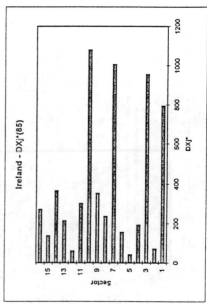

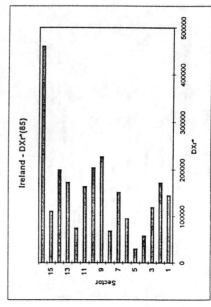

Figure 12.5 Decomposition of gross output for Ireland, 1975, 1985

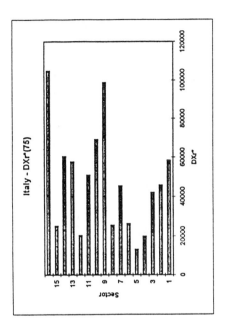

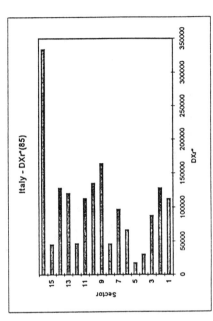

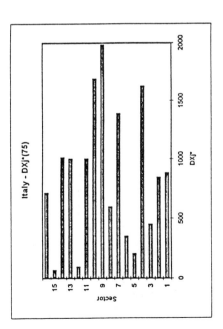

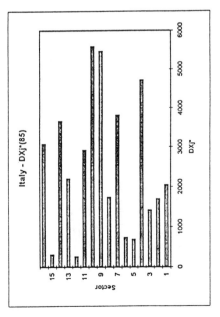

Figure 12.6 Decomposition of gross output for Italy, 1975, 1985

235

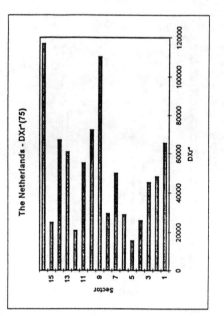

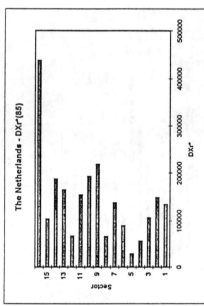

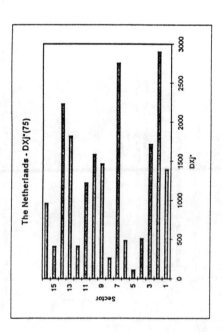

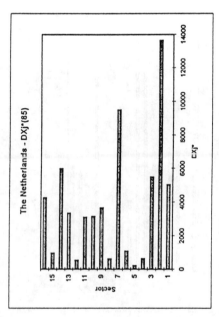

Figure 12.7 Decomposition of gross output for the Netherlands, 1975, 1985

236

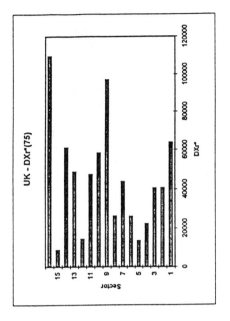

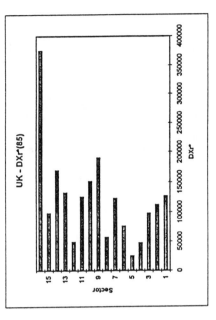

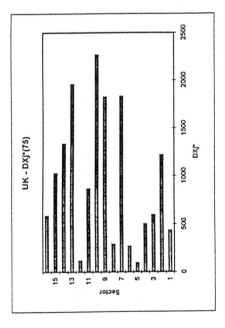

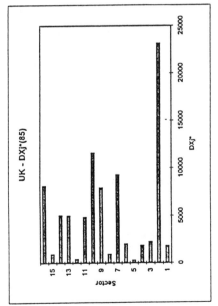

Figure 12.8 Decomposition of gross output for the UK, 1975, 1985

237

5. CONCLUSIONS

The methodology presented here and in a companion piece (Sonis et al. 1996) provides a useful framework for evaluating changes in structural relationships over time as the result of the imposition of changes in macro level trading regimes. In the applications to Europe, the interest focused on the way in which the development of the European Union created differential effects on the degree of integration by country and by sector. Obviously, the methodology provides no insights into the causes and process associated with these changes but it does identify clearly the nature of the changes and provides a basis for further empirical and theoretical analysis. The methodology also complements feedback loop analysis (Sonis et al. 1993, 1995) and generalized structural path analysis methods (Sonis et al. 1997a) that attempt to trace the degree of self influence that might exist in the evolution of relationships.

ACKNOWLEDGEMENT

The authors would like to thank the referees for their comments.

REFERENCES

Boomsma, P., Linden, J. van der and J. Oosterhaven (1991), *Construction of intercountry and consolidated EC input–output tables*, University of Groningen, Mimeo.

Cella, G. (1984), 'The input–output measurement of interindustry linkages', *Oxford Bulletin of Economics and Statistics* **46**, pp. 73–84.

Cella, G. (1986), 'The input–output measurement of interindustry linkages: a reply', *Oxford Bulletin of Economics and Statistics* **48**, 379–84.

Clements, B.J. (1990), 'On the decomposition and normalization of interindustry linkages', *Economics Letters* **33**, pp. 337–40.

Clements, B.J. and J.W. Rossi (1991), 'Interindustry linkages and economic development: the case of Brazil reconsidered', *The Developing Economies* **29**, pp. 166–87.

Dietzenbacher (1992), 'The measurement of interindustry linkages: key sectors in the Netherlands', *Economic Modeling* **9**, pp. 419–37.

Dietzenbacher, E., Linden, J. van der and A.E. Steenge (1993), 'The regional extraction method: EC input–output comparisons', *Economic Systems Research* **5**, pp. 185–206.

Goodwin, R.W. (1980), 'World trade multipliers', *Journal of Post-Keynesian Economics* **2**, 319–44.

Guccione, A. (1986), 'The input–output measurement of interindustry linkages: a comment', *Oxford Bulletin of Economics and Statistics* **48**, pp. 373–77.

Guilhoto, J.J.M., Sonis, M., Hewings, G.J.D. and E.B. Martins (1994), 'Índices de ligações e sectores-chave na economia Brasileira: 1959–1980', *Pesquisa e Planejamento Econômico* **24**, pp. 387–14.

Guilhoto, J.J.M., Sonis, M. and G.J.D. Hewings (1995), 'Using input-output to measure interindustry linkages: a new perspective', *The Developing Economies* **33**, pp. 233–70.

Heimler, A. (1991), 'Linkages and vertical integration in the Chinese economy', *Review of Economics and Statistics* **73**, pp. 261–7.

Milana, C. (1985), 'Direct and indirect requirements for gross output in input–output analysis', *Metroeconomica* **37**, pp. 283–92.

Miyazawa, K. (1976), *Input–Output Analysis and the Structure of Income Distribution*, Springer-Verlag.

Oosterhaven, J. (1989), 'Changing interdependencies between EC-countries', paper presented at the 29th European RSAI Congress, Cambridge, August 1989, and the 9th International Conference on Input-Output *Techniques*, September 1989, University of Groningen.

Schinderinck, J.H.F. (1984), *Interregional Structure of the European Community: Interregional Input–Output Tables of the European Community, 1959, 1965, 1970, and 1975*. The Netherlands: Tilburg University.

Schultz, S. (1973), 'Quantitative criteria for the determination of sectoral priorities', *Asian Economies* **5**, pp. 27–54.

Schultz, S. (1976), 'Intersectoral comparison as an approach to the identification of key sectors', in Polenske, K.R. and J.R. Skolka (eds), *Advances in Input–Output Analysis*, Cambridge: Ballinger, pp. 137–59.

Schultz, S. (1977), 'Approaches to identifying key sectors empirically by means of input–output analysis', *Journal of Development Studies* **14**, pp. 77–96.

Sonis, M. and G.J.D. Hewings (1993), 'Hierarchies of regional sub-structures and their multipliers within input–output systems: Miyazawa revisited', *Hitotsubashi Journal of Economics*. **34**, pp. 33–44.

Sonis, M. and G.J.D. Hewings (1995), 'Matrix sensitivity, error analysis and internal/external multiregional multipliers', *Hitotsubashi Journal of Economics* **36**, pp. 61–70.

Sonis, M., Hewings, G.J.D. and R. Gazel (1995), 'The structure of multiregional trade flows: hierarchy, feedbacks and spatial linkages', *Annals of Regional Science* **29**, pp. 409–30.

Sonis, M., Hewings, G.J.D. and E.A. Haddad (1996), 'A typology of propagation of changes on the structure of a multiregional economic system: the case of the European Union, 1975–1985', *Annals of Regional Science* **30**, pp. 391–408.

Sonis, M., Hewings, G.J.D. and S. Sulistyowati (1997a), 'The structure of the Indonesian economy: a generalized structural path analysis', *Economic Systems Research* (forthcoming).

Sonis, M., Hewings, G.J.D. and K. Miyazawa (1997b), 'Synergetic interactions within pair-wise hierarchy of economic linkages sub-systems', *Hitotsubashi Journal of Economics* **38**, pp. 183–99.

Sonis, M., Oosterhaven, J. and G.J.D. Hewings (1993), 'Spatial economic structure and structural changes in the European Common Market: Feedback Loop input–output analysis,' *Economic Systems Research* **5**, pp. 173–84.

Stone, R.A. (1985), 'The disaggregation of the household sector in the national accounts', in Pyatt, G. and J.I. Round (eds), *Social Accounting Matrices: A Basis for Development Planning,* Washington, DC: World Bank.

Strassert, G. (1968a), 'Möglichkeiten und grenzen der erstellung und auswertung regionalere input–output tablelen', *Schriften zu Regional - und Verkehrsproblem in Industries - und Entwicklungensländern*, Berlin: vol. 2.

Strassert, G. (1968b), 'Zur bestimmung strategischer sectoren milfe von input–output modellen', *Jahrbücher für Nationalökomie und Statistik* **182**, pp. 211–15.

NOTES

1. Belgium, Denmark, France, Germany, Ireland, Italy, The Netherlands and the United Kingdom.

2. Note that the geographic definition of the Rest-of-the-EU will, of course, vary.

13. Regional Industrial Specialization and Patterns of Structural Unemployment in the European Union

John M. Munro and Gustav Schachter

1. INTRODUCTION

This chapter explores the relationship between regional industrial specialization and structural unemployment across the regions of the European Union (EU). At the regional level, there is wide variation in unemployment rates in Western European countries. In the regions used in this chapter, 1986 unemployment rates varied from 3.8 percent in Baden-Wurttemberg to 28.9 percent in Sur (southern Spain); 1993 rates ranged from 3.9 percent in Bayern to 25.9 percent in Sur. Of course, individual regions typically experience a magnification of national economic phenomena. Recent research concludes that income and output convergence among EU regions slowed markedly after the 1960s (Armstrong 1995) and that there has been rather limited responsiveness of regional labour markets to regional shocks (Abraham and Van Rompuy 1995). Krugman (1993) analyses the likely effects of the European Monetary Union and concludes that the European regional disparity problem will worsen.

For this chapter, it is the labour market effects of technical change that make regional industrial specialization of particular interest. Typically, there is a close connection between technical change and labour markets. The supply side is affected by new skills requirements and change of investment location; the impact on labour demand varies widely among sectors and regions. Since technical change is not uniform over time, space, or sector, it has differential effects on labour productivity. Increases in labour productivity may mean a decrease in costs for the firm, a better competitive position and, depending on price and income elasticity, an increase in effective consumer demand finally leading to increased employment. But there could also be a decrease in employment.

Our analytical approach is to compare the level of industrial specialization in different EU regions with the incidence of structural unemployment. The working hypothesis is that regions which are more highly specialized should be more vulnerable to long-term unemployment than regions whose production structure is more similar to the country as a whole. This is because greater flexibility and adaptability in labour market outcomes should be expected in regions which have not concentrated their employment in a few industries. Conversely, we would expect the employment adjustments required by technological change to have impacted regions with higher degrees of specialization more severely.

The chapter begins with reviews of the literature on the measurement of regional industrial specialization and on technology and labour markets. The review sections are followed by empirical information on the extent of structural unemployment in EU regions. Then we develop measures of regional industrial specialization across the system of regions. Regression analysis is used to explore the connections between the degree of regional industrial specialization and the incidence of structural unemployment. The paper concludes with a discussion of policy approaches which could assist in smoothing the impact of new technology on employment in the European Union.

The empirical conclusions of the paper are that EU regions with more specialized economies experienced higher levels of unemployment over the 1986–93 period than regions with more diversified economies. Unemployment was measured in ways which focussed on its structural aspects. One of the causes of structural unemployment is technical change. The policy conclusions of the paper are that technical change should be encouraged but that measures are needed to moderate its effects on the employment situation in regions whose economies are slow to adjust.

2. REGIONAL INDUSTRIAL SPECIALIZATION

The significance and measurement of regional industrial specialization is a venerable topic in economics and geography. Specialization may be measured in terms of output, markets, or – most often used – employment. The theoretical arguments for specialization versus diversification give mixed advice. A region's economy might be expected to be specialized if the various advantages attached to specialization in trade theory are important or if industry-level economies of scale are present.[1] On the other hand, since all industries experience cyclical and secular fluctuations, there may be economic[2] or policy-driven[3] influences which encourage diversity so that fluctuations are moderated across a diverse regional industrial base.

The usual focus of research on the significance of the level of regional industrial specialization has been to study the advantages of diversification (non-specialization), particularly in terms of reducing unemployment or fluctuations in employment. While regional economic structure can be measured in terms of sectoral output, many studies use sectoral employment, probably because interregional differences in unemployment are such a central concern in assessing the extent of regional disparities. It is hypothesized that more diverse regional economies are less subject to the instability in employment which is associated with reliance on single industries which inevitably experience declining markets or technological change. Either can lead to unfavourable effects on regional economic performance. Some studies simply use unemployment to measure instability while others use the divergence between actual and projected employment levels.

Recent summaries of this research are presented in Malizia and Ke (1993) and Siegel et al. (1995). While the conclusions of this research are rather variable (due, perhaps, to differences in geographic areas, in measures of diversification and instability, and in time period), most of it has found that diverse regional economies have less instability.

There are many ways of measuring regional industrial specialization. These include information theoretic measures such as entropy indices, location quotients, measures of inequality based on the Gini coefficient familiar in studies of income distribution, statistical measures of deviation, and concepts derived from portfolio theory. (This last approach is based on the concept that a diverse 'portfolio' of regional industries can be analogous to a risk-minimizing portfolio of securities.[4]) Each of these measures has certain advantages and disadvantages.[5] One of the advantages of measuring the level of regional industrial specialization with Gini-type coefficients, the method used in this chapter, is the extensive knowledge of the properties of such measures.

Another issue in measuring regional industrial specialization is the benchmark against which the structure of a region's economy is to be compared. Some research has used the national distribution of the economy (the approach used in this chapter) while other studies have constructed a 'normal' level of specialization, often equal employment across all industries. Another approach is to compare regions' levels of specialization with each other. Some research has examined changes in specialization levels over time while other studies (for example, Rodgers 1957) look at regional specialization at one point in time.

3. TECHNOLOGY AND LABOUR MARKETS

There has been a considerable research effort to explore the relationships between technical change and employment. According to the recent neo-Schumpeterian emphasis on endogenous technical change, economic forces determine the rate and character of technical change. Sylos Labini (1989, p. 56) states that '(b)ecause a large number of innovations are endogenous, the rate of technical progress is determined by economic impulses'. Some interpretations of economic growth and innovation theory suggest that technology may be treated as a commodity (Romer 1990). Grossman and Helpman (1992) argue that, because of its non-rivalry and non-excludability, technology as an input has continuous spillover effects and can be self-sustaining.

Technical change is closely connected to the institutional and legal system in specific locations. In order to reap maximum returns from their knowledge, individuals and firms desire protection from having immediately to share technological advances. However, technical know-how spreads quickly and other firms easily internalize the externality provided by technological progress of other firms or different localities (Malecki 1991). Technical change is also cumulative with individuals and firms.

Over the long run, technical progress causes an increase in productivity that may be reflected in increases in wages, causing expansion in income and consumption and so increasing employment. Thus, one could conclude that technical change increases employment. However, there is no general agreement on the relationship of technical know-how and labour markets and neither theoretical and empirical research can state definitely the impact of technical change on employment (Nijkamp 1986). The impact of technology on labour markets depends on where, when and how technical change takes place.[6] It can also depend on the type of technical change – product innovation is said to be more likely to have positive effects than process innovation (Katsoulacos 1986).

Changes in the demand for skills induced by technical change may impact the labour market iteratively. Shortages of medium- or high-level skills induce individuals to acquire those skills but, in the meantime, technical change may occur again and those new skills might be pushed out, at least from the regional labour market, by still newer requirements. Recently, technical progress has seemed to encourage flexible production with less division of labour and less specialization, but with higher skill requirements (Kern and Schumann 1984). ' (T)he new generation of technology requires a highly trained labour force equipped with a variety of skills – both those closely linked to production and those related to interaction and coordination within a firm and between a firm and its customers and clients' (Appelbaum and Schettkat 1990, p. 8). Thus, we have a continuous process altering the structure of the economy and of employment.

But both the continuous aspect of technical progress as well as the notion of an interindustry employment equilibrium have been often challenged. Some economists view technical change as fundamentally discontinuous (Freeman et al. 1982). 'Typically, the demand for some grades of labour will decline so much that, even if demand is increasing for labour with other skills and qualifications, the aggregate effect is an overall reduction in employment' (Day and Hanson 1986, p. 312). Retraining an aging blue collar labour pool for high tech jobs often results in a pool of unemployed highly-trained workers ready for the jobs of yesterday, often at the wrong location. Appelbaum and Schettkat (1990) give various examples of success and failure under both market forces and government intervention and demonstrate that the degree of market freedom is not necessarily correlated with effective adjustment to change.

The market may not reach a social optimum in the process of allocating the benefits of technical progress because the degree of monopoly power varies among sectors and innovators may not consider either the consumer surplus created by new products or, on the other hand, the adverse impact they have on profits of existing traditional industries (Grossman and Helpman 1992). While structural unemployment originating in technical change will be moderated and eventually eliminated in the long run, in the short run it becomes a social issue.

4. STRUCTURAL UNEMPLOYMENT

There are several types of unemployment and they have many causes; this pervasive phenomenon is not yet fully understood (Phelps 1995). Our interest here is in the structural variety. Structural unemployment occurs when jobless individuals cannot be absorbed or reabsorbed in the economic system because of some mismatch in location, skills, sector, age, and so on. Certainly, the problem is more than cyclical and, even in a depression, the incentives for innovation are very strong. Some economists assert that structural unemployment is common and that it is tied to technical change; they label this phenomenon technological unemployment. This view is opposed by those who believe in a self-adjusting market mechanism; this group regards 'technical change as either a rather minor, temporary disturbance or as a continuous process which need not and does not deflect the economy from an otherwise smooth equilibrium growth path. Technical change is itself part of the adjustment process' (Freeman et al. 1982, pp. 14–15).

Involuntary industrial unemployment began to be recognized as a possibility between 1870 and 1900 when technical change was outpacing effective demand as a direct result of the income lag of the working class. According to Fano (1991, pp. 266–7):

> Reduced production was the immediate cause of labour displacement, but displacement was related to increased productivity. This was the first direct evidence of technological unemployment, latent in recovery and overt in depression.

Later, the shift in output from manufactured goods to services was viewed as a hope for twentieth-century employment since services tend to experience slower productivity growth. However, as Appelbaum and Schettkat (1990) point out, some services may experience a high rate of productivity growth because of their increasing use of new technology.

In the 1930s 'the depressed condition of the economy was by no means hindering – it was probably even boosting – productivity increases, thus aggravating the problem of unemployment' (Fano 1991, p. 277). Structural unemployment in the stalled recovery of the 1930s persisted because demand did not grow as fast as productivity; technological unemployment increased income inequality but not the propensity to consume. Economic reformers of the time believed that monopoly power created a strong correlation between new technology, increased productivity and price rigidities and that through administered prices they could influence production decisions and reduce unemployment.

5. EUROPEAN UNEMPLOYMENT

After 1970, levels of unemployment rose substantially from their postwar lows in Western Europe. The EEC countries had an average unemployment rate below 2.5 percent in the early 1970s – this peaked at over 10 percent in 1985, then fell to 8 percent by 1990 and has risen since then. A recent survey reviews a wide range of explanations and concludes that 'there does not seem to be any single cause of the rise in European unemployment. Rather, there have been a number of adverse developments' (Bean 1994, p. 615). These include:

* demand shifts combined with nominal wage inertia
* productivity slowdown
* worker militancy
* unemployment benefits
* skills and experience mismatch between workers and jobs

- labour market regulations
- terms of trade changes
- price markups, including higher real interest rates

Bean's survey concludes that only the last two shocks have had a measurable effect on higher levels of unemployment in Europe and that they are augmented by the 'outsider' effect (long-term unemployment has a cumulative impact on future levels of unemployment because of the effects of leaving workers outside the labour market).[7]

6. REGIONAL ASPECTS OF STRUCTURAL UNEMPLOYMENT

A report by the Commission of the European Communities (1991) observed that disparities in regional unemployment rates had been narrowing to some degree but that they were still considerable. Low-income regions[8] and regions in industrial decline typically had high levels of unemployment. However, there were varying levels of unemployment in the core regions of the EU, as well. The uneven impact of technological change may be responsible and regions which are specialized may be more vulnerable. New investment usually seeks the location and the skills that will create the greatest efficiency and profitability. When a shift of investment to new industries occurs, the displaced local workers may not be employable.

Other research into structural unemployment has focused on a possible mismatch between labour supply and labour demand. This mismatch could have occupation, region, industry, age, or a combination of these factors as its defining characteristic. Essentially, the concept of mismatch is founded on comparisons of unemployment and job vacancies. If there are a large number of vacancies in regions with high unemployment, then the mismatch is high. Mismatch is only part of the story of high regional unemployment, but it is the component that is likely to be caused by technical change or reductions in demand for the output of a region's industries. Regions may also, of course, have few job vacancies and high unemployment; in this case the same factors may be at work, but they will be augmented by other macroeconomic influences.

A recent volume of studies on labour market mismatch (Abraham 1991) concludes that regional mismatch is a factor in unemployment levels in several European countries although it does not appear to explain the increase in unemployment rates. Also of interest are the gross flows into and out of regional unemployment (Burda and Wyplosz 1994) and interregional migration.

Another view is that some regions have experienced 'deindustrialization' – the shift of the economy's output and employment away from industry (manufacturing) and towards services. Technological change has an obvious role here. Bluestone and Harrison (1982) assert that a positive evaluation of the success of technological progress must rest on the adaptive capabilities of sunrise industries to absorb the unemployed of sunset industries. However, Cheshire (1991) finds deindustrialization a misleading concept with little long-term relevance for European regions and suggests an emphasis on transformation and the ability of regions to adjust to organizational, sectoral, and spatial change.

In US labour markets, reabsorption of displaced workers is a very slow process. A study of workers displaced from Pennsylvania manufacturing industries between 1982 and 1986 (Jacobson et al. 1993) found that displaced workers experienced declines of 40 percent of predisplacement earnings in the year following displacement and were still averaging 25 percent during the fifth year after job separation. Howland and Peterson (1988) emphasize the handicap which a depressed local economy imposes on successful job search.

A recent volume edited by Rodwin and Sazanami (1991) contains studies reviewing the regional experiences of the UK, West Germany, France, Italy, Spain and Sweden. In general the papers in this work present a pessimistic view of regions' ability to respond to economic transformation without experiencing high levels of unemployment, at least for the 1975–85 period used in most of this research.

7.   STRUCTURAL UNEMPLOYMENT IN EU REGIONS

The analysis in this chapter uses a 55-region system for seven EU countries based on the NUTS 1 system.[9] These regions vary in size – in 1986 the labour force ranged from 7.28 million in Nordrhein-Westfalen (Germany) to 0.27 million in Bremen, also in Germany. Also important for the analysis carried out in this paper, the number of regions per country varies from three in Belgium to 11 in Germany and Italy. No system of regions is perfect, however, and empirical work is often bound by the units for which statistics are published.

Our concept of structural unemployment is based on regional/national comparisons. The definition of structural unemployment is that a region has structural unemployment if either:

A.   Its unemployment rate was above the national average in both 1986 and 1993 *and* its unemployment situation worsened relative to the nation's over this period, or;

B. Its 1993 unemployment level was at least 1.3 times the national unemployment rate.

Table 13.1 shows the 17 regions which met one or both of these criteria.

Table 13.1 EU regions experiencing structural unemployment

Country	Region	Criteria
Belgium	Region Wallonne	A,B
France	Centre-Est	A
	Mediterranee	A,B
Germany*	Bremen	B
	Saarland	B
	Berlin (West)	A,B
Italy	Campania	A,B
	Abruzzi-Molise	A
	Sud	A,B
	Sicilia	A,B
	Sardegna	B
Netherlands	Noord-Nederland	A
Spain	Centro	A
	Sur	A,B
	Canarias	A,B
United Kingdom	South East	A
	Northern Ireland	B

Note: * Former West Germany only.

Sources: Calculated from Eurostat (1989) and Eurostat (1994).

Many former centres of heavy industry are not included in this list. While conventional wisdom might suggest this is an error, recall that our period of interest is 1986 to 1993, by which time much of the restructuring required when heavy industry regions underwent adjustment had already occurred. Also, criterion A for structural unemployment is quite demanding since it requires both unemployment higher than the national average and a relatively worsening position over the 1986–93 period. There are another nine regions which do not meet criterion A but whose unemployment rates in 1993 were higher than the national average but below the 1.3 times threshold of criterion B.

8. REGIONAL INDUSTRIAL SPECIALIZATION AND STRUCTURAL UNEMPLOYMENT

The measure of regional specialization used in this chapter is a Gini-type coefficient calculated to measure differences in regional industrial specialization based on the national industrial structure for each of the seven countries. The calculations are based on 1985 statistics of the number of wage and salary earners by NACE class at the industry level. The number of industries varies from 10 to 24, depending on the country (all but Spain have 19 or more).[10] In general, the fewer the number of industry types the less specialized are regions. Also, more specialization would have been measured if we had used smaller regions.

The analysis could have been done using employment by industry across the total EU economy as the *numeraire* for calculating the specialization coefficients for each region instead of using each region's national industrial employment structure. In the future, this might be appropriate, but the degree of integration of EU factor and product markets for the period covered by the analysis makes the national economies more suitable reference points.

Another variation in methodology would have been to concentrate on specialization in the export sectors of the regional economies. This would be interesting, but data on exports and export employment by industry at the regional level were not available.[11]

Specialization coefficients for each region are presented in Table 13.2. A region which had the same distribution of employment across industries as the national average (maximally diverse) would have a specialization coefficient of 1.0 while one with employment concentrated in one industry (maximally dissimilar from the national distribution and thus maximally specialized) would have a specialization coefficient close to zero.[12]

Regions with structural unemployment are shown in italics. Twelve 'problem' regions are located below the median level of regional industrial specialization (0.755) and five above. Moreover, the bottom quartile (below 0.687 – the 14 most specialized regions) contains ten regions identified as experiencing structural unemployment.

Table 13.2 Regional specialization coefficients

Country	Region	Coefficient	Rank**
Belgium	*Region Wallonne*	0.738	31
(19 industries)	Vlaams gewest	0.893	1
	Bruxelles/Brussels	0.680	44
France	Ile-de-France	0.755	28
(25 industries)	Bassin parisien	0.883	2
	Nord-Pas-de-Calais	0.727	35
	Est	0.772	24
	Ouest	0.763	26
	Sud-Ouest	0.774	23
	Centre-Est	0.819	11
	Mediterranee	0.685	43
Germany*	Schleswig-Holstein	0.688	41
(23 industries)	Hamburg	0.639	48
	Niedersachsen	0.791	18
	Bremen	0.556	53
	Nordrhein-Westfalen	0.794	15
	Hessen	0.830	9
	Rheinland-Pfalz	0.831	8
	Baden-Wurttemberg	0.796	14
	Bayern	0.826	10
	Saarland	0.590	52
	Berlin (West)	0.673	46
Italy	Nord-Ovest	0.709	38
(24 industries)	Lombardia	0.735	32
	Nord-Est	0.870	3
	Emilia-Romagna	0.724	36
	Centro	0.789	20
	Lazio	0.664	47
	Campania	0.690	40
	Abruzzi-Molise	0.675	45
	Sud	0.614	50
	Sicilia	0.599	51
	Sardegna	0.532	54
Netherlands	*Noord-Nederland*	0.848	6
(21 industries)	Oost-Nederland	0.857	4
	West-Nederland	0.845	7
	Zuid-Nederland	0.807	12

Table 13.2 (continued)

Country	Region	Coefficient	Rank**
Spain	Noroeste	0.703	39
(10 industries)	Noreste	0.792	17
	Madrid	0.740	30
	Centro	0.800	13
	Este	0.791	19
	Sur	0.764	25
	Canarias	0.455	55
United Kingdom	North	0.794	16
(21 industries)	Yorkshire and		
	Humberside	0.733	33
	East Midlands	0.721	37
	East Anglia	0.755	29
	South-East	0.784	21
	South-West	0.762	27
	West Midlands	0.687	42
	North-West	0.854	5
	Wales	0.730	34
	Scotland	0.782	22
	Northern Ireland	0.628	49

Notes: * Former West Germany only.
              ** 1 is the most diverse economy.

Source: Calculated from Eurostat (1989).

It would, however, be risky to rely on this analysis to conclude that more highly specialized regions are necessarily associated with a higher incidence of structural unemployment. The reasons for caution are as follows:

1. Structural unemployment should not be measured only by a dichotomous variable. Classifying regions into those with and without structural unemployment is a useful descriptive exercise but the actual level of structural unemployment is important.
2. Three of the least specialized regions (top quartile) are classified in the structural unemployment group.
3. The industrial classification is not identical in all countries. (Spain is the most significant outlier.[13]) Also, the classification may not be optimally suitable for this purpose – a classification with less variation in employment size[14] would have been preferable.

4. We have measured structural unemployment across the total labour market when it might have been more appropriate to use a measure limited to industrial unemployment. For example, it is not clear that the high levels of structural unemployment in southern Italian regions have as much to do with technological innovation in the region's industries as with the persistent inability of the non-agricultural sector (industry and services) to absorb labour released from agriculture (Munro and Schachter 1990).
5. We do not include any measure of the duration of unemployment, yet unemployment probably should be long term to merit the label 'structural'.

9. REGRESSION ANALYSIS

OLS regression analysis was used to address some of these problems. Simply by using regression analysis we address issue 2, issue 1 is addressed by employing measures of the level of structural employment as dependent variables, and issue 3 is addressed by using the share of industrial employment in each region's total employment as a control variable. In the regression equations, regional specialization coefficients and other appropriate variables were regressed on measures of unemployment. In presenting these results, it is important to emphasize that the various equations are not formulated to model all the complex influences on regional unemployment.[15] Our aim was only to show the extent to which interregional differences in various unemployment measures can be explained by interregional differences in industrial specialization.

The variable abbreviations are as follows:

UNEMPRAT = 1993 regional unemployment rate/1993 national unemployment rate (calculated from Eurostat 1994)
UNEMPDIF = 1993 regional unemployment rate − 1993 national unemployment rate (calculated from Eurostat 1994)
UNEMPCH = $UNEMPDIF_{1993}$ − $UNEMPDIF_{1986}$ (calculated from Eurostat 1994 and Eurostat 1989)
INDSPEC = regional specialization coefficient
INDEMP = 1987 regional industrial employment/1987 regional total employment (calculated from Eurostat 1989)
Descriptive statistics for the variables are shown in Table 13.3.

Table 13.3 Descriptive statistics for variables

Variable	Units	Mean	Maximum	Minimum	Standard Deviation
UNEMPRAT	ratio	1.0708	2.0630	0.402	0.3516
UNEMPDIF	decimal rate	0.006454	0.1190	−0.0670	.0384
UNEMPCH	decimal rate	−0.001553	0.0759	−0.0455	0.0228
INDSPEC	index	0.741	0.893	0.455	0.0910
INDEMP	proportional ratio	0.3197	0.470	0.190	0.0668

Table 13.4 Regression results

	Dependent Variable	Constant	INDSPEC	INDEMP	UNEMPCH	Adjusted R^2
(13.1)	UNEMPRAT	2.8983 (9.3346)	−1.7164 (−3.8754)	−1.7398 (−2.8855)		0.4001
(13.2)	UNEMPRAT	2.7141 (8.3724)	−2.2188 (−5.1067)			0.3171
(13.3)	UNEMPDIF	0.19912 (5.8692)	-0.16387 (−3.3861)	−0.22301 (−3.3850)		0.3985
(13.4)	UNEMPDIF	.17552 (4.8312)	−0.22827 (−4.6879)			0.2798
(13.5)	UNEMPCH	0.04475 (1.8601)	−0.00208 (−0.06070)	−0.14001 (−2.9970)		0.1401
(13.6)	UNEMPCH	0.02993 (1.1852)	−0.04251 (−1.2559)			0.0106
(13.7)	UNEMPRAT	2.6285 (9.1811)	−1.7039 (−4.3085)	−0.89583 (−1.5366)	6.0277 (3.7719)	0.5217
(13.8)	UNEMPRAT	2.5055 (8.9980)	−1.9225 (−5.1432)		6.9702 (4.6627)	0.5092
(13.9)	UNEMPDIF	0.16587 (5.5164)	−0.16232 (−3.9083)	−0.11896 (−1.9430)	0.74318 (4.4281)	0.5570
(13.10)	UNEMPDIF	0.14953 (5.0468)	−0.19135 (−4.8111)		0.86833 (5.4591)	0.5334

Results of the regression analysis are presented in Table 13.4 (t-statistics are in parentheses). Multicollinearity should not be a problem; correlation coefficients between all variables used as independent variables in different equations were less than 0.42. Equations (13.7) to (13.10) use UNEMPCH as a proxy for underlying regional tendencies towards structural unemployment in addition to the level of regional industrial specialization.

Equations (13.7) and (13.9) explain more of the variation in the two measures of structural unemployment than do the other equations and both have large and significant coefficients for the industrial specialization measure. The coefficient estimate of −1.7039 in equation (13.7) means that UNEMPRAT, the ratio of regional to national unemployment (mean = 1.0708), declines by 0.17 when the industrial specialization coefficient rises (a more diverse economy) by 0.10. The coefficient estimate of −0.16232 in equation (13.9) means that UNEMPDIF, the difference between regional and national unemployment rates (range is +11.9 percent to –6.7 percent), rises by about 2 percent when the industrial specialization coefficient falls (a more specialized economy) by 0.10.

Regression results for UNEMPCH in equations (13.5) and (13.6) had low adjusted R^2 values and estimated coefficient values which were not significantly different from zero. Otherwise, the various equations produce quite similar estimates of the regression coefficient for INDSPEC. The estimates are larger if we do not include variables reflecting the size of the industrial sector and the underlying tendencies towards structural unemployment but they are still statistically significant at the 1 percent level and large when we do. (Estimates of the coefficients for these control variables themselves are statistically significant, although at a less satisfactory level (10 percent) in the case of INDEMP when UNEMPCH is also included.)

Summarizing the regression results, we can conclude that higher unemployment rates relative to the national level are associated with a more specialized regional economy.

11. CONCLUSIONS

Our research suggests that a region with an economy more specialized than the national average is one which will likely experience difficulty with structural unemployment. This could be caused by technological change or by causes unrelated to direct technical change in the region's industries.

We do not recommend that the problem of regional structural unemployment be solved by restricting or hampering technological change. To quote the principal finding of a National Academy of Sciences study (Cyert and Mowery 1987, p. 18):

> Technological change is an essential component of a dynamic, expanding economy. ... Recent and prospective levels of technological change will not produce significant increases in total unemployment although individuals will face painful and costly adjustments. Rather than producing mass unemployment, technological change will make its maximum contribution to higher living standards, wages, and employment levels if appropriate public and private policies are adopted to support the adjustment to new technologies.

Nor is the direct policy remedy of simply acting to diversify regional economies likely to be feasible. It is generally not desirable to preserve declining industries through subsidies or other preferential measures.

Instead, we emphasize the importance of facilitating the changes required by displaced labour in declining regions and so would strongly endorse the need for policy intervention on both equity and economic grounds. Policy remedies should be ready for implementation before the crisis occurs and should anticipate future technological change (Blazejczak 1991). While actual policies should be designed with multi-instrument and region-specific characteristics (Pompili 1994), we can outline the types of policies which might ease the burdens which technological change can impose on regional labour markets.

1. *Encourage the spread of new technology* Freeman et al. (1982) suggest technology policies that include encouraging firms to adopt radical inventions and innovations, spreading information on technical know-how, and encouraging the use of foreign technology. Such policies are not always viewed as beneficial because the government intrudes into business decisions and sometimes there is simply a transfer of funds or subsidized R&D for some firms and not for others.

2. *Encourage labour market flexibility* Flexible employment may mean contracting out some or all work in a production process. This occurs where where work security prevails (lifetime employment) and has the aim of decreasing expensive fringe benefits. This approach, however, could produce even more insecurity in the labour market, declines in morale, and loss of worker loyalty.

3. *Shorten the work week* This policy approach implicitly treats employment *per se* as providing utility for workers rather than the labour income earned. Many studies on shortening the work week have been completed over the last decade. Guglielmetti (1993) reports on suggestions for an overall reduction of weekly hours in Italy from 40 to 35 with commensurate changes in monthly salary. This could be subsidized by the government. If the necessary production reorganization is possible, the timing of work could be revised but labour unions might object. However, the possibility does exist to diminish hours of work over a long period of time in those sectors where productivity increases allow it. As we know, this did occur for much of the twentieth century.

4. *Focus on re-employment policies* Leigh (1995) analyses a number of policies which focus on securing re-employment of workers displaced by structural change. These include training and retraining programs (with the problematic issue of how these are designed and delivered and who pays for them), targeting unemployment benefits towards re-employment, and providing effective employment services to secure the best possible flow of information between firms and workers.

5. *Use government spending to facilitate adjustment* This type of policy approach could include improving regional infrastructure or shifting public sector employment into regions which have experienced structural unemployment (Rodwin 1991). However, infrastructure upgrades are not a certain remedy for problems which usually have nothing to do with infrastructure quality and moving government employment creates employment problems in the former region (if employees do not move) and does less for the new region (if they do move).

Unfortunately, there is no certain remedy for structural unemployment and society must take advantage of technological progress even when it leads to this problem. Too much control and regulation could kill the incentives for innovation. Nevertheless, structural unemployment is a form of market failure and it should be corrected by having society seek to internalize the externalities imposed on declining firms and their workers. This could be pursued by more rapid retraining for future labour demand or by creating an income safety net for displaced workers. Of course, this is not an easy task for any policy maker and the resulting regional and sectoral discrimination might not be viewed favourably by the public at large or by vested interests. Where active regional development policies are in place, as in the EU, the connections between more diverse regional economies and less vulnerability to structural unemployment should not be overlooked.

REFERENCES

Abraham, K.G. (1991), 'Mismatch and Labour Mobility: some Final Remarks', in Schioppa, F.P. (ed.), *Mismatch and Labour Mobility*, Cambridge: Cambridge University Press.

Abraham, F. and P. van Rompuy (1995), 'Regional convergence in the European Monetary Union', *Papers in Regional Science* **74**, pp. 125–42.

Applebaum, E. and R. Schettkat (1990), 'The Impacts of Structural and Technological Change: an Overview', in Applebaum, E. and R. Schettkat (eds), *Labor Market Adjustments to Structural Change and Technological Progress*, New York: Praeger.

Armstrong, H.W. (1995), 'Convergence among regions of the European Union, 1950–1990', *Papers in Regional Science* **74**, pp. 143–52.

Bean, C.R. (1994), 'European unemployment: a survey', *Journal of Economic Literature* **32**, pp. 573–619.

Blazejczak, J. (1991), 'Evaluation of the long-term effects of technological trends on the structure of employment', *Futures* **23**, pp. 594–604.

Bluestone, B. and B. Harrison (1982), *The Deindustrialization of America*, New York: Basic Books.

Burda, M. and C. Wyplosz (1994), 'Gross worker and job flows in Europe', *European Economic Review* **38**, pp. 1287–315.

Cheshire, P. (1991), 'Problems of Regional Transformation and Deindustrialization in the European Community', in Rodwin, L. and H. Sazanami (eds), *Industrial Change and Regional Economic Transformation: The Experience of Western Europe*, London: HarperCollins.

Commission of the European Communities (1991), *The Regions in the 1990s*, Luxembourg: Commission of the European Communities.

Cyert, R.M. and D.C. Mowery (eds) (1987), *Technology and Employment: Innovation and Growth in the U.S. Economy*, Washington DC: National Academy Press.

Day, H.R. and K.A. Hanson (1986), 'Adaptive Economising, Technological Change and the Demand for Labor in Disequilibrium', in Nijkamp, P. (ed.), *Technological Change, Employment and Spatial Dynamics*, Berlin: Springer Verlag.

Decressin, J. and A. Fatas (1995), 'Regional labor market dynamics in Europe', *European Economic Review* **39**, pp. 1627–55.

Eurostat (1989), *Regions Statistical Yearbook*, Brussels: Office for Official Publications of the European Communities.

Eurostat (1994), *Basic Statistics of the Community*, Brussels: Office for Official Publications of the European Communities.

Fano, E. (1991), 'A "wastage of men": technological progress and unemployment in the United States', *Technology and Culture* **32**, pp. 264–92.

Forsythe, F.P. (1995), 'Male joblessness and job search: regional perspectives in the UK, 1981–1993', *Regional Studies* **29**, pp. 453–63.

Freeman, C., Clark, J. and L. Soete (1982), *Unemployment and Technical Innovation: A Study of Long Waves and Economic Development*, Westport, CT: Greenwood Press.

Gilchrist, D.A. and L.V. St. Louis (1991), 'Directions for diversification with an application to Saskatchewan', *Journal of Regional Science* **31**, pp. 273–89.

Grossman, G.M. and H. Helpman (1992), *Innovation and Growth in the Global Economy*, Cambridge, MA: The MIT Press.

Guglielmetti, P. (1993), 'Orario di lavoro e disoccupazione in Italia', *Rivista Economica del Mezzogiorno*, No.4.

Howland, M. and G.E. Peterson (1988), 'Labor market conditions and the reemployment of displaced workers', *Industrial and Labor Relations Review* **42**, pp. 109–22.

Isard, W. (1960), *Methods of Regional Analysis*, Cambridge, MA: The MIT Press.

Jackson, R.W. (1984), 'An evaluation of alternative measures of regional industrial diversification', *Regional Studies* **18**, pp. 103–12.

Jacobson, L., LaLonde, R. and D. Sullivan (1993), *The Costs of Worker Dislocation*, Kalamazoo, MI: W.E. Upjohn Institute for Employment Research.

Katsoulacos, Y.S. (1986), *The Employment Effect of Technical Change: A Theoretical Study of New Technology and the Labour Market*, Brighton, UK: Wheatsheaf Books.

Kern, H. and M. Schumann (1984), *Das Ende der Arbeitsteilung?*, Munich: C.H. Beck.

Krugman, P. (1991a), *Geography and Trade*, Cambridge, MA: The MIT Press.

Krugman, P. (1991b), 'Increasing returns and economic geography', *Journal of Political Economy* **99**, pp. 483–99.

Krugman, P. (1993), 'Lessons of Massachusetts for EMU', in Torres, F. and F. Giavazzi (eds), *Adjustment and Growth in the European Monetary Union*, Cambridge: Cambridge University Press.

Kurre, J.A. and B.R. Weller (1996), 'Interindustry covariance patterns: too unstable for portfolio variance analysis to be a useful tool?', *Economic Development Quarterly* **10**, pp. 91–103.

Lande, P.S. (1994), 'Regional industrial structure and economic growth and instability', *Journal of Regional Science* **34**, pp. 343–60.

Leigh, D. (1995), *Assisting Workers Displaced by Structural Change: An International Perspective*, Kalamazoo, MI: W.E. Upjohn Institute for Employment Research.

Malecki, E.J. (1991), *Technology and Economic Development: The Dynamics of Local, Regional and National Change*, Harlow, UK: Longman House.

Malizia, E.E. and S. Ke. (1993), 'The influence of economic diversity on unemployment and stability', *Journal of Regional Science* **33**, pp. 221–35.

Morgan, J.N. (1962), 'The anatomy of income distribution', *Review of Economics and Statistics* **44**, pp. 270–83.

Munro, J.M. and G. Schachter (1990), 'An input–output approach to the role of agriculture in development in the Italian South, 1960–1980', *Regional Science Review* **17**, pp. 70–84.

Nijkamp, P. (1986), 'The Triangle of Industrial Dynamics, Labor Markets and Spatial systems, in Nijkamp, P. (ed.) *Technological Change, Employment and Spatial Dynamics*, Berlin: Springer Verlag.

Phelps, E.S. (1995), 'The structuralist theory of employment', *American Economic Review Papers and Proceedings* **85**, pp. 226–31.

Pompili, T. (1994), 'Structure and performance of less developed regions in the EC', *Regional Studies* **28**, pp. 679–93.

Rodgers, A. (1957), 'Some aspects of industrial diversification in the United States', *Economic Geography* **33**, pp. 16–30.

Rodwin, L. (1991), 'European Industrial Change and Regional Economic Transformation: an Overview of Recent Experience', in Rodwin, L. and H. Sazanami (eds), *Industrial Change and Regional Economic Transformation: The Experience of Western Europe*, London: HarperCollins.

Rodwin, L. and H. Sazanami (eds) (1991), *Industrial Change and Regional Economic Transformation: The Experience of Western Europe*, London: HarperCollins.

Romer, P.M. (1990), 'Endogenous technological change', *Journal of Political Economy* **98**, pp. 71–102.

Shelburne, R.C. and R.W. Bednarzik (1993), 'Geographic concentration of trade-sensitive employment', *Monthly Labor Review*, June, pp. 3–13.

Siegel, P.B., Johnson, T.G. and J. Alwang (1995), 'Regional economic diversity and diversification', *Growth and Change* **26**, pp. 261–84.

Sinclair, P.J.N. (1981), 'When will technical progress destroy jobs?', *Oxford Economic Papers*, n.s. 33, pp. 1–18.

Sylos Labini, P. (1989) *Nuove Technologie e Disoccupazione*, Rome: Gius, Laterza e Figli.

NOTES

1. Krugman (1991b) develops a model which emphasizes these influences in creating a core–periphery difference among national regions.

2. External economies of the agglomeration variety may be expected to benefit a range of industries.

3. Many regions have operated policy regimes designed to diversify their economies, often through subsidies or taxation advantages for new industries. Sometimes these policies are effective. For an example of an analytically-derived policy, see Gilchrist and St. Louis (1991).

4. See Lande (1994) and Kurre and Weller (1996) for applications.

5. For studies comparing the various measures see Jackson (1984), Siegel et al. (1995), and Isard (1960, Chapter 7).

6. For a model which directly addresses the employment effects of technical change see Sinclair (1981). This is a general one-sector, short-run model with constant returns and a closed economy, not suitable features for regional analysis.

7. For a United Kingdom regional analysis of this phenomenon see Forsythe (1995).

8. These are mainly regions with large agricultural sectors in Mediterranean countries.

9. The acronym refers to the French-language version of 'nomenclature of territorial units for statistics'.

10. We have also calculated these coefficients at the level of the five NACE industry groups, common across all the countries. These are not reported in this chapter. The regional specialization coefficients are larger (more diverse economies) when they are calculated across five-sector economies. For example, the median value increases from 0.755 to 0.866.

11. See Shelburne and Bednarzik (1993) for a US study which uses industry employment to determine state-level geographic specialization and national export and import propensities to examine the geographic clustering of trade-sensitive industries.

12. For each region we have the distribution of employment by NACE industry sector (Eurostat 1989) and we compare it to the distribution of employment by NACE industry sector for the country. A ratio between country and region is calculated for each industry and the ratios ranked in ascending order. The ratios are then used to calculate Gini-type coefficients using the data organization method suggested in Krugman (1991a) and the calculation method in Morgan (1962). The coefficients define a Lorenz curve for each region to compare the shares of region and country for each industrial sector. The regional industrial specialization coefficients in this chapter are the ratio between the area under the Lorenz curve (comparison of actual regional and national industrial sector employment shares) and the area under a 45-degree line (region and country with identical industrial employment structure).

13. Note, however, that using a finer industrial classification for Spain would have lowered regional specialization coefficients, likely moving one problem region (Sur) below the median value.

14. For example, the 23 industry groups in Germany range in size from 8,800 to 1,502,000 employees and their mean size is 419,000.

15. A study which does this is Decressin and Fatas (1995).

PART FOUR

Globalization and Regional Policy

14. Regional Development and Interorganizational Policy Making in a Pan-European Context

Fabienne Corvers and Peter Nijkamp

1. A NEW FACE OF EUROPE

Europe is going through an unprecedented change, not only politically but also in a regional economic respect. The removal of political borders is bound to have been one of the most important dynamics in regional change in Europe in the 1990s. The European unification and consequent elimination of borders have paved the way to a free movement of people, capital, goods and information. Simultaneously, Eastern Europe has opened its borders and looks towards integration with a new Europe. However, vanishing borders do not automatically imply openness to the benefit of all regions involved. Vanishing borders also means the opening of regional and urban economies to many new social, economic, technological and political influences, introducing an increased competition between city regions in view of economic power (Cheshire and Gordon 1995).

Regions are no longer merely administrative or geopolitical areas, but tend to become increasingly spatial mappings of socioeconomic force fields. The traditional distinction into economic and geopolitical regions has become more relevant in recent years, in particular in Europe where the completion of the internal market has led to a declining importance of national borders. As a consequence, new modes of cooperation are emerging in which nation-states play a less prominent role, but city regions and cross-border regions are gaining more and more importance (see also Nijkamp 1993; Ohmae 1990, 1995). Examples can be found in new modes of cross-border cooperation (for example, Euregions, the Alpes-Adria area, the Rhone-Alpes area). This phenomenon is essentially part of a worldwide development where local or regional economies are finding a new position in a globalization process. Industrial networks are no longer confined by regulatory systems imposed by national administrations. The structure of industrial production has even significantly changed: home-based production is substituted by assembly production where industrial components are acquired via a worldwide network. This means that modern industrial production in a region is largely governed by the regional position in a global open network. A strong regional profile presupposes also a proper metropolitan climate characterized by the presence of connectivity, competence and creativity (the 3C-plus profile) and the absence of congestion, criminality and closedness (the 3C-minus profile). Thus, spatial competitiveness depends on the organization of all human forces in a given space economy (see also Martinotti 1996).

As a result of all these forcefields, we are at present witnessing a search for new regional development strategies, on the basis of a blend of self-reliance and network alliance (Naastepad and Storm 1996). In the promotion of regional (and urban) development in Europe, it has become increasingly useful to distinguish new meso regions which indicate new spatial development trends in the form of corridors and axes and to suggest new strategic cooperation frameworks (Cappellin 1995; Nijkamp et al. 1994). Illustrative examples are the Blue Banana suggested by DATAR (1989) or the European Grape suggested by Kunzmann and Wegener (1991) (for North-western and Central Europe), and the relatively 'new' zone of the Central European Boomerang (Gorzelak et al. 1994). In this context, such European meso regions are abstract spatial constructs which may, however, turn into strategic policy instruments which aim to mobilize resources in order to solve common problems and to exploit a joint spatial potential. Such development zones may then be conceived of as a planning framework aimed at a better use of socioeconomic opportunities, by means of improved activity networks and improved competitiveness of city-regions, leading to new opportunities, particularly related to technologically innovative economic activity. Therefore, it is an important question whether – and under which conditions – new European regional ramifications will be able to reap the fruits of modern technology.

2. EUROPEAN REGIONS AS ECONOMIC PLAYGROUNDS

The most outstanding common feature of European countries and regions is their diversity, politically, economically, socially and culturally. Consequently, a stringent uniform development policy for European regions is bound to fail. It is interesting to observe that in the history of the European Community regional policy issues have always played an important role. Already in the Treaty of Rome (1957) and later on in the Single European Act (1986) and in the Treaty of Maastricht (1992), strong emphasis has been placed on the reduction of socioeconomic discrepancies between regions in Europe. The decisions to create in Europe a joint customs union (1957), a common market (1986) and an economic and monetary union (1992) were taken in the conviction that a better economic integration in the European Community will diminish – in the long run – regional-economic divergences (Armstrong and Taylor 1993). The European search for a balance between efficiency and equity has so far not led to breathtaking results, however. Socioeconomic disparities between all regions in the European Union are still very high, in the order of magnitude of a factor 1 to 6. When in 1975 the European Regional Development Fund (ERDF) was created, it generated high expectations on the reduction of spatial inequalities in Europe. But in practice, the more central and better accessible regions in Europe appeared to be in a better position to grasp new economic and technological opportunities. A centralization of human, economic and technological resources towards the economic core regions in Europe took place, to the detriment of the peripheral regions, where the higher transport and communication costs and the lower levels of skill put the majority of industrial activities at a disadvantage. So, apparently the regional-economic conversion has been a zero-sum game with winners and losers.

In the first ten to fifteen years of the ERDF the main emphasis has been placed on the provision of (subsidies for) infrastructure improvement, such as roads, harbours and airports. The measurable impacts of European regional policy – aiming at a reduction of regional–economic disparities – are certainly not overwhelming. One reason is that infrastructure is at best a necessary condition, but by no means a sufficient condition for achieving a better competitive position (Nijkamp 1995). Both cultural–political and economic–technological factors play a major role in improving the industrial organization of a region. In addition, it ought to be recognized that infrastructure subsidies granted by the EC were only a (small) portion of the total amount of public investment (needed or spent) in a certain area. One should therefore not be surprised to find at best marginal effects of regional policy, although the total GDP of the European Community has increased considerably (Cole and Cole 1993). As a result, the European Union is still characterized by structural regional differences in per capita income and unemployment (Abraham 1996), where the sharpest disparities in regional unemployment are still found in Italy and Spain. For example, in 1990 the highest average unemployment rate in the 10 highest scoring regions in Spain was 28.9 percent. At the same time, the high unemployment regions in Europe tend to have also the lowest average incomes.

It seems thus fairly plausible that in the near future the position of lagging regions in Europe will further worsen if the central areas will benefit more strongly from their agglomeration advantages in a globalizing economy, a situation which will become even more likely if the European Monetary Union eliminates the possibility for nation-specific exchange rate and macroeconomic policies. The question whether regions in Europe will be able to face the new challenges will, among other things, be determined by the functioning of their labour markets, not only in terms of labour costs, but also in terms of flexibility and educational skills (Abraham 1996). This also means that research and development (R&D) policies are of critical importance for regions in Europe. This issue is also recognized by the European Commission which has decided not only to double the budget of the ERDF but also to shift the focal point of regional policy towards regional access to networks, improvement of educational and technological skills, and the impediments and opportunities resulting from regional sustainability policies.

In light of the spectrum of external changes, it is clear that the technological and economic opportunities of European regions and cities are strongly dependent upon the position of these regions within the larger European space-economy and upon their internal structural characteristics and resilience. The *external* position involves two major components, namely (1) the geographical location within Europe such as a central or peripheral location, and far or small distances to political borders, and (2) (non)-physical network links with other parts of Europe, such as road and rail infrastructure and telecommunication facilities (for example, trans-European networks). For example, the economic growth potentials of various parts of a European West–East Development Zone (from Randstad Holland to Warsaw and further) are dependent upon the relationships with adjacent regions in the Baltic Sea Area and in Germany (Löwendahl 1995). The above two characteristics represent particularly the city-regions' level of *accessibility*, that is, the possibility of getting access to new information and communication technology. When we consider the transport links between city-regions in the West and those in the East of the Development Zone, it becomes clear that the first new West–East transport axes will be completed in the unified Germany, where construction plans have reached an advanced stage. Many other Eastern European countries still suffer from backmaintenance and missing links in their road and rail infrastructure, following emerging demands for new infrastructure and new organizational and management structures (Hall 1993). Progress in improvement is, however, essentially slowed down by a lack of domestic (private and public) funding capacity (Kowalski 1992).

The *internal* structural features represent the city-regions' level of *receptivity* to new information and technology. These features include, for example, the composition of the urban economy (such as sectoral structure and firm size), human capital (educational level, and so on), and the availability of (seed) capital (Davelaar 1991). Again, however, Eastern Europe however, misses the typical Western institutional framework which enables the establishment (growth) of small companies. Particularly missing is a supportive infrastructure for small technology-based firms (Dyker 1994).

It is increasingly realized that the actual competitive advantage of (city) regions is brought about by the local presence of science and technology, particularly in research laboratories and enterprises (Hingel 1993). It has become evident that Western European R&D is strongly concentrated in a few 'islands' in each country, whereas the research laboratories and enterprises in these few islands work intensively together in highly exclusive networks. It seems plausible that due to a long history of separation, R&D islands in Western Europe are not very well linked up with those in Eastern Europe. Clearly, there are different types of R&D, such as government-funded R&D and private company R&D, which may have differential impacts on regions. In any case, severe financial stringency nowadays prevents Eastern European scholars from participating in international research networks (Dyker 1994). The isolation of research groups (and individuals) seems even to have intensified since the collapse of the communist system.

Many research results indicate that R&D networks strengthen the position of economic core areas (eventually restructure their economies) and reinforce the peripheral position of other regions in the European Union (see also Kunzmann and Wegener 1991). However, in this respect research findings appear not to be entirely unambiguous. For example, Suarez-Villa and Cuadrado Roura (1993) indicate a regional convergence and even inversion, the latter suggesting a shift of economic power from traditional economic core areas to hinterland or peripheral areas. In Eastern Europe, the major development appears to be a reinforcement of existing regional disparities (or polarization) (Gorzelak et al. 1994). The most urbanized, traditionally most industrialized (except for old industry and mining) and best equipped (infrastructure) regions seem to have recovered most from the negative impacts of the political and economic transformation. Accessibility and receptivity are thus important structuring factors of relationships between zones of (city) regions and between individual (city) regions in Europe. There may be competition between (city) regions, leading to winners and losers and consequently to spatial fragmentation, but there may also be cooperation leading to a joint growth and integration. The answer to such questions is contingent upon many, as yet unknown, future developments and may at best be explored by using some visioning experiments based on scenarios. This will be undertaken in the next section (Section 3). With the help of interorganizational decision making theories we will then analyse in Section 4 what new policy making arrangements will be required in a more integrated

Europe to reduce regional economic inequalities. Section 5, finally, concludes the chapter.

3.   WHAT FUTURE FOR REGIONS IN EUROPE?

As mentioned in the preceding section, all European countries, regions and cities are witnessing nowadays an unprecedented dynamics as a result of both integrating and widening forces which position also Nordic, Central and Eastern-European as well as Mediterranean countries much more clearly on the European map (Nijkamp and van Geenhuizen 1997). It hardly needs any argumentation that the socioeconomic, technological and (geo-)political restructuring in Europe will exert profound – but largely uncertain – impacts in the next decades. Use of new technology and access to transport and communication networks will play a strategic structuring role as the backbone of new European developments ranging from local to transnational scales. European industrial, infrastructural and knowledge networks will form a connecting system between various regions in a heterogeneous European space, not only in a geographical, but also in a socioeconomic and technological sense. Consequently, Europe will likely exhibit a variety of appearances as a result of dissimilar driving forces and varied national and regional policies.

The strategic importance of new networks in the European space economy also provokes many intriguing policy and research questions. Are European regions able to fulfil their strategic economic role and to overcome institutional, financial and sociopolitical impediments? Is the drive towards more mobility, interaction and accessibility in Europe a benefit for all regions and socioeconomic groups or does it lead to new geographical discrimination and segmentation? Is the drive towards a European network society compatible with environmental sustainability and security, or would the modern information society through advanced telematics and electronic highways offer a solution? The driving forces behind these changes can be summarized by means of sets of opposing developments as follows:

a. *Global competition versus regional cooperation* Companies and entire regions are increasingly forced to compete within a global market economy. This means sourcing materials, labour use and marketing over long distances using often fragile networks. On the other hand, particular regions develop tight localized production systems based on strong cooperation between regional partners. In addition, although knowledge has become globally available due to new information and communication technologies, the region provides the entrance to this knowledge through its own resources and its external links with resources located outside the region.

b. *Economic–technical efficiency versus eco-preservation* With economic–technical efficiency as a primary goal, environmental issues may at best be treated as constraints. However, when eco-preservation is the primary goal, the emphasis is on long term stability of ecosystems based on joint interests of man and nature. Eco-preservation presupposes fundamental shifts in human behaviour in favour of long term environmental security and sustainability.

c. *Individualization versus group (community) interests* One can observe a trend for self-realization among individuals by means of consumption of differentiated products and services. In addition, the traditional nuclear family is losing ground to alternative modes of living, leading to a larger number of small households. Closely connected to these trends is the need for flexibility among individuals and organizations, becoming evident in flexible practices such as in working schedules and retirement schemes. When an orientation on group interests prevails, the well-being of the entire community has a high priority with an emphasis on solidarity for inherently weak but important members and interests of socioeconomic groups.

d. *Urban sprawl versus decentralized concentration* Urban dispersal of living and employment sites is leading to an ever-increasing need for commuting, with complex patterns of cross-commuting between city centres and suburbs, and intrasuburban trips. In order to fight the ongoing trend for urban sprawl, various national planning agencies in Europe have now adopted the concept of a compact city as the leading principle. Compact cities aim to favour public transport by high density building, particularly around public transport terminals. At the same time an intermediate form, namely the polycentric or edge city, is emerging.

e. *Growth of large metropoles versus regional equity* There is a trend for a continued growth of large metropolitan areas in the European core. This trend may only be weakened by a targeted regional policy based on equity principles, meaning an orientation of growth towards adjacent and peripheral (or inaccessible) regions.

f. *Accessibility versus isolation* There is no question that the new infrastructure policy in Europe (for example, trans-European Networks) will favour particular regions (mainly metropolitan areas), whereas the relative socioeconomic position of other regions will become more isolated. Europe is likely to become a continent of privileged and less-privileged regions in terms of access to networks.

g. *Market deregulation versus 'social market economy'* There is a persistent trend for deregulation in many fields where authorities have traditionally had a strong grip on the market. However, the model of the 'social market economy' remains valid for administrations which aim to mitigate impacts from disparities in welfare and access to public services.

h. *Bottom-up versus top-down policy action* There is an increasing trend in policy formulation to mobilize the forces of those involved in the field rather than to implement changes by decrees from above. The top-down planning paradigm has increasingly proved incapable of coping with consensus-finding processes involving diverse actors and interests. Bottom-up policy also often means a trend for more flexible and interactive approaches allowing for the participation of more stakeholders in decision making. The new paradigm of 'subsidiarity' in Europe is a new phenomenon which tries to link efficiency to decentralization.

By using the various contrasting forcefields outlined above as an 'envelope' for various future possibilities, a spectrum of multifaceted scenario images of Europe may be constructed reflecting different spatial challenges and opportunities with clear technological implications, that is, Mobile Europe, Techno-Europe, Homebound Europe and Eco-Europe.[1]

The emergence of *Mobile Europe* is rooted in a dominance of forces like individualization, spatial network access, geographical mobility, economic–technical efficiency and urban dispersal. In this image, individual automobility will be maximized regarding coverage of the population and distances at hand. Only the poor are excluded from access to private cars. Congestion remains within limits in the first years through self-adjustment mechanisms. Later, road congestion is reduced by automated guidance systems. In these circumstances, local public transport serves as a feeder to airports and terminals of automatically guided roads. Public transport is increasingly privatized. Among medium and high income groups, there is a persistent preference for suburban lifestyles. Suburbs are being built at low densities and designed to accommodate private cars, at least two per family. Leisure time is spent at far distances from home, car driving being a pleasure in itself. The poor are living in inner city areas and postwar high density suburbs subject to decay. In this Eur-image, the chances for a decline of social cohesion are relatively large. When Europe develops into this direction, opportunities for transport are largely in improved automated driving systems and improved aviation. In transport in Mobile Europe, the leading values are speed, convenience and individual accessibility. Privileged groups can be found in areas with a good access to infrastructure networks.

In the second image, *Techno-Europe*, Europe is a society in which solutions to problems are primarily sought in new technology. In addition, marketing and social acceptance of new technologies are increasingly given attention, in order to advance market adoption. The opportunities of the electronic highway are becoming increasingly popular in households. Teleworking and teleconferencing will be accepted where these can replace physical meetings of people. Car traffic will be fully electronically guided on particular tracks, following the principle of the automatic pilot. On other tracks, car traffic is guided by means of electronic messages which call for intervention with and adjustment of drivers' behaviour. In urban design, technical possibilities of high rise buildings as well as subterranean cities will be fully exploited (the 'third dimension' mobility). Accordingly, transport is increasingly occurring by elevators and bullets in a vertical direction. In this Europe, a strong emphasis is put on education and human capital. This implies a danger of a gap between people that can meet the learning criteria of this technosociety and others who stay behind. When Europe develops in this direction, opportunities for transport are largely in advanced automated driving systems, advanced aviation, vertical people movers, combined horizontal–vertical moving systems, and a further integration of modern telecommunications at home and in the work place. In Techno-Europe, the leading values for transport are speed, accessibility and user efficiency. Leading areas will be those with the best incubation conditions for R&D implementation.

The third image is *Homebound Europe*. This image follows on from an emphasis on community interests and social-democratic values, and from planning for compact cities. European governments increasingly invest in social security, good levels of social housing, job opportunities and public training facilities. There is also a system of almost free public transport within cities. City renewal and design of new city quarters are guided by principles of mixed living and working, and social integration. Subsidization allows for high levels of services within walking/cycling distance from residential housing, thereby decreasing mobility. Local governments particularly invest in local community activities, in order to activate social functions of streets. Based on national feelings of identity, consumers are prepared to pay a relatively high price for goods manufactured locally or regionally. In this Eur-image, planning and policy use advanced bottom-up and mixed approaches in which participation of all stakeholders is at hand. Homebound Europe is the Europe of cohesion, where differences in income are levelled down to a certain degree and solidarity is the leading value. When Europe develops toward Homebound Europe, opportunities for transport are largely in short distance public transport. Leading principles in transport are low user costs and high public accessibility. In this scenario the benefits of cohesion will be accrue to a large of Europeans.

The fourth image, *Eco-Europe*, is the most radical one as it breaks clearly with current trends. Similar to Homebound Europe, the spatial organization of households and firms is increasingly aimed at avoiding a large mobility. Eco-preservation is supported by means of various specific regulations. For example, the user-charge principle is widely accepted in transport which does not meet eco-standards. Eco-principles are also generally used in housing and urban design. In addition, eco-principles are gradually reshaping the industrial landscape of Europe. Reversed logistics and integrated product chain approaches cause fundamental shifts in management and spatial patterns of raw material and energy sourcing, manufacturing and waste treatment. The valuation of time in transport will also change. In Eco-Europe, opportunities for transport are clearly in short-distance vehicles based on eco-principles and mixed public systems for persons and cargo. This image means a clear protection of environmentally vulnerable areas in Europe.

The development of European regions and cities is thus fraught with many uncertainties. Dependent upon the driving forces at hand, cohesion in Europe on various spatial scales may move along an axis with full integration and segmentation as extremes. In Mobile Europe and Techno-Europe, economic/technical efficiency and competition will bring about a reinforcing of existing networks and nodes, whereas extension of networks will only be realized when economically feasible. Accordingly, large parts of Europe will fall outside the major economic and technology nodes and networks, and stay behind in growth and welfare. Such conditions will inevitably lead to large disparities in terms of employment and income levels, and a concomitant massive migration of people in search of better living conditions. This is the image of Europe of segmentation. Otherwise, Europe may move towards equity principles in regional economic policy. In Homebound Europe and Eco-Europe, economic relationships and transport are being developed based upon joint growth and cooperation. Economic activities are directed from large metropolitan areas to peripheral regions by policy measures such as tax incentives, flat rates in long-distance telecommunications, and improvement of traffic infrastructure links with peripheral regions. As a consequence of this regional policy, regional differences in income are levelled down to quite some degree. This is the image of an integrated Europe.

Not all images are equally realistic from the viewpoint of current trends. Mobile Europe is close to current developments, whereas Eco-Europe implies rather drastic breaks with the past. Major constraints to Eco-Europe and to a smaller extent to Homebound Europe are to be found in the present spatial organization of society and lobbies from the transport industry. At the same time, Europe is not homogeneous meaning that particular images are more realistic in some parts of Europe than in other parts. Constraints to the future images of Europe are thus also in the present territorial characteristics of the European regions.

Furthermore, Europe is increasingly facing a global competition with fast growing economies in Asia with low costs of labour and increasingly better-educated people. This implies an evaluation of the images in terms of consequences for the economic competitive power of Europe and leadership in the world economy.

The question of what future there will be for regions in the new European setting depends thus on many background factors, notably international political and economic developments, human and industrial behaviour regarding the use and design of networks in Europe, and the creation and adoption of advanced technology. Thus there is a need for a more thorough reflection on the fundamentals of the behaviour and organization of key actors in Europe regarding the future of European regions. The next section will therefore explore several concepts developed in inter-organizational decision-making theories to analyse the requirements needed for a future European-wide regional policy.

4.   REGIONAL POLICY IN A PAN-EUROPEAN CONTEXT: SOME THEORETICAL REFLECTIONS

The creation of the ERDF in 1975 marked – as outlined above – the official beginning of a European-wide regional policy. Although the objective of Community regional policy has remained the same – reducing regional economic disparities – the underlying ideas or paradigm on how to achieve this objective have changed over the past 25 years. This change in paradigm evolved from being additional to regional policies undertaken by the member states, strongly supply-side oriented and without subnational involvement, to a true Community view on regional development problems with increasing emphasis on a more demand-side type of intervention and stressing the importance of consensus-building mechanisms to involve all relevant actors at all policy levels. The emphasis in the 1970s and beginning of the 1980s was very much on infrastructure provision; by the end of the 1980s the emphasis had shifted towards Research and Technological Development (RTD) as important factors to promote regional competitiveness. Clearly, there is a long chain in policy making, starting off from the formation of objectives to the implementation of policy, but certain characteristics of change are always the same.

In order to understand what the implications of this change in paradigm are for the policy making processes at European, national, regional and local level, this section will go into some theoretical reflections on interorganizational policy making. The fact that the European Union is expanding in membership and deepening in political and economic functioning, poses not only new challenges for the type of (future) regional policy, but also for the way regional policy is formulated, financed and implemented. Will a top-down approach be more effective to reduce regional economic disparities in a pan-European Union or is a bottom-up approach of regional policy required?

Due to several developments, such as decentralization of policies in various countries, decreasing national government revenues and increasing European economic and political integration, the objective of regional policy in general has shifted since the 1980s towards strengthening the region's endogenous development. Making full use of local sources, such as the local labour force, local know-how, local sectoral specialization, local social structure, urban and natural environments in order to create regional economic growth requires an approach far less top-down. The involvement of regional actors becomes essential to achieve the policy objectives of endogenous growth and regional competitiveness. The European Single Market initiative, facilitating the free movement of goods, services, labour and capital, promoted greater concern with the competitiveness and productivity of industries and firms. Against this background, Community regional policy has focused increasingly on assisting the restructuring of regional production systems in order to make regions more competitive. R&D and, more generally, the capacity to innovate and upgrade, particularly in products and processes, are considered to be vital components of regional competitiveness (CEC 1994).

Against this background, the classical top-down approach of policy formulation and implementation is no longer an appropriate framework to analyse the relationship between the way policy processes are organized and the ability to achieve the policy objectives set out. Within the classical approach government is regarded as a real subject: 'the' government is seen as one undivided, monocentric, rational administrative organization. The organization of government is seen as a means, an instrument through which policies are formulated, implemented and evaluated. In order to achieve the policy objectives as efficiently as possible, several organization principles have to be fulfilled, such as unity of command, top-down management, differentiation of tasks and authority, standardization of rules and procedures.

The top-down approach emphasizes the importance of (public) actors and the formal assignments of the organization for the functioning of policymaking processes. The top-down approach has received criticism for coming short in analysing the course of policy processes and the effect of different patterns of interaction on the policy outcomes as it focuses on one central actor. The context in which the actors operate receives less or no attention. The interaction of other actors and their influence on the policy process and therefore policy outcomes are often neglected. Secondly, the top-down approach is sometimes referred to as the law and order perspective as it emphasizes the necessity of government intervention. Privatization initiatives in many traditional government areas in the past decades have questioned the self-evidence of government intervention. And thirdly, the top-down approach gives the idea that as long as government is organized in accordance with several organization principles, achieving policy objectives is a fairly conflict-free, straightforward affair. In case conflicts do occur, a reorganization usually involves a reinforcement of the founding organization principles: more centralization, more control, more rules, more hierarchy.

The counterpart of the top-down approach is the bottom-up approach where government is seen as an 'institutional ensemble' (Toonen 1990). According to this definition, government consists of a multitude of relative independent administrative units at various policy levels that govern the system as a whole through their interactions. These relative autonomous administrative units pursue their own goals, interests and ideas and have their own values, perceptions, resources and means to exert influence. The fact that these units depend on the cooperation or at least non-opposition of other units in order to achieve the policy objectives they have set out, provides ample opportunity for conflicts to occur and influence to be exerted. As a result, the availability of means to influence decision-making processes, such as knowledge, information, exchange, negotiation skills, persuasion techniques, expertise, the ability to form compromises and the ability to steer conflicts, have become alternative ways of achieving policy objectives to the traditional bureaucratic organization structure. The bottom-down approach considers 'the ideal of a neatly symmetrical frictionless organization structure a dangerous illusion' (Korsten and Toonen 1989, p. 45).

In a world that is likely to become ever more interdependent, not only in the sphere of regional and national economies, but also of societies and governments, new ways of formulating, financing and implementing public policies are required. This does not only apply to policy making processes at the national level, but also at the regional level. Regions have to change their way of thinking from regarding themselves as a subnational, merely administrative tier of government to a strategic entity that is linked with the rest of the world. The effect of the European Single Market has been not only an increase in competition between firms and economic sectors, but also between regions. Considering the big differences in economic development between the two hundred or so European regions, business – no longer hindered by trade barriers – will locate there where the locational advantages are best. Therefore, the European Union has tried to enable European regions to grasp these new opportunities by supplementing the 'economic foundation of federalism' (Cappellin and Batey 1993, p. 8) with the principle of subsidiarity in the Maastricht Treaty as well as reforming the way in which Community regional policy is formulated and implemented. Both are considered to give European regions the possibility to exert more influence over their own economic development policies.

The principle of subsidiarity means that each function should be attributed to the lowest efficient decision level within the system of relationships between regions, nation-states and the European Union. Therefore, functions should not be transferred to a superior level when they can be efficiently exercised at a lower level. The reforms of Community regional policy do not only acknowledge the importance of regions, but also build in conditions that make it difficult for national government to ignore regional actors, such as the principle of partnership (Nijkamp 1995).

As the economic opportunities are there – and which will only increase when the European Union expands with new member states – and political possibilities are created, it is up to the regions to use these to their own advantage and conceive new organization and management structures to turn the region from an abstract spatial construct into an instrument of endogenous development. The bottom-up policy approach seems to provide a better framework to succeed in this than the top-down approach, as the bottom-up approach emphasizes consensus-building mechanisms at local and regional level, takes the actual functioning of actors and organizations as a starting point instead of their formal assignments and analyses how these actors interact in a network type of setting.

As public policy seems to be increasingly developed in such 'policy networks' involving public, quasi-public and also private organizations, a policy network can best be analysed in terms of multiplicity, pluriformity, interdependence and interaction.

First, a policy network is made up of a *multitude* of actors who are formally or informally interrelated. Community regional policy is formulated, financed and implemented according to the principle of partnership. This means that, besides national governments, regional and local authorities should also be involved in formulating regional development programmes as well as the social partners within the policy framework set out by the European Commission. The principle of partnership also concerns the financing of the proposed measures, as the European Commission finances only a part of the total costs of regional development projects.

The second characteristic of a policy network is its *multiformity*. The actors differ from one another in terms of assignments, budget, personnel, power, legal status, and so on. The network can be formed around certain policy problems or clusters of resources (Klijn et al. 1995). In a network organized around one policy field, for example, regional policy, the actors can *ceteris paribus* also differ from one another in terms of policy outcomes. The European regions do not only differ widely on economic performance indicators, such as GDP per capita, unemployment rate, annual growth of employment and average household income per region, but they also make up a wide variety of different types of depressed areas. The large economic disparities among regions in the European Union greatly exceed those inside the United States (Corvers 1994). The policy practices developed in the European Union to tackle these regional inequalities vary strongly per region and per member state.

Policy networks are also characterized by the *interdependence* of the actors. Interdependence means that the actors depend upon each other to acquire the means they need to achieve the policy objectives they have set out. Actors will therefore interact with one another as they assume that by means of interacting they will acquire the resources they need. An actor can be considered powerful in a policy network not just because of the resources he/she might be able to mobilize, but also because of the actor's strategic abilities to put these resources to use. Policy is the result of the interaction between the actors. To illustrate interdependence, the European Commission cannot implement a European-wide regional policy without the support – political, technical, financial – of the regions and the member states. In turn, the regions can acquire more resources – particularly financial resources – by involving the member states in their economic development policies and complying to the rules of national government policy programmes just like member states can increase their financial margin of manoeuvre when involving the European Commission in their policy process (and complying to the rules of the Commission). Interdependence refer not only to the difference between the resources an actor has and the resources an actor needs to achieve objectives, but also to the fact that actors can undertake activities that facilitate or obstruct the achievement of objectives of other actors.

Finally, *interaction* in a policy network is displayed in various forms, namely cooperation, collusion, competition and coercion (Bish 1978). Interaction involves some form of negotiation to exchange resources. Actors can interact if they think that by means of cooperation they will both be better off. The mutual benefit can come from jointly seeking a common objective, for example reducing regional economic disparities will make the European Union more competitive as a whole, or from entering into an exchange agreement, for example cross-national cooperation between the police forces of two neighbouring regions.

Collusion is almost similar to cooperation, but imposes costs on third parties that do not take part in the interaction, for example infant industry protection. The term collusion is not optimal to describe this type of cooperation, as it implies secrecy or conspiracy. Many cooperation agreements, especially in the public sector, may generate unintended rather than planned negative consequences for others (which cannot serve as an excuse of course). The police forces of two adjacent regions may agree to stay out of each other's territory even if this is legally allowed, which is at the expense of the citizens' options for calling upon either of two police forces instead of only one.

Competition – as a form of interaction – is related to the two above-mentioned forms. Competition concerns rivalry between two (or more) actors to cooperate with a third actor. Competition is related to cooperation as entering into an agreement with another actor means that this actor's offer was superior to competing alternatives. Collusion is related to competition, as collusion is undertaken by potential competitors to eliminate the competition for favours of a third party. Research funds that require cooperation among researchers in a consortium trigger off competition between researchers for the favours of the main research contracting party to join the consortium.

Coercion, finally, distinguishes between a coerced party and a coercing party. In this form of interaction the coerced party has no option but to meet the requirements of the coercing party or bear some sanction imposed by that party if the requirements are not met. Taxes and laws are two typical examples of coercion: sanctions such as fines or jail are used to encourage citizens to pay their taxes and obey the laws (however, there is no guarantee given whether these taxes and laws are used for the benefit of these citizens). Cross-border cooperation between neighbouring regions, for example, to solve specific border-related problems such as the pollution of a transnational river, can serve as another example of coercion. Traditionally, national governments have considered border affairs a matter of national security which fell under the responsibility of either the Ministry of Defence or Foreign Affairs; regional authorities were not allowed to act upon their own.

If policies are the result of interaction – via cooperation, collusion, competition or coercion – between a multitude of autonomous yet interdependent actors, how can the success of policy networks be measured and, more importantly, what conditions will favour success? Whether the policy objectives set out are actually achieved is not the only criterion to measure the success of policy networks. Equally important is whether the policy network has succeeded in promoting cooperation between the actors, in strengthening their problem-solving capacity, in organizing mechanisms for more structural information exchange, in developing a more democratic, more transparent policymaking process, in formulating policies that are more responsive to the needs of citizens, and so on. The indicators to date, however, are still strongly focused on measuring input and output effects, instead of such behavioural effects.

The changes underlying Community regional policy – as outlined earlier – reflect a shift in policy approach which evolves more bottom-up interaction stressing the importance of consensus-building mechanisms among all relevant actors. Due to the lack of satisfactory new indicators the success of

Community regional policy is still measured in terms of financial additionality: whether there exists a substitution effect with national efforts (withdrawal of national funds) or with private initiatives (unfair competition). Although still experimental, new, more behavioural indicators are being added in order to measure other desirable policy outcomes, such as the development of a strategic framework for regional development and regional innovation, the creation of networks and the promotion of inter- and intraregional cooperation, the identification and preparation of innovation projects in firms, the strengthening of regional R&D and innovation centres located in a region, the optimization in designing new public-private programmes for the promotion of innovation (Corvers 1995).

As different patterns of interaction between actors have different effects on the course of policy processes and therefore produce different policy outcomes, under what conditions will policy networks favour successful policy outcomes? Given the fact that policy networks do not have one central decision and control centre, cooperation problems are likely to occur. Policy networks can succeed in achieving cooperation between autonomous yet interdependent actors and other behavioural effects mentioned above by the following rules of thumb (Klijn et al. 1995).

1. *'Project champion'* the policy network needs a 'project champion', an actor who organizes the structure in which a policy network can develop. Besides organizing the network meetings, sending the invitations, preparing the agenda, diffusing information and the like, a project champion has to be able to open doors, to get political support, to keep an overview of the process(es), to motivate people, to get people to follow their promises, and so on. The organization which takes the lead is therefore less important than the qualities and capacities of the project champion. Policy networks are dynamic processes; the functioning of policy networks involves social engineering.

2. *Achieving win-win situations* the policy network should facilitate bringing about a situation which represents an improvement on the starting position for all actors concerned. This does not mean that all those involved will achieve their objectives to the same extent. What is important is to foster a situation that makes participation in the network more interesting than non-participation.

3. *Activating actors and resources* interaction involves some form of negotiation to exchange resources. The underlying assumption is that actors will be willing to invest their resources in this particular negotiation process. As the success of a policy network – or any network – depends heavily on this willingness, the initial interest and enthusiasm of actors should be

stimulated. Specifying the benefits of participation versus the costs of non-participation is an effective way to achieve this.

4. *Limiting interaction costs* as interaction and negotiation processes also involve costs, it is necessary to prevent actors from pulling out in disillusionment after an enthusiastic start. Interaction costs should be proportionate to the stakes, but win–lose or even lose–lose situations should be avoided, restructured or ended in time. Conflicts can perform an important role in policy networks as they increase the transparency of the issues at stake and the true interests of the quarrelling parties, but they should be prevented from becoming dysfunctional and destructive.

5. *Procuring commitment* the policy network should bring about a situation where actors will make a (serious) commitment to the joint undertaking. Actors will always be aware of the danger that the effect of the joint actions may benefit others or that actors may pull out at crucial moments and leave others (including themselves) with the risks. Commitment can be procured via informal or more formal arrangements, such as covenants, contracts or establishing autonomous legal persons. Another way to procure commitment is by involving actors more in the actual policy process by giving them (shared) responsibilities, including a budget, and/or by setting up a representative Steering Committee.

These rules of thumb cannot guarantee, though, better interaction and better policy outcomes, but they do increase the chances of these things occurring. Although these rules seem fairly straightforward, it requires a whole new way of thinking – a culture change – in public sector organizations at all levels, as these actors are used to thinking in terms of hierarchical relations. But if they manage, then the abstract concept of 'region' can be turned into a strategic instrument promoting regional endogenous growth.

5.   TOWARDS A NEW REGIONAL POLICY IN EUROPE

By distinguishing eight contrasting forcefields this chapter has developed four future-oriented scenarios which emphasize different spatial challenges, political opportunities and technological implications. In an ever widening and deepening European Union the future of regions and cities will not be determined by blueprint policies, but will result from uncertain and contrasting forces. Given the likelihood of continuing economic inequalities between European regions, some form of public intervention will still be needed. In a pan-European context, however, a new type of regional policy is required to successfully combine the elements of equity and efficiency. Given the diversity of Europe – politically, economically, socially and culturally – a uniform development policy for European regions is bound to fail. This paper has argued in favour of a more bottom-up approach to policy formulation, implementation and financing, thereby mobilizing the forces of those involved in the field. As this new policy approach necessitates a drastic change in thinking of these very actors, several pilot programmes in the area of (technology-based) regional development have recently been launched at Community level. This new generation of regional policy programmes consider R&D and more generally the capacity to innovate and upgrade vital components of regional competitiveness. These programmes emphasize regional consensus-building mechanisms and explore the conditions under which consensus-building and, moreover, conflict-solving capacities of actors can be reinforced. Some thoughts on future directions for regional policy making arrangements which are required to reduce regional economic inequalities in a more integrated European Union have been explored in this chapter. It concludes that responsibilities for a successful pan-European regional policy will increasingly have to be shared among relevant actors – public, semi-public and private – for which policy networks provide the facilitating framework for interorganizational policy making arrangements.

REFERENCES

Abraham, F. (1996), 'Regional adjustment and wage flexibility in the European Union', *Regional Science and Urban Economics* **26** (1), pp. 51–75.

Armstrong, H. and J. Taylor (1993), *Regional Economics and Policy,* Second edition, New York/London: Harvester Wheatsheaf.

Bish, R. (1978), 'Intergovernmental relations in the United States', in Hanf, K. and K.F. Scharpf (eds), *Interorganizational Policy Making. Limits to Coordination and Central Control*, London/Beverly Hills: Sage Publications.

Cappellin, R. (1995), 'Regional Economic Development, Regionalism and Interregional Cooperation: the Role of Regions in a Policy for European Cohesion', in Eskelinen, H. and F. Snickars (eds), *Regional Peripheries in Europe*, Berlin: Springer Verlag, pp. 14–19.

Cappellin, R. and P. Batey (eds) (1993), *Regional Networks, Border Regions and European Integration*, European Research in Regional Science no. 3, London: Pion Limited.

CEC (1994), Commission of the European Communities, *Competitiveness and Cohesion: Trends in the Regions*, Fifth Periodic Report on the Social and Economic Situation and Development of the Regions in the Community. Luxembourg: Office for Official Publications of the European Communities.

Cheshire, P. and I. Gordon (1995), *Territorial Competition in an Integrating Europe. Local Impact and Public Policy*, Aldershot: Avebury.

Cole, J. and F. Cole (1993), *The Geography of the European Community*, London/New York: Routledge.

Corvers, F. (1994), 'Economic integration the European way: stronger firms', *Stronger Regions*, MERIT Research Paper.

Corvers, F. (1995), 'The linkage between innovation and regional policy. experiences made with the regional technology plan', paper prepared for the RETI Conference on Economic Development by Innovation, Magdeburg, Sachsen-Anhalt, October 12–13.

DATAR (1989), *Les Villes Européennes*, Paris: RECLUS.

Davelaar, E. (1991), *Regional Economic Analysis of Innovation and Incubation*, Aldershot: Avebury.

Dyker, D. (1994), 'Technology policy and the productivity crisis in Eastern Europe and the former Soviet Union', *Economic Systems* **18** (2), pp. 71–85.

Gorzelak, G., Jalowiecki, A., Kuklinski, A. and L. Zienkowski (1994), 'Eastern and Central Europe 2000', Warsaw: European Institute for Regional and Local Development.

Hall, D. (1993), 'Impacts of economic and political transition on the transport geography of Central and Eastern Europe', *Journal of Transport Geography* **1** (1), pp. 20–35.

Hingel, A. (1993), *Note on 'A New Model of European Development' Innovation, Technological Development and Network-led Integration*, Brussels: CEC.

Klijn, E-H., Koppenjan, J. and K. Termeer (1995), 'Managing networks in the public sector: a theoretical study of management strategies in policy networks', *Public Administration*, **73** (3), autumn, pp. 437–54.

Korsten, A. and Th. Toonen (eds) (1989), *Bestuurskunde: Hoofdfiguren en Kernthema's*, Leiden/Antwerpen: Stenfert Kroese bv.

Kowalski, J. (1992), 'Privatisation Potential in the Transport Sector in Poland', Research Paper, Karlsruhe: University of Karlsruhe.

Kunzmann, K. and M. Wegener (1991), *The Pattern of Urbanisation in Western Europe 1960–1990*, Dortmund: Report IRPUD.

Löwendahl, B. (1995), *Towards a Framework for Spatial Development in the Baltic Sea Area, Baltic Europe in the Perspective of Global Changes*, Warsaw: European Institute for Regional and Local Development, pp. 152–68.

Martinotti, G. (1996), 'Four populations: human settlements and social morphology in the contemporary metropolis', *European Review* **4** (1), pp. 3–23.

Naastepad, C. and S. Storm (eds) (1996), *The State and the Economic Press*, London: Edward Elgar.

Nijkamp, P. (1993), 'Towards a network of regions: The United States of Europe', *European Planning Studies* **1** (2), pp. 149–69.

Nijkamp, P. (1995), *The Region and the Environment in Europe: Whose Concern, Whose Competence?*, Research Memorandum, Amsterdam: Department of Economics, Free University.

Nijkamp, P. and M. van Geenhuizen (1997), 'European transport: challenges and opportunities for future research and policies', *Journal of Transport Geography*, **5** (1), pp. 1–11.

Nijkamp P., Vleugel, J., Maggi, J. and I. Masser (1994), *Missing Transport Networks in Europe*, Aldershot: Avebury.

Ohmae, K. (1990), *The Borderless World*, New York: Sage.

Ohmae, K. (1995), *The End of the Nation State: the Rise of Regional Economies*, New York: Sage.

Suarez-Villa, L. and J. Cuadrado Roura (1993), 'Regional economic integration and the evolution of disparities', *Papers in Regional Science* 72 (4), pp. 369–87.

Toonen, Th. (1990), 'Internationalisering en openbaar bestuur als institutioneel ensemble. Naar een zelfbestuurskunde', Gedeeltelijk uitgesproken als rede bij de aanvaarding van het ambt van hoogleraar in de bestuurskunde aan de Rijksuniversiteit Leiden op 2 november 1990. Den Haag: VUGA Uitgeverij bv.

NOTE

1. The images are mainly taken from the ESF document.

15. Implications of European Union Expansion for Peripheral Regions

Ronald W. McQuaid

---

1. INTRODUCTION

Enlargement of the European Union (EU) to include Central and Eastern European countries (CEECs) has significant economic, institutional, political, security, migration and social implications for the EU as a whole (Laurent 1994; CEC 1995a).[1] The peripheral regions of the existing EU will be particularly influenced by the effects of enlargement upon the EU economy, public policies and public sector budgets (Albrechts 1995; Jackman 1995; Kowalski 1989). This chapter discusses the economic and policy implications of enlargement for the economic development of peripheral regions. Section 2 considers peripherality in the context of the current EU and factors that are influenced by it. Section 3 considers possible economic impacts of enlargement upon peripheral regions and Section 4 considers the impacts of related policies. Conclusions are drawn in the final section. The main findings include the possibility that economic gains from any enlargement could lead to increased 'relative' divergence between groups or regions within the existing EU, the need to fully consider the distributional effects of current policies and the importance of policies to raise the competitiveness of peripheral economies and their populations.

2. PERIPHERALITY IN THE EU

Traditional 'core-periphery' models have been used for analysing the Third World (Hollier 1988), centrally planned economies (Demco 1984) and Europe (Wallace 1990; Clout et al. 1989) in terms of interdependent, multi-directional economic dependency, or geographic location.[2] Generally, peripherality has been considered in terms of the geographical distance of an area from the 'core', with distance being a surrogate for higher transport and communication costs resulting in poorer access to markets and resources such as capital, innovations, and so on.

Peripherality has also been widely used to reflect the stage or level of economic development of regions. Parkinson et al. (1992) identify three broad areas within the EU on the basis of industrial restructuring, with the 'old core', 'new core' and peripheral regions, while Stöhr (1987, p. 189) considers the role of innovation in peripherality, and Williams (1987) distinguishes regions of rapid or slow accumulation of capital. Interestingly this latter classification results in some of the geographically remote EU regions, such as parts of Ireland and Portugal, being included as 'emerging' parts of the economic core.[3] This also raises the issue of the dynamics of change over time, and of how and why previously core regions suffer decline and other regions join the core. The concept of peripherality also raises a number of issues that are key to influencing their economic development, in particular, what are the main interregional frictions and how are they measured, and what are the implications of such friction for market access, inputs, and intraregional linkages. Each of these will depend upon the characteristics of the region (such as industrial structure, infrastructure, factor costs and so on), and the nature of its links to other economies. Each is now considered in turn.

Friction limits access from peripheral regions to others, particularly the core regions, and hence affects costs, risk (for example, the reliability of connections) and type and quality of linkages. The friction between regions is often measured by distance. However, weighted distance as a measure of peripherality may be inappropriate if costs are non-linear. Also, in some cases transport between nodes may be cheaper than from a node to its hinterland.[4] Also the transport of people, ideas and capital may not be closely related to the transport costs of goods, yet these factors are crucial to the competitiveness of organizations in a peripheral region and investment in these regions. Hence, as information technology and knowledge economies become more important peripherality may relate increasingly to the characteristics of the region itself and poor access may not be associated so clearly to geographical distance. Indeed the role of innovation and access to information and so on, suggests that nodes, such as major cities in geographically peripheral regions, may have higher accessibility to such competitive factors than geographically closer locations. Hence the core may be considered as multinodal, non-homogenous and with different overlapping cores based upon different characteristics or functional links.

In terms of access to markets, peripherality will affect particularly those exports sensitive to: transport costs (for example, large low-value goods); staff travel costs, suppliers and customers (including tourists); time (which is becoming the main 'cost' in manufacturing according to Drucker 1990, but more specifically can be important when production is organized in a manner such as 'just-in-time'); certainty (if delivery is highly reliable then the time a delivery takes need not be a significant disadvantage); need for liaison between supplier and customer and the type of liaison; and need for supplier to access market information directly in the markets. Keeble et al. (1988), for instance, identify EU core regions as those in close proximity to centres of demand and peripheral regions being those near few significant markets.

In terms of inputs to manufacturing and service product development and production processes, peripherality influences and is influenced by the characteristics of the region. These factors include industrial structure, the quality and scope of physical and business infrastructures, factor cost and supply, local demand, institutional infrastructure and networks, agglomeration economies and technological development which are all important to the development of peripheral regions. Hence, in addition to interregional relationships (for example, in terms of communication costs), overlapping intraregional factors relating to inputs and production networks need to be fully considered. For instance external ownership of plants may also determine location and relocation decisions of branch plants (Bachtler and Clement 1990) although their views may be influenced by the available communication infrastructure (McQuaid et al. 1996).

Peripherality may also lead to disadvantages in the supply of specialist services, skilled labour (especially as more flexible work patterns may result in specialists concentrating in the 'core' where their market is larger and more easily accessed), access to innovation and capital. While peripherality may be associated with lower factor costs, such as labour, the European Commission (CEC 1994) suggests that macroeconomic harmonization may lead to upward pressure on wages in peripheral regions, and so a reduction in their cost advantages. There is thus great pressure to improve learning, education and training, increase labour market flexibility and raise productivity in peripheral regions to increase or maintain competitiveness and to retain and create employment opportunities and improve wages.

Technological inputs include access to, and effective utilization of, new technologies, propensity to innovate and opportunities for skilled staff so that they may be attracted to or retained in the region. Clearly technology is important in the development of new and improved products and production processes and peripherality may hinder technology transfer and indigenous technological development. Hansen (1992) has suggested that the innovative regional *milieux* is important for development. However, Campagni (1995) argues that while *innovative milieux* (that is, wide synergies among local actors which give rise to fast innovation processes) are present in lagging regions in the EU, they are rare and present only in potential and not fully developed forms (due to lack of entrepreneurship or 'backward' social environment, and so on). Direct and indirect (for example, public procurement) policies, institutional factors and contrasting interfirm links have all been important in the development of successful technological regions (for example, Hall et al. 1987).

Will the rise of information technology and the knowledge industries eliminate geographic peripherality? The new information technologies and rising importance of knowledge industries and occupations may reduce the geographic disadvantages of peripherality, with access to knowledge rather than distance determining peripherality. Florida (1995) argues that regions must provide the crucial inputs required for knowledge-intensive economic organizations to flourish.[5] However, the characteristics of peripheral regions and their access to key sources of knowledge and use of that knowledge may still leave them economically marginal. Empirically, Richardson and Gillespie (1996) found that the major communications infrastructure investment in the Scottish Highlands and Islands created some employment, but that this was mostly from inward investment seeking relatively skilled labour at low cost and not from indigenous firms. Hence current EU policies to improve information infrastructure may be a necessary but not a sufficient condition for economic development in peripheral regions.

Such developments in these knowledge industries emphasizes the importance of the links between peripheral regions and the global economy and nodes making up a global rather than primarily EU core. Regions may increasingly be interdependent and integrated and become focal points for economic, technological, political and social organization as the nation-state is squeezed between accelerating globalization and rising regional economic organization (Florida 1995). There is likely to be an associated shift of focus from emphasizing national competitiveness to one which revolves around the concepts of economic and environmentally sustainable advantage at the regional as well as at the national, or global, scale.

Finally, intraregional links, infrastructure and institutions are also important. Krugman (1991) argues that the concentration of economic activity in space is due to the increasing returns to scale in production. These are because of 'spillovers' from the pooled labour market, relating to inputs from supplier industries, and so on, and information and technological factors within industries. Dynamic interindustry clusters may also lead to agglomeration economies (Doeringer and Terkla 1995). The competitive pressures within a region are important and Porter (1990) argues that a demanding home market is crucial to the development of an industry.[6]

However, it is not simply the existence of certain industries, but also the networks of formal and informal relations between organizations that are important for regional growth (Mazzonis 1989) and for small business formation (McQuaid 1996). The question arises, if social, institutional and other networks are important between firms, do these networks and the factors influencing these networks vary systematically across space? Storper (1995) argues that the region is the locus of 'untraded interdependencies' such as labour markets, public institutions and locally or nationally derived rules of action, customs, understanding and values (p. 205). Hence regional policies which support regional institutions may become more important. The national and EU budgetary constraints due to enlargement (discussed below) may put increased strain on such institutions.

Given these complexities concerning peripherality, it is not possible to provide a definite set of peripheral regions here. However, in the context of this paper the peripheral regions can be taken as those both geographically and functionally peripheral, specifically the Objective 1 and Objective 6 regions in Scandinavia, Greece, Ireland, Italy, Portugal, Spain and the UK (shown in Figure 15.1 and discussed further below). Clearly some parts of the above regions (possible eastern Ireland) are more strongly linked to the core and the arguments in this paper also apply to many other regions such as those under Objectives 2 and 5b.

In summary, it is important to consider how the different aspects of peripherality relate to characteristics of the regions and their interconnections with other global and EU areas. This suggests that policies to deal with the consequences of enlargement for peripheral regions need to cover a range of intra- and interregional issues, and economic development policies must reflect these issues and assist in developing develop the necessary physical and non-physical infrastructure to achieve increases in the competitiveness of the regions and their populations.

3. ECONOMIC IMPLICATIONS OF ENLARGEMENT

The significant implications for existing peripheral regions of an enlargement of the EU include those directly affecting their economies in terms of trade, investment and migration together with, as considered in the following section, those influencing resource and budget support for peripheral regions.

Standard economic theory suggests that enlargement will lead to greater economic growth and economic welfare across the EU (for example, Armstrong and Taylor 1993) and greater ability to compete with non-EU economies in the global economy.

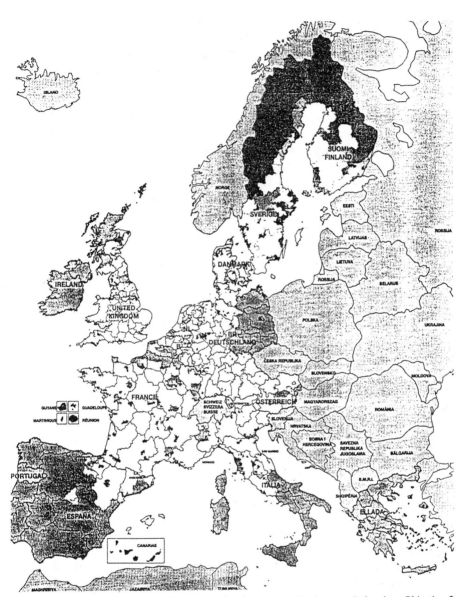

Objective 1 (1994–99): Economic adjustment of regions whose development is lagging. Objective 2 (1994–96): Economic conversion of declining industrial areas. Areas partially eligible under Objective 2. Objective 5b (1994–99): Economic diversification of rural areas. Areas partially eligible under Objective 5b. Objective 6 (1995–99): Development of sparsely populated regions.

Source: European Commission.

Figure 15.1 Areas eligible under the regional objective of the structural funds (1994–99)

The European Commission appears to promote this view (CEC 1995a), claiming that its current policies should result in EU growth (CEC 1995b) and that even lagging regions will gain (although, with the exception of East Germany, not as much as the EU average, CEC 1993a), assuming that the reforms in CEECs do not fail. However, the reduction in border effects on trade and transportation networks due to expansion may have centralizing effects on production, together with a shift towards the CEECs. This could lead to an improvement in the economic position of the whole EU, but with greater divergence between its regions, as peripheral regions may benefit relatively less (or not at all) compared to the other regions.[7]

While trade and investment should increase throughout the EU, the CEECs are in a good position to improve these through potential comparative advantages in some industries and some production that would otherwise be located elsewhere in the EU would shift to them (Jackman 1995). The education standard of the workforces in many of the Visegrad countries is high and labour costs low. They are also geographically near the core of the existing EU and have good transport and communication links to the main EU economies, are closer to the core markets than many existing EU peripheral regions, have had considerable recent private EU investment (for example, in Hungary and the Czech Republic) and are developing legal and financial institutions for a market economy. Relevant language skills are also widely available, and there are cultural links in many cases. In some industries the non-peripheral EU economies will have advantages in marketing to new CEEC markets and so improve their economies of scale and specialization advantages relative to the peripheral regions. Hence increased trade and investment will affect the industrial structure of all regions, and policies need to be targeted to support local and regional economies in the CEECs and the EU to make such adjustments quickly, efficiently and effectively. A number of studies shed light upon these issues.[8]

Bröcker and Jäger-Roschko (1996) argue that, for manufacturing industries, some CEECs (and former Soviet Union countries) may diversify away from industries that were previously competing with existing EU peripheral regions, hence increasing opportunities for these regions. Using a partial equilibrium trade model they argue that empirically the eastern Europe reforms and enlargement should not harm existing peripheral regions and some areas (such as Greece) may gain due to geographic proximity. However, the relative growth in the peripheral regions may be lower than in the rest of the current EU, so increasing divergence of relative wages and living standards across the EU.

Using a gravity model[9] Wang and Winters (1991) and Winters and Wang (1994) estimated the trading potential (for the mid 1980s) of the CEECs including the Soviet Union if they had liberalized trade. The results indicated that trade within CEECs and with developing countries would not increase, but trade with industrialized countries would have grown by factors of three to thirty. They estimated that for the four Visegrad countries potential and actual exports from France were US$5748m and $501m respectively giving a net potential of US$5247 of increased exports. For (West) Germany, Italy and the UK the net potential export increases were US$9075m, $4744m and $4083m respectively (including East Germany does not significantly alter the relative results). Hence, not surprisingly, Germany would gain most from increased trade in absolute and relative (to GDP) terms, while more distant countries (and hence geographically peripheral regions) would gain less.

Similarly, van Bergeijk and Oldersma (1990) used a gravity model with 49 countries for 1985 and estimated that while CEECs would gain most from improved trade, the western flank of Europe (France, UK and Benelux) would be relatively unfavourably placed compared to Germany, although there are net welfare gains. While the results of such models will be affected by the assumptions and model structure, they do correspond with expectations, and also with trading patterns before the Second World War and 'Cold War' since in 1938 some 30 percent of Hungary's and Poland's imports came from Germany (Berghahn 1996). In summary, the new members will provide a market for EU goods, but given their geographical proximity this should place the core economies at an advantage compared to peripheral regions.

Investment from the core EU member states may be directed to CEECs rather than to the existing EU periphery. This is particularly the case where close contact between producer and customer is required. Non-EU inward investment may well be attracted there for similar reasons as well as closer proximity to the core market than in the existing EU peripheral regions. However, the earlier discussion in this chapter noted the importance of other factors, such as labour and capital productivity, the institutional framework, and hence the comparative advantages of the CEECs are not necessarily sufficient for their development.

Enlargement is likely to lead to potentially large migration from CEECs (linked to 'pull' factors of better opportunities and to 'push' factors of job losses following restructuring) which may increase labour supply but also social and political tension in 'core' countries. It may also slow outmigration from the peripheral regions of the current EU (EU-15) due to the greater competition for job opportunities in the more prosperous parts of the EU (see Begg 1995), although there will be new opportunities in the new member states and from the increased economic growth.

Hence the enlargement of the EU to include Visegrad and possibly other CEECs is likely to move the centre of economic gravity of the EU eastwards, reinforcing the relative importance of economies such as Germany's, but placing western and south-western peripheral regions at an increased relative disadvantage compared to the remainder of the EU. However, enlargement will also have important direct and indirect effects upon all regions through impacts upon macroeconomic policies, particularly the EU budget and transfers at the national level, and on regional policies. These are now considered in turn.

4. POLICY IMPLICATIONS OF ENLARGEMENT

4.1 Macroeconomic Policies

Even without enlarging the EU significant budget changes affecting peripheral regions are occurring. Policies to meet the target criteria for financial and monetary convergence, including the single European currency, puts pressure on reducing government deficits in most member states and may lead to deflationary pressures (Smith 1992) in the short run.[10] The enlargement of the EU would exacerbate this by placing further pressure on both the EU regional and other budgets and on the budgets of existing member states who may need to increase their net contributions to, or reduce their net receipts from, the EU. This section briefly considers the implications for peripheral regions of EU related macroeconomic policies and then of EU regional policies.[11]

Macroeconomic policies across the EU are important to peripheral regions for, among other reasons, helping to set an economic environment to promote the economic development of the EU economies, and to transfer resources between member states, regions, individuals and groups. The CEC (1995a, p. 5) argue that such policies will provide EU-wide benefits by helping to provide a stable macroeconomic environment with a credibly implemented plan to restore public finances, leading to lead to a virtuous 'crowding in' effect, whereby short-term investment and employment is encouraged due to improved confidence of the private sector and a reduction on the risk-premium on interest rates. However, there are likely to be diverse regional impacts that vary by member state. For instance, the private sector 'crowding in' investment may be located differently from that cut in public investment, possibly resulting in a relative increase in core regions rather than peripheral ones, while changes in the type of public investment may lead to further structural problems for different parts of the labour market.

Many of the EU policies such as the proposals set out in the 'White Paper' on Competitiveness (CEC 1993b) and the EU Employment Strategy (CEC 1995b), have direct or indirect impacts upon regions and may disadvantage peripheral regions (Begg and Mayes 1991). All fiscal and monetary policies result in the transfer of resources from some individuals, organizations and groups to others, through taxes, expenditure and prices and these will have a spatial dimension. For example, high interest rates result in major transfers between borrowers (individuals, governments and so on) and savers, and there are often relatively large transaction costs associated with these EU transfers.

Similarly, the Common Agricultural Policy (CAP) has led to significantly higher prices – paid by all members of society (Jackman 1995) and is regressive in the sense of prices and tax raised to fund it impinging relatively more on those with lower incomes, while resources are transferred to individuals or organizations linked to the farming industry. Indeed much CAP support is directly targeted at those who own or lease land, so only those local people who are relatively wealthy (at least in capital terms) receive the bulk of the support. CAP may favour the wealthier regions (Ardy 1988) while Mediterranean peripheral regions may be particularly disadvantaged (Franzmeyer et al. 1991). As the Central and East European countries likely to join an enlarged EU are more agriculturally based than existing member states, they would make relatively high demands on the CAP budget (if CAP was not reformed), but also CAP would form a major component of fiscal transfers to these countries. Estimates vary of the impact of enlargement upon the CAP budget, and a high estimate is that the impact of the Visegrad countries joining would more than double the CAP cost by an additional 37 billion ECU per year (Anderson and Tyres 1993). Clearly such budget increases would be impossible unless the EU decided to significantly increase the budget as a share of EU GDP, with most of the increase being directed towards the new CEEC members, and further reform of the Structural Funds is required.

The implications for existing peripheral regions is that their share of existing structural and other funds would be likely to decline in absolute and relative terms, and so there would be diversion of GDP from their member state to the CEECs. There is likely to be considerable resistance from the main member states or regions having to fund any increase in the EU budget and from those likely to lose funding, including the possible rise of groups such as the Northern League in Italy (Curbelo and Alburqueque 1993), especially if not compensated by greater growth.

The transfer of EU funds to poorer regions or groups could be achieved through the use of automatic transfers, as is common within most member states.[12] Indeed the MacDougall Report (CEC 1977) argued that a system of explicit and automatic transfers within the EU was important for moving towards political and economic union. Without such automatic stabilizers to redistribute the gains and losses from further economic integration there will be 'stagnation of the integration process, and at the worst result in secession and dissolution' (CEC 1977, p. 60). However, pan-EU automatic transfers are still largely absent.

There is a potential contradiction that while interregional/community fiscal transfers are widely accepted within countries to reduce the income differences resulting from uneven development, such political support may be lacking when it comes to significant transfers between member states in the EU (Goodhart 1990; MacKay 1995b). If automatic transfers were introduced many would be directed at the new CEECs (given their low incomes) and peripheral regions with large proportions of elderly, unemployed etc. It is difficult to envisage high levels of financial and political support from existing member states as for this to have a meaningful impact the budget would need to be large, which may be difficult to control. However, while the current EC budget is only around 1 percent of the GDP of the EU it is significant as it is often targeted at limited groups (for example, specific industries or young unemployed people and so on) so the impact on these is relatively large.

The indirect implications of EU enlargement on the budgets of the individual member states are also important. The macroeconomic policies discussed above are likely to lead to cuts in member state public expenditure and budget deficits in many countries, which may in turn reduce regional support policies and mainstream budgets such as education and welfare which are of particular importance to peripheral regions.

The move towards a European Monetary Union and a single currency will also influence the development of member states and their regions through changes in monetary and fiscal policy and budget constraints discussed above and changing the focus from member states to the EU in terms of external balances of trade. This could lead to exchange rates which take little account of impacts upon peripheral regions through removing exchange rate variations as a national policy option. Krugman and Venables (1990) argue that small countries engaging in mutual and equal reductions in barriers to trade with larger countries may suffer ambiguous effects (welfare gains through competition and economies of scale but wage declines and possible loss of industry) so they should 'undervalue' their currency.

Krugman (1993) suggests that the European Monetary Union will increase regional disparities, while Abraham and Van Rompuy (1995) also imply a worsening of disparities, especially if there is a limited responsiveness of labour to regional shocks. Similarly, monetary policy will be focused on the needs of the EU as a whole (or specific members) with relatively less weight given to the needs of individual nations or regions. While this is currently a problem for regions within a member state, the disconnection between local circumstances and those influencing the monetary policy are in general likely to become greater as monetary policy is determined at a larger scale.

4.2 European Regional Policies

The regional policies of the European Union and its predecessors are discussed elsewhere (for example, Dignan 1995). The EU policies relating to the Structural Funds[13] have consistently been to improve indigenous growth of assisted regions (see for instance CEC 1995c), so that convergence is reached through bringing the poorer regions up to the levels of the wealthier ones. The main policy responses of many cities in peripheral regions were upgrading and extending their strategic communications infrastructure (Dawson 1992) to reduce the 'friction' of the physical distance from the EU core, hence allowing diffusion of innovation, and so on. Parkinson et al. (1992) found that agglomeration economies remained important with control and command functions predominantly in the core regions. One result of major infrastructure and other investment in the main cities of the peripheral regions may be to exacerbate the intraregional differences, perhaps reinforcing a system of cities (Pred 1977) which are well linked together, but have poor links to the economies of their hinterlands.

Other important policy responses to the structural implications of the macroeconomic policy factors of the enlargement of the EU have focused upon capital, labour and related infrastructure (see, for instance, CEC 1995a, b). For example, improving competitiveness of firms in peripheral regions, through innovation, capital investment, 'export' initiatives marketing; labour market policies such as labour migration (although barriers such as language remain), flexible working, wages and non-wage costs, improving the supply of labour (education, training and the related lifelong learning) and ensuring access for disadvantaged groups; and improved communications and infrastructure.

The Single European Market raised the issue of its impact upon peripheral regions (Begg 1989) and was linked to the development of Structural Funds to promote the development of lagging regions and assist those with declining industries (such as agriculture) and subsequently regional policy was reformed. The main types of regions aided were Objective 1 or lagging regions (including most of the most geographically peripheral regions), Objective 2 regions undergoing industrial decline (spread throughout the traditionally industrial areas of the EU), Objective 5b regions covering economic diversification of rural areas, again usually geographically peripheral and Objective 6 for the very sparsely populated Nordic peripheral regions. While the budget from 1994–99 is 170 billion ECU, after 1999 it is likely that many of the resources would be diverted from existing peripheral regions (except perhaps those with extremely low GDP or the new Nordic members) to the potential new members.

Table 15.1 Annual per capita aid allocation in objectives 1/2/5b/6 areas 1994–99 (ECU at 1994 prices)

	Objective 1	Objective 2	Objective 5b	Objective 6	Objectives 1–6
Austria	120	31	35	–	30
Belgium	95	40	29	–	30
Denmark	–	45	25	–	24
Finland	–	45	35	107	49
France	143	43	38	–	38
Germany	145	37	26	–	40
Greece	225	–	–	–	225
Ireland	262	–	–	–	262
Italy	117	39	31	–	58
Luxembourg	–	19	33	–	35
The Netherlands	115	42	31	–	24
Portugal	235	–	–	–	235
Spain	188	51	64	–	135
Sweden	–	32	34	110	22
United Kingdom	115	43	48	–	33
EUR-15	170	42	35	109	62
Total ECU mn	93972	15352	6860	697	138201
Percentage of all Structural Funds	68%	11.1%	5.0%	0.5%	100%
Percentage of EU population covered	26.6%	16.4%	8.8%	0.4%	100%

Notes:
Excludes Community Initiatives.
Figures are rounded.
a) including Objective 3 which obtained 9.4 percent of Structural Funds, Objective 4 which received 1.6 percent, and Objective 5a which received 4.4 percent.

Source: Data from CEC (1996).

The importance of Structural Funds to specific member states and regions, particularly the poorest and most geographically ones, is clearly seen in Table 15.1. This shows the per capita distribution in eligible regions or areas of the main geographically focused ERDF funds (excluding the many Community Initiatives which are for particular purposes such as adjusting to declines in textiles, shipbuilding or the defence industries). It shows the importance of

Objective 1 funding, particularly for the Mediterranean countries, Ireland and geographically peripheral parts of the UK (primarily the Scottish Highlands and Islands and Northern Ireland) and Objective 6 funding in peripheral regions in Sweden and Finland.

Portugal, Greece, Ireland and Spain receive much higher per capita aid nationally (although Ireland's recent growth means that it no longer has such a low per capita GDP). The first three countries are covered entirely by Objective 1, while the table also shows the importance, in per capita terms, for the populations of Objective 1 (and Objective 6) funding for peripheral regions in other countries. Among the other countries the Objective 1 areas receive particularly high contributions compared to the overall per capita allocations of all Structural Funds (Objectives 1 to 6) within each country. Indeed allocations for Objective 1 and 6 in these regions generally received three to five times the per capita average for the country as a whole. Structural Funds are only part of the EU expenditure and the national figures for each country do not take account of the net contributions of the country to the EU budget (with Germany making the largest net per capita contribution to EU funds in 1995). However, it is likely that the poorer regions within wealthier countries, such as Sweden and the UK, contribute relatively less than wealthier regions and so the figures are likely to reflect relative net contributions also.

Should the Visegrad states enter the EU then the average EU GDP level would fall and areas such as Ireland and the Highlands and Islands would move over the eligibility threshold of 75 percent of average GDP and so no longer be eligible for Objective 1 status, losing resources (unless the regulations were changed). Also, if the Visegrad countries joined and received Objective 1 status (as their economic position would warrant), then data (CEC 1993a) suggest that they might be eligible for 26 billion ECUs, almost half of the existing EU budget.[14] Baldwin (1993) estimates that the net cost to the EC budget of admitting the four Visegrad countries would be 58.1bn ECU per annum and it would take 30 years for them to reach an average per capita GDP of 75 percent of the average, so the cost would be ongoing for the foreseeable future. This is because their GDPs are low; they would contribute little in revenue but be eligible for considerable aid and are heavily dependent upon agriculture. They have a population of around 64 million concentrated in Poland (38 million). Maresceau (1992) also suggests that the annual aid budget to the CEECs would be 25 times that of current aid to the five southern EU countries. Similarly these countries would have a greater claim on the other Structural Funds than most existing EU countries. While EU regional policy is currently relatively well funded, but there may be a crisis if expectations are not met, due perhaps to weak macroeconomies (Armstrong 1996; Cappellin 1995).

It is possible that to replace Structural Funds that may be diverted to the CEECs after 1999, peripheral regions may seek to link together to gain EU financial support. However, the basis of this support may be to transfer funds to placate the demands of these regions rather than to genuinely improve regional economic development. For example, groups of peripheral regions (for example, sharing a sea) may have few economic links and efforts to promote such links, in order to get EU funds, may divert them from other policies that would give a greater economic impact. There may, of course, be other rationales for such groupings, such as the need to deal with common environmental issues.

Transportation is of particular importance to peripheral regions and the potential new members. Within the EU there has also been considerable interest in ensuring that policies relating to the provision of transportation infrastructure should not hinder economic development, and should promote the development of disadvantaged peripheral regions (Biehl 1986; Button et al. 1995). The desire for greater integration through the Single European Act acted as a catalyst for the development of various strands of transport policy particularly with respect to the role of infrastructure. The European White Paper on Growth, Employment and Competitiveness (CEC 1993b) argues that improved Trans-European Networks are important for stimulating economic growth and will be important for integrating CEECs. Ironically, greater accessibility due to improved transportation networks may increase the centralization of production and distribution facilities following the greater integration due to the Single European Market and so hinder the development of peripheral regions.

The Common Transport Policy of the EU has traditionally been concerned with the harmonization and liberalization of transport operations within the Union although the recent emphasis has been on the development of Master Plans for different transport modes including the development of new networks where their absence causes isolation or hampers the development of part of the Union's territory (CEC 1992, 8). However, Nijkamp (1995) notes that the quality of the communication infrastructure in nodal centres, interoperationality (especially between national systems) and intermodality and integration (between short and long distance transport) will be important to integrate all EU regions with transport network.

5. CONCLUSIONS

There are significant institutional, political, and economic implications of the enlargement of the EU to include Central and Eastern European countries. This chapter has argued that these will have particularly significant direct and indirect impacts upon existing peripheral regions of the EU. As the EU is enlarged then the centre of economic gravity (in terms of trade flows and investment) is likely to move eastwards, and reinforce the economic dominance of the existing EU core. Although overall greater EU growth may result, this will, *ceteris paribus*, increase divergence and the relative economic peripherality of existing EU peripheral regions (with the possible exception of Greece with its greater proximity to CEECs). Support will need to continue to be given to promote economic development of the existing EU peripheral regions, especially indigenous development, given the increased competition for inward investment from CEECs, although the emphasis upon different types of support given may vary from those of the past.

It was argued that the notion of peripherality is complex and its implications multifaceted and that the core may be considered as multinodal, non-homogenous and with different overlapping cores based upon different characteristics or functional links. Hence, analysis of policies related to the development of peripheral regions will need to deal with a range of factors including interregional links involving capital, labour and physical, communications infrastructure together with intraregional links and local infrastructure and institutions, and so on. It is important that such policies are used to increase the competitiveness of regions and to genuinely support their economic development, within the wider social and environmental contexts. The potential of such policies being seen primarily as attempts to maximize national shares of EU funding, with their use and distribution being almost secondary, must be overcome.

In terms of funding through the EU, the existing peripheral regions may again become relatively more peripheral as they have much greater competition for funds, and less political influence within an enlarged EU. The cost of enlargement to EU budgets together with European Monetary Union convergence criteria and other budgetary pressures, are likely to lead to relative cuts in member state public expenditure and budget deficits in many countries, which may in turn reduce regional support policies and mainstream budgets such as education and welfare which are of particular importance to peripheral regions, although their relative scale may be small.

Enlargement will also need to result in the fundamental reform of the main EU programmes. These changes will have significant redistributive impacts (upon individuals, organizations, and regions) who benefit from existing or new programmes and on those who fund the higher expenditure (for example, perhaps through higher taxes, interest rates paid or prices). However, if the policy changes are designed to increase economic welfare and to take account of the impacts upon the development of peripheral regions (and of particular groups in society) then some of these factors may be ameliorated. It is crucial, therefore, to consider fully the spatial impacts of all existing and future changes in mainstream national and EU funding programmes and their impacts upon the development of all regions.

There are a number of options on how to deal with the possible expansion of the EU, each with differing implications for financial or other support, migration, access to EU markets, and political integration and so on. Three of the potential options include: first, the CEECs (or initially a few of them such as the Visegrad countries) could be given full membership of the EU with reform of main EU policies (especially CAP) and institutions, and an increased EU budget (which would have repercussions for peripheral regions and national budgets in an era of extreme budget pressure on member states). Second, the EU could adopt a multi-tier membership approach with different states receiving different levels of support and integration into policies, for example varying membership of the Single European Currency reducing the benefits of integration but allowing national exchange rate and other policies to reflect the needs of their regions. Third, the CEECs could be given an associate status with financial aid and improved access to European markets for goods and services (although reductions in world trade barriers may make this relatively less important). Clearly various combinations and levels of economic and political integration into the EU are possible. The improvement of trade and greater integration of the CEEC countries is important for them and the EU as a whole and should increase overall economic welfare. A major challenge will, however, be to ensure that economic gains from any enlargement do not result in increased divergence between groups or regions through the EU.

REFERENCES

Abraham, F. and P. Van Rompuy (1995), 'Regional convergence in the European Monetary Union', *Papers in Regional Science* **74**, pp. 125–42.

Albrechts, L. (1995), 'Shifts in Europe and their impact on the European spatial structure', in Hardy, S., Hart, M., Albrechts, L. and K. Katos (eds), *An Enlarged Europe: Regions in Competition*, London: Jessica Kingsley Publishers.

Anderson, K. and R. Tyres (1993), *Implications of EC Expansion for European Agricultural Policies, Trade and Welfare*, London: Discussion Paper 829, CEPR.

Ardy, B. (1988), 'The national incidence of the European Community budget', *Journal of Common Market Studies* **26** (4), pp. 401–29.

Armstrong, H.W. (1995), 'Convergence amongst regions of the European Union', *Papers in Regional Science* **74**, pp. 143–52.

Armstrong, H.W. (1996), 'Discussion paper for the Jean Monnet group of experts', *Regional Policy and Structural Aid*, Hull: Centre for European Union Studies.

Armstrong, H.W. and J. Taylor (1993), *Regional Economics and Policy*, London: Harvester Wheatsheaf.

Bachtler, J. and K. Clement (1990), *The Impact of the Single European Market on Foreign Direct Investment in the United Kingdom*, London: HMSO.

Baldwin, R. (1993), *Towards and Integrated Europe*, London: CEPR.

Begg, I. (1989), 'The regional dimension of "1992" proposals', *Regional Studies* **23**, pp. 368–76.

Begg, I. (1995), 'Factor mobility and regional disparities in the European Union', *Oxford Review of Economic Policy* **11**, pp. 96–112.

Begg, I. and D.G. Mayes (1991), *A New Strategy for Social and Economic Cohesion after 1992*, Luxemburg: Office for Official Publications of the European Communities.

Berg, A. and J. Sachs (1992), 'Trade reform and adjustment in Eastern Europe: the case of Poland', *Economic Policy* **14**.

Berghahn, V. (1996), *Quest for Economic Empire*, Oxford: Berghahn Books.

Bergeijk, P.A.G. van and H. Oldersma (1990), 'Détente, market-orientated reform and German unification: potential consequences for the world trade system', *Kyklos* **43**, pp. 599–609.

Biehl, D. (1986), *The Contribution of Infrastructure to Regional Development*, Brussels: Commission of the European Communities.

Bröcker, J. and O. Jäger-Roschko (1996), 'Eastern reforms, trade, and spatial change in the EU', *Papers in Regional Science* **75**, pp. 23–40.

Button, K.J. and E.J. Pentecost (1993), 'Regional service sector convergence', *Regional Studies* **27**, pp. 623–36.

Button, K.J., Leitham, S., McQuaid, R.W. and J.D. Nelson (1995), 'Transport and industrial and commercial location', *Annals of Regional Science* **29**, pp. 189–206.

Campagni, R.P. (1995), 'The concept of innovative milieu and its relevance for public policies in European lagging regions', *Papers in Regional Science* **74**, pp. 317–40.

Cappellin, R. (1995), 'Regional development, federalism and inter-regional cooperation', in Eskelinen, H. and F. Snickars (eds), *Competitive European Peripheries*, Berlin: Springer.

CEC (Commission of the European Communities) (1977), *MacDougall Report, Report of the Study Group on the Role of Public Finance in European Integration, Vols. 1 and 2*, Luxemburg: Office for Official Publications of the European Communities.

CEC (1987), *Third Periodic Report from the Commission on the Social and Economic Development of the Regions of the Community*, Luxemburg: OOPEC.

CEC (1992), *Transport Infrastructure,* COM(92) 231 Final, Luxemburg: OOPEC.

CEC (1993a) *Trade and Foreign Investment in the Community's Regions: The Impact of Economic Reform in Central and Eastern Europe. Report by the National Economic Research Associates*, Luxemburg: OOPEC.

CEC (1993b), *Growth, competitiveness and employment: the Challenges and Ways Forward into the Twenty-first Century*, Luxemburg: OOPEC.

CEC (1994), 'Competitiveness and cohesion', *Fifth Periodic Report from the Commission on the Social and Economic Development of the Regions of the Community*, Luxemburg: OOPEC.

CEC (1995a), *White Paper on the Preparation of Associated Countries of Central and Eastern Europe for Integration onto the Internal Market of the Union*, Luxemburg: OOPEC.

CEC (1995b), *The European Employment Strategy: Recent Progress and Prospects for the Future*, COM(95) 465 Final, Luxemburg: OOPEC.

CEC (1995c), *The New Regional Programmes under Objectives 1 and 2 of Community Structural Policies*, COM(95) 111 Final, Luxemburg: OOPEC.

CEC (1996), *First Cohesion Report*, COM(96) 542 Final, Luxemburg: OOPEC.

Clout, H., Blacksell, M., King, R. and D. Pinder (1989), *Western Europe: Geographical Perspectives*, London: Longman.

Collins, S. and D. Rodrik (1991), *Eastern Europe and the Soviet Union in the World Economy*, Washington, DC: Institute for International Economics.

Curbelo, J.L. and F. Alburqueque (1993), *Economic and Monetary Union, Stabilization Policies and Developmental Planning in the Peripheral Regions of the EC*, Research Paper 14, Glasgow: European Policies Research Centre, Strathclyde University.

Dawson, J. (1992), 'Peripheral cities in the European Community: challenges, strategies and prospects', *Public Policy and Administration* 7, pp. 9–20.

Demco, G. (ed) (1984), *Regional Development Problems and Policies in Eastern and Western Europe*, London: Croom Helm.

Dignan, T. (1995), 'Regional disparities and regional policy in the European Union', *Oxford Review of Economic Policy* 11, pp. 64–95.

Doeringer, P.B. and D.G. Terkla (1995), 'Business strategy and cross-industry clusters', *Economic Development Quarterly* 9, pp. 225–37.

Drucker, P.F. (1990), 'The emerging theory of manufacturing', *Harvard Business Review*, May–June, pp. 94–102.

Florida, R. (1995), 'Toward the learning region', *Futures* 27, pp. 527–36.

Franzmeyer, F., Hrubesch, P., Seidel, B., Weise, C. and I. Schweiger (1991), *The Regional Impact of Community Policies*, Luxemburg: OOPEC.

Goodhart, C. (1990), 'An approach to European currency unification', *Lloyds Bank Annual Review* 3, pp. 194–207.

Hall, P., Breheny, M., McQuaid, R.W. and D. Hart (1987), *Western Sunrise – The Genesis and Growth of Britain's Major High-Tech Corridor*, London: George Allen & Unwin.

Hansen, N. (1992), 'Competition, trust and reciprocity in the development of innovative regional milieux', *Papers in Regional Science* 71, pp. 95–105.

Hollier, G.P. (1988), 'Regional Development', in Pacioe, M. (ed.), *The Geography of the Third World*, London: Routledge, pp. 232–70.

Jackman, R. (1995), 'Regional policy in an enlarged Europe', *Oxford Review of Economic Policy* 11, pp. 113–25.

Keeble, D., Offord, J. and S. Walker (1988), *Peripheral Regions in a Community of Twelve Member States*, Luxemburg: OOPEC.

Kowalski, L. (1989), 'Major Current and Future Regional Issues in the Enlarged Community', in Albrechts, L., Moulaert, P., Roberts, P. and E. Swyngedouw (eds), *Regional Policy at the Crossroads*, London: Jessica Kingsley Publishers.

Krugman, P. (1991), 'Increasing returns and economic geography', *Journal of Political Economy* **99**, pp. 483–99.

Krugman, P. (1993), 'Lessons from Massachusetts for EMU', in Torres, F. and F. Giavazzi (eds), *Adjustment and Growth in the European Monetary Union*, Cambridge: CUP.

Krugman, P. and A.J. Venables (1990), 'Integration and the Competitiveness of Peripheral Industry', in Bliss, C.J. and J.B. de Macedo (eds), *Unity with Diversity in the European Economy: the Community's southern frontier*, Cambridge: CUP.

Laurent, P.H. (1994), 'Widening Europe: the dilemmas of community success', *AAPSS* **531**, pp. 124–40.

Linnemann, H. (1966), *An Econometric Study of International Trade Flows*, Amsterdam: North-Holland Publishing Company.

Mazzonis, D. (1989), 'Small firm networking, co-operation and innovation in Italy viewed by an agency engaged in actions for stimulating the technological upgrading of industry', *Entrepreneurship and Regional Development* **1**, pp. 61–74.

MacKay, R.R. (1995a), 'Non-market forces, the nation state and the European Union', *Papers in Regional Science* **74** (3), pp. 209–31.

MacKay, R.R. (1995b), 'European Integration and Public Finance: the Political Economy Of Regional Support', in Hardy, S., Hart, M., Albrechts, L. and A. Katos (eds), *An Enlarged Europe: Regions in Competition*, London: Jessica Kingsley.

Maresceau, M. (1992), 'The European Community, Eastern Europe and the USSR', in Redmond, J. (ed.), *The External Relations of the European Community: The International Response to 1992*, London: St. Martins Press.

McQuaid, R.W. (1986), 'Production functions and the disaggregation of labor inputs in manufacturing plants', *Journal of Regional Science* **26** (3), pp. 595–603.

McQuaid, R.W. (1996), 'Social networks, entrepreneurship and regional development', in Danson, M. (ed.), *Small Firm Formation and Regional Economic Development,* London: Routledge.

McQuaid, R.W., Leitham, S. and J.D. Nelson (1996), 'Accessibility and location decisions in a peripheral region of Europe – a logit analysis', *Regional Studies* **30** (6), pp. 579–88.

Nijkamp, P. (1995), 'Borders and barriers in the new Europe: impediments and potentials in new network configurations', in Coccossis, H. and P. Nijkamp (eds), *Overcoming Isolation: Information and Transport Networks in Development Strategies for Peripheral Areas*, Berlin: Springer.

Parkinson, M., Bianchini, F., Dawson, J., Evans, R. and A. Harding (1992), *Urbanisation and the Functions of Cities in the European Community*, Brussels: European Commission.

Porter, M. (1990), *The Competitive Advantage of Nations*, London: Macmillan.

Pred, A. (1977), *City Systems in Advanced Economies*, London: Hutchinson.

Richardson, R. and A. Gillespie (1996), 'Advanced communications and employment creation in rural and peripheral regions: a case study of the

Highlands and Islands of Scotland', *Annals of Regional Science* **39**, pp. 91–110.

Smith, J. (1992), 'European Monetary Arrangements and National Economic Sovereignty', in Amin, A. and M. Dietrich (eds), *Towards a New Europe? Structural changes in the European economy*, London: Edward Elgar.

Stöhr, W.B. (1987), 'Regional economic development and the world economic crisis', *International Social Science Journal* **112**, pp. 187–97.

Storper, M. (1995), 'The resurgence of regional economics, ten years later, the region as a nexus of untraded interdependencies', *European Urban and Regional Studies* **2**, pp. 191–221.

Wallace, W. (ed.) (1990), *The Dynamics of European Integration*, London: RIIA/Pinter.

Wang, Z.K. and L.A. Winters (1991), *The Trading Potential of Eastern Europe*, Discussion Paper No. 610, London: CEPR.

Williams, A.M. (1987), *The Western European Economy: a Geography of Post-war Development*, London: Hutchinson.

Winters, L.A. and Z.K. Wang (1994), *Eastern Europe's International Trade*, Manchester: Manchester University Press.

NOTES

1. At Copenhagen on 22–23 June 1993 the EU Heads of Government agreed that associated CEECs could become members, although no timetable was set. Three of the Visegrad-4 countries (Poland, the Czech Republic and Hungary) plus Estonia and Slovenia, seem most likely to be allowed fuller integration with the EU first. Much future analysis of related issues is expected under the EC's Agenda 2000 programme.

2. A fundamental policy issue is whether to target individuals or client groups who are on the periphery of society or the economy, or to target areas or regions which are geographically or functionally peripheral. This, however, also raises issues of how to define a peripheral area (for example, in terms of the characteristics of an area rather than by the geographic location) and also of intraregional versus interregional differences. These approaches are not mutually exclusive.

3. There are also different levels of peripherality (for example the ultra-peripherality of the French overseas territories) and also differences between entire countries being peripheral (for example, Ireland) or regions being peripheral in terms of their own country, or of the wider EU economy.

4. The concentration of research upon manufacturing industries often introduces a bias where it fails to reflect the economic structure of regions by ignoring 'exportable' services and primary industries that may be fundamentally important to them. The scale of regions and choice of the centre of the

region (for example, the population centre or production centre may not be the same) will also influence results.

5. These include: manufacturing infrastructure of interconnected vendors and suppliers (on a global basis); a human infrastructure that can produce knowledge workers and facilitates the development of a team orientation, organized around lifelong learning; a physical and communication infrastructure which facilitates and supports constant sharing of information, the electronic sharing of data and information, just-in-time delivery of goods and services, and integration into the global economy; and capital allocation and industrial governance systems attuned to the needs of knowledge-intensive organizations.

6. Although the home market for different industries could be considered as being regional, national or EU.

7. There is a debate as to whether convergence of the peripheral region economies towards the core in terms of GDP per capita, unemployment and so on is taking place, and even with slow convergence the current relative problems of these regions and the speed of any such convergence still poses a problem. Based on EC evidence (CEC, 1987, 1994) there were great disparities across the EU with peripheral regions increasingly disadvantaged. Evidence suggests that convergence does not occur in all periods, with Button and Pentecost (1993) arguing that there was no significant convergence of GDP per capita across the EU during the 1980s. Similarly, Armstrong (1995) found only slow income and output convergence after the 1960s. The migration of people from the periphery to the core may not fully counter regional disparities (Begg 1995).

8. The inclusion of tradable services in such analysis may have uncertain effects on some of these studies as, for example, tourism may benefit some remote regions, but business services may follow different patterns from manufacturing, especially financial services which may concentrate in specific nodes. In addition even within one sector regional models need to take into account types of firms and inputs may be heterogeneous, invalidating assumptions of similar and constant elasticity of substitution between inputs (McQuaid 1986).

9. This was based on the robust Linnemann (1966) type model and fitted to 76 market economies. Collins and Rodrik (1991) found somewhat similar results using a methodology based upon empirically breaking aggregate export figures for countries and allocating it to specific country trade shares.

10. The targets include a maximum deficit of 3 percent and a maximum total public debt of 60 percent of GDP, although the actual reductions in deficit at the EU level may be lower if EU bonds to fund expenditure in policy areas

such as the Trans-European Networks are not included in the public deficit targets. The economic rationale for such exclusion is limited although the expenditure would be important for many regions.

11. This may cause tension between those member states currently recipients of the Cohesion Fund aiming at bringing those who are currently the poorest (Greece, Ireland, Portugal and Spain) towards the level of other EU states, against the new countries who would come in as the poorest and hence have a greater claim for funding, based upon their lower levels of development and incomes. This would be exacerbated if the view was taken that regional policy should be limited to bringing regions up to a minimum level rather than to eventual convergence of incomes, and so on.

12. MacKay (1995a) argues that market solutions alone will not lead to cohesion and balanced regional development and that automatic stabilizers involving regional transfers are essential and 'natural' in advanced economies as assumptions that spatial inequalities are temporary and minor are not realistic.

13. The four main Structural Fund funding devices are the European Regional Development Fund, the European Social Fund, the Agriculture Guidance and Guarantee Fund and the Financial Instrument for Fisheries Guidance, the first two being particularly important for regional policies.

14. The per capita GDP of these countries ranged from 22 percent of the EU-15 average for Slovakia to 45 percent for the Czech Republic. However, it should be noted that the GDP figures for the Central and East European countries are probably unreliable and underestimates (Berg and Sachs 1992).

16. A Meta Analysis of the Impact of Infrastructure Policy on Regional Development

Kenneth Button and Piet Rietveld

1. INTRODUCTION

The timing, nature and extent of infrastructure provision forms an explicit part of most countries regional economic policies. Within this general pattern there are, however, some discernible differences in approach. Many countries have taken the position that infrastructure has an important influence on the location of industrial development and have used a proactive approach to infrastructure provision. Another view is that infrastructure provision should be reactive in the sense of ensuring that a region's economic development is not impeded by a lack of infrastructure – any potential shortage stemming from the perceived public good nature of much infrastructure.[1]

These issues have received much attention in recent policy discussions in several parts of the world. An interesting example is provide by Europe. Developments both within the European Union (EU) and, linked to this, with regard to the policies of such institutions as the European Bank for Economic Reconstruction and Development towards the post-communist societies of central and eastern Europe, have led to renewed interest in ensuring that infrastructure policy should at least not hinder economic developments.[2] In particular, while the Common Transport Policy of the EU has traditionally been concerned with the harmonization and liberalization of transport operations within the Union, the Treaty of Maastricht explicitly brings up the issue of transport networks (Title XII) and master plans for high-speed rail, combined transport, motorways and inland waterways have been developed (Commission of the European Communities 1992).

Since one of the justifications for this wider European interest in transport infrastructure at all levels is to meet social and regional objectives, and in particular to assist in the integration of peripheral areas into the Community, there is a need to more fully understand the importance of such infrastructure on industrial location and economic development more generally. In fact, firm evidence of the nature of the links involved and their quantification is still missing – indeed much of the EU policy in this regard stems primarily from belief rather than from concrete, quantitative analysis.[3] Further, the issue is becoming more important as developments take place in the former communist states of eastern and central Europe. To ensure that their economies are more completely integrated with those in the current European area adequate and appropriate infrastructure will need to be in place. If policies with this as an end goal are to be successfully put in train then a firmer understanding of the links between infrastructure provision and economic development is required.

The aim of this chapter is to add a small amount to this understanding. The initial sections examine the arguments and evidence surrounding the role which transport and related infrastructure plays in stimulating economic development and in influencing the location of economic activities. It is used to set the subsequent empirical analysis in context. The main focus of the quantitative work is on the extent to which the knowledge that has already been gleaned from a variety of case studies provides a solid basis upon which to base conclusions regarding the future direction of infrastructure policies.

2. INFRASTRUCTURE AND PRODUCTIVITY

What exactly is meant by infrastructure? The provision of adequate infrastructure is often seen as a necessary prerequisite for economic advancement but, while economists are generally rather particular in the ways in which specific goods are categorized, the definition of infrastructure (sometimes equally opaquely referred to as 'social overhead capital') tends to be vague and imprecise. Lakshmanan (1989) talks of the term as 'often employed in a loose impressionistic manner'. Where there have been efforts at delineation, the tendency is frequently to look at particular physical features and to offer lists of such characteristics – Nurske (1966), for instance, lists features such as: 'provide services basic to any production capacity'; 'cannot be imported from abroad' and 'large and costly installations'. Hirschman (1958), in defining social overhead capital, lists sectors, namely, 'In its widest sense, it includes all public services from law and order through education and public health to transportation, communications, power and water supply as well as such agricultural overhead capital as irrigation and drainage systems. The hard core of the concept can probably be restricted to transportation and power'. More recently, these characteristics have tended to be outlined in rather more technical terms and, in particular, the possible relevance of notions such as information flows (Youngson 1967) and, as a particular case of externalities, of public goods (Andersson 1991; Andersson and Kobayashi 1989), have been examined.

While definitions are very important, here we tend to shy away from getting too deeply involved in the issue and to adopt the easy way out by following the spirit of Jacob Viner's wisecrack that 'economics is what economists do' and simply treat infrastructure as 'what most people consider it to be'. From a strict definition perspective this may be seen as a form of passing the buck but in practical terms and, given the nature of the chapter, it seems unlikely that it will lead to any substantive degree of confusion.

There has recently been something of an upsurge of interest by policy makers in the role which transport, communications and other infrastructure plays in stimulating economic development. From an intellectual perspective this can, looking back at the literature of the past century or so, be seen to fit in with a cyclical pattern of changing academic interests. More pragmatically, a number of key factors can, perhaps, be highlighted as being of specific relevance for the 1990s. There have been major technical advances in telecommunications that require new infrastructure if they are to be fully exploited, although the exact nature of this infrastructure is not always agreed upon. With more conventional forms of transport, rapidly rising demand in the 1970s and 1980s at a time of relatively limited investment and replacement expenditure means that many existing facilities require refurbishment and additional capacity is required under current policies to match forecast demand. Bottlenecks already exist and pressures for improvements for key links in the network are already a reality.

As part of this increased interest, by both policy makers and academics, the whole questioning of the mechanisms of supply and control have also come under review. In many countries the role of the state in providing infrastructure has been the subject of detailed debate.

The exact importance of infrastructure as an element in the economic development process has long been disputed.[4] Much seems to depend upon the degree to which supply considerations are thought important. The Keynesian approach, epitomized by the Harrod–Domar framework, indicates that causality runs from economic exploitation to income and infrastructure generation. In contrast, Classical economics is essentially supply driven and transport and other infrastructure are generally seen as important elements in the production function. Much of the recent work follows the Classical mode in looking at the links between infrastructure provision and economic development through some form of aggregate production function analysis. It has sought to see how well it, and its individual elements, explain economic performance.[5]

The usual format is to take a production function of the standard form

$$Y = f(L, K, J) \tag{16.1}$$

with Y indicating output; L labour; K the stock of private capital and J the stock of public capital.[6] The relevant parameters are then estimated (often employing a Cobb–Douglas specification) using either time-series data for a particular area – such as Aschauer's (1989) work in the USA – or by cross-sectional analysis across regions – such as Biehl's (1986, 1991) work on the European Union.

Many of the early studies, especially from the US, at the national and state levels, provided statistically significant and apparently robust evidence that well-designed and operated infrastructure can expand the economic productivity of an area. Aschauer, for example, looking at data covering the period 1949 to 1985, concluded that a 1 percent increase in the public capital stock could raise total factor productivity by 0.39 percent. Munnell (1992) tabulates output elasticities of public capital derived from US studies in the 0.03 to 0.39 range although with a preponderance of results toward the upper end of the range. Similar positive findings are recorded by Biehl (1991) regarding the European Union.

More recently, these studies have been subjected to a variety of criticisms. Gramlich (1994) offers a summary but, briefly, the key points include the following. First, while econometric studies may throw up positive correlation between economic performance and the state of infrastructure, the direction of causation is not immediately clear. Wealthier areas may simply have more resources for infrastructure provision. The efforts at testing for causality are, as yet, minimal.[7]

Second, as seen above, the term infrastructure is a flexible one with no agreed definition and simply taking official accountancy data may disguise important measurement, qualitative and definition factors.

Third, the way in which infrastructure is managed and priced may be as important as the provision of infrastructure *per se* (Winston 1991). In terms of policy, therefore, account must be taken of the short-term levels of utilization, maintenance and so on in addition to the stock of, and investment in, infrastructure.

Fourth, even within the very vague notion we have regarding what constitutes infrastructure, there are numerous sectors and elements.[8] From a policy perspective it is, therefore, important to isolate the roles of, say, transport, energy and softer infrastructure such as law, education, business services and defence in influencing macroeconomic performance.

Fifth, as more studies have emerged they are producing much wider ranges of results. As Morrison (1993) puts it, 'A clear consensus about the impacts of infrastructure investment has as yet been elusive, at least partly because different methodologies generate varying results and implications'. In a recent study Sturm and de Haan (1995) deploying US and Dutch data, for instance, point to the fact that the data series in most studies looking at the economic effects of public capital are neither stationary nor cointegrated and, thus, conclusions that public capital has a positive effect on private sector productivity are not well founded. Equally, Jorgensen (1991) has questioned the basic premise underlying the use of a production function approach. This sensitivity may, of course, go beyond simple matters of technique if there is, in fact, no underlying relationship.

3. INFRASTRUCTURE, EMPLOYMENT AND EQUITY

In addition to the theme of productivity, another issue which has received much attention is the impact of infrastructure investment on employment. There are potentially two major ways in which infrastructure affects employment. The first concerns the substitution/complementarity effects that may occur between production factors due to infrastructure availability. The second relates to the differentiated impacts infrastructure investments may have on the competitive position of regions or countries.

According to the standard theory of the firm, an improvement in an external input such as infrastructure can be interpreted as a shift in the production function with the effect that less private inputs are needed to produce the same volume of production. In the standard case of a Cobb–Douglas production technology, this would lead to a decrease in both private capital and employment. With other technologies one may arrive at situations whereby a reallocation takes place between private capital and employment. In the transport sector there seems to be a tendency for infrastructure investments to result in more capital-intensive methods of production. Investments in ports, for instance, facilitate the use of large container ships implying greater capital intensity in the way transport services are supplied. Similar arguments can be applied to links in transport networks such as wider canals.

This is not the entire story, however, because higher productivity in a competitive environment, through a lowering of prices, will also stimulate demand. In addition to the substitution effect away from labour, therefore, there will also be a demand effect generating an increase in overall production and a higher demand for labour services. An important factor in determining the overall impact of these forces is the price elasticity of demand – if it is high then one may anticipate a large increase in production volumes and thus also potentially in employment. Since different sectors make use of infrastructure with differing intensities so production costs will change at different rates. Shifts will take place between sectors leading to employment growth in those with high price elasticities and higher intensities of infrastructure use, and decline of employment in other types of sectors. Nothing a priori can be said about the sizes of these effects but there is no automatic reason to anticipate that overall employment effects would be positive.

Another perspective concerns interregional or international competition. Transport infrastructure improvements can lead to decreases in transport costs and hence stimulate interregional trade. The intensity of competition increases because sectors in regions which were formerly sheltered are now confronted by cheap imports. The result is that while consumers in these regions may be able to buy at lower prices, employment in these sectors in such regions declines. In exporting regions an increase in employment may be anticipated. The theory of trade, therefore, predicts that in each region employment in some sectors will expand while in others it will contract as a result of the infrastructure improvement. The overall impact on a region will depend on, amongst other things, its sectorial structure. The flexibility of the labour force is also important and a rigidity can mean that employment loss in one sector cannot be completely compensated for in others (Rietveld 1995).

These conclusions contradict the widely held belief that infrastructure investments have a large impact on employment. The possible reason is that in many cases new infrastructure does lead to high growth rates of economic activity in its immediate surroundings. Closer inspection, however, usually reveals that such growth is mainly a matter of differential growth within regions. Locations near access points to roads, for example, grow at a higher rate than the regional average whereas locations further away grow at lower rates.

It should be noted that the majority of firms that relocate move a very short distance. Relocation of firms in response to infrastructure improvements mainly occurs at a local scale and is not a major cause of differences in regional growth rates. A study of the location behaviour of firms with more than 10 employees in the eastern part of the Netherlands, for example, found that 75 percent of those that relocated did so to places in the same municipality (Bruinsma et al. 1997). A closer inspection reveals that in the relocation process, 42 percent of the firms remained at approximately the same distance from the nearest ramp of a highway, 41 percent moved to a closer location and 16 percent moved further away. Such findings underline that the rapid growth in the number of firms that is sometimes observed at particular places near newly improved highways is to a considerable extent the consequence of relocation within regions. These relocation processes are, of course, quite relevant at a local level but from a broader regional or national perspective they are less important.

Another issue concerns the effects of infrastructure supply on regional divergence. As indicated above an improvement of transport infrastructure leads to changes in interregional and international trade patterns. These changes imply that a trend towards specialization has a positive impact on aggregate welfare. However, from a distribution aspect there may be adverse effects, including job losses in regions where industries are not sufficiently competitive to stand competition by suppliers from elsewhere. It is not possible to come up with a general diagnosis whether the relocation of economic activity as a consequence of improved transport has a positive or negative effect on regional inequalities.

Much depends on the existing quality of infrastructure. Krugman (1991) indicates that, in a simple core–periphery context, it is plausible in an early phase of transport infrastructure development between core and periphery that there will be a tendency towards spatial concentration at the core. In later phases a reverse tendency may be observed. The background to this is that in the base situation with very high transport costs, there will be a dispersed production pattern; each region produces the products it needs because transport costs are too high to make trade profitable. When infrastructure improvements reduce transport costs a process of specialization takes place allowing for the exploitation of economies of scale in production. As long as transport costs remain relatively high, a plausible location of production is the core. It is here that most consumers are found. The volume of transport flows to the periphery is much smaller compared with the situation with production taking place in the periphery. This holds as long as the difference in production costs between core and periphery is smaller than the difference in the implied transport costs. When transport costs are very low one may expect that the ultimate location of production is dictated by costs of production and it is probable that this will lead to a shift away from the core with its expensive production factors to the cheaper periphery. Thus, as the infrastructure linking core and periphery improves there is a first stage with a tendency from dispersed production towards production in the core, and a second stage with a shift from the core to the periphery. This would imply that in the long run the periphery will benefit from infrastructure improvement.

This is not the complete picture because it only deals with infrastructure improvements between core and periphery and ignores infrastructure improvements within core or periphery. Most countries tend to give priority to infrastructure projects in the core and this leads to a negative impact on competitiveness of the periphery. A good example is the construction of the high speed rail system in Europe which clearly has an adverse effect on interregional equity (Bruinsma and Rietveld 1993).

4. META ANALYSIS

Meta analysis, while certainly not circumventing all of the limitations associated with traditional reviewing procedures, would seem to offer at least a partial way forward in terms of bringing together some of the empirical works which has looked at links between infrastructure investments and various aspects of economic performance. It is, in simple terms, the use of formal statistical techniques to sum up a body of separate but similar studies. Glass (1976) offers a formal definition,[9] namely that meta analysis refers to the statistical analysis of a large collection of analysis results from individual studies for the purpose of integrating the findings. In connotes a rigorous alternative to the casual, narrative discussions of research studies which typify our attempts to make sense of the rapidly expanding research literature.

Equally, meta analysis has been defined in *The Economist* (1991) as the deviations found in lots of studies of the same thing. If the deviations are randomly scattered around zero then there is no effect. But if they cluster off to one side, the meta analysis shows that something is going on, even if the individual results may not be significant in themselves.

It, therefore, provides a series of techniques that allow the cumulative results of a set of individual studies to be pulled together. In doing this it can not only help to provide more accurate evaluations of quantitative parameters but may also offer insights into phenomena for which no specific study currently exists. It can also, in certain circumstances, help to pinpoint political bias and to provide more clearly defined valuations of the economic costs and benefits from the plethora of data that exists. It can act as a supplement to more common literary type approaches when reviewing the usefulness of parameters derived from prior studies and help direct new research to areas where there is greatest need.

The idea of meta analysis has a relatively extensive history, especially with respect to replicated physical experiments and it has been widely employed in psychology and medical research, but its application to microeconomic issues has, especially given the extensive growth in empirical work, until now been remarkably limited. Some of the few recent examples include the examination of causes of X-inefficiencies across a range of different industrial studies and of estimated values of environmental externality costs, and the study of the links between turnover and absenteeism.[10] It offers several advantages over conventional procedures – by conventional reviewing techniques we mean studies which list results of previous work and debate their prose and cons in a literary fashion with the aim of isolating superior work or analysis which may be used as the basis for further analysis or decision making.

There is the problem that the output of most traditional reviews tends to be in the form of taxonomies of findings without any specific attempt to relate these to the review's purpose. In consequence such reviews seldom meet the needs of those engaged in quantitative forecasting. Added to this is the subjectivity that tends to accompany a basically literary type approach. Further, the result of any statistical verification procedure can be a greater degree of conflict in the outcome than exists in the base studies themselves. Although disagreements amongst findings is itself not bad – it suggests a need for seeking an explanation for the diversity – traditional methods do not normally attempt more than a description of the problem.

Second, there is the problem that traditional reviewing, because it does not necessarily embrace sound statistical practice, is usually scientifically unsound. A common problem is that if a majority of studies come up with similar conclusions these are accepted on a sort of voting basis irrespective of the quality of the data used or reliability of techniques employed. Meta analysis, while not entirely solving this problem, can at least indicate the sensitivity of results to the type of data used and methodology employed. Finally, the traditional review process is frequently inefficient because of the difficulties of mentally handling a large number of different findings.

5. META ANALYSIS OF INFRASTRUCTURE INVESTMENT STUDIES

The meta analysis conducted in this paper makes use of 28 estimates of the output elasticity of public infrastructure investment.[11] These studies are diverse in that they cover a range of countries, employ a variety of techniques, involved various levels of spatial aggregation and were conducted at different times. The sources embrace both published and unpublished findings.

The study selection process was one of simply scanning the literature and taking those studies which provide comparable results. This procedure clearly suffers from several of the defects which can be levelled against meta analysis (for example, the lack of comprehensive coverage and an excessive focus of just one output measure) but the aim is to offer supplementary analysis to conventional literary reviews and to concentrate on exploring quantitatively some of the assertions which previous reviews have made. The findings are intended to be indicative.

While there are a variety of quantitative techniques available to explore the results of sets of studies, the analysis here employs a standard least squares procedure to conduct a meta-regression analysis. It broadly follows the general form for a meta-regression analysis as set out by Stanley and Jarrell (1989):

$$b_j = \beta + \Sigma \alpha_k Z_{jk} + u_j \quad j = 1, 2, ..., L, \quad *k = 1, 2, ..., M , \tag{16.2}$$

where b_j is the reported estimate of the relationship of interest in the j-th study from a total of L studies; β is the summary value of b, Z_{jk} are variables that reflect the relevant characteristics of an empirical study that could explain variations amongst studies; α_k are the coefficients of the M different study characteristics which are controlled for and u_j is the error term.

The actual variables included in this case are selected to elicit some quantification of the types of effect that may influence the values of public sector infrastructure investment output elasticities derived in econometric studies. The output elasticity E_i is a result of the production function (16.1). It is defined as the percentage change in output caused by an increase in the infrastructure stock of 1 percent. In the standard case of a Cobb–Douglas production function it simply coincides with the parameter associated with J. More explicitly, to do this involves estimating the following equation:

$$E_i = \alpha + \beta_1 X_{i1} + \beta_2 X_{i2} + \beta_3 X_{i3} + \beta_4 X_{i4} + \beta_5 X_{i5} + \beta_6 X_{i6} + \beta_7 X_{i7} + \beta_8 X_{i8} + \varepsilon \quad (16.3)$$

where
E_i :   is the estimated elasticity derived in study i;
X_1:   takes the value of 0 for US studies and 1 otherwise;
X_2:   takes the value of 0 for national studies and 1 otherwise (regional, urban);
X_3:   takes the value of 1 for cross section data and 0 otherwise;
X_4:   takes the value of 1 if pooled time series-cross sectional data is used and 0 otherwise;
X_5:   takes the value of 1 if the study is in first differences and 0 otherwise;
X_6:   takes the value of 0 if the publication was prior to 1991 and 1 otherwise;
X_7:   takes the value of 0 if a Cobb–Douglas specification was used and 0 otherwise;
X_8:   is gross national product per capita.

The estimated equation provides a relatively good overall fit to the data (see the results in Table 16.1) although the significance of individual variables is often low. It also provides confirmation for some of the conclusions reached in a rather more intuitive manner in a number of the recent literary reviews. The magnitude of the α coefficient is broadly in line with the general level of national output elasticity found in Munnell (1992) and the negative sign and scale (albeit only at a low level of statistical significance) of the X_2 variable, provides confirmation of the importance of the level of aggregation when assessing the magnitude of output elasticities.

There is considerable debate in the literature about the desirability of estimating elasticities in terms of differences in order to deal with the problem of common trends (Hulten and Schwab 1991; Sturm and Haan 1995). It is still debatable whether this transformation is statistically desirable (Munnell 1992) but what does emerge from the meta analysis is that elasticities derived from equations involving differences (variable X_5) seem to produce lower estimates than those calculated directly. There is also an indication that there has been something of a decline in the elasticity values that have been calculated over time (the X_6 variable) which may be a reflection of improved data sources or of more careful econometric analysis not captured in the other variables included in equation (16.2).

Table 16.1 Meta regression results

Variable	Estimate	Standard error	t-value	Prob>|t|	Standardized estimate	Correlation with dependent variables
α	0.343	0.230	1.488	0.153	0.517	0.547
X_1	0.240	0.108	2.219	0.029	−0.315	−0.260
X_2	−0.140	0.127	−1.106	0.282	−0.163	−0.091
X_3	−0.104	0.158	−0.660	0.517	−0.074	−0.050
X_4	−0.033	0.117	−0.283	0.780	−0.169	−0.181
X_5	−0.076	0.095	−0.796	0.436	−0.278	−0.226
X_6	−0.124	0.080	−1.552	0.137	0.163	0.027
X_7	0.095	0.114	0.823	0.416	−0.075	−0.417
X_8	−0.003	0.009	−0.322	0.751		

$R^2 = 0.153$ Total sum of squares = 1.388

$F(8, 19) = 2.498$ Residual sum of squares = 0.676

Interestingly, the dummy variable indicating whether a study was of US origin or not is highly significant and suggestive of the fact that US studies, other things equal, tend to produce lower elasticities than do studies conducted elsewhere.[12] Theoretically this can be explained in terms of the substantial base level and quality of infrastructure found in high income countries and the scale, scope and density economies which accompany this. Additional infrastructure in this context may provide little additional potential stimulus especially if the economy enjoys flexible labour and private capital markets. What it does imply, however, is that previous surveys which have, in the main, tended to concentrate on the North American literature may, assuming the direction of causation is from infrastructure investment to economic stimulus, have been underestimating output elasticities in many parts of the world.

6. CONCLUSIONS

Public sector infrastructure investment has reemerged as a major topic of political and economic interest in many countries. Quantitative information on the detailed importance of such investments is, though, still relatively scant. That which is available is normally of a case study variety. It is important not only to ensure that sufficient infrastructure is made available but also to ensure that excessive investments are avoided with all the resources costs this can entail.

This meta analysis has brought together, within a meta-regression framework, the results of a number of macro level studies, that have sought to add quantification to the debate by calculating the output elasticity of public sector infrastructure investment. It has not been concerned with matters such as direction of causality but has, instead, focused more narrowly on the extent to which it is possible to explain, relatively rigorously, why a substantial body of scientific studies have produced quite wide variations in their estimations.

The results of this small-scale meta analysis suggest that variations in estimates stem from a variety of sources, some of which can be explained by the nature of the economies under review but others are more closely linked to the study methodology employed. In particular, the attention paid in many surveys to the situation in North America may be misleading if their findings are extended without modification to other geographical regions.

REFERENCES

Andersson, A.E. (1991), 'Infrastructure and the Transformation of the C-society', in Thord, R. (ed.), *The Future of Transportation and Communication*, Borlange: Swedish National Road Administration.

Andersson, A.E. and K. Kobayashi (1989), 'Some Theoretical Aspects of Spatial Equilibria with Public Goods', in Andersson, A.E., Batten, D.F., Johansson, B. and P. Nijkamp (eds), *Advances in Spatial Theory and Dynamics*, Amsterdam: North Holland.

Aschauer, D.A. (1989), 'Is public expenditure productive?', *Journal of Monetary Economics* **23**, pp. 177–200.

Aschauer, D.A. (1990), 'Why is Infrastructure Important?', in Munnell, P. (ed.), *Is There a Shortfall in Public Capital Investment?*, Conference Series, 34, Boston: Federal Reserve Bank of Boston.

Aschauer, D.A. (1994), 'Infrastructure and macroeconomic performance: direct and indirect effects', paper to *OECD Conference on Capital Formation and Employment*, Amsterdam.

Bajo-Rubio, O. and S. Sosvilla-Rivero (1993), 'Does public capital affect private sector performance? An analysis of the Spanish case, 1964–88', *Economic Modelling* **10**, pp. 179–85.

Berdt, E.R. and B. Hansson (1991), *Measuring the Contribution of Public Infrastructure Capital in Sweden*, Stockholm: National Bureau of Economic Research Working Paper 3842.

Biehl, D. (1986), *The Contribution of Infrastructure to Regional Development*, Brussels: Regional Policy Division, European Communities.

Biehl, D. (1991), 'The Role Of Infrastructure In Regional Development', in Vickerman, R.W. (ed.), *Infrastructure and Regional Development*, London: Pion.

Bruinsma, F.R. and P. Rietveld (1993), 'Urban agglomerations in European infrastructure networks', *Urban Studies* **30**, pp. 919–34.

Bruinsma, F.R., Rienstra, S.A. and P. Rietveld (1997), 'Economic impacts of the construction of a transport corridor: a multi-level and multi-approach case study for the construction of the A1 highway in the Netherlands', *Regional Studies* **31**, pp. 391–402.

Button, K.J. and S.M. Jongma (1995), *META-analysis Methodologies and Microeconomics*, Trace Discussion Paper TI 95-143, Amsterdam: Tinbergen Instutute.

Christodoulakis, N. (1993), *Public Infrastructure and Private Productivity: A Discussion of Empirical Studies and an Application to Greece*, Athens: Athens University of Economics and Business.

Commission of the European Communities (1992), *Transport Infrastructure*, Document COM(92) 231 Final, Brussels: CEC.

da Silva Costa, J., Ellson, R.W. and R.C. Martin (1987), 'Public capital, regional output and development: some empirical evidence', *Journal of Regional Science* **27**, pp. 419–37.

Eberts, R.W. and M.S. Fogarty (1987), 'Estimating the relationship between local public and private investment', Working Paper 8703, Cleveland: Federal Reserve Bank of Cleveland.

Evans, P. and G. Karras (1994), 'Is government capital productive? Evidence from a panel of seven countries', *Journal of Macroeconomics* **16**, pp. 27–9.

Ford, R. and P. Poret (1991), *Infrastructure and Private Sector Productivity*, OECD–ESD Working Paper 91, Paris.

Fukuchi, T. (1978), 'An analyse economico-politique d'un developpement regional harminise', *Collections de L'Insee, Serie C* **61**, 227–53.

Glass, G.V. (1976), 'Primary, secondary, and meta-analysis of research', *Educational Researcher* **5**, pp. 3–8.

Gramlich, E.M. (1994) 'Infrastructure investment: a review essay', *Journal of Economic Literature* 32: 1176–96.

Hakfoort, J.R., de Haan, J. and J.E. Sturm (1993), 'Investeringen in infrastructuur en economische groei', *ESB*, 670–72.

Hirschman, A.O. (1958), *The Strategy of Economic Development*, New Haven, Conn.: Yale University Press.

Holtz-Eakin, D. (1992), 'Public sector capital and the productivity puzzle', National Bureau of Economic Research Working Paper 4122.

Hulten, C.R. and R.M. Schwab (1991), 'Public capital formation and the growth of regional manufacturing industries', *National Tax Journal* **44**, pp. 12–34.

Jorgenson, D. (1991), 'Fragile statistical foundations: the macroeconomics of public infrastructure investent', comment on Hulton and Schwab (1991) when presented at the American Enterprise Institute Conference on Infrastructure Needs and Policy Options for the 1990s, Washington: AEI.

Keeler, T.E. and J.S. Ying (1988), 'Measuring benefits of a large public investment: the case of the US Federal-aid Highway System', *Journal of Public Economics* **36**, pp. 69–85.

Kelijian, H.H. and D.P. Robinson (1995), 'Infrastructure productivity: a razor's edge', mimeo, University of Maryland.

Krugman, P. (1991), *Geography and Trade*, Cambridge: MIT Press.

Lakshmanan, T.R. (1989), 'Infrastructure and Economic Transformation', in Andersson, A.E., Batten, D.F., Johansson, B. and P. Nijkamp (eds), *Advances in Spatial Theory and Dynamics*, Amsterdam: North Holland.

Lynch, M. (1994), 'Applied economics: linking transportation policy and economic growth', paper to Canadian Transportation Research Forum Conference, Victoria.

Lynde, C. and J. Richmond (1992), 'The role of public capital in production', *Review of Economics and Statistics* **74**, pp. 37–44.

McQuaid, R.W., Nelson, J.D., Leitham, S. and J.W. Esslemont (1993), 'European regional policy, transport infrastructure and economic development', Proceedings of Seminar E, PTRC 21st Annual Conference, University of Manchester Institute of Science and Technology.

Mera, K. (1973), 'Regional production functions and social overhead capital: an analysis of the Japaneses case', *Regional and Urban Economics* **3**, pp. 157–86.

Merriman, D. (1990), 'Public capital and regional output: another look at some Japanese and American data', *Regional Science and Urban Economics* **23**, pp. 436–48.

Morrison, C.J. (1993), 'Macroeconomic relationships between public spending on infrastructure and private sector productivity in the United States', in Mintz, J.M. and R.S. Preston (eds), *Infrastructure and Competitiveness*, Ottowa: John Deutsch Institute for the Study of Economic Policy.

Munnell, A.H. (1992), 'Infrastructure investment and economic growth', *Journal of Economic Perspectives* **6**, pp. 189–98.

Nurske, R. (1966), *Problems of Capital Formulation*, Oxford: Basil Blackwell.

Pinnoi, N. (1994), 'Public infrastructure and private production: measuring relative contributions', *Journal of Economic Behaviour and Organisation* **23**, pp. 127–48.

Prud'homme, R. (1993), 'Assessing the role of infrastructrure in France by means of regionally estimated production functions', paper to a workshop on *Infrastructure, Economic Growth and Regional Development*, Jonkoping.

Ratner, J.B. (1983), 'Government capital, employment and the production function for US private output', *Economic Letters* **13**, pp. 213–7.

Rietveld, P. (1995), 'Transport infrastructure and the economy, *Investment, Productivity and Employment*, Paris: OECD.

Sarafoglou, N., Anderson, A., Holmberg, I. and O. Ohlsson (1994), 'Spatial infrastructure and productivity in Sweden', paper presented at the 34th European Congress of the Regional Science Association, Groningen.

Seitz, H. (1993), 'A dual economic analysis of the benefits of the public road network', *Annals Regions Science* **27**, pp. 223–39.

Seitz, H. (1994), 'Public infrastructure capital, employment and private capital formation', paper to OECD Conference on Capital Formation and Employment Amsterdam.

Stanley, T.D. and S.B. Jarrell (1989), 'Meta-regression analysis: a quantitative method of literature surveys', *Journal of Economic Surveys* **3**, pp. 161–70.

Sturm, J.E. and J. de Haan (1995), 'Is public expenditure really productive? New evidence for the USA and the Netherlands', *Economic Modelling* **12**, pp. 60–72.

Tatom, J.A. (1991), 'Public capital and private sector performance', *Federal Reserve Bank of St Louis Review* **73**, pp. 3–15.

Tatom, J.A. (1993), 'Paved with good intentions: the mythical national infrastructure crisis', *Policy Analysis* **196**.

Toen-Gout, M.W. and M.M. Jongeling (1993), 'Investeringen in infrastuctuur en economische groie', *ESB*, pp. 424–7.

Vickerman, R.W. (1991), 'Transport Infrastructure in the European Community: new developments, regional implications and evaluation', in Vickerman, R.W. (ed.), *Infrastructure and Regional Development*, London: Pion.

Youngson, A.J. (1967), *Overhead Capital, A Study in Development Economics*, Edinburgh: Edinburgh University Press.

Winston, C. (1991), 'Efficient transportation infrastructure policy', *Journal of Economic Literature* **5**, pp. 113–27.

The Economist (1991), 'Under the metascope', *The Economist* **319** (7707), pp. 93–4.

NOTES

1. If infrastructure is a public good then, left to the market, conventional economic wisdom would support government action either as a direct supplier or as a motivator for expanded supply through such measures as subsidies to the private sector or reciprocal regulations. The difficulty is that in conventional economic terms few forms of infrastructure exhibit to any significant extent the characteristics which one normally associates with 'publicness', that is, public goods are goods with a particular kind of externality that embraces the ideas of non-rivalry and non-excludability. Transport, communications and similar infrastructure are, however, frequently congested and, while on parts of a network one user's

consumption may have a negligible impact on others, this is certainly not universally the case.

2.   See also Vickerman (1991) and McQuaid et al. (1993) for discussions of the more recent developments in EU transport infrastructure policy.

3.   This is not to say that there has been no work done on the overall importance of transport and other public infrastructure for economic development. Aschauer (1989) and Biehl (1986) offer, for instance, examples of macro studies of the importance of infrastructure.

4.   There is also literature at a more micro level, and in particular work has been undertaken at the regional or local project level on the impact of individual pieces of infrastructure. This is an extremely important topic but outside of the scope of this chapter. What should be said is that the empirical evidence to date on the link between infrastructure investment and industrial location can at best be described as ambiguous.

5.   A separate, more theoretical approach is to use duality theory applied to a restricted profit function to determine the net benefits which private manufacturing firms obtain from public services. Seitz (1993), for instance, uses this approach to look at the benefits of the German public road network. Munnell (1992) offers some comment on the limitations of this methodology.

6.   There are variations on this and Prud'homme (1993), for instance, favours $Y = f(L, K, J, F)$ where F stands for the functionaries (those employed in the public sector).

7.   The study of public expenditure by US cities by Eberts and Fogarty (1987) explores this issue and produces inconclusive results about causality.

8.   While the vast majority of these macro studies look at public infrastructure as a whole a small number have focused on particular elements, such as Keeler and Ying's (1988) work on the productivity of the US highway system.

9.   Stanley and Jarrell (1989) adopt a somewhat shorter definition, namely, 'Meta analysis is the analysis of empirical analysis that attempts to integrate and explain the literature about some specific important parameter'. More exactly, the object of meta analysis is effect size, where this is defined as $g = (u_e - u_c)/\sigma$ where, u_e is the mean of the experimental group; u_c is the mean of the control group and σ is the standard deviation of the control group. Effect size renders the size of individualized studies concerning some phenomena comparable and suitable for analysis. To

combine results in a meta analysis it is, thus, assumed that size effect is a standard measure of empirical effect which can be treated as constant across the literature.

10. For a survey of the applications of meta analysis in economics see Button and Jongma (1995).

11. These estimates were taken from the following studies (in some instances studies offer more than one estimate derived, for example, using alternative techniques): Aschauer (1989, 1990, 1994); Bajo-Rubio and Sosvilla (1993); Berdt and Hansson (1991); Christodoulakis (1993); da Silva Costa et al. (1987); Evans and Karras (1994); Ford and Poret (1991); Fukuchi (1978); Hakfoort et al. (1993); Holtz-Eakin (1992); Hulten and Schwab (1991); Kelijian and Robinson (1995); Lynch (1994); Lynde and Richmond (1992); Mera (1973); Merriman (1990); Pinnoi (1994); Prud'homme (1993); Ratner (1983); Sarafoglou et al. (1994); Seitz (1994); Tatom (1991, 1993); Toen-Gout and Jongeling (1993).

12. There is correlation between X_1 and X_8 and omission of the nationality dummy results in the X_8 coefficient taking a positive and significant sign. Since the US is a high income country it may be that countries with high GDP per capita do have lower elasticities rather than there being an explicitly nationality effect in play.

17. On the Relation between Information Development and Economic Development: an Econometric Analysis

Yoshiro Higano and Guoping Mao

1. INTRODUCTION

Information development in its original sense refers to the process in which the information-oriented socio-economy has become mature through the diffusion of information-related innovations into the activities of the society.

Information activities involve (a) those activities which create, produce, dispose of, teach, deliver, or provide knowledge, information, data, or messages and (b) those activities which produce the information machines or the information materials for the activities of (a). Information development is now taking place in various forms in every field of the society – economy, culture, daily life, and so on.

Information development has a strong impact on regional development, and accelerates both the national and international economic development. Information development 'has contributed a valuable sense of the way in which services are leading economic change' (Marshall and Wood 1992, p. 1255). The information development 'is better viewed as a process and as a productive force and ... from this perspective its impact is not limited to spatial organization of industries as it also alters production methods' (Amirahmadi and Wallace 1995, p. 1745). Information industries have the potential to create regional economic impacts equal to or greater than manufacturing industries (Porterfield and Pulver 1991).

Through information development during the last decade, information technologies are not only used for activities within a nation but also for international activities. A considerable portion of technical change which drives economic growth is due to the diffusion of innovations through local research and development. Economic growth is enhanced by developments in telecommunications, but these do not only facilitate business activities within the region, but also the flow of ideas, goods, money, and so on, between the region and the rest of the world. Also, books imported from abroad are important for the education which further enhances the local R&D.

From the 1960s, the study of information development in the developed countries has made great progress (Machlup 1962; Porat 1977; Katz 1986, and so on). All those studies have provided substantial evidence which shows the process and the trend of information development in the developed countries. But, very few studies have been made of developing countries.

In this study, we take the cases of Shanghai (a rapidly-developing metropolitan city in the developing country) and Japan (a highly-developed country) as examples of economic development which has been enhanced and oriented outwardly by information development. In the last 30 years, Japan has implemented a series of policies and programmes for promotion of information development. We look at how much information development contributed to economic development, and how Japanese information development occurred. In the case of Shanghai, which is the largest centre of economy, culture, education, research, technology, international trade, banking and information in China, this city is expected to play a central role in the economic development of China as a whole in the future.

First, we present synthetic indicators of information development based on principal components analysis and factor analysis. Subsequently, we will specify an econometric model of economic development, and estimate the impact of the information development on economic development.

Information development in Japan may provide clues to the future for Shanghai. So, we will also compare economic development in Shanghai with that of Japan based on the indicators of average or per capita ratios.

2. ESTIMATION OF INFORMATION DEVELOPMENT

2.1 Indicators of Information Development

The socioeconomic information development is comprehensive as a concept. First, we categorize indicators of information development into five, and calculate the characteristic value of each indicator by the principal components analysis. Next, based on those characteristic values, we calculate the synthetic indicator of the socioeconomic information development.

Based on the past studies, indicators of information development are categorized into five as follows:

1. Information development capabilities (CI). In order to promote information development, it is necessary to have highly qualified

scientists and technicians, advanced technology, and capital. They may be called information development capabilities (abbreviated to 'the capabilities'). Here, we assume that the indicator of the capabilities is dependent on: production of computers; researchers[1] and persons engaged in information activity;[2] expenditure on R&D; value added of publishing and printing; and telecommunication circuits.

2.   Education (E). Education is an activity that produces, develops, explains, teaches, and diffuses knowledge or experience. Education actively promotes enhancing human desire for information, advancing technology of information disposal, and popularizing information activity. Here, we assume that the indicator of education is dependent on: the ratio of education expenditure to GNP; the ratio of university graduates to the population in a given year; stock of books, expenditure on education and culture; and teachers.[3]

3.   Information development in the economy (EI). This implies the rise in the ratio of information products and information services to gross output in the national economy. EI is a measure of the impact of information industries on national production. Here, we assume that the indicator of information development in the economy is dependent on: the ratio of value added of information industry[4] to GNP; the ratio of information labour to the total labour force;[5] and per capita value added of the information industry.

4.   Information development in society (SI). This implies the rise in the outfit status of information goods, information services and information means in society. We assume that the indicator of information development in society is dependent on: engineers and technicians, computers in use; public telephones; postal expenditure; and public libraries.

5.   Information development in daily life (LI). This implies the rise in the consumption status of information goods and services, and in the diffusion status of information means in daily life. Here, we assume that the indicator of information development in daily life is dependent on: telephone subscribers; diffusion rate of TV; expenditure on transportation and communication in daily life; and expenditure on education.

Table 17.1 summarizes statistical data for those five indicators, and lists the data sources of Shanghai and Japan.

Table 17.1   The indicators of information development

Information development	Statistical data	Unit	Shanghai variable	Japan variable	Data source
Capabilities CI	Production of computers	number/100persons	SPC	JPC	1
	Researchers	person/100persons	SPR	JPR	1
	Persons engaged in information	person/100persons	SPI	JPI	2
	Expenditure on R&D	10dollars/person	SPRD	JPRD	1
	Value added of publishing and printing	100dollar/person	SPPV	JPPV	1
	Telecommunication circuits	circuit/1000persons	SPTC	JPTC	1
Education E	Ratio of educational expenditure to GNP	%	SREG	JREG	1
	Ratio of university graduates to population	%	SRGP	JRGP	1
	Stock of books	book/person	SPB	JPB	1
	Teachers	person/100persons	SPT	JPT	1
in the economy E1	Expenditure on education and culture	dollars/person	SPEE	JPEE	1
	Ratio of value added of information industry to GNP	%	SRIG	JRIG	3
	Ratio of information labour to total labour	%	SRIL	JRIL	2
	Value added of information industries	10dollars/person	SPIV	JPIV	3
in the society S1	Engineers and technicians	person/100persons	SPET	JPET	1
	Public telephones	number/1000persons	SPPT	JPPT	1
	Postal expenditure	100dollars/persons	SPPE	JPPE	1
	Computers in use	number/10000persons	SPC	JPC	4
	Public libraries	number/100persons	SPL	JPL	1
in daily life L1	Telephone subscribers	%	SPTS	JPTS	1
	Diffusion rate of TV	%	SDTV	JDTV	1
	Expenditure on transportation and communication	100dollars/household	SHE1	JHE1	1
	Expenditure on education	100dollars/household	SHR2	JHE2	1

Source 1: Data for Shanghai are cited from Shanghai Statistics Bureau (1987–1992) and data for Japan are cited from Management and Coordination Agency of Japan Statistics Bureau (1953–1992).
Source 2: Data for Shanghai are recalculated from Source 1 and data for Japan are cited from Source 1 and Economic Planning Agency of Japan (1984, p. 1676).
Source 3: Data for Shanghai are recalculated from Source 1 and data for Japan are cited from Source 1 and Economic Planning Agency of Japan (1985, p. 25).
Source 4: Data for Shanghai are cited from Source 1 and data for Japan are cited from Source 1 and Japan Association of Information Disposal and Development (1988, p. 69).

2.2 Estimating the Level of Information Development

The characteristic values of the indicators (capabilities, education, economy, society, and daily life) are calculated by using principal components analysis as follows:

1.   Information development capabilities (CI)
Shanghai: SCI = 0.454SPC + 0.500SPR + 0.490SPI + 0.060SPRD + 0.369SPPV + 0.405SPTC
Japan: JCI = 0.383JPC + 0.397JPR + 0.398JPI + 0.417JPRD + 0.423JPPV + 0.429JPTC

2.   Education (E)
Shanghai: SE = 0.476SREG + 0.402SRGP + 0.485SPB + 0.381SPT + 0.481SPEE
Japan: JE = 0.215JREG + 0.493JRGP + 0.473JPB + 0.501JPT + 0.486JPEE

3.   Information development in the economy (EI)
Shanghai: SEI = 0.583SRIG + 0.593SRIL + 0.555SPIV
Japan: JEI = 0.596JRIG + 0.580JRIL + 0.555JPIV

4.   Information development in the society (SI)
Shanghai: SSI = 0.458SPET + 0.487SPPT + 0.436SPPE + 0.463SPC + 0.385SPL
Japan: JSI = 0.458JPET + 0.411JPPT + 0.477JPPE + 0.428JPC + 0.459JPL

5.   Information development in the daily life (LI)
Shanghai: SLI = 0.488SPTS + 0.522SDTV + 0.458SHE1 + 0.529SHE2
Japan: JLI = 0.530JPTS + 0.441JDTV + 0.516JHE1 + 0.508JHE2

The synthetic value of socioeconomic information development (SEI) is calculated as follows.

Shanghai: SSEI = 0.454SCI + 0.443SE + 0.448SEI + 0.455SSI + 0.436SLI
Japan: JSEI = 0.459JCI + 0.455JE + 0.458JEI + 0.439JSI + 0.424JLI

The calculated indicators are shown in Figure 17.1 (the indicators of Shanghai in 1952 are normalized to one).

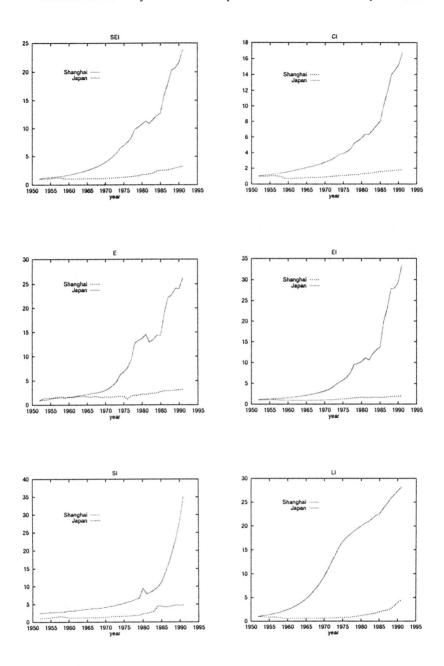

Figure 17.1 Shanghai and Japanese information development

3. ANALYSIS OF INFORMATION DEVELOPMENT

3.1 The Level of Information Development

The synthetic level of Shanghai information development (SSEI) increased three times from 1952 to 1991, and the average growth rate was 3.1 percent per year. On the other hand, the synthetic level of Japanese information development (JSEI) increased 24 times in the corresponding period, and the average growth rate was 8.5 percent. Japanese information development had taken off in the early 1960s, and has grown at full speed from the 1970s. Shanghai information development had made little progress until open policy and economic reform started in the early 1980s.

In 1952, the level of Shanghai information development was nearly equal to that of Japan, but, the level of Shanghai in 1991 was only 13.5 percent of that of Japan, which almost corresponds to the level of Japan in 1968. Shanghai had been left far behind Japan in those 25 years in terms of information development. The comparison between Shanghai and Japan is summarized in Table 17.2.

Table 17.2 Comparison of information development

Information development in	Characteristic value of 1991		Average growth rate (%)	
	Shanghai *	Japan	Shanghai	Japan
Capabilities	1.838 (1963)	16.769	1.6	7.6
Education	3.190 (1970)	26.154	3.0	9.2
Economy	1.937 (1964)	33.350	1.7	9.1
Society	4.784 (1973)	35.153	4.1	7.0
Daily life	4.455 (1965)	28.171	3.9	8.8
Synthetic level	3.235 (1968)	23.887	3.1	8.5

Note: * year in which the Japanese level corresponds to Shanghai's 1991 level.

3.2 The Characteristics of Information Development

At the start of 1952, the level of socioeconomic information development of Shanghai was nearly equal to that of Japan. Now the level in Japan in seven times greater than that of Shanghai. The cause of the big gap can be explained by factor analysis.

Factor loading is the correlation coefficient between original data and new indicators. The factor loading of the socioeconomic information development of Japan (JSEI), the correlations of the capabilities (JCI) information development in the economy (JEI) and education (JE) with JSEI are very high. It shows that Japanese socioeconomic information development is greatly dependent on strengthening the capabilities, developing education and applying information to production. In Shanghai, on the other hand, the factor loading shows that the correlations of the capabilities (SCI) and information development in the society (SSI) with SSEI are high. We can see that the slow process of the socioeconomic information development in Shanghai is because neither education nor information development in the economy has a strong effect on SSEI.

Why are the contributions of the capabilities, education and information development in the economy to SSEI so little in Shanghai? We analyse the reasons further below.

The factor loading shows that the main factors which strengthen the capabilities in Japan are increasing the research expenditure and enhancing telecommunication ability. From 1952 to 1991, Japanese telecommunication circuits (per 1,000 persons) in Japan increased from 0.35 to 7.6, of which the average growth rate was 8.2 percent (in Shanghai it was from 0.036 to 1 and the average growth rate was 8.9 percent); the average growth rate of value added of publishing and printing per 100 persons was 14.4 percent (that of Shanghai was 3.4 percent); and the average growth rate of per capita expenditure on R&D was 19 percent (that of Shanghai was 2.8 percent). So, it is observed that Japanese information development capabilities have been greatly strengthened in those 40 years. In Shanghai, the main factor for expanding the capabilities was the increase in researchers and the persons engaged in information activities. During the 40 years, the average growth rate of researchers per 100 persons was 6.1 percent in Shanghai (that of Japan was 4.7 percent). The average growth rate of the persons engaged in information activities per 100 persons was 1.2 percent (that of Japan was 3.1 percent). Due to a shortage of research funds (the factor loading of the expenditure on R&D to the capabilities was very small) the improvement of basic conditions for information creation and development was made very slowly. As a result, Shanghai's capabilities are still very weak in total.

In Japan, the main factors accounting for education development were the fostering of a number of talented persons and increasing educational expenditure. The ratio of the university graduates to the population increased from 0.03 percent in 1952 to 0.37 percent in 1991 (that of Shanghai had increased from 0.1 percent to 0.28 percent), the average growth rate of teachers per 100 persons was 0.9 percent (that of Shanghai was 1.7 percent) the average growth rate of per capita expenditure on education and culture was 15.5 percent (that of Shanghai was 9.7 percent). In Shanghai, the factors affecting the development of education were the stock of books and the increase in educational expenditure. Fostering talented persons has fallen behind Japan. The development of education has played a very important role in promoting socioeconomic information development in Japan. In Japan, information development in the economy was accounted for by the rapid development of information industries. In the past 40 years, carrying forward the R&D, education, and services of post and telecommunications, encouraging the manufacturing of information machines and equipment and introducing competition into the market of information services all gave an impetus to information development in the economy. The ratio of value added of information industries to GNP in Japan increased from 16.2 percent in 1952 to 37.9 percent in 1991 (that of Shanghai only increased from 16.6 percent to 20.2 percent). In Shanghai, there is no such striking factor affecting SEI according to the factor loading analysis.

To sum up the above, Japan increased expenditure on R&D and education, and implemented policies which outfitted information infrastructure, fostered talented persons and promoted information industries. Such policies rapidly made the information-oriented socio-economy in Japan. In Shanghai, on the other hand, the synergy of those factors on information development was weak because of a shortage of expenditure on R&D, delay in fostering talented persons and the weakness of the information infrastructure. As a result, Shanghai information development has fallen behind Japan.

4.   INFORMATION DEVELOPMENT AND ECONOMIC DEVELOPMENT

4.1 The Measurement of Economic Development

Generally speaking, the concept of economic development is differentiated from the concept of economic growth. Simply, economic growth means an increase in production, that is, a growth in output. The best yardstick to measure economic growth is gross national product (GNP). On the other hand, the concept of economic development is comprehensive. The common definition of economic development involves economic growth, improving material welfare, eliminating poverty and illiteracy, changing industrial structure and output structure, technical progress, and so on. Economic development has multiple goals, and is multifaceted. So, we have no single data which could exactly and adequately capture the multifaceted essence of economic development, and could describe its intricate process. In this chapter, we consider the following data to construct a single indicator of the process of economic development: gross national products (GNP); per capita national income (PNI); technical progress (TP);[6] and life expectancy (LE).

The synthetic values of economic development (ED) of Shanghai and Japan are respectively calculated by the principal components analysis as follows:

Shanghai: SED = 0.512SGNP + 0.513SPNI + 0.525STP + 0.446SLE
Japan: JED = 0.500JGNP + 0.503JPNI + 0.506JTP + 0.491JLE

The synthetic values of economic development show that the average growth rate of Shanghai economic development was 4.9 percent and that of Japan was 6.3 percent in the 40 years from 1952 to 1991. The calculated indicators of economic development in Shanghai and Japan are depicted in Figure 17.2, in which the level of 1952 is normalized to one.

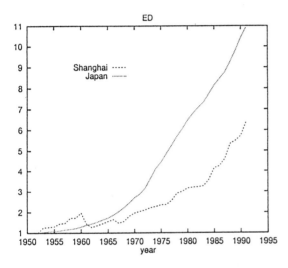

Figure 17.2 The levels of economic development of Shanghai and Japan

4.2 The Model of Economic Development

Neoclassical economic growth theory assumes that per capita national income (Y/L) is a function of the capital–labour ratio (K/L) that is, the rate of economic growth is dependent on the growth rate of the capital–labour ratio.

Here, we assume that economic development is dependent on both the capital–labour ratio and information development. We define the following model of economic development:

$$ED = A_0 \, PK^{\alpha} SEI^{\beta},$$
(17.1)

in which ED is the calculated level of economic development, PK is the capital–labour ratio, SEI is the synthetic level of information development, A_0, α, and β are parameters.

Using data of the period from 1973 to 1991, economic development in Shanghai is described by the model as follows (the figures in the brackets are t-values).

$$SED = 3.630 \; SPK^{0.395} \; SSEI^{0.312}$$
$$(10.60) \quad (5.86) \quad (2.57)$$
$$R^2 = 0.98450 \text{ and S.E.} = 0.04.$$

Also, using data from 1969 to 1991, economic development in Japan is described as follows:

$$JED = 1.657 \; JPK^{0.399} JSEI^{0.328}$$
$$(7.42) \quad (9.05) \; (6.25)$$
$$R^2 = 0.99438 \text{ and S.E.} = 0.03.$$

4.3 The Impact of Information Development on Economic Development

Based on these models, we summarize the estimates of the factor contribution to economic development in Shanghai and Japan in Table 17.3.

Table 17.3 Factor contribution to economic development

	Average growth rate		Growth rate of factor input		Contribution	
	Shanghai	Japan	Shanghai	Japan	Shanghai	Japan
Capital–labour ratio	10.7	10.5	4.3	4.2	71.1	60.0
Information development	5.5	8.9	1.8	2.8	28.9	40.0
Economic development	6.1	7.0	6.1	7.0	100.0	100.0

The impact of information development on economic development in Shanghai was 28.9 percent, compared to 40.0 percent in Japan. The difference is due to the difference in the information economy. Shanghai is now at the initial stage of information development. Japan is at the mature stage of the high information-oriented society. The difference in the stage of information development had taken shape at a different level of economic development.

The average growth rate of the capital–labour ratio and the factor input of the capital–labour ratio to economic development in Japan (10.5 percent, 4.2 percent) are both nearly equal to that in Shanghai (10.7 percent, 4.3 percent). However, the contribution of the capital–labour ratio in Japan is obviously lower than in Shanghai. It could be viewed that as a highly capital-equipped economy. Japan has already entered a phase of the diminishing marginal contribution of the capital–labour ratio to economic development.

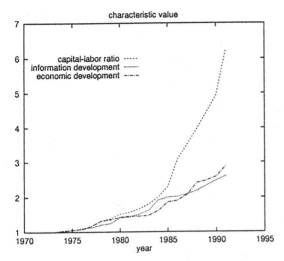

Figure 17.3 Changes in C–L, SEI and ED of Shanghai

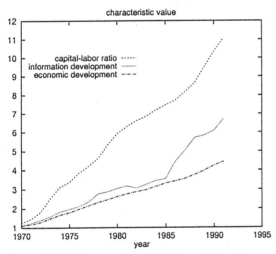

Figure 17.4 Changes in C–L, SEI and ED of Japan

Figures 17.3 and 17.4 depict the changes in the capital–labour ratio (C–L), the synthetic indicator of information development (SED) and the synthetic indicator of economic development (ED) in Shanghai and Japan, respectively (we normalize all those indicators of Shanghai in 1973 and Japan in 1969 to one to compare them with each other).

Figures 17.3 and 17.4 shows two important points which are worthy of note. First, not only in a developing area like Shanghai but also in a developed country like Japan, information development is congruous with economic development. We can conclude that in the future modern society the most important determinant of economic development will be information development, though the contribution of information development on economic development is not so strong now. Furthermore, the curve of information development in Japan is always drawn above the curve of economic development, which means that information development has grown more rapidly than economic development. In Shanghai, on the other hand, the curve of information development is sometimes (1973–1981, 1987–1991) drawn below the curve of economic development, and is sometimes (1982–1986) drawn above it. So, it is considered that the contribution of information development on economic development in Japan was larger than that in Shanghai.

Second, not only in Shanghai but also in Japan the curve of the capital–labour ratio is drawn far above the curve of economic development (Shanghai is so from 1985), which means that the capital–labour ratio has grown more rapidly than economic development. It could be considered that at present in Shanghai and even in Japan the main motive force of economic development had been the intensification of the capital–labour ratio.

5. CONCLUSION

The main findings of this study are summarized as follows. There is a clear difference in the effect of information development between a developing region like Shanghai and a highly developed region like Japan. From the case studies of Shanghai and Japan, we conjecture that in the modern economy the backwardness of economic development in developing countries is just backwardness in information development. The backwardness of information development involves weak capabilities, backwardness of education and immature information development in the economy.

It is necessary for the economy in China to place even greater emphasis on information development in order to attain a high level of economic growth.

REFERENCES

Amirahmadi, H. and C. Wallace (1995), 'Information technology, the organization of production, and regional development', *Environment and Planning A* **27**, pp. 1745–75.

Economic Planning Agency of Japan (1984), *New Information Theory* (in Japanese), Tokyo: Ministry of Finance of Japan, Printing Bureau.

Economic Planning Agency of Japan (1985), *Approaches Towards the Computation of the Information-oriented Economy* (in Japanese), Tokyo: Ministry of Finance of Japan, Printing Bureau.

Japan Association of Information Disposal and Development (1988), *White Book on Information Development* (in Japanese), Tokyo: Japan Association of Information Disposal and Development.

Katz, R.L. (1986), 'Measurement and cross-national comparisons of the information work force', *The Information Society* **4**, pp. 231–77.

Machlup, F. (1962), *The Production and Distribution of Knowledge in The United States*, New York: Princeton University Press.

Management and Coordination Agency of Japan Statistics Bureau (1953–1992), *Japan Statistical Yearbook (1953–1991)*, Tokyo: Japan Statistical Association and The Mainichi Newspapers.

Marshall, J.N. and P.A. Wood (1992), 'The role of services in urban and regional development: recent debates and new directions', *Environment and Planning A* **24**, pp. 1255–70.

Porat, M.U. (1977), *Information Economy, Volume 1, Definitions and Measurement*, Report of the US Department of Commerce, PB-286762.

Porterfield, S.L. and G.C. Pulver (1991), 'Exports, impacts and locations of services producers', *International Regional Science Review* **14** (1), pp. 41–59.

Shanghai Statistics Bureau (1987–1992), *Shanghai Statistical Yearbook (1986–1991)*, Beijing: China Statistics Publishing Corporation.

NOTES

1. Natural science research institute, social science institute and synthetical science research institute.

2. Based on definition of Porat's 'the primary information sector', but researchers and teachers are not included here.

3. Universities, colleges, technical schools, middle schools, primary schools, kindergartens, the schools for blind and deaf-mute, and so on.

4. This is the same same as Porat's definition of 'the primary information sector'.

5. This is the same as Porat's definition of 'the primary information sector'.

6. The technical progress in Shanghai (STP) is estimated based on the following production function:

$$Y = 1.196 \ K^{0.555} L^{0.589} \exp(0.014t),$$

$$R^2 = 0.99132, \text{S.E.} = 0.06,$$

in which Y is GNP (10 million yuan), K is capital stock (10 million yuan), L is labour input (10 thousand), t is time variable (year, 1970 = 1, ..., 1991 = 22).

18. Global Opportunities and Regional Strategies: Contrasting Canada's Technology Triangle and Australia's Multi-Function Polis

Paul Parker

1. INTRODUCTION

Globalization and the increasing knowledge intensity of the economy have led many regions to promote regional development based on high-technology industries. The process of technology creation and transfer is often assumed to be globally uniform, yet advocates of 'high-tech' development use conflicting conceptual frameworks. A top-down approach has been used by many central governments to mobilize resources to promote the development of selected centres. An international example of this approach is the Multi-Function Polis (MFP), proposed by the Japanese Minister for International Trade and Industry to his Australian counterpart, in which a new Pacific city for the exchange of technology and culture was to be established. However, the top-down approach has been widely criticized and the bottom-up approach has been promoted as an alternative with its emphasis on building local capacity and creating partnerships and networks. An example of this approach in the high-technology sector is Canada's Technology Triangle (CTT) where the four cities of Cambridge, Guelph, Kitchener and Waterloo formed a joint marketing arrangement and firms formed industry-based and export networks. The CTT and MFP were both initiated in 1987 so an evaluation of their initial achievements and limitations will be provided. An important finding is the influence of local and external actors in both case studies. This implies that rather than rely exclusively on either external or internal resources, there is a need to integrate the top-down and bottom-up models into a model of local–global partnership to achieve high-tech development.

The promotion of high-tech industry is a common strategy for regions seeking to improve their position in the global economy and an extensive literature has evolved (Beck 1992; Britton 1996; Castells and Hall 1994;

Glasmeier 1987; Malecki 1991; Markusen et al. 1986; Massey et al. 1992; Preer 1992; Smilor et al. 1988). The globalization of the economy is perceived as both a threat and an opportunity for regional development. Increased international competition is perceived as a threat as companies shift their production facilities to low cost regions and cause a 'hollowing out' of industrial economies as part of the new international division of labour (Bluestone and Harrison 1982; Dicken 1992). On the other hand, improved access to international markets means greater potential sales for high value goods and services produced locally. The rapid exchange of information using advanced telecommunication technologies has increased the rate of technology creation and diffusion. Both products and processes have become more information intensive. The challenge facing many regions is how to implement a high-tech growth strategy to produce high value, knowledge intensive goods and services.

High-tech industries are generally concentrated in the metropolitan centres at the top of national and international urban systems where information networks are the most dense and financial, human and infrastructure resources are the greatest (Castells and Hall 1994). The high wages and rapid growth potential associated with high tech firms make them desired by virtually all governments. As a result, lower order cities and peripheral regions in industrialized countries and developing countries alike want to increase their relative position in these industries. Advocates such as Partridge (1993) argue that even rural states can achieve employment growth in high tech industries by the right mix of government expenditure and taxation policies. The creation of new technology and the promotion of high-technology firms is thus a topic of direct interest to regional scientists as regions attempt to redirect their economies to specialize in this sector.

Regional development strategies are often divided into two competing approaches. The first approach is based on a top-down model in which central government initiates a strategy to attract external public and private investment to stimulate growth in a designated region. In the second model the emphasis is on a bottom-up strategy of building local capacity, especially local human and institutional resources. Network formation among firms is important to raise the ability of small and medium-sized firms to engage in large projects and to achieve agglomeration benefits. The inclusion of actors from university, industry and government is considered to be important in the creation of a sustained innovative milieux (Aydalot and Keeble 1988; Maillat and Lecoq 1992). In general, top-down initiatives attempt to create high-tech regions by the attraction of firms to the region while bottom-up initiatives concentrate on building local capacity and entrepreneurship.

The two general models are examined by the use of two case studies located outside the global technology leaders of the United States, Japan and Europe.

Instead, Australia and Canada were chosen as countries trying to increase their technology base to counter their traditional reliance upon natural resource extraction and processing industries and to augment their traditional small and domestically focused manufacturing base. Fears of job losses from restructuring and the hollowing out of old manufacturing centres and the shift of employment to lower wage areas motivated the promotion of high-tech industries to counter these trends. The evaluation of the case studies identifies weaknesses in the original models and calls for the integration of the two development approaches into a model of local–global partnership for high-tech development based on the building of local capacity through partnerships with local and external actors.

2. THE TOP-DOWN MODEL

Many national governments have sought to stimulate the development of high-tech centres or technopoles (Malecki 1991; Savoie 1992). Castells and Hall (1994) review many of these initiatives, including the Multi-Function Polis (MFP) in Australia. In each case, the national government has a defined vision or set of policy objectives and implements a programme to establish the technopole. In some cases, greenfield sites are chosen and in others existing urban centres are selected for the expansion of an adjacent site or particular industries. In general, a few urban centres at the top of the urban hierarchy maintain a dominant role in the creation and dissemination of new technologies. The concentration of knowledge, communication and information networks along with specialized financial, technical and business services in these centres creates a comparative advantage for further technological developments. Castells and Hall (1994) and others thus recognize the agglomeration benefits of new firms entering high-tech industries where others are already located and the resulting reinforcement of the technopole role of metropolitan centres (London, Paris, Tokyo, and so on). The more interesting test is the extent to which smaller centres can also become technopoles and stimulate regional development based on high tech industries.

The general top-down model is based on the active role of external actors: central governments, private banks and transnational firms (Figure 18.1). Jobs, wealth and a larger local tax base are created by the injection of funds from outside the region. This approach has often been adopted by governments seeking to promote high-tech industries in particular regions or growth centres. The key inputs are external investment in response to improved infrastructure and fiscal incentives provided by federal, state or provincial governments. The development process is depicted as largely independent of the local region. Instead, the process is based on key policy decisions by central governments and the satisfaction of location factors set by external firms and loan criteria set by banks with external head offices.

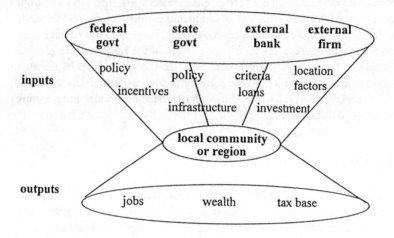

Figure 18.1   Top-down model

The case study used to evaluate this type of initiative is the MFP in Australia. It was established to serve as a Pacific centre for the exchange of technology and culture with input from not only national, but also international sources (MITI 1987). The objectives of the proposal will be identified and its initial performance evaluated.

3.   THE BOTTOM-UP MODEL

The bottom-up approach has emerged as a fundamental challenge to the top-down approach (ECC 1990; OMMA 1992). The large-scale projects and growth pole emphasis of top-down policies have been replaced in many countries with an emphasis on the indigenous potential of a region and its technological capability (Stöhr 1981; Stöhr and Taylor 1981). Increased local processing and value added activities were often depicted as independent of global processes. Coffey and Polese (1984, 1985) proposed a stage model of local development based on local entrepreneurship and business expansion.

In Canada, the federal government had attempted to stimulate regional development for decades through a series of federal departments and programmes (Savoie 1992). By the 1980s these top-down efforts were considered by many to have failed and the emphasis in industrial policy shifted to sectors rather than regions. Two region-based initiatives remained (Atlantic Canada Opportunities Agency and Western Diversification Program) but operated with reduced budgets. In Australia, attempts in the 1970s to stimulate new growth centres under the Whitlam Labor government received much less funding over a much shorter period than the regional programmes in Canada. In both countries these programmes were generally considered unsuccessful and were replaced with calls for a bottom-up model of development. The Canadian government created the Community Futures Program in the mid 1980s to stimulate a bottom-up approach based on the cooperation of several local communities to gain funding under this national programme.

More fundamentally, national groups such as the Economic Council of Canada joined local groups in calling for a shift to bottom-up strategies (ECC 1990). The failure of top-down programmes to delivery the expected redistribution of regional fortunes has led many to reject such programmes. Instead of a mandate defined by a national policy, objectives are determined at the local level, typically through a strategic economic planning process and the promotion of local level networks, partnerships and entrepreneurship (Bryant and Preston, 1987). An emphasis is placed on enhancing local human resources through training and increased participation, on building the capacity of local institutions and on creating innovative financing tools to provide greater access to capital (OMMA 1992). The development of high-tech industries linked to local educational and research resources has also been advocated (Science Council of Canada 1990). Entrepreneurship and other processes to increase the value of local resources are promoted as central features of this approach (Figure 18.2).

An alternative form of the bottom-up or local economic development model emphasizes local initiatives and entrepreneurship set within the context of external processes and trends. Bryant and Preston (1987) and Albrechts et al. (1989) depict the local economic development process in Canada and Europe as emphasizing local capacity and initiative within the context of external forces such as federal governments, transnational corporations and globalization processes. In this way the bottom-up process overcomes the criticism that it fails to see beyond the community boundary and often results in wasteful duplication of effort.

The case study selected to evaluate a bottom-up approach to high-tech development is the CTT. It was initiated as a result of the shared objectives of four small cities (Cambridge, Guelph, Kitchener and Waterloo) who decided to create a shared regional identity, Canada's Technology Triangle or

CTT, rather than compete among themselves and duplicate development efforts.

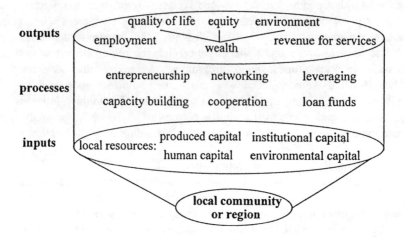

Figure 18.2   Bottom-up model

4.   CASE STUDIES: ORIGINS, LOCATIONS AND OBJECTIVES

A brief description of each case study (MFP: Multi-Function Polis; CTT: Canada's Technology Triangle) will be provided and then comparisons made. First, the origin, location and objectives of the two proposals will be compared. Both regions identified information technologies, environmental management and education as three key industries for promotion. The link between research capacity at universities and technology transfer to industry will be examined using data on spin-off firm creation and patent applications.

The origins of the CTT and MFP were both found outside of their respective countries. In 1987 the Japanese Minister for International Trade and Industry was hosting his Australian counterpart, the Minister for Industry and Commerce, when he suggested that Australia could follow the example of Japan's technopolis programme by establishing a Pacific centre for the exchange of technology and culture (MITI 1987). The proposed 'Multi-Function Polis' would benefit both countries by providing Japan with access to new technologies at the research stage and a new model of high amenity urban lifestyles, while Australia benefited from the transfer of Japanese technologies to stimulate production and job creation. The needs of both countries were depicted as complementary and the proposal received endorsement from both national governments.

The international proposal for the MFP had no predetermined site so after the Australian and Japanese governments agreed on joint objectives, a competition was held to determine where it should be located. Four of the six Australian states submitted bids and in 1990 the South Australian capital, Adelaide, was selected as the MFP site. Adelaide had a 1991 population of 1.2 million and offered a single 1800 hectare site for the project located 15 km north of the central business district (the Gilman/Dry Creek site). The objectives of the MFP evolved from the initial Japanese proposal through a series of intergovernmental negotiations first between the national governments of Japan and Australia and then between the Australian national government and the state of South Australia. In 1992 the objectives were declared in a joint federal–state statement (Table 18.1).

Table 18.1 MFP Australia objectives

To create or establish:
    a model of conservation of the natural environment and resources
    a model of environmentally sustainable development
    a model of equitable social and economic urban development
    a national focus for economic, scientific and technology development of international significance
    leading centres of innovation in science, technology, education & the arts
    a focus for international investment in new technologies
    a model of productive interaction: among industry, R&D, education and commercial interests
    an international centre of innovation and excellence in urban development

Source: Commonwealth of Australia and State of South Australia (1992).

The globalization of the economy and increased international competition through the reduction of trade barriers, especially under NAFTA, stimulated the formation of Canada's Technology Triangle (CTT). In 1987 the economic development officers of the four neighbouring cities (Cambridge, Guelph, Kitchener and Waterloo) each represented their communities at a large trade show in the United States. They recognized the inefficient duplication of effort represented by having four separate booths, four sets of literature, four sets of staff and four sets of travel expenses. As well, they believed that their communities could gain more international recognition by working together as a single larger unit. These local actors then started the process to form the CTT to increase the international profile and competitiveness of their region. They recognized that the attraction of new investment to any of the four cities would have positive effects on their own community through increased employment and local market opportunities. The objectives of the initiative extended beyond business attraction to include the promotion of local networks across city boundaries.

The CTT consists of four small cities in south-western Ontario. Waterloo, Kitchener and Cambridge form a continuous urban chain along the western side of the triangle with Guelph forming the third point approximately 30 kilometres to the east. The proximity of the cities results in a shared labour market with internal commuting. Kitchener is the largest city with a 1991 population of 180,000. The other three cities each had a population of nearly 100,000 for a regional population of approximately 500,000. Access to the CTT is facilitated by its proximity to Toronto with the Toronto international airport being a one-hour drive and downtown Toronto a one-and-a-half-hour drive.

The objectives of the CTT were based on the shared aspirations of the four cities. A joint CTT (1994) publication declared that cooperation and technology were the foundation for their combined economic growth. The shared goal was to promote the region as one economic unit and to draw on the complementary strengths of each city. The images created by promotional material included: computer programmers creating revolutionary software, white coats in labs making microbiological breakthroughs and state-of-the-art robotic assembly lines. These images represent the computer specialization at the University of Waterloo, the life sciences emphasis at the University of Guelph and the advanced manufacturing systems used in some Cambridge and Kitchener plants. However, more than images would have to be created if the cities were to succeed in creating a dynamic high-tech regional economy. Local firms were identified in 13 science and technology industries with a total of 13,000 workers in the early 1990s. Six of these industries employed 1000 or more workers: computer hardware and software, environmental technologies, manufacturing (including design and development), industrial automation, telecommunications and energy (Lindsay and Lindsay 1994).

5. INITIAL MFP/CTT DIFFERENCES AND SIMILARITIES

The MFP and CTT had significant institutional differences. Unlike the MFP, the CTT had no Development Corporation with federal funding to support staff, research, administration and marketing efforts. There was no International Advisory Board as assembled for the MFP (MFP Australia

1994a). No mandate was received from the federal government and most importantly, there was no core site or physical separation from the local community. Indeed, the CTT has been called a virtual office with no substantial resources to achieve its goals. Instead, the CTT institutional structure consisted of new combinations of pre-existing organizations. For example, a combined economic development committee was formed with representatives from the Economic Development Departments of the four cities. The provincial government gave a small initial grant toward new promotional material and, once established, the provincial and federal governments used the CTT name to promote and represent the region.

The institutional initiative of forming Canada's Technology Triangle was heralded by some as a symbol of firm and institutional networking (Crane 1992). In contrast, Zeidenberg (1995) asserted that the CTT had neither the budget nor the capacity to develop networking or to access venture capital for small innovative firms. While the formal CTT committee remained a joint marketing initiative of the four cities, the successful creation of the regional image has been used by other organizations to develop their own networks. For example, computer industry networks were not created or dictated by the CTT committee, but instead were promoted as an example of membership across the region and as a means to facilitate interaction and exchanges among computer firms and related university and government partners. A CTT Export Network also was formed to promote exports from small and medium-sized firms. Firms were matched with university students who prepared a marketing plan for the firm to enter the American market.

Similarly, local groups identified venture capital as a constraint to the expansion of new high-tech firms and then responded to this need. A private proposal for venture capital funds was advocated by the President of Zief Industries and presented to the federal government. Community response was demonstrated by the community loan fund coordinated by the Community Opportunities Development Agency (CODA) having subscribed more capital by mid 1996 than the comparable Toronto community loan fund (Born 1996). The major Canadian banks targeted the region as a priority area for investment in high-tech firms with pilot programmes for new lending criteria for these firms. The federal government initiated a Community Investment Program in 1996 and the CTT was selected as one of the pilot areas. This programme required the cooperative participation of industry, local government and educational institutions along with a commitment for local sources to replace the federal government as the source of operating funds over a six-year period.

Despite the institutional differences, the MFP and CTT proposals shared several needs. Both urban centres needed to restructure their old manufacturing base and respond to the globalization of markets and increased free trade. Both needed to create employment opportunities to combat rising unemployment in the early 1990s. Local communities also wanted to improve their environmental quality and to clean up and redevelop old industrial lands. Overall, there was a desire to improve the quality of life and to improve access for diverse social groups.

6. MFP INITIAL EVALUATIONS

When they learned that the MFP was to be located on the Gilman site in Adelaide, some Adelaide residents rejected the proposal outright. This opposition was articulated by a variety of community groups and two Adelaide academics who wrote a series of articles and books on the subject (Harwood 1990a–f; MFPACCP 1991b; Smith 1990, 1991, 1992). Local opposition was recognized by the government-appointed MFP Community Consultation. The panel concluded that community views support the national concept based on its international linkages, the enhancement of Australia's international competitiveness and the promotion of an innovative culture, yet held serious objections to the MFP–Adelaide urban development (MFPACCP 1991a, p.1). Despite the economic, environmental and social opportunities promised, the primary objections were the inappropriateness of an advanced technology approach for the development of human values, the MFP contribution to population pressures and environmental risks, its ecological unsustainability, the contribution to an increasing dominance of the Australian economy by multinational corporations and foreign investment, and the diversion of scarce resources and increasing pressure on the economy in pursuing elitist enclave developments (MFPACCP 1991a, p.1)

Despite the efforts of the Community Consultation Panel, the timing of events implied that community issues were of little importance to MFP decision makers. The Community Consultation Panel presented its report in August 1991 after allowing community groups an opportunity to react to the feasibility study completed in May. However, in July the state and federal governments had announced the start of the project with an initial operating budget of $12 million (Smith 1992, p. 5).

In addition, the conclusion reached by the Panel, that the majority of the community saw the project as acceptable and that it should proceed, was challenged by Smith (1992). Many of the submissions supported the MFP provided that certain conditions were met. The Panel recognized this support and made recommendations to meet many of the conditions. In contrast, Smith (1992) regarded the submissions as a rejection of the MFP because the conditions could not be met.

Further consideration is needed to clarify some of the environmental debate surrounding the proposed MFP. The formal environmental impact assessment procedure examined many of the issues raised in earlier debates, including: geotechnical uncertainty, groundwater and water quality, public health and air quality, biological environment, social impacts, transport needs, economic issues, infrastructure requirements, waste disposal, management of the site, and the desirability of alternative sites (SAOPUD 1992, p. 6). The need to rectify the environmental damage already inflicted on the Gilman site presented both a problem and an opportunity. The problem was that the site appeared unattractive and it was perceived to be hard to attract investors. However, the problems of renovating damaged urban environments are worldwide, so the successful restoration of environmental quality on the site could demonstrate innovative environmental management and restoration services and expertise which could be exported.

Environmental management had been identified as one of the growth industries of the 1990s and was selected in the 1991 feasibility study as one of the three sectors to target for MFP initiatives. As a result, the problems on the site created opportunities to demonstrate environmental rehabilitation expertise. One of the principal strategies proposed was to excavate lakes on the site to provide stormwater retention areas and to use the fill to construct urban village platforms for residential, industrial and commercial use (SAOPUD 1992). The proposed MFP development was to be innovative and provide high-technology housing for a population of 30–50,000 which would allow for the integration of residential, commercial and industrial development. At the Gilman site, the proposed allocation of land use was: 43 percent urban, 23 percent lakes and canals, 34 percent open space/urban forest (SAOPUD 1992, p. 8). Despite the limitations of evaluating a concept plan with general rather than specific data on what firms and processes would be located on the site, the Office of Planning and Urban Development concluded that the major potential environmental impacts identified could be managed (SAOPUD 1992). In contrast to the social and environmental debate over the viability of the MFP, initial CTT evaluations largely focused on economic issues.

7. CTT INITIAL EVALUATIONS

Smith (1993, p. 4) noted that 'The success of the (Waterloo) regional economy can only be explained by its adaptability. And the source of that adaptability must be entrepreneurial drive'. The success of the region was chronicled by Larry Smith in a series of reports for the Region of Waterloo (which includes the cities of Waterloo, Kitchener and Cambridge, but excludes Guelph) (Smith 1993, 1995). Between 1987 and 1994 the regional economy grew at double the provincial rate (23 percent in contrast to 11 percent). The Waterloo Region grew at a faster rate than any other Canadian census metropolitan area east of British Columbia. Only the cities of Vancouver and Victoria grew faster in the 1987–94 period with a buoyant wood products sector and substantial investment and immigration from Asia (Smith 1995). Employment growth in the region (16 percent 1987–94) outpaced Ontario (4 percent) by an even wider margin (Smith 1995). A growing agglomeration of high-tech firms was identified by several researchers (Bathelt and Hecht 1990; Denomme 1996; Jung 1994). This growth was expected to continue as reported in a 1995 survey of high-tech firms in the City of Waterloo. Employment in the 63 responding firms averaged only 5 employees at start-up, but grew to an average of 51 employees in 1995 and was expected to rise to an average of nearly 100 employees over the next five years (Whitney & Co. 1995). Overall, 92 percent of the firms expected to grow with an estimated creation of 2290 jobs in 50 of the respondent firms.

  The overall success of the CTT economy was argued to be based on six key factors: entrepreneurship, export focus, education, infrastructure, suppliers and quality of life (Borovilos cited in Lindsay and Lindsay 1994, p. 28). Entrepreneurship grew rapidly, as indicated by the number of individuals reporting proprietorship as their occupation on the census (16,240 persons in 1991). The 49 percent increase over the 1981–91 period in Waterloo Region nearly doubled the 28 percent increase in Ontario as a whole (Knafelc 1995). Entrepreneurship was particularly important in the high-tech sector as demonstrated by 95 percent of the science and technology firms in the City of Waterloo having been established in the region (Whitney & Co. 1995). Wright (1991) reported similar results from a survey of 164 high-tech firms in Mississauga and the CTT. The survey included firms in business machines, aircraft and parts, communications and electronics, plastics and synthetics, drug and medicine, scientific instruments and other machinery sectors. The location factor most often cited was familiarity with the region (81 percent of respondents). This finding is interpreted as reflecting the role of entrepreneurs in the establishment of firms in the region where they lived. Transportation (70 percent) and availability of skilled labour (64 percent) were also common responses and reflect conventional location criteria to provide access to markets, to suppliers and to required skilled workers. However, the availability of these resources in many communities enables the familiarity of entrepreneurs (for example, with the city where they went to university) to be a determining factor in location decisions.

  Filion and Rutherford (1996) cast doubt on the assertion that the region's manufacturing base is restructuring toward a high-tech 'knowledge intensive' future. The image of Ontario's 'economic miracle' region is based on a low unemployment rate (a 1994 average of 6.6 percent in contrast to the provincial average of 9.6 percent) (Statistics Canada 1995). However, Rutherford (1995) notes that the low unemployment rate is achieved by a substantial decline in participation rates (especially among females) from pre-recession record levels of 76 percent in 1986 to 72 percent in 1991. Despite this decline, participation rates remain well above the provincial average (67 percent). Youth unemployment also remains problematic as workers aged 15–24 suffered the greatest decline in employment during the recession of the early 1990s. Zeidenberg (1995) goes further to assert that nearly 20 percent of the region's labour force is unemployed when those receiving employment insurance and welfare are combined with those who have withdrawn from the labour market.

The ability of the Waterloo regional economy to continue to outperform the provincial economy was also questioned. The Jung (1994) survey of 221 small and medium-sized firms in Kitchener and Waterloo did not identify significant inter-firm cooperation at the local level. Instead, the firms were fully integrated into the Southern Ontario industrial network and to a lesser extent into other Northeast North American industrial regions. Key attributes of successful 'flexible specialization' regions such as the Third Italy, Silicon Valley and some industrial districts in Los Angeles are argued to be absent in the Waterloo Region. Intense regional linkages and cooperation among firms are emphasized in these successful regions as the means to downplay competition and deploy joint product development and marketing (Scott 1992; Storper and Scott 1989). Networking among computer firms is acknowledged, but overall Filion and Rutherford (1996, p. 267) 'conclude that not only is Waterloo Region at best weakly networked, it is wide open to fluctuations occurring within the Southern Ontario industrial belt which is particularly sensitive to cycles affecting the car industry'.

8. EDUCATION AND RESEARCH RESOURCES

Majoribanks (1990, p. 1) stated that 'The primary objective of the University of Adelaide's Strategic Plan is to promote closer cooperation with industry and to maximize its links with industry, commerce and government as an integral part of its research management strategy'.

The educational and research institutions in the CTT and MFP share several attributes. Three universities are located in each region and they are complemented with additional specialized research and manufacturing institutions. The University of Adelaide, Flinders University and the University of South Australia are all located in Adelaide. The University of

South Australia's Levels campus is adjacent to the expanded MFP/Technology Park site and has a tradition of working on applied projects of direct interest to industry. The University of Adelaide has the strongest research reputation of the three universities and is represented on the MFP Australia Board by its Vice Chancellor for Research. Total external research funding from government and industry sources to the University of Adelaide was approximately $30 million per year in the early 1990s (University of Adelaide 1994). Flinders University is located in the southern part of Adelaide, but participates in several joint research projects and cooperative research centres with the other universities and industrial partners. In some cases, researchers from all three universities have joined together in the same project.

The three universities in the CTT are the University of Waterloo, University of Guelph and Wilfrid Laurier University. The University of Waterloo is the largest with a total of 24,000 students. It boasts a large cooperative education programme with nearly 9000 students alternating academic terms with work terms in 24,000 companies worldwide (Maclean's 1994, p. 72). Specializations include engineering, information technology, mathematics and computer science. The University of Guelph has 15,000 students and specializes in agriculture, veterinary medicine, life sciences and bio-technology (Maclean's 1994, p. 67). Wilfrid Laurier University is smaller with 8,000 students, yet has a strong reputation in specialized areas such as music and business administration (Maclean's 1994, p. 74). In addition, the Connestoga College of Applied Arts and Technology offers 65 diploma or certificate programmes that are skills and career oriented.

Specialized institutions that contribute to the region's technical capacity include the Ontario CAD/CAM Centre in Cambridge which offers professional services in computer aided design/manufacturing. Its services include planning, evaluation, and training for specialized tasks. The Canadian Industrial Innovation Centre is located in Waterloo and provides assistance to entrepreneurs and innovators. The range of assistance available covers marketing, finance, appraisal, patenting, prototype development, and research.

The need for special assistance to transfer technology from the university environment to commercial ventures is recognized at universities in both the CTT and MFP. The University of Adelaide incorporated Luminis Pty. Ltd. as its commercial development company to promote and to facilitate collaboration between the university and industry. Its objectives are to promote technology transfers, research opportunities/consultancies, and to provide project management. Since 1990, it has operated as a management company to encourage the commercial development of intellectual property and to hold equity interests in several university spinoff firms.

The University of Waterloo has a Technology Transfer and Licensing Office within its Research Office and the University of Guelph has an Industrial and Innovation Services unit that promotes research expertise, technology acquisition, research support and business development. Although no office specializes in technology transfer at Wilfrid Laurier University it has a Research Centre for the Management of New Technology (REMAT) within its School of Business and Economics. An Institute for Innovation Research is located at the University of Waterloo. Given these institutional initiatives to promote technology transfer from university to commercial application, a review of related performance measures is required.

9. PERFORMANCE MEASURES: PATENTS

The strength of links between university research and commercial application can be measured in several ways. The licensing of technologies developed on campus can generate income for a university and many universities are active in this field. Within Canada, the University of Waterloo has a longstanding reputation for earning more from licenses than other universities. Much of the income gained by the University of Waterloo is from computer software and this income stream is declining ($1.6 million in 1992, $1.4 million in 1994) with changes in the types of software being used and the practice of transferring software rights to private companies (often spinoffs from the university) (AUTM 1993, 1995). Other universities, especially those with large medical schools, are increasing their number of licenses (and the associated income) and are expected to surpass Waterloo income levels in the future.

The overall level of university income generated from licenses remains small in Canada in comparison to that of universities in the United States. The number of income-generating licenses held by the 11 Canadian institutions which responded to the annual Association of University Technology Managers (AUTM) survey rose from 158 to 242 between 1992 and 1994. In comparison, American universities reported an increase from 2632 to 3560 income-generating licenses over the same period and held approximately fifteen times as many licenses. An even larger difference appeared in the income generated. Reported license income to Canadian universities rose from $4.2 to $5.8 million while that for American universities rose from $173 to $266 million over the 1992–94 period (AUTM 1993, 1995). Australian universities have been less active in this area, but license revenue and patent royalties became higher priorities in the 1990s and activity is expected to grow.

Prior to gaining income from commercially successful inventions, the intellectual property rights to these inventions need to be established. The application for and issue of patents is a standard means to establish intellectual property rights. The largest commercial market for these inventions is in the United States and many inventors apply to have their discoveries recognized there. US patent data thus provide a measure of the creation of new inventions and technology from various international as well as national sources. A comparison is provided for registered US patents held by residents of MFP Australia's host city (Adelaide) and the CTT cities (Waterloo, Guelph, Kitchener and Cambridge) (Table 18.2).

Table 18.2   US patents by MFP and CTT inventors, 1991–95

Address of inventor assignee	MFP Adelaide #	%	CTT Cambridge, Guelph, Kitchener, Waterloo	%
University	4	14	23	8
Local spinoff	3	10	8	3
Other local firms	12	42	103	34
US firm	3	10	90	30
Individual(s)	4	14	74	24
Federal government	3	10	4	1
Total	29	100	100	100

Source: CNIDR, 1996 US Patent and Trademarks data base.

Patents with an interest held by the Universities of Adelaide, Waterloo and Guelph are identified as well as those by their spinoff companies. No patents were found under the name of the Universities of South Australia, Flinders or Wilfrid Laurier. The assignees holding the rights to the patent are further divided into local firms, US firms, individuals or the federal government. Local firms and individuals account for 50 percent or more of the patents in each city. The role of US firms is particularly strong in Guelph and Waterloo where subsidiaries include a research function in their range of activities. The foreign ownership of the research results as well as the plants has been identified as a limitation in Canada's technological development (Britton 1987). Although Adelaide is a larger urban centre its residents hold fewer US patents. This pattern is explained in part by the greater difficulty in pursuing US opportunities from Australia. The pattern holds not only for universities, but also for private firms and individuals as shown in Table 18.2.

To consider the broader context of CTT patents, the AUTM annual survey provides an indication of the level of patent activity for ten of the largest Canadian universities. A university may choose not to respond to the survey if they have no activity in this area, but it could also indicate a lack of a responsible office or specialized staff to support technology transfer. Over the 1992–94 period UBC reported applying for, and being issued, more US patents than any other Canadian university (AUTM 1993, 1994, 1995). The universities of Toronto, Queens and Alberta were also very active and came next in the ranking. The University of Waterloo lodged 36 applications and had 14 US patents issued during this three-year period. This indicates that although the University of Waterloo is one of Canada's top five university sources of patented research, it is not unique and other universities are important sources of new technology as well.

To explore the potential for universities to contribute to local and regional economic development, one needs to look beyond aggregate patent numbers to the processes by which technology is transferred to local industry. Two of these processes, the formation of spinoff firms and the networking of research groups with companies, will be explored. The formation of spinoff companies is well recognized at the University of Waterloo where over 100 spinoff firms have been identified and approximately 30 of them reported research links with the university (TTLO 1994). The University of Adelaide has also been active in this area with several firms (Repromed, Integrated Silicon Design, Bresatec, GroPep and Enterovax) being created as subsidiaries of Luminus, the commercial development company owned by the university. For a more detailed examination of the processes emphasized by the top-down approach in the MFP and the bottom-up approach in the CTT, a review will be made of recent changes in the information technology industry.

10. INFORMATION TECHNOLOGY FROM THE TOP DOWN, MFP

Information technology is one of the fastest growing industries in the 1990s and is considered central to the high-tech aspirations of both the MFP and the CTT. However, the approach emphasized to develop the information technology industry differed sharply between the two areas. In the CTT an emphasis was placed on small firm creation (entrepreneurship) and growth.

This bottom-up approach was built on links to local education and research resources as many firms either hired students or were created by students or faculty from local universities. Initial university research may have led to the establishment of the firm or the firm could create partnerships through contract research at the university. In contrast, the top-down approach to stimulating the information technology industry is to attract external funds to the region, typically from central government sources or to attract external firms (typically transnational) to the region (Figure 18.1).

The information technology industry in the MFP benefited directly from inputs from central government and external firms. The inclusion of Technology Park and Science Park as part of the MFP integrated the state government's initiatives at promoting high-tech development in South Australia. Technology Park promoted itself as the oldest and most successful research park in Australia (MFP Australia 1994b). Its initial success was strongly supported by defence expenditure and the establishment of defence-affiliated research and development firms. Local success was thus achieved by the infusion of federal funds in the form of defence contracts. The importance of defence funds in supporting high-tech firms has been well documented in the United States during the rapid growth phase of Silicon Valley and other nodes of high-tech firms. The role of central government remained high in the expansion of the MFP even though the federal government reduced its role and the state government increased its commitment (note the removal of Australia from the project title). In 1997 the role of the MFP Development Corporation was expanded as it was restructured to incorporate the Urban Projects Authority, the Projects Group of the SA Tourism Commission and the Strategic Planning Group of the former Department of Information Industries (MFP 1997a).

The information technology sector was identified as one of three priority sectors for promotion in South Australia. An IT 2000 Vision called for South Australia to attract multinational IT companies as part of their global strategy. These multinationals would then serve as the source of skill transfers to local firms (SAEDA 1994, p. 11). In 1994 three major firms were attracted as part of this strategy: Motorola Australia, Australis Media, and Electronic Data Systems (EDS). Motorola decided to build its Australian Software Development Centre in Technology Park to service its worldwide business interests. By the year 2000 it is expected to employ 400 software engineers (SAEDA 1994, p. 12). Australis Media Ltd. chose Technology Park as the site for its national customer service centre to serve its pay-tv operations. By the year 2000 operations are projected to grow to support 1000 jobs at its purpose-built facility (SAEDA 1994, p. 11). EDS was the successful bidder to gain the state government contract for the outsourcing of its information and computer service needs. EDS and the state government agreed to jointly establish an Information Industries Development Centre which aims to 'create a centre of excellence in the software and services industries by providing market access, business advisory services and technology support services' (MFP Australia 1995, p. 16).

The information industries centre would also serve as a focal point in the first stage of the MFP urban development (Mawson Lakes) expected to house a population of 10,000 adjacent to Technology Park and the Levels campus of the University of South Australia. Telstra, Australia's leading telecommunications information services provider, is the initial provider of information infrastructure with the community being serviced by an interactive broadband infrastructure and a range of services and applications (MFP 1997c). The 1996 decision by the state government to proceed with the urban development gave impetus to the MFP strategy (MFP 1996). More information technology firms are to be attracted and the 'Smart City Australia' project was launched to achieve this objective (MFP Australia 1994a, p. 17; MFP 1996).

The Smart City Australia project 'underpins the MFP vision of a continuously innovative and enterprising community by providing an IT&T strategy and architecture, guided by a technology partner, to coordinate delivery of services to meet the full spectrum of community needs, from home offices to health care' (MFP Australia 1995, p. 16).

These achievements were based on a top-down model where development is achieved by inputs from central government and external firms investing from outside the region. Although the emphasis was on this external attraction, it should be noted that local initiatives were also active. In particular, the Signal Processing Research Institute was established in 1992 and is a joint venture between MFP Technology Park and the Universities of South Australia, Adelaide and Flinders (MFP 1997b). Tenants include the Institute for Telecommunications Research, the Cooperative Research Centre for Sensor Signal and Information Processing and the Australian Information Technology Centre. Other university-based research projects of commercial interest to the information technology industry included work on integrated circuit design. Many projects are part of the ongoing research and development activities of local researchers and in general have little to do with the MFP and its activities. The same research and commercialization process was underway in the CTT, where it was given much greater recognition as a bottom-up form of economic development.

11. INFORMATION TECHNOLOGY FROM THE BOTTOM UP, CTT

Information technology is a fast growing sector within the Canadian economy. It trebled the national growth rate during the 1980s and had sales of $40 billion in 1990. Nearly half of this activity took place within Ontario (CTN 1996). A key to success in this sector is the ability to sustain ongoing product innovation through scientific research and development. Most of these firms invest 10 percent or more of revenues in R&D, with the result that information technology firms account for 35 percent of industrial R&D in Canada or $1.8 billion annually (CTN 1996). Many of the firms are high growth and export oriented with 90 per cent of sales being outside of Canada. The common challenges faced by these firms has lead them to seek local networking opportunities.

An example of successful local networks is the Computer Technology Network which was formed in 1991 to facilitate the exchange of information among high-tech firms in the CTT. An initial meeting was held among representatives from the Waterloo-based spinoff firm, Mortice Kern Systems Inc., the Information Technology Research Centre at the University of Waterloo, the City of Waterloo and the local Office of the Ontario Ministry for Industry, Trade and Technology. Monthly breakfast meetings and special seminars are organized on topics such as software licensing, software copyright, patent protection, finding partners and obtaining investment funds (CTN 1996).

An electronic Internet directory is provided of the 60 companies in the CTT area engaged in continuous research and development related to the production of computer hardware, telecommunications hardware or packaged software and services (CTN 1996). A further 50 support companies are listed to identify a range of related services. The creation of the Computer Technology Network in 1991 was a natural evolution from smaller networks formed earlier by university researchers and their company partners.

An example of earlier network formation is the Institute for Computer Research (ICR) which was formed in 1982 to foster excellence in computer research at the University of Waterloo. It promotes synergy among researchers, provides efficient access to shared central hardware and software services and serves as a focal point for research interaction with industry (ICR 1995). The Institute has approximately 100 faculty members who are either individual members of ICR or are members of one of the thirteen formally federated groups within ICR. Each federated group is a team of researchers working on one or more related projects under a general title, such as: computer communications, computer graphics, logic programming and artificial intelligence, pattern analysis and machine intelligence, and so on (ICR 1995).

The Institute for Computer Research (ICR) draws on public and private sector support to enhance the computer research environment at the University of Waterloo. The ICR also serves as a focus for interaction with industry. It maintains a Corporate Partner Program through which it attempts to develop and maintain research relationships between university and industrial researchers. The partners include some of the largest Canadian and international information technology firms: Apple Canada, Bell Canada, Bull HN Information Systems, Digital Equipment of Canada, Hewlett-Packard (Canada), IBM Canada, The Mutual Group, NCR Canada, Northern Telecom Canada and WATCOM. An endowment fund is derived from Corporate Partners' contributions and used to support: a weekly colloquia, an Evening Lecture series, a Distinguished Visitors Program, a modest programme of grants to provide seed money for new and innovative projects, and post graduate scholarships to attract the best students to computer-related academic programs (ICR 1995). ICR regularly invites research presentations and visits by industry and serves as an information and contact agent for such interactions.

The major public sector support for the ICR is derived from the National Science and Engineering Research Council of Canada (NSERC) and its substantial Infrastructure Grant to operate a shared research support facility with three hardware and four software technicians (ICR 1995). Within the Institute, each research group maintains its own network of public and private support. Some research projects are supported by NSERC grants while others are funded by government departments, agencies and a broad range of private firms. In some cases research results have led to new products which warranted the formation of a spinoff company where researchers were able to commercialize their products and hire management and financial specialists to expand corporate operations. An example of the network maintained by one of these groups (PAMI) is provided next.

The purpose of the Pattern Analysis and Machine Intelligence Group (PAMI) is to advance the state-of-the-art in machine intelligence with an emphasis on knowledge-based systems, computer vision and robotics. Significant applications for contract research and transfer of technology to industry include: robot vision, computer graphics and animation, path planning and control; Canadian Space Projects on autonomous robotics and vision; remote sensing; biomolecular sequence alignment and analysis; process monitoring, classification and prediction; application of inductive learning to clinical diagnosis and prognosis; unconstrained character recognition; computer 3-D visual inspection of circuit boards; and image processing and optimal pattern layout on surfaces (ICR 1995).

Much of the research carried out in the PAMI Laboratory is closely integrated with the concerns and problems of industry. As a result, many research projects have involved the transfer of technology to organizations such as: AASTRA Aerospace, Alberta Research Council, Bell-Northern Research, Computer Devices Company, Diffracto, Alias Research, The Canadian Space Agency, Defence Research Establishment, Dynacon, Environment Canada, Fiat, General Motors Canada, General Motors, Hughes Aircraft, IBM, International Submarine Engineering, Leathercam, NCR Canada, Northern Telecom, Ontario Ministry of Transportation, Rotoflex International, SPAR Aerospace, Syncrude Canada, Taran Furs, TASC (The Analytical Sciences Corporation,) Thomson CSF, Toronto Sick Children's Hospital, Virtek Vision Corporation (ICR 1995)

Virtek Vision Corp. is a spinoff firm established in 1986. It maintains a strategic relationship with the PAMI lab to gain access to specialized personnel as well as the latest research and technical developments in the lab. The firm develops and supplies machine vision, 3-D laser projection technology and machine intelligence systems to the leather goods, aerospace and construction industries (ITRC 1996; TTLO 1994). In 1994 Virtek incorporated a US subsidiary with its headquarters in Boston to spearhead international sales. Over 90 percent of its products are exported with the US as the principal market. Specialized products, such as the Virtek Laser Edge ply alignment system for the construction of composite materials are used by customers including Boeing, Lockheed, British Aerospace and Short Brothers (Virtek 1997).

The PAMI lab is one of several labs where research projects have been funded by national research organizations as well as industry. The results of this university-based research have also given rise to a spinoff firm which has grown from a local base to supply a growing international market. Similar bottom-up or entrepreneurial initiatives started most of the science and technology firms operating in Waterloo in the 1990s (Whitney & Co. 1995). The focus on small firms risks overlooking the larger external firms which have chosen to locate in the CTT. Large American firms (AT&T, Hewlett-Packard, NCR, Raytheon, and so on) are also present in the CTT, however, these subsidiaries typically have weaker links with local universities than the smaller local firms and most emphasis for future growth is placed on the locally created firms. The experience of the CTT and MFP needs to be compared to determine whether or not the case studies adhere to the top-down and bottom-up models presented earlier.

12. DISCUSSION

The CTT and MFP Australia were established in the same year, but their principal sponsors and techniques of promoting development differed (Table 18.3). The narrow objectives of the CTT were achieved as the three levels of government (local, provincial and federal) all promoted the region using the single name instead of the list of individual city names. However, local awareness of the new name remained limited and calls were made for the simple committee structure to be replaced with a more substantial organization. In contrast, the ambitious objectives of the MFP to create a new model of sustainable urban development proved difficult to achieve in the short term and the new development corporation formed to lead MFP activities found itself facing financial uncertainty when the Australian government announced that it would not extend funding beyond June 1996 (MFP 1997b). Overall, the limitations and overlaps of the top-down and bottom-up models need to be reconsidered in light of the experience of these two regions.

MFP Australia represents a top-down approach to high-tech development and was initially criticized heavily. The perception that the MFP was a large externally-driven project about to transform an unsuspecting part of Australia eased as the economic boom of the 1980s was followed by the recession of the early 1990s and no foreign investment materialized. The recession also increased interest in potential job-creating projects. The change in South Australian state government was potentially damaging, but the opposition which had been very critical of the MFP became supportive of the project when they gained power. The state government increased its role as the principal source of funds for MFP Development Corporation operations. Additional project and capital funding was drawn from the federal government (Building Better Cities Program), local government (infrastructure) and industry (utilities and information technology infrastructure) (MFP 1997b).

Local input to the planning process was achieved through the elitist model of involving the most senior representative from the peak agency in each sector (Conservation Council of South Australia and South Australian Council of Social Services), initially as consultants, and then as members of the Community Advisory Council. The approach involved local consultation to identify the aspects of predetermined proposals which raised local opposition. The Social Issues Study and the Community Consultation Panel both identified sensitive social issues, but both failed to gain local approval of the approach which had been considered secretive and elitist. The establishment of a Community Advisory Council was to provide a new means of local involvement with representatives from five named organizations (Conservation Council of South Australia, South Australia

Council of Social Services, Local Government Association of South Australia, United Trades and Labour Council of South Australia and the Chamber of Commerce and Industry of South Australia Inc.) and three others with expertise in environmental health, education and local community interests (MFP Development Act 1992, section 26). However, by 1995 there was optimism that the new structures would provide greater community involvement than in the past (Deslandes 1995).

Table 18.3 Summary of MFP and CTT attributes

	MFP	CTT
Year established	1987	1987
Initial sponsors	Australian/Japanese governments	City councils
Subsequent sponsors	South Australian government	City councils and firms
Institutional structure	New development corporation, advisory committees	Committee of existing officials
Principal objective	Create model of high tech and sustainable urban development	Promote single image of a high tech region
Principal means to promote information technology industry	Attract external firms	Promote networks and local spinoff firms
Examples of external	Motorolla Australis Media EDS (Electronic Data Systems)	AT&T NCR Hewlett-Packard
Examples of university spinoff firms	Integrated Silicon Design Bresatec Ltd. Repromed	Virtek Watcom Open Text

The top-down approach to planning was matched by the promotion of information technology industries through the attraction of external firms to the region. Success in attracting Motorolla, Australis Media and EDS was noted earlier. However, the bottom-up process of spinoff firms being created by researchers at local universities was also found, at the University of Adelaide in particular. This implies that bottom-up processes are also underway in Adelaide and that the opportunity exists to link the two processes to enhance the ability of the MFP to meet its objectives. Indeed, the emphasis of MFP activities has shifted over time as the initial emphasis on external attraction has been balanced by more recognition of the importance of local partners. The disbanding of the International Advisory Board when the federal government cut its funds in 1996 symbolizes this shift. However, the selection of Silicon Valley as a model and the adoption of strategies from Collaborative Economics, a subsidiary of the Stanford Research Institute, which advocates the formation of clusters of related firms and the promotion of their interaction, requires greater emphasis on local firms and research capacity (MFP Australia 1996). International partnerships continued to be promoted, such as the decision in 1995 to become a member of Joint Venture: Silicon Valley, but the importance of local clusters or groups was also recognized as being of strategic importance.

While the MFP changed to increase local input in the development process, the examination of the CTT as a rapidly growing region based on entrepreneurship and networking in the information technology industry overlooked many external factors. Investment that supported the reported high rates of economic growth included major external firms such as Toyota which opened a car production facility in Cambridge in the late 1980s and then expanded it in the mid 1990s. Even in the information technology industry, the successful networking among the computer firms was not restricted to local participants and local initiatives. The involvement of some of the leading computer firms in the world was important to stimulate the achievements in research that led to the formation of spinoff firms which export 80–90 percent of their products. Rather than considering the top-down and bottom-up models as mutually exclusive, a closer examination identifies elements of both models in operation in both case studies. A hybrid model is thus proposed as a better means to represent local–global partnerships to successfully promote high-tech development (Figure 18.3).

The global–local model draws strengths from both the top-down and bottom-up models and allows for flexible application in particular regions. The implicit argument is that neither external nor internal resources alone are sufficient to achieve high-tech development. MFP Australia could not succeed as a high-tech enclave based on the limited external funding offered by the federal government. Instead, it needed to make links with local research parks (merge with Technology Park and Science Park), universities (adjacent location to University of South Australia, representation on boards and committees) and community groups (representation on committees).

Ironically, the inclusion of local partners became the only way for the MFP to survive as the federal government decided in 1996 to withdraw its funding. Conversely, the success of the computer industry network in the CTT is based on their inclusion of external partners. Local actors took the lead role in starting research projects that attracted external funding from both the public and private sectors, but the external inputs were of critical importance to undertake the research. New firms were started as inventions were patented and then commercialized in spinoff firms. Networks were formed among university researchers and industry partners. Local production capacity grew, firms exported most of their output as production was aimed for international markets, employment rose from an average of 5 employees per firm at start-up to 51 employees per firm in 1995 and future growth is expected (Whitney & Co. 1995). The overall result was increased employment and growth in the regional economy based on the combination of local and external resources.

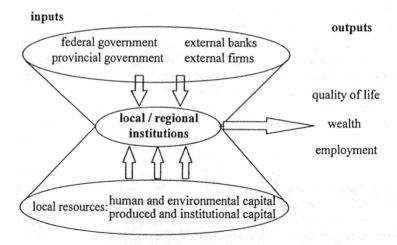

Figure 18.3 Local–global partnership model

13. CONCLUSION

MFP Australia and the CTT share the objective to promote high-tech development, but have very different structures and approaches. The MFP represents a top-down approach where national and international proponents advocated the creation of this high-tech centre. In contrast, the CTT represents a bottom-up approach where four small cities decided to recognize their complementary strengths and to cooperate in development efforts that would be mutually beneficial. Popular evaluations of these initiatives in the mid 1990s concluded that the CTT was a success while the MFP was a failure. However, the initial conclusion that a bottom-up approach is required to succeed overlooks many details. A review of some of the most successful elements of the CTT indicates that it is not local capacity in isolation that has created growth and employment. Instead, it is the creation of networks that link local groups to national and international interests that have resulted in the greatest success. Indeed, when these networks are examined in detail, their origins are found to precede the formation of the CTT. In this context, the CTT simply represents another manifestation of cooperation and collaboration among local institutions rather than the cause of such cooperation.

External links are an important component of the development process in the CTT. They are not limited to partnerships on individual research projects, but extend to the investment in manufacturing and development facilities, such as those owned by AT&T, NCR, Hewlett-Packard and Raytheon. Conversely, the MFP emphasis on the attraction of external firms overlooks the local networks formed by research groups at the three local universities and their collaboration with industry in several Cooperative Research Centres. Local firms were also required to form the clusters to attract related firms in the development strategies advocated by Collaborative Economics for MFP implementation. The competing top-down and bottom-up models are thus replaced with a model of local–global partnership as the preferred model for high tech development.

Given this local–global partnership model, initiatives to create stronger links between the MFP and local research groups and firms are considered essential for success to be sustained. The incorporation of other research park initiatives (Technology Park and Science Park) and strengthened links with local universities are steps in this direction. Indeed, the integration of education, high tech employment and residential areas with reduced environmental impacts has become the dominant feature of the MFP and its first stage of urban development at Mawson Lakes in Adelaide. The experiences of the MFP and CTT thus offer lessons for other regions attempting to promote high-tech development. International linkages are important to achieve innovations of international importance and to gain shares of export markets. However, local capacity also needs to be built through networks that link local private, public, education and research organizations.

ACKNOWLEDGMENTS

The author would like to thank the many individuals who assisted with this research by participating in interviews or providing information. The Social Sciences and Humanities Research Council of Canada provided valuable financial assistance. The University of Adelaide and the University of Waterloo provided valuable institutional support. The comments and suggestions of the referee and editors improved the quality of the chapter. Any errors or omissions remain the responsibility of the author.

REFERENCES

Albrechts, L., Moulaert, F., Roberts, P. and E. Swyngedouw (1989), 'New Perspectives for Regional Policy and Development in the 1990s', in Albrechts, L., Moulaert, F., Roberts, P. and E. Swyngedouw (eds), *Regional Policy at the Crossroads: European Perspectives*, London: Jessica Kingsley, pp. 1–9.

AUTM (Association of University Technology Managers) (annual) Summary of annual survey results, unpublished report to respondents.

Aydalot, P. and D. Keeble, (1988), *High Technology Industry and innovative environments,* London: Routledge.

Bathelt, H. and A. Hecht (1990), 'Key technology industries in the Waterloo region: Canada's technology triangle', *The Canadian Geographer* **34** (3), pp. 225–234.

Beck, N. (1992), *Shifting Gears: Thriving in the New Economy*, Toronto: Harper Collins Publishers Ltd.

Bluestone, B. and B. Harrison (1982), *The Deindustrialization of America,* New York: Basic Books.

Born, P. (1996), 'Community opportunities development agency overview', unpublished seminar presentation, Executive Director, CODA: Cambridge.

Britton, J. (1987), 'High Technology Industry in Canada: Locational and Policy Issues of the Technology Gap', in Breheny, M. and R. McQuaid (eds), *The Development of High Technology Industries: An International Survey,* London: Croom Helm.

Britton, J. (1996), 'High tech Canada', in Britton, J. (ed.), *Canada and the Global Economy: The Geography of Structural and Technological Change*, Montreal and Kingston: McGill-Queen's University Press, pp. 255–72.

Bryant, C. and R. Preston (1987), *A Framework for Local Initiatives in Economic Development*. Economic Development Bulletin No. 1, Economic Development Program, Waterloo: University of Waterloo.

Castells, M. and P. Hall (1994), *Technopoles of the World: The making of 21st Century Industrial Complexes,* London: Routledge.

CNIDR (Centre for Networked Information Discovery and Retrieval) (1996), US Patent and Trademark Office data. http://patents.cnidr.org/access.access.html

Coffey, W.J. and M. Polese (1984), 'The concept of local development: a stage model of endogenous regional growth', *Papers of the Regional Science Association* **55** pp. 1–12.

Coffey, W.J. and M. Polese (1985), 'Local development: conceptual bases and policy implications, *Regional Studies* **19**, pp. 85–93.

Commonwealth of Australia and State of South Australia (1992), *Agreement on MFP Australia*, Canberra and Adelaide. June.

Crane, D. (1992), 'Communities taking charge of their economic futures', *Toronto Star,* 2 April

CTN (Computer Technology Network) (1996), 'Finding the common ground in Canada's Technology Network', CTN Home Page http://www.ctn.org March.

CTT (Canada'sTechnology Triangle) (1994), *Canada's Technology Triangle*, brochure.

Denomme, M. (1996), 'Networking within the Kitchener–Waterloo Software Development Agglomeration: implications for local and regional economic development', BES senior honours essay, Department of Geography, University of Waterloo: Waterloo, Ont. unpublished.

Deslandes, M. (1995), 'Chair, Community Advisory Council, interview', 3 February.

Dicken, P. (1992), *Global Shift,* 2nd edn, London: Harper and Row.

ECC (Economic Council of Canada) (1990), *From the Bottom Up. The Community Economic Development Approach*, Ottawa: Minister of Supply and Services.

Filion, P. and T. Rutherford (1996), 'Manufacturing Miracles? The Restructuring of Waterloo Region's Manufacturing', in Filion, P., Bunting, T. and K. Curtis (eds), *The Dynamics of the Dispersed City: Geographic and Planning Perspectives on Waterloo Region,* Publication Series No. 47. Department of Geography, Waterloo: University of Waterloo, pp. 239–71.

Glasmeier, A. (1987), 'Factors governing the development of high tech industry agglomerations: a tale of three cities', *Regional Studies* **22** (4), pp. 287–301.

Harwood, J. (1990a), 'Multifunction secrecy', *Australian Society* **9** (11), pp. 4–5.

Harwood, J. (1990b), 'The six billion dollar plan: Eco-Speak and multi-function politics', *Adelaide Review* **79**, pp. 6–7, August.

Harwood, J. (1990c), 'Selling the Polis: the challenge of the century', *Adelaide Review* **80**, pp. 3–5, September.

Harwood, J. (1990d), 'A very peculiar Polis', *Adelaide Review* **81**, pp. 8–9, October.

Harwood, J. (1990e), 'Rocky Polis Show', *Adelaide Review* **82**, pp. 6–7, November.

Harwood, J. (1990f), 'When prophecy fails', *Adelaide Review* **83**, pp. 6–7, December.

ICR (Institute for Computer Research, University of Waterloo) (1995), http://www.icr.uwaterloo.ca/ICR/brochure/brochure.html pages dated 23 June.

ITRC (Information Technology Research Centre) (1996), http://www.itrc.on.ca/SuccessStories/virtek.html

Jung, H-J. (1994), 'An evaluation of the local production network system in the context of the flexible production paradigm: a case of small and medium-sized enterprises in Kitchener–Waterloo', PhD dissertation, School of Urban and Regional Planing, Waterloo: University of Waterloo, Ont. unpublished.

Knafelc, P. (1995), 'Community benchmarks of proprietorship: a proxy for entrepreneurship and indicative measure of economic development', MAES major research paper, Local Economic Development Program, Waterloo: University of Waterloo, unpublished.

Lindsay, R. and W. Lindsay (1994), 'Canada's technology triangle: cooperation nets a positive response', Supplement to *Trade and Commerce Magazine.*

Maclean's (1994), 'The Fourth Annual Ranking: Universities 1994 special issue', *Maclean's,* 14 November.

Maillat, D. and B. Lecoq (1992), 'New technologies and the transformation of regional structures in Europe: the role of the milieu', *Entrepreneurship and Regional Development* **4**, pp. 1–20.

Malecki, E. (1991), *Technology and Economic Development: the dynamics of local, regional and national change,* New York: Longman Scientific and Technical.

Marjoribanks, K. (1990), 'Your link to a better future', in *University of Adelaide Annual Report,* Adelaide: University of Adelaide, pp. 1–2.

Markusen, A., Hall, P. and A. Glasmier (1986), *High Tech America,* Boston: Allen & Unwin.

Massey, D., Quintas, P. and D. Weil (1992), *High Tech Fantasies: Science Parks in Society, Science and Space,* London: Routledge.

MFP Australia (1994a), *Annual Review 1993/94: The Face of our Future*, Adelaide: MFP Australia.

MFP Australia (1994b), MFP Australia's Technology Park, List of tenants, Adelaide, unpublished. November.

MFP Australia (1995), *Annual Review 1994/95*, Adelaide: MFP Australia.

MFP Australia (1996), *Annual Review 1995/96*, MFP Australia: Adelaide, http://www.mfp.com.au/AnRep96.htm

MFP (1996), MFP Smart City Go-Ahead, Media Release. http://www.mfp.com.au/mfpsmart.htm 28 October.

MFP (1997a), Operational structure of the MFPDC, http://www.mfp.com.au/whatmfpd.htm

MFP (1997b), Information Update: February, http://www.mfp.com.au/Febinfo.htm

MFP (1997c), The IT&T Advantage Telstra will bring to Mawson Lakes. Media Release, http://www.mfp.com.au/telstram.htm 18 February.

MFPACCP (MFP Adelaide Community Consultation Panel) (1991a), *Report.* Volume 1, *Conclusions and Recommendations*, Canberra: Australian Government Publishing Service, August.

MFPACCP (MFP Adelaide Community Consultation Panel). (1991b), *Report.* Volume 2, *Submissions*, Canberra: Australian Government Publishing Service, August.

MITI (Japan, Ministry of International Trade and Industry) (1987), 'A Multi-Function Polis Scheme for the 21st Century: Basic Concept', reprinted in *A Tale of New Cities: Japan's plans for Australia*, undated.

OMMA (Ontario Ministry of Municipal Affairs) (1992), *International Forum on Community Economic Development Proceedings*, February 12–14, OMMA, Toronto: Intergovernmental Committee on Urban and Regional Research.

Partridge, M. (1993), 'High-tech employment and state economic development policies', *The Review of Regional Studies*, pp. 287–305.

Preer, R. (1992), *The Emergence of Technopolis: Knowledge Intensive Technologies and Regional Development,* New York: Praeger.

Rutherford, T. (1995), 'Control the ones you can: production, restructuring, selection and training in Kitchener region manufacturing, 1987–92', *The Canadian Geographer* **39** (1), pp. 30–46.

SAEDA (South Australia Economic Development Authority) (1994), *Annual Report 1993/94*, Adelaide: SAEDA.

SAOPUD (South Australia, Office of Planning and Urban Development, Assessments Branch) (1992), *Gilman/Dry Creek Urban Development Proposal Assessment Report*, Adelaide: SAOPUD.

Savoie, D. (1992), *Regional Economic Development: Canada's Search for Solutions* 2nd edn, Toronto: University of Toronto Press.

Science Council of Canada (1990), *Firing up the Technology Engine: Strategies for Community Economic Development,* Ottowa: Science Council of Canada.

Scott, A. (1992), 'The collective order of flexible production agglomerations: lessons for local economic development policy and strategic choice', *Economic Geography* **68** (3), pp. 219–33.

Smilor, R., Kozmetsky, G. and D. Gibson (1988), *Creating the Technopolis: Linking Technology Commercialization and Economic Development.* Cambridge: Ballinger.

Smith, J. (1990), *Australia- Going, Going, Gone? A Critique of the Multifunction Polis Project*, Bedford Park, South Australia: The Flinders Press.

Smith, J. (1991), *The High Tech Fix: Sustainable Ecology or Technocratic Megaprojects for the 21st Century?*, Aldershot, Hants, UK: Avebury.

Smith, J. (1992), *The Beginning of the End? Technology, The Environment and MFP-Australia*, Canberra: Kalgoorlie Press.

Smith, L. (1993), *Dynamic Profile of the Economy of Waterloo Region*, Kitchener: Regional Municipality of Waterloo.

Smith, L. (1995), *Dynamic Profile of the Economy of Waterloo Region*, Kitchener: Regional Municipality of Waterloo.

South Australia Parliament (1992), *MFP Development Act 1992*, No. 24 of 1992, Adelaide.

Statistics Canada (1995), *Labour Force Annual Averages 1989–94,* Ottawa: Government of Canada, Catalogue 71–529.

Stöhr, W. (1981), 'Development from Below: the Bottom-up and Periphery-inward Development Paradigm', in Stöhr, W. and D. Taylor (eds), *Development from Above or Below?*, Toronto: John Wiley and Sons, pp. 39–72.

Stöhr, W. and D. Taylor (eds) (1981), *Development from Above or Below?*, Toronto: John Wiley and Sons.

Storper, M. and Scott, A. (1989), 'The Geographical Foundations and Social Regulation of Flexible Production Complexes', in Wolch, J. and M. Dear (eds),

The Power of Geography: how territory shapes social life, Boston: Unwin Hyman, pp. 21–40.

TTLO (Technology Transfer and Licensing Office) (1994), *Spin-off Company Profiles*, Waterloo: Office of Research, University of Waterloo.

Virtek (1997), *About Virtek*. http://www.virtek.ca/xprofabt.htm.

Whitney & Co. (1995), *City of Waterloo Strategic Development Plan: Future Business Parks and Employment Areas*, Waterloo: City of Waterloo.

Wright, J. (1991), 'Technological development in Mississauga and Canada's technology triangle: a calibrated application of the product life cycle', Masters thesis, Department of Geography, Waterloo: Wilfrid Laurier University, unpublished

University of Adelaide (1994), *University of Adelaide Annual Report*, Adelaide: University of Adelaide.

Zeidenberg, J. (1995), 'Lost in the technology triangle', *This Magazine*, January.

19. An Empirical Study of a Planning Process to Form an Effective Vision for a Region

Yoshinobu Kumata, Tatsuro Sakano and Jisheng Liu

1. VISION AS AN ENTITY IN GLOBAL RESTRUCTURING

An image of a place, an identity of a city, and a vision of a region are relatively new entries into our vocabulary which are gaining importance in city and regional planning. Since the 'I Love New York Campaign', selling an image of a place is considered one of the important tools for a city and regional transformation. Old industrial cities in the US and Europe which have lost their economic bases try to sell their new image as leading post industrial cities for inviting investments from the world.

Due to globalization and informatization, the city system has been facing a fundamental change. Diversification of international networks and strengthening of ties among cities across the boundaries of nation-states create new opportunities. The principal role in regional development is now shifting from state government to local government and non-governmental organizations (NGOs). Local governance became a key word in various developmental projects in the UN and in the international association of municipalities. But when we look closely at the reality of local governance, the meaning of locality is found to be quite obscure. The political boundaries do not correspond to the economic activities. Newly emerging NGOs are changing the traditional role and structure of communities.

It is becoming harder for local residents to control their own destinies against the forces of global restructuring. Under this situation, new planning tools are expected to be invented so that they bring a new system of governance and increase the self-actualization capability of a region. A vision is conceived as one of such tools. However, it is reported that place marketing and city identity campaigns do not necessarily change the reality of regions (Paddison 1993). If reality does not change, the rosy dreams expressed in visions fade away. It is necessary to find the nature of effective visions and the process which produces them.

2.   FROM A MECHANISTIC MODEL OF PLANNING TO A LINGUISTIC MODEL

A plan is a set of information which controls actions to achieve a certain goal. The style of planning can be categorized by the way of producing the information and of controlling actions. With this perspective, the definition and characteristics of a vision as an entity of regional planning will be delineated in a comparative way with the existing planning models.

In a stable environment, a common goal is relatively easy to set and collaboration is effectively achieved through preset routines of action programmes. The model of organizing complex activities is called mechanistic since the goal is automatically achieved once the routines are set.

The origin of this model can be traced back to 'Scientific Management' proposed by Frederic Taylor (Taylor 1947). The principle of 'Scientific Management' had been very influential for all sectors in industry as well as government for the last half century (Salko and Sakano 1984). However, the theoretical validity of the model was not well understood until Harvard Simon justified the model from the point of efficiency in information processing (March and Simon 1958). Ironically, it was the time when the mechanistic model was beginning to lose its effectiveness in an acceleratingly changing environment. In this situation, a more flexible mechanism was required. Then alternative models were proposed by many researchers of management science and of planning. Long-range planning (Steiner 1969) and strategic planning (Anthony 1965; Lorange and Vancil 1977; Ansoff 1979), for example, are among such genres. Although there were a variety of models, they were essentially modelled upon cybernetics. Russell Ackoff (1981) delineates the essence in his model of planning. Cybernetic models of planning possess higher capabilities of adaptation and learning than mechanistic ones since information is incessantly being produced by monitoring environment and by evaluating actions, thus enabling recourse actions and the achievement of a certain goal in a changing environment. With limited capability to forecast the future, an optimum plan at one time is no longer optimum at another time in the future. The only promising way is not to look for an optimum plan but to incorporate a process of cybernetic control into planning.

Although the cybernetic model possesses higher flexibility, the limit of the model is clear from two respects. This model cannot solve the problem of value conflicts because it assumes only one ultimate goal toward which other sub goals are coordinated. In a pluralistic society, however, it is impossible to set a meta-goal in theory and practice. To put it another way, the cybernetic model assumes the hierarchical structure of societal organization. Hierarchically organized systems, as Galbraith (1973) put it, have less capacity for information processing if compared with network type organizations, especially in a densely connected environment. Emery and Trist (1965) clearly recognized that densely connected agents/actors create a totally different environment from the one sparsely connected. Kaufman and Holland found that densely connected parts eventually show self-organizing properties without any single controlling part in some critical conditions in their studies on the origin of life and neural network (Waldrop 1994). However, self-organizing principles are not well understood, at least at a societal level. Fundamental conditions of flexibility to adapt to this newly emerging environment are diversity and initiatives of various actors in a region. Yet, the nature of the mechanism about how to integrate actions without suffocating initiatives is not understood well. Transparency of the process and delegation of power may be the necessary conditions, but they are not sufficient.

In this study we propose language as a promising model of this type of self-organization. Language has several interesting characteristics. A symbol in a language contains various meanings. Therefore, interpretations often conflict among different interpreters. Despite this conflict, communication is possible because they share the procedure to decode the meaning according to the context. If a plan is shared by various actors in the same sense as language, every actor can interpret appropriate meanings according to the unique situations he/she faces, thus maintaining social integrity.

A blueprint or preset routine of action usually designates only one meaning, thus narrowing the margin of interpretation and becoming obsolete in changing contexts. A vision of a region may function differently. It provides a common image of the future, upon which actors can find a meaning of the collaborative planned activities and tailor strategies for their future actions. Vision formulation is expected to play an important role in adapting to the turbulent environment. However, the importance of sharing a positive image of the future by many influential actors has not been given proper consideration in the design planning process. Despite its importance, there are very few empirical studies on vision formation except our own (Liu and Kumata 1993). The study of vision formation in actual planning process will bring deeper understanding of the new model of planning.

Most Japanese local governments recognize the vital significance of vision formulation as the base and core of their plans, but few have organized appropriate planning processes to form an effective vision shared by leading actors in their regions. Through questionnaires answered by many local governments, the chapter proposes a promising new planning process to amalgamate various actors' images of the future of the region, and shows an empirical evidence that the process is considered accepted by the local governments.

3. PARADIGM SHIFT OF PLANNING IN JAPAN

Table 19.1 illustrates the shifting scope and definitions in planning paradigms that have been prevalent in Japan. The time frames, across the rows, are decadal with A = 1950–1960; B = 1960–1970; C = 1970–1980; D = 1980–1990; E = 1990 onwards. The criteria used to plot the shifting paradigms including the model of citizen or image of citizen, the degree and quality of participation of citizens in planning, the perceived model of the planner's role or position, the strategic aim of planning, the planning orientation in terms of the direction that the process took, the typology and the name of the actual plan produced, and major concerns that were addressed by these plans.

The table seems complicated at first glance but there is a continuing trend behind it. The demands of citizens have been constantly diversified over a period of 50 years. When basic human needs are not satisfied at the take off period of economic development, priority about the allocation of public resources is clear and the consensus is easily attained. But once basic human needs are satisfied, higher order demands are developed and diversified. Therefore, standardized services produced by mass production processes do not fit into the newly emerging situation. Citizens are no longer consumers of public services, but are clients to be served through the process of consultation. Now, we are going into the stage where self-realization is the prime concern of citizens. At this stage, the factor which determines the level of satisfaction is not the quality of service produced by others but the experience of participaton in the process of planning.

Self-realization cannot be attained by consuming goods and services. It can only be achieved through the experience of participate in the process of planning. In effect, as demands become diversified, the process of planning becomes flexible, the role of citizens turns from passive to active, planners become facilitators, and visions gain importance as effective forms of plans.

Table 19.1   Paradigm shifts of planning in Japan

Criteria	A 1950–1960	B 1960–1970	C 1970–1980	D 1980–1990	E 1990–
Model of citizen	Worker to be accommodated	Consumer to be supplied	Client to be served	Guest to be satisfied	Actor to perform
Meaning of participation	'Begging' for living arrangements	Suggestions for improving living conditions	Asking for necessary public services	Demanding satisfactory environment	Ordering what and how to be provided and served
Model of planner	Engineer	Manager	Designer	Consultant	Producer
Strategic aim of planning	Providing basic amenity	Establishing economic security	Acquiring club membership	Winning respect for success	Offering self realization
Planning orientation	Less cost	More income	Better quality	Higher satisfaction	Richer fulfilment
Typology of plan	Physical plan	Economic plan	Multi-object plan	Multi-life style plan	Live-show drama plan
Name of plan	Master plan	Development plan	Integrated development plan	Vision + original plan	Participation process
Major concern in planning	Jobs, housing, food, health	Eduction, public facilities, transportation, quantity of goods	Welfare services, higher education, living infrastructure	Group-wise public services, information, environment, culture	Global contribution, restructuring industries, decentralizing power

4. DEVELOPMENT OF MUNICIPAL PLANNING SYSTEM IN JAPAN

Looking back at the development of Japanese planning systems since the Second World War, there are four transitional stages. Before the Local Government Act of 1969 was passed, local governments at municipal level were not required to make a comprehensive plan. In 1950 the National Development Act was passed. In the Act, the comprehensive developmental plans at four regional levels were legalized; at national level, prefectural level, regional level, and a special regional zone level. During this period, planning was a job for the national and the prefectural governments. The role of municipal governments was mainly to execute the standard procedures set by the national government. The model of planning was mechanistic, but when the period of economic growth in the 1960s came to an end, the necessity to bring the decisions nearer to people was gradually recognized. Developmental plans at regional and prefectural levels were no longer sufficient to meet the variety of needs at the local level. This was the context when the Local Government Act of 1969 was passed and it had been required for the municipal governments to make a comprehensive plan.

In 1969, the Ministry of Home Affairs gave notification of the scheme of the comprehensive plan, based on which all the municipal governments make almost identical structures of comprehensive plans; the three tier system. The first tier corresponds to the most abstract level of the plan, describing values, guidelines and ultimate aims. The second tier describes specific goals and the policy structure. The third tier is the most concrete level of the plan, which contains action programmes. Actually, only 10 percent of the municipal governments had already made their own comprehensive plans at the beginning and it took ten years for 90 percent of the municipal governments to have finished making their plans of the first tier. The second and the third tiers were delayed on average for another ten years. The main reason for this delay was the lack of organizational and personnel capability of planning. Therefore, during the 1970s, the second stage, consulting resources were introduced from outside to formulate the plans. Outside planners were professionals with special knowledge and techniques in planning. The main task was goal-setting based on the long-range forecasts usually for the next 10 to 15 years. But they were not familiar with the local situation with which they were supposed to be involved. Consequently, their plans were often criticized for lack of feasibility.

But through the experience of the second ten years, municipal governments were acquiring planning capability. Most of them set up planning departments during this stage. Based on this capability, they were able to make plans themselves and tried to overcome the lack of feasibility. They tried to integrate budgetary process and to coordinate the actions of various departments. In addition, the system of planning control was eagerly introduced. In 1990, almost 100 percent had made the second and the third tiers of the plans. These two plans were systematically reviewed and revised on average every three and five years respectively. In effect, through the third stage, planning became one of the administrative routines or everyday activities. Obviously, the cybernetic model had been influential in improving the system of planning during this stage.

While the shift in the balance from goals and visions to concrete actions leads to higher feasibility, plans are losing attractiveness to the people. Searching for new meanings and possibilities for the future through reflection on values and reformulating visions cannot be expected from the routine kind of planning activity firmly established in the third stage. There should be some radical departure from the existing practice, in particular in the coming fourth stage, where cities and regions face a fundamental change due to globalization and informatization as mentioned earlier. Reconsidering vision formulation is one such step.

5. THE EXTENT OF VISION'S DIFFUSION AND THE DEGREE OF UNDERSTANDING

Within the three tier system of planning, a vision is in practice defined in the first tier. The term 'vision' is commonly used by planning officials. However, the formal definition is not found in the documents issued by the ministry. Furthermore, it cannot be found even in the academic literature. The definition of 'vision' and its role in planning are not made clear in theory and practice. The planner's perception of the definition and its role affects the effectiveness of planning. On the contrary, the lack of a formal definition may confuse the meaning of the term.

Therefore, first, we conducted a survey in 1994 by questionnaires to 470 planning officials in 235 local governments in Japan.[1] The survey revealed that about 90 percent of the official planners in local governments share the same ideas about 'vision' and that they recognize its importance in planning. The points most planners agree on are summarized below.

1. 'Vision' is a desirable future image of a region, which is worked out by the collaborative efforts by a local government and residents.
2. 'Vision' is a framework which gives a direction for all the actors in a region and which coordinates various actions of not only intra-governmental activities but also private–public relationships.

3.   'Vision' is a medium through which a value system is restructured, a grand strategy is formulated, and fundamental rules of a new city game are shared by the actors in a region.

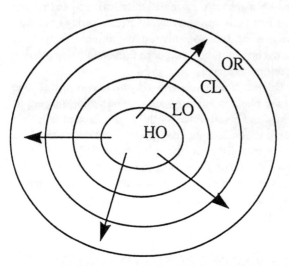

HO: High-ranked officials   Rate of diffusion: 92 percent
LO: Low-ranked officials   Rate of diffusion: 68 percent
CL: Community leaders   Rate of diffusion: 45 percent
OR: Ordinary residents   Rate of diffusion: 26 percent

Figure 19.1 Diffusion of 'vision'

In effect, it is not explicitly recognized but tacitly understood that vision is not a type of plan which directly controls the behaviour of local actors, but a framework which enfolds contextual information, within which each actor can find the meaning of one's behaviour. Despite the lack of formal definition, there exists in practice a consensus among at least official planners. However, the survey also showed that 90 percent of the local governments think their visions are not shared by the residents and that about 60 percent of them think the existing planning processes are limited in improving the situation. Based on these results, we proceeded with the second survey[2] to obtain more detailed information about the extent of vision's diffusion and the degree of understanding by the residents in the cities.

The data obtained are the subjective judgments of the official planners. They may not reflect reality. However, the survey shows several interesting points.

In almost all the local governments, their future visions are summarized and symbolized in a few key words or catchphrases. Table 19.2 shows the percentage of the residents who recognize that such phrases represent the visions. It is revealed that there is a big diffusion gap between the government officials and the residents. The percentage of the residents is lower than that of the officials. To see in more detail, 92 percent of the high-ranked officials is the highest, following 69 percent of the low-ranked officials, 45 percent of the community leaders and 26 percent of the ordinary residents respectively. These data indicate the diffusion of vision proceeds in the same order; first from the high-ranked officials to the low-ranked officials, and through the community leaders to the ordinary residents. This process is depicted in Figure 19.1. When the distance from the centre of diffusion is longer, the message becomes weaker, thus decreasing the rate of diffusion.

Table 19.2 Rate of diffusion among various local actors

Actor*	Rate of diffusion										
	−10%	20%	30%	40%	50%	60%	70%	80%	90%	100%	Ave.
OR	38.24	15.67	20.06	6.90	11.60	3.45	2.19	1.25	0.63	0.00	26%
CL	13.66	12.11	17.39	5.59	19.88	7.45	8.70	7.14	4.04	4.04	45%
LO	2.37	3.56	6.82	4.45	13.06	4.75	16.62	21.96	11.57	14.84	68%
HO	0.59	0.59	0.30	0.30	5.03	1.48	3.85	7.69	13.31	66.86	92%

*OR = Ordinary residents
CL = Community leaders
LO = Low-ranked officials
HO = High-ranked officials

To acknowledge key phrases as the representation of 'vision' is one thing and to understand the vision is another. The acknowledgment is a very first step to a deeper understanding. In this study, five different aspects of understanding are surveyed; (1) understanding of a vision's influence on daily life and community, (2) understanding of a vision's desirability to a community, (3) understanding of government actions to achieve the goal, (4) understanding of the role of residents in the vision, and (5) understanding at the level that a resident or an official can explain to other residents or officials. Tables 19.3 and 19.4 show the percentage of the average residents and the officials who understand 'vision' in the five aspects.

In each aspect, the level of residents' understanding is lower than the average of the government officials. Especially, the percentage of the residents who can explain 'vision' to other residents is very low. In addition to that, the patterns of understanding differ strikingly between the residents and the officials. While for the officials, the understanding of government actions to achieve the goal is highest at 61 percent, the highest understanding for the residents is that of the visions' desirability at 35 percent. The understanding of visions' influence on daily life and community is the second highest, 41 percent and 25 percent respectively, for both of them. These data show the tendency that the officials understand 'vision' in connection with their daily jobs while the intuitive value judgment comes first in the case of residents' understanding. Because the officials make a vision without paying much attention to the residents, it is quite difficult for residents to interpret it into their everyday language.

Table 19.3 Degree of understanding for the average government officials

A Understanding of visions' influence	41.0%
B Understanding of visions' desirability	38.4%
C Understanding of government actions	61.0%
D Understanding of residents' role	10.0%
E Can explain to other residents of officials	22.6%

Table 19.4 Degree of understanding for the average resident

A Understanding of visions' influence	24.9%
B Understanding of visions' desirability	34.5%
C Understanding of government actions	16.1%
D Understanding of residents' role	5.3%
E Can explain to other residents of officials	2.0%

The contrast between the highest rate of the officials' understanding about the necessary government actions and the very low rate of the residents' understanding about their own roles does imply that the languages used in the worlds of officials and that in the community of the residents are different and that vision is mostly written in an official's language. The only possible way for the residents to understand vision is through their intuitive value judgement. As the previous survey revealed, most official planners expect vision to work as a framework which gives a direction for all the actors in a region and which coordinates various actions. But without proper understanding, it is difficult for the residents to translate the values expressed in the vision into roles and actions. The existing vision does not function as expected because the language of officials is not understandable to other actors in a region, specifically to the ordinary residents. If this is the case, sharing a language is one of the important foundations for mutual understanding.

6. DESIRABLE PLANNING PROCESS AND CITIZEN PARTICIPATION

Under the existing institutional setting of the Japanese political decision-making system, local governments are the prime actors in making and monitoring comprehensive plans. Almost all the governments have their own planning departments. According to our survey, in 96 percent of the governments, the planning departments take charge of this job. In addition to the formal responsibility, evidence shows that the planning departments take strong leadership in formulating plans. For example, 59 percent of the catch-phrases which symbolize 'vision' are devised by them. This figure can be understood as the indicator of their strong influence if compared with the fact that the mayors' contributions in this regard is only 17 percent (see Table 19.5).

Table 19.5 Initiatives to conceive of the key phrases of vision

Planning team	59.4%
Mayor/Governor	17.0%
Community leader	0.3%
Consultant/Think tank	6.4%
Councillor	0.3%
Resident	1.5%
Others	15.4%

However, the planning divisions usually set up joint meetings or committees to coordinate various divisions. This practice established mainly during the third stage to increase feasibility. These committees are set up in 90 percent of the governments. In the other 10 percent, they utilize regular meetings which are already set up for the purpose of general coordination. It is also common to hold out-house committees for the authorization of the plans. This type of committee is set up by 92 percent of the governments. The members are designated by the governments. Academics, community leaders and city councillors are the most favoured nominees of the governments. In more than 80 percent of the governments, the persons of these three categories are designated as committee members (see Table 19.6). After passing this committee, the city councils vote on the plans.

Based on the observation above, the four subprocesses of planning are delineated: (1) a first draft is produced by a planning department, (2) it is refined by a coordination process in an interdepartment meeting, (3) based on the refined draft, a proposal to a government is worked out by an out-house committee, and (4) the proposal is finalized as an official plan by voting in a city council meeting. It is confirmed by the survey that these processes proceed sequentially in most of the governments. This standard process of planning is shown in Figure 19.2.

Table 19.6 Members appointed in out-house committees

Academics	88.6%
Representative of community organization	81.9%
Representative of residents	55.2%
Councillors	81.1%
Executive officials	40.9%
Others	17.3%

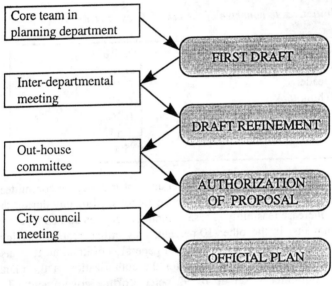

Figure 19.2 Standard process of planning

As mentioned earlier, however, the problem of this standard process is well recognized. The process has a certain limit of diffusion and obstructs the understanding of 'vision' by the residents. To overcome this problem, various measures for mutual communication and participation are taken deliberately by the governments. In 46 percent of the governments, public hearings are carried out, and in 22 percent, participative organizations are set up. Public surveys are conducted by 92 percent, and 26 percent of them gather essays about desirable future from public (see Tables 19.7 and Table 19.8). In our previous study (Liu et al. 1995), it is confirmed that the lack of opportunities for mutual learning is one of the critical factors which obstruct vision sharing. If we categorize the types of opportunities and communication channels in Tables 19.7 and 19.8 from this standpoint, the data show the tendency that less interactive participation opportunities and channels are used more often than high interactive ones. A public opinion survey, for example, is most commonly used among the channels of communication in Table 19.8, but it is less interactive than others. Public hearings are another example used in the highest rate among the participation opportunities, but it is also less interactive than other opportunities. The lack of interactivity can explain at least partially the limits of the existing planning process.

Table 19.7 Citizen participation opportunities used in planning

Public hearing	45.5%
Participative organization newly set up	21.8%
Existing participative organization	8.8%
Neighbourhood meeting	16.1%
Other	30.3%

Table 19.8 Other communication channels used in planning

Public opinion survey	91.8%
Gathering essays on desirable future from public	26.4%
Interviews with community leaders	17.3%
Computer network/BBS/E-mail	0.3%
Telephone/Facsimile interview	1.2%
Other	24.5%

Table 19.9 Citizen participation opportunities open at different planning stages

Planning stage	Opportunities open
Stage 1: first draft	51.8%
Stage 2: draft refinement	24.2%
Stage 3: authorization of proposal	20.6%
Stage 4: official plan enactment	15.8%

In addition to the types of participation opportunities and communication channels, the timing in which stage of planning they are set up seem to be another important factor which affects the process of vision sharing. To grasp the existing pattern, the data are summarized in Tables 19.9 and 19.10. Table 19.9 shows in which stage of planning the opportunities of citizen participation are held open to the residents. The figures are the percentage of the governments which set up any type of participation opportunities shown in Table 19.7. In the same way, the percentage of the other communication channels which are set up at different planning stages are tabulated in Table 19.10.

Table 19.10 Other communication channels open at different planning stages

Planning stage	Channels open
Stage 1: first draft	82.7%
Stage 2: draft refinement	23.6%
Stage 3: authorization of proposal	8.5%
Stage 4: official plan enactment	4.5%

Judging from the diffusion pattern of vision depicted in Figure 19.1, it seems natural to conjecture that the participation opportunities are expanding as the process proceeds from the centre of planning to the periphery. However, the actual pattern is reversing. As against expectations, the percentages are higher in the early planning stages. Other communication channels also show quite a similar tendency although the rate of decrease is much steeper. It used to be said that governments propose their plans after deliberate consideration. It has usually been criticized that residents are kept away from the early stage of planning and are given limited options at the final stage. But contrary to the common image, the fact is that the core teams of the governments try to gather public opinion at the early stage through various participation opportunities and communication channels. Then, they close their windows gradually to avoid unexpected interference from the public as the final stage of planning comes to an end. By doing so, the risk of starting the process all over again is reduced. In addition to that, the feeling of participation is stronger when they can participate at the beginning. In this sense, the process is considered to be rational.

However, as analysed previously, the process has a deficiency in the extent of diffusion and the level of understanding. To find out the appropriate type of opportunity setting, it is necessary to examine the relationship further between the patterns of opportunity setting and those two factors. Table 19.11 shows such a relationship. The average diffusion rate to the ordinary residents is calculated from the data used in Table 19.2. The degree of understanding is calculated from the data used in Table 19.3. To simplify the analysis, the data are summarized in one indicator by counting the numbers checked in the five aspects of understanding. If this indicator is 5, it means that the residents understand all five aspects of vision. If this is 0, it means that they do not understand any of the five aspects of it. Theoretically, actual values will be scattered between 0 and 5. As for the patterns, they are categorized in nine patterns. Table 19.10 shows that public hearings and participatory organizations which are set up specifically for planning are the two major opportunities. Therefore, the patterns of opportunity setting are categorized by the combination of these two types of opportunities. In the table, PH denotes public hearing and PO denotes participatory organization. The numbers which follow the abbreviations are obtained by counting the number of stages at which these opportunities are held open respectively. In the case that both opportunities are not set up in any of the four stages, O is marked in the table. The result shows a couple of interesting facts about the patterns of opportunity setting.

Table 19.11 Patterns of participation opportunity and vision sharing

Patterns of opportunity	Diffusion rate	Level of understanding
PO4	51%	2.84
PO3	39%	2.15
PO2	37%	1.72
PO1	29%	1.39
PH4	25%	1.37
PH3	27%	1.41
PH2	22%	N.A.
PH1	26%	N.A.
O	23%	1.28

First, both the diffusion rate and the understanding level of public hearing are lower than those of participatory organization. Public hearing is less interactive than participatory organization. The low level of diffusion and understanding can be explained as the result of low interactivity. Secondly, when participative organizations are set for each of the four stages, the diffusion and the understanding level record the highest score. If this number of stages drops, both scores become low. However, the difference among four categories of public hearing is negligible. In effect, public hearing does not improve the process of vision sharing in the above two aspects, while setting participative organization upgrades the levels significantly. The implications of these facts are summarized in three points. First, low interactive opportunity does not improve the vision sharing process. Secondly, high interactive opportunities can improve the process. Thirdly, such participative opportunities will achieve the highest diffusion rate and understanding level when they are set at every four stages of planning. In other words, high interactive opportunities should operate concurrently with each stage of in-house planning from beginning to end. Contrary to the ideal process, however, the low interactive opportunities are set up only at the beginning of the stage of planning in the existing process.

7. LESSONS FROM THE JAPANESE EXPERIENCE

The planning process in Japan has changed its style for over the last fifty years. In each stage of social and economic development, new planning styles were invented to tackle the problems peculiar to each stage. When the basic human needs are not satisfied at the takeoff period of economic development, priority about the allocation of public resources is clear and the consensus is easily attained. But once the basic human needs are satisfied, higher orders of demands have been developed and diversified. Central control by the state government cannot deal with every aspects of these diversified local matters. Some of the local governments manage to find their own future options by themselves beyond state control. Recently, it is not rare that the state government relies on the ideas invented by local governments. Information is one of the sources of power. The state government cannot keep the dominance of information. The balance of power is tilted towards decentralization in a long-term perspective.

Planning and public decision making are the product of culture and history of each society. In most Asian countries, strong central governments have been predominant. The reason may partly be cultural and historical. But the general trend which Japan has experienced seems common. Decentralization and strengthening local governance soon or later will be one of the primal political issues. However, it is not easy to break down the tight institutional control.

Most Japanese local governments claim that citizen participation is important. However, most participation opportunities are low interactive. They are set up at the early stage of planning, but gradually close their windows to avoid the unexpected interference from the public towards the final stage.

Fundamental conditions of flexibility to adapt to the new global restructuring are diversity and initiatives of various actors in a region. Transparency of the process and delegation of power may be the necessary conditions, but they are not sufficient. Most governments officials think transparency and delegation of power are necessary. But at the same time they fear losing control in the decision-making process. Their fear is not just emotional and irrational since the existing theory of planning does not explain the mechanism about how to integrate actions without suffocating initiatives of various actors.

In this chapter, we proposed an alternative view of planning. To understand and to adapt to a new situation, we need a proper language. Lack of proper language makes the chances of adaptation quite low. But since the existing language was created to describe the past situation, a new language has to be created. Vision formulation should be understood as an effort to create a new common language to adapt to a new situation. Creating a new language requires all the actors to transform the semantic structure of their language, by which values and action implications of a vision are assessed according to the contexts they face. Transforming semantic structure is not an easy task especially when different languages are spoken. As a matter of fact, our study shows that the languages used in the worlds of officials and that of the residents are different and that a vision is mostly written in an official's language and not in resident's language. Therefore, it is difficult for the residents to translate the values expressed in the vision into roles and actions. This lack of common language is considered one of the main causes of the fear by officials of loosing control.

But the lack of common language can be an advantage in creating a new one. A language corresponds to a world view. Therefore, a variety of languages can be a source of creativity. Synthesizing different world views into a vision means establishing common ground for all actors to play harmoniously. Again this is not an easy task. It is not well known how to achieve this. Our survey shows the evidence that low interactive opportunity does not improve the vision-sharing process and that high interactive opportunities will achieve the highest diffusion rate and understanding level when they are set at every stages of planning.

Redesigning legal and institutional frameworks and developing new communication technologies opens the possibility of improving our planning capability. But the institutional framework and the technology do not automatically solve the problems. It is much more important to understand the nature of cognitive processes in planning and the conditions to affect these since this brings us the fundamental knowledge.

REFERENCES

Ackoff, R.L. (1981), *Creating the Corporate Future*, New York: John Wiley and Sons, Inc.

Ansoff, I. (1979), *Strategic Management*, London: Macmillan Press.

Anthony, R.N. (1965), *Planning and Control Systems*, Cambridge, MA: Harvard Business School.

Emery, F.E. and E. Trist (1965), 'The causal texture of organizational environments', *Human Relations* **18**, pp. 129–38.

Galbraith, J. (1973), *Designing Complex Organizations*, Reading, MA: Addison–Wesley.

Liu, J.S. and Y. Kumata (1993), 'A study on an approach to create the vision of new capital', papers on City Planning No.28, City Planning Society of Japan.

Liu, J.S., Kumata, Y. and T. Sakano (1995), 'An empirical study on a vision of a region and its enactment process through planning', *Planning Administration* No.45, Japan Society of Planning Administration.

Lorange, P. and R.F. Vancil (1977), *Strategic planning Systems*, Englewood Cliffs, NJ: Prentice–Hall.

March, J. and H.A. Simon (1958), *Organizations*, New York: John Wiley and Sons, Inc.

Paddison, R. (1993), 'City marketing, image, reconstruction and urban regeneration', *Urban Studies*, **30** (2), pp. 339–49.

Salko, R. and T. Sakano (1984), 'Taylor's scientific management', S3 paper No.84-01, Department of Social Systems Science, University of Pennsylvania.

Taylor, F.W. (1947), *Scientific Management*, New York: Harper and Row.

Waldrop, M. (1994), *Complexity*, Harmonsworth: Penguin Books.

NOTES

1. The first survey was conducted in 1994.

   Method: Questionnaire by fax

   Sampling: Two officials in charge of comprehensive planning from 47 prefectural governments and 188 municipal governments, which are classified into three categories by the size of the population: (1) below 50,000; (2) 50,000 to 10,000; (3) 100,000 to 3,000,000; and (4) above 3,000,000

   Period: September 1994 to January 1995

   Response rate:51.3 percent

2. The second survey was conducted in 1995.

   Method: Questionnaire by mail

   Sampling: One official in charge of comprehensive planning from 47 prefectural governments and 687 municipal governments, which equals all the city governments in Japan

   Period: November 1995 to December 1995

   Respose rate: 49.7 percent

Index

Abraham, F. 296
Abraham, K.G. 247
accessibility of regions 268, 269, 271,
   287–8
   see also geography, as a factor in
      regionalization;
      telecommunications
Ackoff, R. 37–5
Adelaide, University of 353, 354, 356,
   357, 359
agglomeration
   benefits, high-tech industries 343, 352
   of FDI, relationship to transaction
      costs and trade in producer
      services 102–24
   and local choice of Japanese
      electronics firms in East Asia
      127–41
   relationship to peripherality 288, 289,
      297
   triggered by globalization 6, 7
   see also interregional trade flows in
      the service industries
Agosin, M.R. 151–2
agricultural sector
   impact of improvement of production
      efficiency on manufacturing in
      South 89–99
   wage rates in terms of Krugman
      equilibrium 80–81, 83–4, 86–9
Albrechts, L. 345
Alpes-Adria euroregion 265
Amirahmadi, H. 326
Anderson, K. 150–151, 159
APEC (Asia Pacific Economic
   Cooperation Council) 27
Appalachian Regional Development
   Commission 34–6
Appelbaum, E. 245, 246
application of regional science,
   weaknesses in 32–3, 40, 42
Arad, R.W. 180

Aschauer, D.A. 312
ASEAN nations, Japanese FDI within
   102, 133
Asian NIEs, FDI in 102
Assisted Relatives Class immigrants,
   Canada 191, 192, 197
associate EU status, option of 302
Association of University Technology
   Managers (AUTM) survey 355,
   357
Atlantic Canada Opportunities Agency
   345
Australia, Multi-Function Polis (MFP)
   see Multi-Function Polis
   (MFP)/Canadian Technology
   Triangle (CTT), technology creation
   in
Australis Media Ltd 358, 364
autarkic equilibrium 64–7, 70, 73–4
automated driving systems 272, 273
automatic transfers within EU 295–6

Baldwin R.E. 150, 299
Bangalore regional economy, India 27
Bartik, T.J. 133, 134
Batey, P. 277
Bean, C.R. 246
Bergstrand, J.H. 13, 170, 187
Berry, B.J.L. 40
Biehl, D. 312
Blue Banana zone 266
Bluestone, B. 248
bottom-up approach
   to regional policy making within
      Europe 272, 276, 277, 278, 280,
      282
   to technology creation 20–21, 341,
      342, 344–6, 358, 360–362, 365,
      366–7
Bröcker, J. 292
Brussels School models 40
Bryant, C. 345

Richardson, R. 289
Ries, J. 191
Rietveld, P. 18–19
Rodrik, D. 4
Rosenbloom, J.L. 134
Rosser, J.B. 39, 40
Rosser, V. 40
Route 128 regional economy, USA 27, 37
rules of origin 54, 58, 60
Rutherford, T. 352–3

Sakano, T. 21
San Antonio/Austin regional economy,
    Texas 37
Sanso, M. 13
Sanyo Electric 128, 135
Schachter, G. 16–17
Schettkat, R. 245, 246
Scheurwater, J. 154
Schmenner, R.W. 134
Schott, J.J. 150, 153
Schultz, S. 215
Schwab, R.M. 134
Science Park, South Australia 358, 365
'Scientific Management', principles of
    374
sectoral variability *see* extraction
    method, as tool in identifying key
    sectors
Self-employed Class immigrants, Canada
    191, 192, 194, 195, 196–7
sensitive dependence on initial
    conditions (SDIC) 39
service industries *see* interregional trade
    flows in the service industries
Shanghai *see* information development in
    Japan and Shanghai
Sharp 128, 135
Siegel, P.B. 243
Signal Processing Research Institute,
    South Australia 359
Silicon Valley regional economy, USA
    27, 37, 353, 358, 365
Simon, H. 374
Singapore, Japanese investment in 128
Single European Act (1986) 266, 300
Single European Market 297, 300
size and structure of economy,
    relationship between 229

skill shortages 244–5
skilled (professional) labour 119–21,
    123, 124, 244–5, 288, 352
slaved variables 40
'Smart City Australia' project 359
Smith, D.F. 134
Smith, J. 350
Smith, L. 351
Snape, R. 150–151
Social Issues Study, MFP 363
social market economy versus
    deregulation of market 271–2
social returns to human capital 37
social sciences, potential
    interdisciplinary linkages with
    regional science 33–4
Sonis, M. 16, 215, 218, 220, 221, 228,
    238
Sony 128, 135
South Australia, University of 353–4,
    359
South, industrialization in *see*
    industrialization, pattern of in the
    South
Southwest/Grand Rapids region,
    Michigan 207, 209
spatial diversity and globalization,
    overview of 3–22
spatial general equilibrium model of FDI
    agglomeration
  analysis assumptions 115
  basic setup 108–10
  comparative static analysis 115–21
  complexities involved with 105
  equilibrium conditions 110–112
  international investment, analysis of
    within model 121–3
  symmetric equilibrium 112–15
specialization 17, 315, 353
  see also regional industrial
    specialization and patterns of
    structural unemployment in the
    EU
spinoff firms resulting from university
    research 354, 356, 357–9, 361, 362,
    365, 366
Stackelberg duopoly *see* trade; general
    equilibrium analysis of patterns and
    gains from trade